汉英论语类读

Chinese-English New Classification of the Analects of Confucius

编　　译　牛青坡
英文审校　［美］司徒彬（Charles Stubin）

河南人民出版社

图书在版编目(CIP)数据

汉英论语类读 = Chinese - English New Classification of the Analects of Confucius / 牛青坡编译. — 郑州 : 河南人民出版社, 2022. 3
ISBN 978 - 7 - 215 - 11862 - 1

Ⅰ. ①汉… Ⅱ. ①牛… Ⅲ. ①《论语》- 注释 - 汉、英②《论语》- 译文 - 汉、英 Ⅳ. ①B222. 2

中国版本图书馆 CIP 数据核字(2021)第 212807 号

河南人民出版社 出版发行
(地址 : 郑州市郑东新区祥盛街 27 号 邮政编码 : 450016 电话 : 65788072)
新华书店经销　　河南瑞之光印刷股份有限公司印刷
开本 710 毫米 × 960 毫米　1/16　印张 33
字数 470 千字
2022 年 3 月第 1 版　　2022 年 3 月第 1 次印刷

定价 : 128. 00 元

编排说明

1. 以天地人、仁义礼智信等儒家思想为纲要，将《论语》中有关政治、经济、教育、文化、农工商、生老病死等内容进行分类，共归 16 大类、83 小类。

2. 一章只归一类，即不重复归类。当一章涉及几项内容时，选择一项核心内容归类。如子路第 13.9 章讲孔子到卫国，见人丁兴旺，说先富之、再教之，将此章归类为“民”，未归“周游列国”。

3. 各章均由原文、篇章号、注释、白话译文、英译、英译注等部分构成。原篇章号放在原文、白话译文、英译后的括号内。

4. 注释以促进对原文理解为原则，对原文的部分字、词、句依照出现的顺序，根据所列的参考书或个人理解，进行说文解字式的注释。受篇幅所限，基本不列明其出处，不设注释号码。

5. 各章独立注释。当一个词在上下几章都出现时，各章均做注释，免得交叉参考，以节省阅读时间。

6. 当多部参考书对一字的解释不一样时，通常将列上多个注释，这也是需进一步研究的对象。如乡党（10.06，51 衣）中的“寝衣”注释为“当时的被子，睡衣”，因为何晏注为“今之被也”，而今人注为“睡衣”。

7. 根据《新华字典》注音，使用拼音加汉字法，此字首选单音常用字。

8. 对所有人物，依据手边资料，均做简介。由于孔子弟子的身份，文中基本自明，汉语中不再另外标注“孔子弟子”等字。

9. 人物常出现字和名，字在先，名在后，分别对字和名注释，不厌其烦，旨在明确人与事的关系，也便于增强记忆。比如颜渊（12.05，01

天)“子夏曰:‘商闻之矣,死生有命……。’”分别注释为“子夏:姓卜名商,字子夏”和“商:姓卜名商,字子夏”。

10. 对于原文省略的内容,注释时通常使用括号表示。

11. 对10 仁、72 周游列国两节的内容,分别按其类别、出访时间的先后顺序进行排序。其他各节的内容,均按其在《论语》中出现的先后顺序排列。

12. 为方便英语读者,对有关人、事、时间、地点以及背景等知识,提供英译注。

13.“子”译成 Master。The Master 专指孔子本人。其他人称“子”的,在 Master 后加姓氏拼音等。原文一章中出现仅指孔子的“子”时,“子”白话译为“孔子”,英译为“The Master”。只出现“孔子”的,“孔子”白话译为“孔夫子”,英译为“Confucius”。同时出现“孔子”、仅指孔子的“子”或“夫子”的,依照全章意思,白话、英译要么为“孔子”和“The Master”,要么为“孔夫子”和“Confucius”。

14. 对部分类别名称的说明:

(1)天:《论语》49 处涉及“天”,选其中 7 章来说明天的概念。

(2)自然:道法自然,归为天道类。

(3)有关人的本性、共性、规律性的论述。

(4)小人:为人性的一面,依俗语“先小人后君子”排在君子前。

(5)乐:是礼仪的重要成分,与五常并列一类。

(6)帝:指尧、舜、禹及夏、商、周朝代的最高统治者。

(7)君:指诸侯,仅次于帝王的阶层。

(8)士:大夫之下的官职,有志之人,读书人,注释中未再细分。

(9)仕:当官,为一种职业,归为分工大类。

(10)政:指政治、政务、行政等有关安民兴国之类的内容。

(11)贫富与盗:贫富事关政治,盗又事关贫富,归为政法。

(12)器:是用具,属于生活的一个组成部分。

(13)气:是气人的气,不同于怨、忧,是人生一态。

(14)骂:指斥责,不是通常“用脏话、粗野的话侮辱人”的意思。

(15)高人:指受孔子尊敬的几位名士,如伯夷、叔齐等。

(16)孔子:是对孔子的特写,包括孔子的事迹、对孔子的评价。

(17)周游:孔子周游列国之事,按其出现顺序排列。

(18)岁月:有孔子一生的总结,对年轻人的期待和对社会发展的预见。

自　　序

《论语》是我国儒家智慧的经典,是人类智慧的结晶,也是我国国泰民安的理论基础,故有半部《论语》治天下之说。两千多年来,特别是自汉武帝独尊儒术以来,《论语》的很多思想已经深深扎根于中华大地,成为重要的民族精神来源之一,直接影响了很多人的思维习惯。要想明白中国人之所以为中国人,要想明白我们行为背后的推动力量,没有《论语》,恐怕会丢失一条重要线索。

《论语》对于人生,从吃穿、做人、立志、求学、成家、立业,到治国、理政等,都给出了具体可行的操作步骤。全球畅销书《高效能人士的七个习惯》(*The 7 Habits of Highly Effective People*)的七分之三直接就是《论语》514 章中的 3 章,即“2. Begin with the end in mind(先行其言而后从之(02.13,14 信)(注:02.13 指《论语》第 2 篇 13 章,‘14 信’指本书第 14 节,下同),5. Seek first to understand, then to be understood[不患人之不己知,患不知人也(01.16,34 修身)],7. Sharpen the saw[工欲善其事,必先利其器(15.10,43 工)]”。足见《论语》具有国际性、指导性。

《论语》内容丰富,智慧众多,但较零散。前些年,本人为学《论语》将其 514 章内容分成 16 大类 81 小类,纳入一本书中,书名《论语类读》。2015 年 11 月 7 日,《论语类读》要出版了,为了促销,我想到免费赠送此书的英文版。于是我从网上下载英国人理雅各先生(James Legge)在 1876 年前后出版的《论语》英译本。经复制、粘贴,很快《论语类读》英文版就形成了。这居然成了本书的起点,完全出乎我的意料。

为了负责起见,我以湖南出版社汉英对照版《四书》(*The Four*

Books)为依据对它进行校对。首先,将书中所用的人名地名由威妥玛式拼法(Wade System)改为大家熟悉的汉语拼音(Chinese Phonetic Alphabet)。比如改王孙贾 Wang-sun Chia 为 Wangsun Jia, 孟武 Mang Wu 为 Meng Wu, 子夏 Tsze-hsia 为 Zixia 等。

其次,统一词汇。比如"君子",理雅各先生在翻译"君子无所争,其争也君子(03.07)"中的"君子"时,用的是 the student of virtue(有品德的学生)、Chun-tsze("君子"的威妥玛拼音);在翻译"子谓子产:有君子之道(05.16)"中的"君子"时,用的是 a superior man(有上等品质的人);在翻译"文质彬彬,然后君子(06.18)"中的"君子"时,用的是 the man of virtue(有品德的人);而在"后进于礼乐,君子也(11.01)"中,用的是 accomplished gentlemen(有成就的绅士)。同一词的这些不同翻译需要统一。

最后,修改明显的错误。比如"乡原,德之贼也(17.13)",此处乡原的含义是"老好好、不倒翁"。理雅各先生译为"Your good, careful people of the villages are the thieves of virtue",大意是:"你们乡村中善良、认真的人,是品德方面的盗贼。"显然,善良认真的人不是"乡原"。

随着工作的深入,我发现越来越多的问题。比如,"我未见好仁者恶不仁者(04.06,10 仁)",大意是真正的好人不厌恶坏人,如同老子的"不善者,吾亦善之,德善(《道德经》第49 章)"一样。理雅各的译文是"I have not seen a person who loved virtue, or one who hated what was not virtuous",意思是:"我既没有看到过任何喜爱仁德的人,也没有见过讨厌没有仁德的。"与原文不符。

考虑到一百多年来,有关《论语》的研究成果层出不穷,汉语、英语都在发展,突然间,头脑中冒出一个简单的想法:自己翻译《论语类读》,更简单的想法是,在一个春节(2016 年)期间完成。

第一,基于对原文每一个字、词、句子的理解和注释,直接由古文翻译成英语,不经过现代汉语翻译的过程,因为我个人认为古文译成白话文会降低阅读效率,还会损失信息。

第二,意思优先,字字落实。若古文有暗含的字,添加,但放在括号内。比如，“子曰：‘食夫稻，衣夫锦，于女安乎？’”（17.21，80 丧）（宰我）“曰：‘安。’”师徒二人均有言外之意。故翻译时把此言外之意放在括号中。

第三，人名地名使用音译。古代姓名主要有姓、名、字三部分，长辈对晚辈、地位高的对地位低的，可以叫名，相反只能用尊称或者称其字。

第四，增加注释，提供《论语》的背景知识，便于国内外读者理解。

第五，遵守传统，统一词汇。如孔子译成 Confucius（孔夫子）。“子”译成“Master”。“The Master”专指孔子本人。其他称“子”的人，在“Master”后加姓氏，比如“曾子”译为“Master Zeng”。

第六，语言是活的。对《论语》的研究成果尽量吸收，择善而从。比如杨伯峻先生关于“四体不勤”（18.07，41 农）的一条注释，赵阳先生有关“子路共之”（10.27，04 自然）、“攻乎异端”（02.16，68 攻）的见解等。

2015 年 12 月 1 日，我开始翻译。万万没想到，不少汉字很难找到对应的英语，看似简单的一个字，有时花一天甚至几天，都百思不得其解。2016 年春节假期过后，仅仅译到第 3 章第 5 节（15）礼乐，不足四分之一。

两个多月艰难的翻译，一次又一次让我怀疑自己的能力，一次又一次想到放弃。一到要放弃时，就响起一个声音：“力不足者，中道而废。今女画。”（06.12，02 道）一点点的进步，增多一点点的信心。不知不觉中，我必须要完成此书的使命感增强了。一不做，二不休，我投入所有可用时间，下班后、出差中，哪怕十分八分钟，都要翻译。到 2016 年 8 月中旬，第一草稿完成。

为了减少错误，邀请美国老朋友查尔斯·斯图宾先生（Mr. Charles Stubin）帮我把关。他的中文名是司徒彬，我称他司徒老师。他的母语是英语，他使用汉语近 60 年，曾经在中国台北专门学汉语多年，对中文诗词情有独钟。中国一改革开放，他就来中国考察，曾在美国芝加哥附近的孔子学院讲课，平时看《红楼梦》《三国演义》《西游记》《三体》等名著。2015 年 9 月中秋节前，我到美国看望他，一天晚饭时下着小雨，刮着小风，听他低吟："萧条秋雨夕，苍茫楚江晦。时见一舟行，濛濛水云外。"这是清朝王士祯的诗，吟诵正合时宜。

2016 年 8 月 17 日，他同意审校此稿，先修改《论语类读》英译本的第一章"天道"和最后一章"岁月"。司徒老师做事极为认真，一个字、一个词地打磨，全力以赴，花费大量时间。经过他一修改，译文变得简单、顺畅。比如，"子曰：'天何言哉？四时行焉，百物生焉。天何言哉？'"（17.19，01 天）他修改后的译文甚是优雅。

2016 年 9 月 1 日，我发给他更多内容，包括仁、义、礼、智、信、礼乐。10 月 12 日，他来函："对你的翻译，做了一番挣扎之后，我遗憾地说：'我完成不了这项任务。'你的英语语言技巧不能胜任此项工作，我的编辑技巧不够高，不能把你的翻译变成流利、地道的英语。另外，很多很多汉语词句（古文），让我稀里糊涂，不知所云……我想很多研究《论语》的人会受益于好的白话翻译。"

他的"白话"二字给我重大启示。对我国古文读者，若正确理解了文中的字、词，原则上不需要白话翻译。若对古文的字、词理解错了，白话翻译也白翻，所以原计划没有白话。但是，对外国读者，白话则大不相同。这样，我从头开始将《论语类读》的英语译文逐段逐句逐字翻译成现代汉语即白话文，再将白话文对照古文，判定正误，反复进行汉译英，英译汉，使两种语言语义互换，一一对应，如同做完算术题验算一样，让表达更近原意。

2017 年 2 月 7 日，白话文翻译完成。经过两次全面的自校，至 2017 年 8 月底《汉英论语类读》的全部翻译完成，包括现代汉语译文、英语译文及注释。在此期间，司徒彬先生一直给予鼓励、帮助和指导，还将英语书名修改为："Chinese-English New Classification of the Analects of Confucius"，直译为"孔子论语的汉英新分类"。

司徒老师对此书继续把关。为了便于审校，书稿用大号字打印，装订成册，快递到美国，由他直接在书稿上修改，只修改英语，而古文、白话文只作为修改时的参考。2017 年 9 月 15 日，他收到书后，开始埋头苦干，至 2017 年圣诞节前，完成修改任务，寄回书稿。

司徒老师修改的《汉英论语类读》稿子，让我爱不释手。《汉英论语类读》共514章，他从英语正文到注释都做了全面、认真、细微的修改，少则几个词，多则整章重译一遍，使英语译文切合我所理解的白话文，通顺易懂。满纸的修改，字字皆辛苦，使我感激不尽，感慨万千：汉语博大精深，而英语也很复杂。

2017年12月30日，我开始依据司徒老师所做的修改完善书稿，经过4个月完成全部书稿。在此过程中对其中一些内容，我还重新做了补充或修改，而其英语译文，司徒老师也把了关。从他修改的英译文中，我学到了活的英语。比如，“三省吾身”（01.01，05 人），我用“introspect”表示“内省”，这是词典上给出的，故译成“introspect myself three times”，他将“introspect”修改为“question”（问），简单易记。“拜下，礼也”（09.03，12 礼），讲“磕头，是礼节”，我用的是“knock my head”，他干脆用“ketou”，这就是“磕头”的拼音，西方人明白，简捷痛快。特别是“食不厌精，脍不厌细”（10.08，52 食）一章，最初翻译以孔子为主语，审校时恢复了原文的祈使句，使之更具指导价值。

在各位专家的帮助下，《汉英论语类读》终于初步完成了。由《论语类读》促销赠送英语版的初心，演变成花费巨大精力翻译《论语类读》，使之丰富为《汉英论语类读》，是我做梦也没有想到的。而且想都不敢想的是，这客观上完成了《论语》的英语重译、英汉互译。

在翻译过程中，我认真参考了手边现有的《论语》各种权威版本，如三国何晏本、宋代朱熹本，当代杨伯峻、张岱年、于丹等的注释注译本，以及河南人民出版社的赵阳版本。同时阅览了300多篇有关《论语》的最新研究论文，尤其是附后直接引用的论文，博采众长，尽最大努力使此书对《论语》的理解接近原意。受篇幅所限，所有注释基本上没有编号，也未列明出处，谨对各注译者表示歉意和衷心的感谢。英语翻译由美国朋友司徒老师把关、审校，他付出了巨大的心血，没有他的修改，此书只是半成品，对他表示由衷的感谢。在翻译的两年多时间里，我得到家人的理解与支持，也向他们表示真挚的感谢。

此书抛砖引玉，重在应用。世界每年单纯因吃药不当，造成意外死亡的数目触目惊心，而 2500 年前孔子就吃药提出“丘未达，不敢尝”，足见《论语》不是空洞的教条，而有重大现实意义。

君子闻过则喜。由于《论语》博大精深，本人田父献曝，智疏学浅，水平有限，虽竭尽全力，仍有多处百思不得其解，因此《汉英论语类读》所给出的中英文译文、注释一定相对肤浅，甚至错误百出，贻笑大方，真诚欢迎各位读者、师长不吝赐教。

牛青坡

2020 年 6 月 26 日

Preface

Charles Stubin

To borrow a phrase from the great 20th Chinese scholar/philosopher, Feng Youlan, Confucius(551 BC-479 BC) was "the First Teacher". The core of his teachings can be found in *The Analects*, or *Lunyu*(论语). Confucius's teachings continue to be the foundation of Chinese culture today.

There have been a number of English Translations of *The Analects* in the past, but Mr. Qingpo Niu's translation breaks new ground. He has reorganized *The Analects* into new categories by subject, making Confucius's thoughts more readily accessible on such matters as Benevolence, Righteousness, Heaven, Nature, Filial Piety, etc.

Since *The Analects* were written in Classical Chinese, they can be very hard to understand. Classical Chinese can be very spare, almost cryptic. While a few passages in *The Analects* are easily understood, such as the famous "san ren xing" (三人行), or "when walking in a group of three", many, if not most, passages are difficult to comprehend in the original Classical Chinese.

Mr. Niu has translated *The Analects* into Modern Chinese, thus making it accessible to millions of readers who have never studied Classical Chinese. To bring the message of the wisdom of Confucius to non-Chinese readers, he then translated the Modern Chinese text into idiomatic English. Additionally, he has added extensive notes, explaining names and events which the modern readers will find helpful.

英文序译文

司徒彬（Charles Stubin）

借用20世纪伟大的华人哲学家和学者冯友兰的话说，孔子（公元前551－公元前479）是“第一任”老师。其教育思想的核心可以从《论语》中找到。孔子的教育思想今天依然是中华文化的根基。

《论语》的英语翻译，过去已有一定数量的版本了。但是，牛青坡先生的翻译有新的突破。他将《论语》按科目重新进行了分类，使读者更容易理解孔子的思想，比如仁、义、天、自然、孝等。

《论语》是用文言写成的，理解起来非常困难。文言文简约精炼，但难免晦涩难懂。当然，《论语》中有一些章节还是比较容易理解的，比如“三人行”，即“三个人结伴行走”，但是很多章节（即使不是太多）的原文不太容易理解。

牛先生将《论语》译成现代汉语（白话文），让成千上万从未接受过文言文训练的读者理解起来没有障碍。为了让母语非汉语的读者分享孔子的智慧，他将《论语》由现代汉语翻译成地道英语。另外，他还增加了大量的注释，介绍人物和事件，这对现代读者很有帮助。

目 录

一

One

天道

The Way of Heaven

01

天 Heaven

王孙贾问曰:“与其媚于奥,宁媚于灶也。何谓也?”子曰:“不然。获罪于天,无所祷也。”(03.13)

【白话译文】

王孙贾问:“有个说法:‘与其向室神奥献媚,还不如向灶王爷献媚。’它是什么意思呀?”孔子说:“不是这回事。如果一个人得罪了天,任何祷告都帮不了他。”(03.13)

【英译】

Wangsun Jia(1) asked, “There is a saying: ‘Should one toady to the kitchen God Zao rather than to the household God Ao(2). ’ What does it mean?” The Master(3) said, “Not so. Any prayer does not help one if he is guilty against Heaven(4). ” (03.13)

【注释】王孙贾(音 jiǎ 钾):姓王孙,名贾,卫灵公的大夫。曰:说。媚:巴结、讨好。于:对、向。奥:室中最高的神,居西南角。灶:灶王爷。子:孔子(公元前551年9月28日—公元前479年3月9日[J15]),姓孔名丘,字仲尼,周朝鲁国人,今山东人,伟大的思想家和教育家,儒家学派的创始人。然:是的、正确的。获罪:得罪。天:天君、天神、上天、万物的主宰。无:没有。所:……的人、事、地等,助词,放在动词前。祷(音 dǎo 导):祷告。无所祷也:没有可祷告的了。

【英译注】This dialogue probably occurred in 495 BC, the 15th Year of Duke Ding of the State of Wei. Confucius had a hard time seeking a position there at the age of 57. (1) Wangsun Jia: Surname Wangsun, first name Jia, a senior official in charge of military affairs at the State of Wei. (2) Ao: the highest god at a household staying at the southwest corner of a house. (3) The Master: Confucius. (4) Heaven: the God of Heaven or the dominator of everything and everyone on the earth.

仪封人请见,曰:"君子之至于斯也,吾未尝不得见也。"从者见之。出曰:"二三子,何患于丧乎? 天下之无道也久矣,天将以夫子为木铎。"(03.24)

【注释】仪:仪地,今河南兰考县。封人:镇守边疆的官。请见:求见。曰:仪封人说。至于斯:到这里来。尝:曾经。未尝不得见也:从来没有见不上的。从者:随从。从者见之:跟随孔子的随从弟子,让他拜见了孔子。出曰:仪封人出来说。二三子:弟子们;朋友们。何:为什么。患:担心。丧:丧失周礼。何患于丧乎:何必担心周礼无法恢复呢。无道:无仁政。久:很长。天:天君、上天。夫子:孔子。为:当作。木铎:天子发布政令时摇的木舌大铜铃。

【白话译文】

仪地的边防官请求拜见孔子,说:"哪位君子到这里,都没有拒绝我见他的机会。"他随从孔子的弟子见到了孔子。会见出来后,他说:"朋友们,你们为何担心恢复不了周礼? 世上很久没有天道了。上天将任命你们老师的职位相当于木舌铜铃,指引方向。"(03.24)

【英译】

A boundary guard commander at the frontier town of Yi(1) asked to be presented to Confucius, saying, "When any superior man comes here, I have never been denied the chance to meet with him." He met with Confucius by following his disciples. As he came out after the meeting, he said, "Friends, why do you worry about not being capable to recover the Rites of Proprieties of the Zhou Dynasty? The Way of Heaven(2) has long been absent from the world. Heaven will appoint your master to be like the bell with its wooden clapper(3) and he will show us the Way."(03.24)

【英译注】(1) Yi: A frontier town at the State of Zheng, current Lankao County, Kaifeng City, Henan Province. (2) The Way of Heaven: The laws of social and natural development; the right principles, just doctrines for politics, good government administrations, etc. (3) the bell with its wooden clapper: The bell was used by the emperor to announce administration policies, while a bell with a metal clapper was applied to announce a military action or policy.

子曰:“大哉尧之为君也!巍巍乎!唯天为大,唯尧则之。荡荡乎!民无能名焉。巍巍乎!其有成功也。焕乎,其有文章。”(08.19)

【注释】大:伟大。哉:啊。尧:古代圣帝。为君:做君主。巍巍:崇高。乎:呀。唯:只有。天:天君、上天。为:是。大:最高大。则:效法。之:天。荡荡:(他的恩德)广大。民:百姓。名:形容、称说。民无能名焉:百姓不知道用什么语言来称赞他啊。有:取得。成功:丰功伟绩。焕:辉煌。文章:礼仪制度。

【白话译文】

孔子说:“圣帝尧,多么伟大啊!天,多么崇高啊!只有天最伟大!只有尧帝尊崇和效法天的宏大准则。他对人民的恩德是多么浩荡和广博啊!他们无法用言语来歌颂他。他的丰功伟绩是多么崇高、伟大啊!他的礼仪制度,是多么灿烂辉煌啊!”(08.19)

【英译】

The Master said, “How great was Yao(1) as the saintly emperor! How lofty is Heaven! Only Heaven is supreme! It was only emperor Yao who revered and emulated its grand criteria. How vast and mighty is his grace upon the people who could not find the right words to eulogize him! How eminent and majestic are his great achievements and abundant merits! How splendid and glorious are his protocols and institutions of the Rites of Proprieties!” (08.19)

【英译注】(1) Yao: Yao is regarded as the ancient Chinese legendary saintly emperor, name Fangxun. As the chieftain of Taotang's Tribe, he united many tribes and was good for hydraulic work and agriculture development.

司马牛忧曰:"人皆有兄弟,吾独亡。"子夏曰:"商闻之矣,死生有命,富贵在天。君子敬而无失,与人恭而有礼,四海之内皆兄弟也。君子何患乎无兄弟也?"(12.05)

【注释】司马牛:姓司马名耕,字子牛,传其兄宋国大夫桓魋(音huán环 tuí 颓)作乱被追杀,全家出逃,似无兄弟。亡(音 wú 吴):无、不。子夏:姓卜名商,字子夏。商:姓卜名商,字子夏。有命:有命运在。天:天君、天神、上天、万物的主宰。在天:在于天的给予。敬:做事严肃认真。而:但,却。失:错。与人:对人。恭:谦逊、礼貌。四海:天下。皆:都是。患:愁。

【白话译文】

司马牛忧虑地说:"人都有兄弟,除了我没有。"子夏说:"我听说:死、生是由命运决定的,财富、权力是由上天事先安排的。如果一位君子工作严肃认真,不出差错,按照礼节恭敬地对待别人,四海之内所有人都是他的兄弟。一位君子为什么要忧虑没有兄弟呢?"(12.05)

【英译】

Sima Niu(1) said anxiously, "All have brothers, except me." Zixia(2) said: "I have heard that one's death and life are predetermined by fate, and one's wealth and power are prearranged by Heaven. All the people within the four seas(3) are his brothers if a superior man works earnestly and carefully, free from faults, and deferentially treats people according to the Rites of Proprieties. Why is a superior man anxious because he has no brothers?" (12.05)

【英译注】(1) Sima Niu: Surname Sima, first name Niu, Confucius's disciple. It was said that his brother Huantui, a senior officer of the State of Song, staged an armed rebellion, and was a fugitive convict sentenced to death. Thus his whole family left home and he seemed no brother. (2) Zixia: Surname Bu, first name Shang, style name Zixia, Confucius's disciple. (3) the four seas: The country within the boundary of south, north, east and west seas. Chinese originally thought that the country was surrounded by four seas.

子曰:"莫我知也夫!"子贡曰:"何为其莫知子也?"子曰:"不怨天,不尤人,下学而上达。知我者其天乎!"(14.37)

【注释】鲁哀公十四年(公元前481年)春,西狩获麟,孔子71岁,感慨道穷,叹此语,2年后逝世。莫我知:没人了解我。也夫:啊。子贡:姓端木名赐,字子贡。何:怎么。为:做、看待、认识。其:他人。子:你。何为其莫知子也:你怎么看待他人不了解你呢。天:天君、天神、万物的主宰。尤:责怪、怨恨。下学:下学人间事。而:但,却。上达:上知天命。其天乎:大概只有天吧。

【白话译文】

孔子说:"哎!没有人理解我啊!"子贡说:"要是没人理解你,你做些什么呢?"孔子说:"我既不怨天,又不怪人。我学习世态人情,进而感知上天的道理。大概能理解我的,是天吧!"(14.37)

【英译】

The Master said(1), "Alas! No one understands me!" Zigong(2) said, "What do you do if no one understands you, my Master?" The Master said, "I neither complain against the Heaven nor blame the man. I study the affairs of men, and grasp the Principles of Heaven. It is probably Heaven who understands me!" (14.37)

【英译注】(1) When Confucius was 71 years old, a unicorn was caught in a hunting expedition at the western State of Lu in the 14th Year of Duke Ai (481 BC). He said this, lamenting his doctrines were unaccepted by the state rulers. (2) Zigong: Surname Duanmu and first name Ci, style name Zigong, Confucius's disciple.

孔子曰:"君子有三畏:畏天命,畏大人,畏圣人之言。小人不知天命而不畏也,狎大人,侮圣人之言。"(16.08)

【注释】三:三项。畏:敬畏,因为深远不可测故敬畏,害怕。天:上天。命:命令、命运,不可抗的自然和社会发展规律。大人:伟人、领袖、伟大人物。圣人:至德之人。言:言论。而:因此、因而。狎(音 xiá 霞):亲近而不庄重,亵渎。

【白话译文】

孔夫子说:"君子敬畏三件事:敬畏上天的指令,敬畏伟大人物,敬畏圣人的言论。小人不理解上天的指令,因而他不敬畏,亵渎伟大人物,轻视和侮辱圣人的言论。"(16.08)

侮(音 wǔ 五):轻慢、怠慢。

【英译】

Confucius said, "A superior man stands in awe of the following three: He stands in awe of the Mandates of Heaven(1); he stands in awe of a great man; and he stands in awe of the words of the saints. An inferior man does not understand the Mandates of Heaven, so he is not awed by them; he blasphemes a great man; and he slights and insults the words of saints." (16.08)

【英译注】(1) the Mandates of Heaven: The objective laws for natural and social developments. They were thought to be orders or mandates from Heaven because those could not be understood by human beings at Confucius's times.

子曰:"予欲无言。"子贡曰:"子如不言,则小子何述焉?"子曰:"天何言哉?四时行焉,百物生焉。天何言哉?"(17.19)

【注释】予:我。欲:想。无:不。言:说话。子贡:姓端木名赐,字子贡。小子:弟子。何:什么。述:传述。何述:述何,传述什么。焉:呢。天:上天、天下主宰。四时:四季。行:运行。生:生长。

【白话译文】

孔子说:"我不想说话了。"子贡说:"如果老师你不说话,那么我们作你的弟子还学习、传播什么呢?"孔子说:"上天说

了什么？四季走了又来，万物生生不息。上天非要说什么吗？”(17.19)

【英译】

The Master said, “I would rather not speak anymore.” Zigong[1] said, “If you, my Master, do not speak, what can we, your disciples, learn and transmit?” The Master said, “What does the Heaven say? The four seasons come and go, and all things live and grow. What does Heaven have to say?” (17.19)

【英译注】(1) Zigong: Surname Duanmu and first name Ci, a style name Zigong, Confucius's disciple.

02

道 The Way of Heaven

子曰：“富与贵，是人之所欲也，不以其道得之，不处也。贫与贱，是人之所恶也，不以其道得之，不去也。君子去仁，恶乎成名？君子无终食之间违仁，造次必于是，颠沛必于是。”(04.05)

【注释】欲：想、要、愿意。所欲：想要的东西。其：代词，这，此，那，那些。道：正道，正当合理的方法和手段；天下通达之理，摸不着，看不见，但作用无限。得：取得、达到。之：富与贵。处：占据。贫：缺钱。贱：职位低。不以其道：(外部因素，非自己)不遵守那个正道。得：遭受、遭遇、沦落到(贫贱)。不以其道得之：“由于外部环境的原因，如政治的黑暗、君主的无能

【白话译文】

孔子说:"发大财、当高官,是一个人想要的。如果不按道德和正义的方式获得这些,我是不要的。没有钱、职位低,是一个人讨厌的。如果由于天下不道不正(使我)遭受贫贱,我是(没有怨言)接受它们的。如果一名君子放弃了仁德,他怎么成就他的名声?一名君子即使在吃一顿饭的短时间内,也从来不会违背仁德的要求。在仓促的那一瞬间也不会,即使无家可归和贫困潦倒也不会。"(04.05)

【英译】

The Master said, "Great wealth and high rank are what one desires. If they are acquired by a way not in conformity with morality and justice, I do not take them. Poverty and lowly position are what one detests. If they are acquired as a result of immorality and injustice under heaven, I would accept them (without complaint). How can a superior man accomplish his good name if he forsakes the virtue of superior benevolence? A superior man never violates the requirements of superior benevolence, even in the short time that he takes to eat a meal. Neither does he leave it in a moment of haste, nor does he forsake it even if he is homeless and miserable." (04.05)

等,被动地沦为贫贱。"[J01] 不去也:不放弃,接受。恶(音 wù 务):憎恶。去:抛弃。恶(音 wū 乌)乎:如何、怎样。成:成就。名:名誉、名声。终食:吃完饭。间:时间。违:背离。无终食之间违仁:一顿饭的工夫也不背离仁德。造次:仓促间。必:一定。于:按。是:这,这样。必于是:必须按仁德办。颠沛:穷困,受挫折。

子曰:"朝闻道,夕死可矣。"(04.08)

【注释】此章孔子以忧国忧民之心,感叹大道难得。朝:早晨。闻:听见、听说。道:社会、政治的最好制度和选贤任能的最佳体系等。夕:晚上。可矣:可无悔无恨了。

【白话译文】

孔子说:"假如我早上能听到最适合政府管理和个人行为的崇高思想体系,晚上我可以死而无憾了。"(04.08)

【英译】

The Master said, "If in the morning I could hear the supreme doctrines(1) best for a governmental administration and personal behaviours, I might die without regret in the evening." (04.08)

【英译注】(1) This section laments the fact that the supreme doctrines are rarely heard in the society.

冉求曰:"非不说子之道,力不足也。"子曰:"力不足者,中道而废。今女画。"(06.12)

【注释】冉求:姓冉名求,字子有。说(音 yuè 月):悦,愉快。子:老师,孔子。之:的。道:学说。力:(我的)能力。者:停顿或假设语气词。中道而废:半途而废。今:现在。女(音 rǔ 辱):汝,你。画:止,画地自限。今女画:现在你自我限制了自己。

【白话译文】

冉求说:"不是我不喜爱你的学说,是我的能力不够,不能实施它。"孔子说:"如果你的能力不够,你走到半道才走不下去。现在你还没有开始,就限制了你自己。"(06.12)

【英译】

Ran Qiu[1] said, "It is not that I do not admire your doctrines, but my ability is insufficient to practice them." The Master said, "If your ability is insufficient, you cannot go further than halfway. Now you limit yourself beforehand." (06.12)

【英译注】(1) Ran Qiu: Surname Ran and first name Qiu, style name Ziyou, Confucius's disciple.

子曰:"谁能出不由户? 何莫由斯道也?"(06.17)

【注释】出:外出。由:经过。户:房门。何:为什么。莫:没有人。由:经过。斯:这。道:正道。也:呀。

【白话译文】

孔子说:"谁可以不走房门而离开房间? 为什么一个人不走这条正道呢?"(06.17)

【英译】

The Master said, "Who can leave a room without going by the door? Why doesn't a person go on by this righteous way[1]?" (06.17)

【英译注】(1) Confucius took metaphor of the door for the righteous way that everyone should follow.

子曰:"齐一变,至于鲁,鲁一变,至于道。"(06.24)

【注释】齐:齐国,姜太公的封地。鲁:鲁国,为周公的封地,周公传说是西周礼仪制度的制定者。至:达到。道:先王大道。

【白话译文】

孔子说:"齐国一旦改革,可以达到鲁国的状况。鲁国一旦改革,可以达到先前圣王建立的周朝礼仪标准。"(06.24)

【英译】

The Master said, "Once the State of Qi(1) is reformed, it can reach the status of the State of Lu(2). And once the State of Lu is reformed, it can meet the criteria of the Rites of the Zhou Dynasty established by the previous saintly emperors." (06.24)

【英译注】(1) the State of Qi: A state granted to Duke Jiang Ziya in 1027 BC, currently in eastern Shandong Province, when the Shang Dynasty was overthrown by the Zhou Dynasty. (2) the State of Lu: A state granted to Duke Dan of the Zhou Dynasty in 1027 BC, who was the younger brother of King Wu and established etiquette regulations for the Zhou Dynasty, currently in southern Shandong Province. Confucius was born and brought up here.

子曰:"邦有道,危言危行;邦无道,危行言孙。"(14.04)

【注释】邦:国。有道:政治清明。危:正直。言:主动对人讲话。行:行为。无道:政治黑暗。孙(音 xùn 训):逊,谦让。

【白话译文】

孔子说:"如果一个国家公平合理,一个人可以直率说话,正直行动。如果一个国家腐败不公,一个人可以正直行动,但谦卑说话。"(14.04)

【英译】

The Master said, "If a state is just and fair, one may speak straightforwardly and behave righteously. If a state is corrupt and unfair, one may behave righteously, but speak humbly." (14.04)

公伯寮愬子路于季孙。子服景伯以告,曰:"夫子固有惑志于公伯寮,吾力犹能肆诸市朝。"子曰:"道之将行也与,命也;道之将废也与,命也。公伯寮其如命何!"(14.38)

【白话译文】

公伯寮在季孙面前诽谤子路。子服景伯把这告诉孔子,并说:"季孙思想上真的被公伯寮迷惑了。我有力量能处决公伯寮,陈其尸体于市场或宫厅之外。"孔子说:"如果我的学说流行起来,取决于天命。如果我的学说消亡,也取决于天命。公伯寮能够对天命做些什么呢?"(14.38)

【注释】公伯寮(音 liáo 辽):姓公伯名寮,字子周。愬(音 sù 素):诉,告发,诽谤。子路:姓仲,名由,字子路。于:向。季孙:鲁国正卿姓季孙,名斯,谥(音 shì 是)桓,史称季桓子,公元前 505 年至公元前 492 年在位。子服景伯:姓子服名伯,谥号景,鲁国大夫。以:把这。告:告诉(孔子)。夫子:季孙。固:本来;通"故",连词,所以,因此。惑:迷惑。志:思想。于:被。力:力量。肆:处死罪人,陈尸示众(的地方)。诸:之于。市朝:市场。吾力犹能肆诸市朝:我的力量还能杀死他(公伯寮)陈其尸于市。道:主张、原则。将行:得到推行。也:助词,表停顿。与:同"欤(音 yú 余)",表感叹。命:天命。废:废弃。如命何:对天命能怎样。

【英译】

Gongbo Liao(1) slandered Zilu(2) in front of Jisun(3). Zifu Jingbo(4) notified Confucius of this and said, "Jisun has truly been deluded in his thought by Gongbo Liao. I still have the strength to execute Gongbo Liao and expose his corpse at a market or outside the palace." The Master said, "If my doctrines prevail, it depends on the mandates of Heaven. If my doctrines perish, it also depends on the mandates of Heaven. What can Gongbo Liao do to the mandates of Heaven?" (14.38)

【英译注】(1) Gongbo Liao: Style name Zizhou, his life unknown. (2) Zilu: Surname Zhong, first name You, style name Zilu, Confucius's disciple. (3) Jisun: Surname Jisun, first name Si, posthumous title Huan, chief minister (505 BC – 492 BC) of the State of Lu during the regimes of Duke Ding and Duke Ai. (4) Zifu Jingbo: Surname Zifu, first name of Bo, posthumous title Jing, a high official of the State of Lu.

子曰:"人能弘道,非道弘人。"(15.29)

【注释】弘:发扬光大。道:天下通达之理、规律,看不见,作用大。人能弘道:人能使道扩大,德才大者道随之大,德才小者道随之小。非道弘人:道不使人的德才扩大。

【白话译文】

孔子说:"一个人可以弘扬天道,但天道不能促进、提升一个人的品德和才华。"(15.29)

【英译】

The Master said, "A man can promote and expand the Way of Heaven, but the Way of Heaven cannot advance and enhance the morals and talents of a man." (15.29)

子曰："君子谋道不谋食。耕者，馁在其中矣；学也，禄在其中矣。君子忧道不忧贫。"(15.32)

【注释】谋：求。道：天下通达之理，摸不着，看不见，但作用无限。食：衣食。耕：种地。馁（音něi）：饥饿，饥饿问题、吃饭问题。在其中：在这中间。耕者，馁在其中矣：种地的事，其中有吃饭的问题呀。学：读书学习。禄：做官俸禄。忧：担心。贫：贫穷。

【白话译文】

孔子说："君子追随天道而不谋求生计。农夫在耕种中解决饥饿问题。学者因为学习才获得官俸。君子担心自己不知晓天道，而不担心自己的贫穷。"（15.32）

【英译】

The Master said, "A superior man pursues the Way of Heaven rather than seeking sustenance. A farmer deals with hunger problem while planting. A scholar obtains an official's salary because of studying. A superior man is anxious about his not perceiving the Way of Heaven but not about his own poverty." (15.32)

子曰："道不同，不相为谋。"(15.40)

【注释】道：主张、理想。同：相同。相：共同。为谋：商议。不相为谋：没法一起谋划。

【白话译文】

孔子说："两个人的思想体系不同，他们一起谋划不成一件大事。"（15.40）

【英译】

The Master said, "When ideologies of two persons are different, they cannot successfully plan an important thing together." (15.40)

子曰:"礼云礼云,玉帛云乎哉? 乐云乐云,钟鼓云乎哉?" (17.11)

【注释】礼、乐的道是本,器物是表,器物用来传道,体现出礼、乐。云:呀,语气词。玉:玉礼器。帛(音 bó 伯):丝织品。云:说。哉:吗。玉帛云乎哉:云玉帛乎哉,说的就是玉帛吗。乐(音 yuè 月):乐曲、乐舞。钟鼓:打击乐器。钟鼓云:云钟鼓,说的是钟鼓。

【白话译文】

孔子说:"礼啊! 礼啊! 礼说的仅仅就是玉石和丝绸吗? 乐啊! 乐啊! 乐说的仅仅就是钟、鼓吗?"(17.11)

【英译】

The Master said[1], "Alas, the Rites of Proprieties! Alas, the Rites of Proprieties! Do the Rites of Proprieties only speak of gems and silk? Alas, the Music! Alas, the Music! Does the Music only speak of the drum and bell?" (17.11)

【英译注】(1) This chapter discusses the contents and forms of rites and music. The Way of Nature of the Rites and Music is intrinsic, while their utensils are extrinsic. The utensils are used to express the Way of Nature and present what the etiquette or music is.

03

德 Morals

子曰："德不孤，必有邻。"(04.25)

【白话译文】

孔子说："如果一个人不缺少良好的品德，必然有很多人愿意与他为邻。"(04.25)

【英译】

The Master said, "If one is not short of good morals, there must be many people wishing to be his neighbors." (04.25)

【注释】德：有德的人；德是把道贯彻到心中而不失掉的好品质。孤：少、寡。不孤：不少，宽厚。邻：与他相处者。德不孤，必有邻：仁德宽厚的人，惠人益人，会有很多人跟随他、亲近他。

子曰："中庸之为，德也。其至矣乎！民鲜久矣。"(06.29)

【白话译文】

孔子说："符合中庸的行为，是一种道德行为。中庸很完美啊！但很长时间，在人民当中找不到它了。"(06.29)

【注释】中：正，中间，不偏不倚，无过无不及。庸：平常（道理）。中庸之为：依中庸标准做事的行为。德也：符合道德标准。其：第三人称代词，它，指中庸。至：最高、顶点。民：百姓。鲜（音xiǎn 显）：少，缺少。久：很久。民鲜久矣：很久以来，百姓很少有人按中庸标准做事了。

【英译】

The Master said, "A behaviour consistent with the Golden Mean[1] is a kind of morality. Ah! The Golden Mean is perfect! But it has been missing among the people for a long time." (06.29)

【英译注】(1) Golden Mean: One concept of Confucius School that combines two Chinese characters "Zhong" and "Yong". "Zhong" is "middle", without inclination to either side, and denotes the correct course to be pursued by all under heaven. "Yong" is "no change" and denotes the fixed principle regulating all under heaven.

子曰:"泰伯,其可谓至德也已矣。三以天下让,民无得而称焉。"(08.01)

【白话译文】

孔子说:"称泰伯具有完美品德,当之无愧。他三次让王位给他最小的弟弟,因此,人们找不到合适的词语称赞他。"(08.01)

【注释】泰伯:姓姬,周代古公亶(音 dǎn 胆)父的长子,为吴国始祖,公元前 1100 年前后逃至南蛮,让位给弟弟季历,季历传周文王,文王传武王,武王于公元前 1027 年伐纣,灭商朝。至:最高尚。三:多次。让:让王位。民:百姓。无得:找不到合适的词。称:赞扬(他)。

【英译】

The Master said, "Taibo[1] deserved being called a person of perfect morals! He three times offered the throne to his youngest brother, so the people could not find the right phrases to praise him." (08.01)

【英译注】(1) Taibo: Surname Ji, first name Taibo, the eldest son of three sons of chieftain Gugong Danfu of Zhou Clan at South of Qishan Mountains, currently at Shaanxi Province. His youngest brother Ji Li had a virtuous and able son Chang and his father desired to pass his throne to Ji Li. He and his another brother Zhongyong perceived this and fled to Southern China around 1100 BC as the creator of the State of Wu. Ji Li's son Ji Fa overthrew the Shang Dynasty in 1027 BC.

子曰:"有德者必有言,有言者不必有德;仁者必有勇,勇者不必有仁。"(14.05)

【注释】有:拥有、获得。德:道德、品德。者:的人。必:一定。言:言论、名言。勇:勇气,勇敢。

【白话译文】

孔子说:"有大德的人一定说了一些名言,但说了一些名言的人不一定就有大德。有仁德的人一定具有勇气,但具有勇气的人不一定就有仁德。"(14.05)

【英译】

The Master said, "One who possesses great morals must have spoken famous sayings, but those who have spoken famous sayings may not necessarily have great morals. A man of superior benevolence must possess courage, but those who possess courage may not necessarily possess the virtue of superior benevolence." (14.05)

子曰:“骥不称其力,称其德也。”(14.35)

【注释】骥:千里马。称:值得称赞。其:它的。力:气力。德:美德。

【白话译文】

孔子说:“骥是千里马,被称赞的不是它的力气,而是它的品德。”(14.35)

【英译】

The Master said, “Ji[1], a superior horse, is not praised for its stamina but for its moral character.” (14.35)

【英译注】(1) Confucius appreciated a winged steed for its subordinate moral to serve its master other than its strength to run fast and endurably.

或曰:“以德报怨,何如?”子曰:“何以报德?以直报怨,以德报德。”(14.36)

【注释】或曰:有人说。以:用。德:恩德。报:报答。怨:怨恨。何如:怎么样。直:正直。

【白话译文】

有人问:“用恩德报答怨恨,你看如何?”孔子说:“为什么用恩德报答怨恨?用正直报答怨恨,而用恩德报答恩德。”(14.36)

【英译】

Someone asked, “What do you think of requiting hatred with grace?” The Master said, “Why is hatred requited with grace? One requites hatred with uprightness and requites grace with grace.” (14.36)

子曰:"由,知德者鲜矣。"(15.04)

【白话译文】

孔子说:"由! 懂得品德的人,很少啊!"(15.04)

【英译】

The Master said, "You[1]! Oh, it is few who understand morals." (15.04)

【注释】由:姓仲名由,字子路。知:懂得。德:道德、品德、恩德。者:的人。鲜(音 xiǎn 显):稀少,缺少。

【英译注】(1) You: Surname Zhong, first name You, style name Zilu, Confucius's disciple.

齐景公有马千驷,死之日,民无德而称焉。伯夷、叔齐,饿于首阳之下,民到于今称之。其斯之谓与?(16.12)

【白话译文】

齐景公死时,有 4000 匹马,但人们没有发现他的一样行为值得称赞。伯夷、叔齐,在首阳山下饿死,他们一直到今天还被传颂。大概这能够告诉我们一点有关品德方面的东西吧?(16.12)

【英译】

Duke Jing[1] of the State of Qi possessed four thousand horses at his death, but the people could not find his single deed worthy

【注释】齐景公:姓姜名杵臼(音 chǔ 楚 jiù 旧),齐国国君,公元前 547 年至公元前 490 年在位。驷(音 sì 四):四匹马。死之日:死时。民:百姓。无:(对他)没有。德:德行。称:称颂。民无德而称焉:他没有品德值得百姓称颂呀。伯夷:姓墨,名允字公信。叔齐:姓墨,名致字公达。首阳:首阳山。其:大概。斯:这个意思。之谓:说的是。与:吧。其斯之谓与:大概说的就是这个意思吧。

【英译注】(1) Duke Jing: Surname Jiang, first name Chujiu, a Duke of the State of Qi from 547 BC to 490 BC. (2) Boyi and Shuqi: Boyi was the elder son of a monarch of the

of praise. Boyi and Shuqi(2) starved to death at the foot of the Shouyang Mountains(3), but they are extolled down to today. May this possibly tell us something of morals? (16. 12)

State of Guzhu in the Shang Dynasty, and Shuqi was his younger brother. Their father appointed Shuqi as his successor. After their father died, Shuqi gave the throne to Boyi, while Boyi respected their father and refused it. They all fled to the State of Zhou. Later they remonstrated with the King of the State of Zhou not to overthrow the last emperor of the Shang Dynasty. When the Zhou succeeded, they sadly ran into Shouyang Mountains and refused the food from the Zhou Dynasty, and died from hunger strike. (3) Shouyang Mountains: Located at current Yuncheng City, Shanxi Province.

子曰:"乡原,德之贼也。"(17.13)

【白话译文】

孔子说:"在一个乡镇,一个表面老实的人,既不得罪谁,也不辨别善恶,实际上是一个破坏道德的卑鄙的人。"(17.13)

【英译】

The Master said, "At a town, an ostensibly honest man who neither offends anybody nor distinguishes clearly between right and wrong is actually a mean man who undermines morals." (17.13)

【注释】乡:12500户为一乡,此指乡里、一个地方。原(音yuàn愿),古字通"愿",忠厚老实[15]。此指随人所愿,不得罪人。乡原:一说,到一乡、一地,就揣摩人情,顺意而为,博得好感;二说,古字"乡"与"向"同,见人就向人投其所好,随其趣向,曲意逢迎。贼:破坏者。乡原,德之贼也:好好先生,不讲是非,言行不一,以媚于世,以博取忠厚之名,是对仁德民风的败坏啊。

子曰:“道听而涂说,德之弃也。”(17.14)

【白话译文】

孔子说:“一个人在路上听到什么,不经证实马上就传播出去,这是有道德的人所唾弃的作风。”(17.14)

【英译】

The Master said, “A person hears something on the road and then at once spreads it unverified, which is a style cast aside by moral people.”(17.14)

【注释】道:路。而:就、却。涂:途、路程。说:传播。弃:丢失、废置。道听而涂说:路上听了就传,必多错误。德之弃:道德所唾弃的。

子张曰:“执德不弘,信道不笃,焉能为有,焉能为亡?”(19.02)

【白话译文】

子张说:“如果一个人遵守道德不坚定,信仰天道不全心,那么他存在与否,有什么关系?”(19.02)

【英译】

Zizhang(1) said, “What does it matter that such a man exists or not if he neither follows the morals firmly nor believes the Way of Heaven with all his heart?”(19.02)

【注释】子张:姓颛(音 zhuān 砖)孙,名师,字子张。执:实行。德:道德、品德。弘:今天的“强”字,坚强、坚定。信:信仰。道:正道、主张、原则。笃:坚定。焉:怎么。能:能够。为:算是。有:存在。焉能为有:(这种人)怎么能算作存在。亡(音 wú 吴):无、不,不存在。焉能为亡:怎么能算作不存在(有没有这种人无所谓)。

【英译注】(1) Zizhang: Confucius's disciple, surname Zhuansun, first name Shi, style name Zizhang.

子夏曰:"大德不逾闲,小德出入可也。"(19.11)

【注释】子夏:姓卜名商,字子夏。大德:大是大非。逾:超越。闲:木栏,界限。小德:细枝末节。出入:不一致,有差距。可:可以,没问题。

【白话译文】

子夏说:"在关键品德上不超越界限,但在末节问题上有灵活性是可以的。"(19.11)

【英译】

Zixia(1) said, "One does not overstep the bounds on critical virtues, but it is all right that he is flexible on minor matters." (19.11)

【英译注】(1) Zixia: Confucius's disciple, surname Bu, first name Shang, style name Zixia.

04

自然 The Nature

子曰:"岁寒,然后知松柏之后彫也。"(09.28)

【注释】寒:严寒。知:明白、看清。之:语助词,取消句子的独立性。后:在……后,在一般草木落叶或枯萎后。彫:《说文》"半伤也","小小受伤,生机不减"[J02]。后彫也:在其他树木落叶之后,(松柏)还保持绿叶茂盛,郁郁葱葱;何晏"大寒之岁,众木皆死,然后知松柏小雕伤"。

【白话译文】

孔子说:"到了一年寒冷时,才知道在其他树木落叶之后,只有松树柏树还郁郁葱葱。"

【英译】

The Master said, "It is not until the year turns cold, and other trees shed their leaves that we see that the pine and the cypress remain green."

色斯举矣,翔而后集。曰:"山梁雌雉,时哉时哉!"子路共之,三嗅而作。(10.27)

【注释】色:(人的)神情改变。斯:(野鸡)就。举:飞走。矣:啦。翔:飞翔。而后:一会儿。集:汇合起来,落到某处。曰:(孔子)说。山梁:山岭。雌:母。雉:野鸡。时哉:懂得时宜呀。子路:姓仲名由,字子路。共(音 gōng 公):通"供",供给、投食。嗅:(鸡)用鼻子辨别气味。而:并且、就。作:啄食。

【白话译文】

看到人的面色变化,野鸡立刻飞了起来,盘旋着,很快落在一块。孔子说:"啊,在山梁上的母野鸡,它们真知道好时机啊!它们真知道好时机啊!"子路投食,它们三番五次观望,而后开始啄起来了。(10.27)

【英译】

Seeing a person's countenance change, pheasants flew up instantly, hovering round, and soon settled together. The Master said, "Oh, the hen pheasants on the hill ridge! They truly know the right opportunity! They truly know the right opportunity!" When Zilu(1) threw them some food, they observed it three times and then started to peck at it. (10.27)

【英译注】(1) Zilu: Surname Zhong, first name You, style name Zilu, Confucius's disciple.

二
Two

人
Human Being

05

人 Human Being

曾子曰:“吾日三省乎吾身。为人谋而不忠乎?与朋友交而不信乎?传不习乎?”(01.04)

【白话译文】

曾子说:“每天我三次就如下内容反省自己:为别人处理事务,我竭尽全力吗?与朋友相处,我对他们诚信吗?老师传授给我的东西,我练习了吗?”(01.04)

【注释】曾子:姓曾名参(音 shēn 申),字子舆,鲁国南武城人,今山东平邑县人。吾:我。日:每天。三:多次。省(音 xǐng 醒):自我检查。乎:于、对。身:自身。为(音 wèi 慰):给、替。谋:谋划、办事。忠:尽心、竭力。乎:吗。交:交往。信:诚信。传(音 chuán 船):传授,教给学生的知识。习:(自己)通晓、熟悉。

【英译】

Master Zeng[1] said, “Every day I question myself three times[2] on the following: Do I exhaust myself when I handle affairs for others? Am I faithful to my friends when I get along with them? And do I practice what I am taught by my masters?” (01.04)

【英译注】(1) Master Zeng: Confucius's disciple (505 BC – 436 BC), surname Zeng, first name Shen, and style name Ziyu, a person from Nanwucheng, the State of Lu, currently at Pingyi County, Shandong Province. (2) three times: Many times, not limited to three times.

有子曰:“信近于义,言可复也。恭近于礼,远耻辱也。因不失其亲,亦可宗也。”(01.13)

【注释】有子:姓有,名若,字子有,孔子弟子,小孔子43岁。他或他的弟子可能参与了《论语》的编纂,因为只有他与曾子、冉子、闵子是《论语》中称“子”的孔子弟子。《史记》载他的身材面貌与孔子相似,孔子刚去世时,孔子弟子一致立他为师,对待他如同对待孔子一样。信:信约、约定。近于:符合。义:道义。言:承诺。可:能够、可以。复:履行、实行。恭:恭敬。远(音 yuàn 院):远离。因:依靠、凭借。失:丧失。其:自己的。亲:可靠的人或原则。宗:主、可靠、靠得住。因不失其亲,亦可宗也:对此句的解释争议较大,大体意思是依靠可靠的人,做事也就有把握了。

【白话译文】

有子说:“当一个人与他人的约定接近正义,他就可以兑现他的承诺。一个人的恭维态度接近于礼仪,他就可以远离耻辱。如果信赖了可靠的人,一个人就可能牢靠地达到目标。”(01.13)

【英译】

Master You[1] said, “One can carry out his promise when his agreement with others is close to righteousness. One can keep away from humiliation when his deference is nearly consistent with the Rites of Proprieties. And one may be ensured to achieve a goal if trustworthy persons are relied upon.[2] (01.13)

【英译注】(1) Master You: Confucius's excellent disciple, surname You, first name Ruo. He was recommended by his classmates to teach them after their Master Confucius died. It is believed that his disciples partially edited *The Analects*. (2) This sentence's meaning is controversial, with the following translations for reference: (A) A thing can be reliable if a proper intimate person is depended upon. (B) The principles, which do not deviate from earnest teachings of one's parents, can be his reliable guides and standards to handle daily affairs.

子游曰:“事君数,斯辱矣。朋友数,斯疏矣。”(04.26)

【白话译文】

子游说:“一个人伺候君主太频繁就会受到污辱。一个人与朋友交往太频繁,就会受到疏远。”(04.26)

【英译】

Ziyou(1) said, “One can be insulted when he attends upon his sovereign too frequently. And one can be estranged from his friends when he associates them too frequently.”(04.26)

【注释】子游:姓言,名偃(音yǎn眼),字子游,吴人。事:侍奉。数(音shuò硕):屡次,频繁。斯:就、那么。辱:(招致)侮辱。事君数,斯辱矣:侍奉国君频繁,以为是熟人了,忽视礼节,就会招致侮辱呀。朋友:劝告朋友;与朋友交往。疏:(被)疏远、疏薄;“朋友数,斯疏矣”值得深思,别说朋友为何疏远,就是当初亲密的夫妻,有多少为何疏远,甚至成了路人了。

【英译注】(1) Ziyou: Surname Yan, first name Yan, style name Ziyou, Confucius's disciple from the State of Wu.

子曰:“中人以上,可以语上也;中人以下,不可以语上也。”(06.21)

【白话译文】

孔子说:“对中等以上水平的人,可以与他讨论重大事情。对中等以下水平的人,不可以与他讨论重大事情。”(06.21)

【注释】中人:德、才、智分为上中下三等,中等者为中人。可以:能够(向他)。语(音yù玉):和别人一起谈论、交流。上:上等的德才智,高深的修养学问。

【英译】

The Master said, "With someone who is above average, one can discuss weighty matters, but one cannot discuss weighty matters with someone below average." (06.21)

子曰:"知者乐水,仁者乐山;知者动,仁者静;知者乐,仁者寿。"(06.23)

【注释】知(音 zhì 志):智,智慧。者:的人。乐(古音 yào 耀,今音 lè 勒):喜爱,自得其志,劳从其愿,故愉悦。水:运其才智以治世,如水流不止。山:山之安固,自然不动。动:日进故动。静:无欲故静。寿:长寿。

【白话译文】

孔子说:"智慧的人热爱河流,仁德的人热爱高山。智慧的人活跃,仁德的人安静。智慧的人享受自我,仁德的人享受长寿。"(06.23)

【英译】

The Master said, "A man of wisdom loves a river(1) and a man of superior benevolence loves a mountain(2). A man of wisdom is lively and a man of superior benevolence is tranquil. And a man of wisdom enjoys himself and a man of superior benevolence enjoys longevity." (06.23)

【英译注】(1) river: It can generally be a stream, river, lake, and ocean that shows flexibility of wisdom. (2) a mountain: It is secure, stable, and reliable, and thus referred to superior benevolence.

子曰："志于道，据于德，依于仁，游于艺。"（07.06）

【注释】志：心意、志向。于：在。道：社会或自然的规律，或者周代的礼仪制度。志于道：目标在道。据：根据、执守、靠着。德：道贯彻到心中而不失掉者。依：依靠、凭借。游：游弋。艺：礼、乐（音 yuè 月）、射、御、书、数，为孔子所教的六门课程。

【白话译文】

孔子说："把一个人的理想放在探索天道上，培养和保持自己的高尚道德，遵守仁义，自娱自乐在六艺之中。"（07.06）

【英译】

The Master said, "Set one's ambitions on seeking the Way of Heaven(1), cultivate and keep one's lofty morals, abide by superior benevolence, and amuse oneself in the six arts(2)." (07.06)

【英译注】(1) Way of Heaven: It could be the system of the Rites of Proprieties or right ideology in the Zhou Dynasty. (2) six arts: They were the Rites of Proprieties, Music, archery, carriage driving, *Book of History*, and mathematics, six courses taught by Confucius.

子曰："兴于诗，立于礼，成于乐。"（08.08）

【注释】兴：振奋，修身。于：从，由于。诗：学《诗经》。兴于诗：诗篇使人振奋。立：立身。礼：礼节。立于礼：礼法使人立足于世。成：成人、学成。乐（音 yuè 月）：乐曲、乐舞。成于乐：音乐使人学有所成（乐是孔子所教的最后内容）。

【白话译文】

孔子说："一个人通过《诗》振奋起来，通过礼仪让自己在社会上站得稳，通过礼乐完成他的学业。"（08.08）

【英译】

The Master said, "One inspires himself by *Poems and Odes*(1), establishes himself well

【英译注】(1) *Poems and Ode*: Currently called *Book of Poetry*, containing 305 songs, odes, and epics. (2) Music is the last course

in society by the Rites of Proprieties, and accomplishes his learning by Ritual Music(2)." (08.08)

taught by Confucius. One could accomplish his learning after finishing this course.

子曰:"知者不惑,仁者不忧,勇者不惧。"(09.29)

【注释】知(音 zhì 志):智,智慧。者:的人。惑:迷惑。忧:忧愁。惧:畏惧。

【白话译文】

孔子说:"智慧的人不迷惑,仁义的人不忧愁,勇敢的人不畏惧。"(09.29)

【英译】

The Master said, "A man of wisdom is not perplexed, a man of superior benevolence is not anxious, and a man of courage is fearless." (09.29)

子曰:"不得中行而与之,必也狂狷乎!狂者进取,狷者有所不为也。"(13.21)

【注释】不得:得不到。中:中正,不偏不倚,中庸之道。行:言行。与:交往。之:他。不得中行而与之:我找不到言行中庸的人而与他交往。必也狂狷乎:只能交往激进或保守的人了。必:一定。狂:狂放者。狷(音 juàn 倦):拘谨,保守。进取:进取善道,一意向前,知进不知退。不为:畏缩不前,该做的不敢做。

【白话译文】

孔子说:"如果我找不到奉行中庸之道的人去交往,我必须选择激进的人或胆小的人。激进的人迫不及待善意进取而不顾危险,但是胆小的人太谨慎以至于有些

事当做而不做。”（13. 21）

【英译】

The Master said, “If I cannot find the people of Golden Mean[(1)] to get along with, I must select either a zealous man or a timid man. A zealous man is eager to advance for goodwill regardless of danger, but a timid man is too cautious to do something necessary.” (13.21)

【英译注】(1) Golden Mean: The Way of Nature always kept on at the center, impartially. Confucius selected two extremes to illustrate the Way.

子贡问曰：“乡人皆好之，何如？”子曰：“未可也。”“乡人皆恶之，何如？”子曰：“未可也。不如乡人之善者好之，其不善者恶之。”（13. 24）

【注释】子贡：姓端木名赐，字子贡。乡人：全乡人，一乡 12500 家。好（音 hào 号）：喜爱。之：他一个人或一件事。未可也：不能肯定呀。恶（音 wù 务）：憎恨。乡人之善者：全乡的好人。其：乡人。其不善者：全乡的坏人。

【白话译文】

子贡问道：“全乡的人都喜欢一个人，你认为他怎么样？”孔子说：“不那么好。”“全乡的人都厌恶他，你认为他怎么样？”孔子说：“也不那么好。不如全乡的好人都喜欢他，全乡的坏人都厌恶他。”（13. 24）

【英译】

Zigong[1] asked, "How do you think about a person who is liked by all the people in a town [2]?" The Master replied, "Not so good." "How do you think about that he is detested by all the people in a town?" The Master said, "Not so good either. It is no better than that he is liked by all the good people and detested by all the bad people in the town." (13.24)

【英译注】(1) Zigong: Surname Duanmu, first name Ci, style name Zigong. (2) town: An administrative unit as a township, which was composed of 12, 500 households at Confucius's time.

子路问成人。子曰:"若臧武仲之知,公绰之不欲,卞庄子之勇,冉求之艺,文之以礼乐,亦可以为成人矣。"曰:"今之成人者何必然?见利思义,见危授命,久要不忘平生之言,亦可以为成人矣。"(14.13)

【白话译文】

子路问如何成为完美的人。孔子说:"如果他像臧武仲一样智慧,像公绰一样清心寡欲,像卞庄子一样勇敢,像冉求一样多才多艺,再加上用礼、乐培养外在的品质,他就可以成为完美的人了。"稍后,他补充道:"今天完美的人何必这样?如果一个人不见利忘义,祖国危险时能不惜生

【注释】子路:姓仲,名由,字子路。问:讨教。成人:完美的人。若:如果具备。臧武仲:臧孙纥(音gē哥),鲁国大夫。之:的。知(音zhì志):智,智慧。公绰:孟公绰(音chuò辍),鲁国大夫,属于孟孙氏家族。不欲:克制、不贪婪。卞庄子:鲁国卞邑大夫,勇敢有力,一次战争中杀敌70人(一作10人)而死,传说能与虎独斗,留刺双虎故事。冉求:姓冉、名求,字子有。艺:多才多艺。文:修饰。以:用。亦:也就。何必:为什么一定。然:这样。危:危险。授命:献出生命。久:长久。要:古时的"约"字,穷困。平生:平时。言:诺言。

命，长期遭受贫困时也不忘当初的诺言，他就可以认为是完美的人了。”(14.13)

【英译】

Zilu[1] asked how one could become a perfect man. The Master said, "One can become a perfect man if he is as wise as Zang Wuzhong[2], as ascetic as Gong Chuo[3], as brave as Master Bian Zhuang[4], and as versatile as Ran Qiu[5], plus that he cultivates his external qualities by the Rites of Proprieties and Ritual Music." Later he added, "Why must a perfect man of today be like that? If one does not forsake good for the sake of gold, does not spare life when his motherland is in danger, and he does not forget his original promises even when he long suffers from poverty, he can be reckoned as a perfect man." (14.13)

【英译注】(1) Zilu: Confucius's disciple, surname Zhong, first name You, style name Zilu. (2) Zang Wuzhong: First name Sunge, last name Zang, a senior official of the State of Lu, famous for his wisdom. (3) Gong Chuo: From Mengsun family in the State of Lu, well-known for his pure heart and few desires. (4) Master Bian Zhuang: A senior official of the State of Lu. He was brave and killed 70 (or 10) persons of enemy in a battle, full of strength to solely fight with a tiger. A story tells that he had two tigers killed once. (5) Ran Qiu: Confucius's disciple, surname Ran, first name Qiu, style name Ziyou, with multiple talents.

子曰：“人无远虑，必有近忧。”(15.12)

【注释】无：没有。远：长远的。虑：谋划。近：眼前的。忧：忧患。必有近忧：一定就会有即将到来的忧患。

【白话译文】

孔子说：“一个人对未来缺乏长远谋虑，他一定会有近在眼前的忧愁。”(15.12)

【英译】

The Master said, "If one lacks forethought for the future, he must have anxieties about immediate matters." (15.12)

子曰:"巧言乱德。小不忍,则乱大谋。"(15.27)

【注释】巧言:花言巧语。乱:败坏。小:小事,细节。忍:忍耐、检点。大谋:大事、要事。

【白话译文】

孔子说:"轻佻的语言会破坏道德。在小事上缺乏忍耐,会破坏重大计划。"(15.27)

【英译】

The Master said, "Guileful words may vitiate morals. And lack of forbearance in trifles may spoil a great plan." (15.27)

子曰:"性相近也,习相远也。"(17.02)

【注释】性:人的本性。相:相互。近:接近。习:耳闻目睹,反复练习,习俗、习惯。远:疏远,差别很大。习相远:由于习俗的熏陶、耳闻目睹,(人与人)大不一样了。也:句末语气词,表示判断、肯定。

【白话译文】

孔子说:"人与人,本质上是相近的,但通过习染变得大不相同。"(17.02)

【英译】

The Master said, "People are alike by nature, but become widely different by practice." (17.02)

子曰:"不知命,无以为君子;不知礼,无以立也;不知言,无以知人也。"(20.03)

【注释】知:懂得。命:天命。无以:就不能。为:成为。立:立身处世。知言:辨别他人言语的是非。知人:了解他人善恶、本性、品质。

【白话译文】

孔子说:"一个人不理解天命,他就不能成为君子;不理解礼仪,他就不能在社会上立身;不理解一个人的言语,他就不能真正懂得这个人。"(20.03)

【英译】

The Master said, "One cannot become a superior man if he does not perceive the Mandate of Heaven; one cannot establish himself in society if he does not perceive the Rites of Proprieties; and one cannot truly know a person if he does not perceive his words." (20.03)

06

小人 An Inferior Man

子曰:“君子周而不比,小人比而不周。”(02.14)

【注释】周:合群、团结。比(音 bì 闭):勾结。

【白话译文】

孔子说:“君子团结他人而不拉帮结派,但是小人拉帮结派而不团结他人。”(02.14)

【英译】

The Master said, “A superior man unites others and does not collude with them, but an inferior man colludes with others and does not unite them.” (02.14)

子曰:“君子喻于义,小人喻于利。”(04.16)

【注释】喻:通达。义:正义。利:财利、私利、谋利益。另一种读法:“子曰:‘君子,喻于义。小人,喻于利。’”君子:掌权者。喻:晓喻、教育、开导。于:在。义:道义,如三纲五常之类。喻于义:在道义上,进行教育、开导。小人:百姓。利:获利或谋生手段。

【白话译文】

孔子说:“君子非常明白的是正义,而小人明白的仅是私利。”(04.16)

【英译】

The Master said, "A superior man well knows righteousness and an inferior man only knows selfish gains.[(1)]" (04.16)

【英译注】(1) Another translation: A superior man is educated with righteousness, and an inferior man is educated with measures to make a life.

子谓子夏曰:"女为君子儒,无为小人儒。"(06.13)

【注释】谓:告诉,对……说。子夏:姓卜名商,字子夏。女(音rǔ辱):汝,你。为:做。儒:博学先王之道,有学问的人,分为君子和小人。君子:人格高贵。小人:品格平庸、低下。

【白话译文】

孔子对子夏说:"你要成为具有君子素质的学者,不要成为具有小人素质的学者。"(06.13)

【英译】

The Master said to Zixia[(1)], "You want to be a scholar with qualities of a superior man, and not be a scholar with qualities of an inferior man." (06.13)

【英译注】(1) Zixia: Confucius's disciple, surname Bu, first name Shang, style name Zixia.

子曰:"君子坦荡荡,小人长戚戚。"(07.37)

【注释】坦:平直、宽广,豁达、开朗。荡荡:平坦。坦荡荡:豁达开朗,胸怀大度。长:经常。戚戚:忧愁。

【白话译文】

孔子说:"君子坦荡开朗,小人常悲哀、心胸狭窄。"(07.37)

【英译】

The Master said, "A superior man is optimistic and magnanimous, while an inferior man is frequently grievous and narrow-minded." (07.37)

子曰:"君子成人之美,不成人之恶。小人反是。"(12.16)

【注释】成:成全、助长。人:别人。美:好事。恶(音 è 饿):不良行为。反:相反。是:这样。小人反是:小人的做法与此相反。

【白话译文】

孔子说:"君子帮助他人做好事,不做坏事。小人正相反。"(12.16)

【英译】

The Master said, "A superior man helps others do good deeds but not do evil ones. And an inferior man just does the opposite." (12.16)

子曰:"君子和而不同,小人同而不和。"(13.23)

【注释】和:和谐,和睦,协调,不同的东西和谐地配合,如八音的和谐,五味的调和。同:相同,附和,相同者混合,人云亦云。和而不同:追求和谐,但不盲目附和。

【白话译文】

孔子说:"君子通过独立表达他的观点达到整体和谐,但不附和他人。小人通过含糊地表达他的观点附和他人,而不达整体和谐。"(13.23)

【英译】

The Master said, " A superior man acquires overall harmony[1] by expressing his opinions independently, but does not echo others. And an inferior man echoes others by expressing his opinions ambiguously, but does not acquire overall harmony. " (13.23)

【英译注】(1) harmony: It is a perfect status reached by unique elements, like a piece of wonderful music work in ancient China played collectively by eight unique instruments of metal, stone, string, bamboo, gourd, clay, leather, and wood other than monotonically by one instrument only.

子曰:"君子易事而难说也。说之不以道,不说也;及其使人也,器之。小人难事而易说也。说之虽不以道,说也。及其使人也,求备焉。"(13.25)

【注释】易事:易于与人相处共事。说(音 yuè 月):悦,愉快。难说:不易取得他的欢喜。以:按照。道:正道。及:等到。其:他。使:任用。器之:量才而用。难事:难共事。易说:易于欢心。求备:求全责备。

【白话译文】

孔子说:"为君子工作是很容易的,但取悦他却很难。如果错误地取悦他,他是不高兴的。当他选择人服务他时,他会因才使用。为小人工作是很难的,但取悦他却很容易。按错误的方式取悦他,他是快乐的。当他用人时,求全责备。"(13.25)

【英译】

The Master said, "It is easy to work for a superior man, but difficult to gratify him. If one tries to gratify him wrongly, he will be unhappy with it. When he chooses people for service, he employs them based on their talents. It is hard to work for an inferior man, but easy to gratify him. He will be happy if he is gratified wrongly. When he uses people, he demands perfection and finds faults with them."(13.25)

子曰:"君子泰而不骄,小人骄而不泰。"(13.26)

【注释】泰:安静坦然。骄:傲慢无礼。

【白话译文】

孔子说:"君子安详但不骄横,小人骄横但不安详。"(13.26)

【英译】

The Master said, "A superior man is composed but not arrogant. And an inferior man is arrogant but not composed."(13.26)

子曰:"君子上达,小人下达。"(14.24)

【注释】上:本,德义、仁义。达:通达。下:末,财利、器艺,农工商各业。小人下达:小人通达于财利。

【白话译文】

孔子说:"君子通达上层建筑,小人通达基础建设。"(14.24)

【英译】

The Master said, "A superior man has a good sense in the superstructure[1] and an inferior man has a good sense in the infrastructure[2]." (14.24)

【英译注】(1) superstructure: Morals, benevolence, righteousness and so on, even the Way of Heaven. (2) infrastructure: Selfish gains, profits, basic living skills, and others.

子曰:"君子求诸己,小人求诸人。"(15.21)

【注释】求诸己:对自己求全责备。求诸人:对别人求全责备。

【白话译文】

孔子说:"君子严格要求自己完美,小人严格要求他人完美。"(15.21)

【英译】

The Master said, "A superior man strictly demands perfection on himself, and an inferior man strictly demands perfection on others." (15.21)

子曰:"君子不可小知,而可大受也。小人不可大受,而可小知也。"(15.34)

【注释】不可:不可以使用。小:小事。知:考验(他);智慧、聪明。而:而是。可:可以(让他)。大:大事。受:承担。大受:受大,承担大事重任。

【白话译文】

孔子说:"君子不可在小事上显示聪明,但可以承担重大任务。小人不可以承

担重大任务，但可在小事上显示聪明。”（15.34）

【英译】

The Master said, “A superior man cannot show his wisdom in small matters, but can undertake great tasks. And an inferior man cannot undertake great tasks, but can show his wisdom in small matters.” (15.34)

子夏曰：“小人之过也必文。”（19.08）

【注释】子夏：姓卜名商，字子夏。之：的。过：错。必：一定。文（音 wèn 问）：掩饰。

【白话译文】

子夏说：“如果小人犯了错，他一定会掩饰它。”（19.08）

【英译】

Zixia said, “If an inferior man makes a mistake, he must whitewash it.” (19.08)

【英译注】(1) Zixia: Confucius's disciple, surname Bu, first name Shang, style name Zixia.

07

君子 A Superior Man

子曰:“君子之于天下也,无适也,无莫也,义之与比。”(04.10)

【白话译文】

孔子说:“对于天下的事,君子没有偏爱的,也没有轻视的。只要符合正义的,他就去做。”(04.10)

【英译】

The Master said, “For anything under the sky, a superior man neither favours it nor slights it. He does whatever is in compliance with righteousness.”(04.10)

【注释】之于:对于。天下:天下人和事。无:不、没有。适(音 dí 笛):亲近、厚待。无适也:没有必须亲近的,没有一个模式确定必须这么做。莫:疏远、冷淡。无莫也:没有必须疏远的,没有一个模式确定必须不这么做。义:适宜、妥当;正义。之:的。与:就。比:接近、并列。义之与比:义无亲疏,怎么符合义,就怎么做。

子曰:“君子欲讷于言而敏于行。”(04.24)

【白话译文】

孔子说:“君子对自己的要求是:说话慎重精练,行动勤奋机敏。”(04.24)

【注释】欲:愿意、要求(自己)。讷(音 nè):迟钝,话少,谨慎。言:主动对人说话。敏:勤奋、机敏。行:行动、行为。

【英译】

The Master said, "A superior man requires himself that he speaks cautiously and concisely and behaves industriously and resourcefully." (04.24)

子谓子贱:"君子哉若人!鲁无君子者,斯焉取斯?"(05.03)

【注释】谓:评论。子贱:姓宓(音 fú 伏)名不齐,字子贱。若:此。君子哉若人:君子呀,此人。鲁无君子者:(假如)鲁国无君子。斯焉:此人。取:学到。斯:此品德。斯焉取斯:此人从哪里学到了这种品德。

【白话译文】

孔子评论子贱说:"这个人是君子啊!如果鲁国没有君子,他能够从谁那里取得他的好品德呢?"(05.03)

【英译】

The Master commented on Zijian(1), "Ah, this man is a superior man! If there were no superior men at the State of Lu, from whom could he have acquired his good morals?" (05.03)

【英译注】(1) Zijian: Confucius's disciple, surname Fu, first name Buqi, style name Zijian, from the State of Lu or the State of Song.

子谓子产:"有君子之道四焉:其行己也恭,其事上也敬,其养民也惠,其使民也义。"(05.16)

【注释】鲁昭公二十年(公元前522年),子产卒,孔子30岁,闻之,为之出涕,赞扬之。谓:评论。子产:姓公孙名侨,字子产,郑国贤相,郑穆公之孙。四:四项。其:他。行己:自己行为。恭:庄重。

【白话译文】

孔子评论子产说："他有四种君子的品德：他举止恭敬，服侍国君敬重，教养百姓恩惠，役使百姓公正。"（05.16）

事：侍奉。上：国君。敬：尊敬。养：教育、养活。惠：恩惠。使：役使。民：百姓。义：符合时宜、时机恰当。

【英译】

The Master commented on Zichan(1), "He has four virtues of a superior man: he behaved himself deferentially, served his sovereign reverently, nourished the common people favorably(2), and employed the people justly." (05.16)

【英译注】(1) Zichan: Surname Gongsun, first name Qiao, style name Zichan, grandson of Duke Zhengmu, an excellent diplomatist and wise prime minister of the State of Zheng during regimes of Duke Jian and Duke Ding from 554 BC to 522 BC. When he died, Confucius was 30. (2) He gave the State's agricultural lands to the common people and collected a favourable tax from them.

子曰："质胜文则野，文胜质则史。文质彬彬，然后君子。"（06.18）

【注释】质：朴实自然。胜：多于、超过。文：文采，修饰。则：就，那么。野：粗野。史：言词华丽，虚伪轻浮。彬（音 bīn 宾）：兼备相宜。

【白话译文】

孔子说："一个人重视内在品质而忽视外在优美，就显得粗野。他注重外在优美而忽视内在品质，就显得虚浮。当他很好平衡了内在品质和外在优美时，他就是一名君子。"（06.18）

【英译】

The Master said, "One seems boorish when he emphasizes intrinsic quality but ignores extrinsic excellence. He seems superficial when he focuses on extrinsic excellence but ignores intrinsic quality. When he well balances both intrinsic quality and extrinsic excellence, he is then a superior man." (06.18)

子曰:"君子博学于文,约之以礼,亦可以弗畔矣夫!"(06.27)

【注释】博:广泛。于:在。文:遗留典籍。约:约束自己。之:他;毛奇龄说,博约是两事,文礼是两物。此为以礼约文,以约约博,博在文,约文又在礼。[2] 以:用。亦:也就。弗:不会。畔(音 pàn 判):叛,背叛,违道、背离(君子之道)。矣夫:啊,强烈感叹词。

【白话译文】

孔子说:"君子广泛学习历史文献,用礼仪约束他的学习,这样他就可以不离经叛道了!"(06.27)

【英译】

The Master said, "A superior man extensively studies the historical documents, and restrains his studies within the boundary of the Rites of Proprieties, and thus he may not be heretical and deviate from the true teachings!" (06.27)

曾子曰:“可以托六尺之孤,可以寄百里之命,临大节而不可夺也。君子人与?君子人也。”(08.06)

【注释】曾子:姓曾名参(音 shēn 申),字子舆,鲁国南武城(今山东平邑)人。托:(承担他人)临终嘱托。六尺:六尺指15岁以下,七尺指成年。孤:死去父亲的幼儿(幼君主)。寄:寄托。百里:国家。命:政权。临:遇到。大节:紧要关头。夺:屈服。人:此人。君子人与:此人是君子吗。也:啊。

【白话译文】

曾子说:“一个人可以受托照顾六尺高的孤儿王子,可以把方形边长100里的国家命运委托给他,且他在生死关头不变节投降。这样的人是君子吗?是的,他是君子。”(08.06)

【英译】

Master Zeng(1) said, “A man can be entrusted to care for an orphan prince of six *chi*(2), can be authorized with the fate of a duke's state squared with a side of 100 *li*(3), and does not yield his integrity at a critical life-and-death juncture. Is such a man a superior man? Yes, he is.” (08.06)

【英译注】(1) Master Zeng: Confucius's disciple (505 BC – 436 BC), surname Zeng, first name Shen, and style name Ziyu, a person from Nanwucheng, the State of Lu, currently Pingyi County, Shandong Province. (2) an orphan prince of six *chi*: A prince aged younger than 15 years with height of six *chi*, currently about 138 centimeters as 1 ancient *chi* was 23 centimeters. (3) 100 *li*: The side of the squared state was 100 *li*, currently equal to about 50 kilometers. *Li* is Chinese unit of length equal to half a kilometer today.

子曰:“论笃是与,君子者乎? 色庄者乎?”(11.21)

【注释】论:讲话。笃:诚实。是:宾语前置词。与:赞许。论笃是与:说话诚恳,就给予赞扬。君子者乎:(此说话诚恳的人)是君子吗。色:外表。庄:庄重。

【白话译文】

孔子说:“仅仅因为一个人只是说话真诚,就可以一定肯定他的为人吗? 这个人真正是君子吗? 或者他表面看起来是庄重的人?”(11.21)

【英译】

The Master said, “Can a person be highly regarded simply because he only talks sincerely? Is he really a superior man? Or does he appear solemn superficially?” (11.21)

棘子成曰:“君子质而已矣,何以文为?”子贡曰:“惜乎,夫子之说君子也! 驷不及舌。文犹质也,质犹文也。虎豹之鞟,犹犬羊之鞟。”(12.08)

【注释】棘子成:卫国大夫。质:本质,品质(好)。已:可以。矣:了。君子质而已矣:君子品质好就可以了。何:为何。以:采用。文:表面的仪式。为:呢,反问语气词。子贡:姓端木名赐,字子贡。惜:可惜,遗憾。夫子:棘子成。之:的。说(音 shuō):陈述,解说。驷:四匹马拉的华丽车辆。不及:赶不上、比不上。舌:舌头,一解“说出的话”;二解“文采飞扬、修养高深的言论”。驷不及舌:一解“一言既出,驷马难追”;二解“驷马豪车,比不上文采飞扬的言论”。犹:像,同。鞟(音 kuò 扩):去毛

【白话译文】

棘子成说:“君子培养内在品质就够了。为什么他需要培育外在优美呢?”子贡说:“可惜,先生你这么评说君子啊! 四匹马拉的豪华车子,无法超越美妙的言辞。

外在的形式，好似内在的品质；反之亦然。虎豹的皮，去掉了外皮上的毛，与光秃秃的犬羊皮没大的区别。”（12.08）

的兽皮，皮革。虎豹之鞟：虎豹的皮革；没了毛，如同犬羊的皮革。

【英译】

Ji Zicheng(1) said, "It is enough for a superior man to cultivate his intrinsic qualities only. Why need he cherish his extrinsic excellence?" Zigong(2) answered, "How pity is it for you a gentleman to speak of a superior man! A gorgeous carriage drawn by four horses can not overtake brilliant speech. The extrinsic form is similar to the intrinsic quality, and vice versa. The hide of a tiger or leopard whose fur has been skinned is not much different from the bald hide of a dog or goat." (12.08)

【英译注】(1) Ji Zicheng: The senior official of the State of Wei, located at current Weihui City, Henan Province. (2) Zigong: Confucius's disciple, surname Duanmu and first name Ci, style name Zigong.

子曰："博学于文，约之以礼，亦可以弗畔矣夫。"（12.15）

【白话译文】

孔子说："一个人广泛学习历史文献，用礼仪约束他的学习，这样他就可以不离经叛道了！"（12.15）

【注释】博：广泛。文：遗留典籍。约：约束自己。之：他。以：用。亦：也就。弗：不会。畔（音pàn判）：叛，背叛，违道（君子之道）。矣夫：啊，强烈感叹词。

【英译】

The Master said, "One extensively studies the historical documents, and restrains his study within the boundary of the Rites of Proprieties, then he may not be heretical and deviate from the true teachings!" (12.15)

子曰:"君子道者三,我无能焉:仁者不忧,知者不惑,勇者不惧。"子贡曰:"夫子自道也。"(14.30)

【注释】三:三项素质。道:行为标准。无能:未能做到。者:的人。忧:忧愁。知(音 zhì 治):智,智慧、聪明。惧:恐惧、畏惧。子贡:姓端木名赐,字子贡。夫子:孔子。自道:自我表述,子贡认为孔子做到了这些。

【白话译文】

孔子说:"君子能做到的三件事,我还做不到:仁者没有忧虑,智慧者不会迷惑,而勇敢者不会恐惧。"子贡说:"我老师关于君子的说法,正好道出了他所做到的。"(14.30)

【英译】

The Master said, "I fail to do three things that a superior man does: a man of superior benevolence is free from anxiety; a man of wisdom is free from perplexity; and a man of courage is free from fear." Zigong[(1)] said, "What my Master talks about a superior man exactly describes what he does." (14.30)

【英译注】(1) Zigong: Surname Duanmu and first name Ci, style name Zigong, Confucius's disciple.

子曰:"君子义以为质,礼以行之,孙以出之,信以成之。君子哉!"(15. 18)

【注释】义以为质:以义为根本。质:根本。之:君子、君子之道。行:推行。孙(音 xùn 训):逊,谦让。出:语言表达。信:忠诚。成:完成。

【白话译文】

孔子说:"君子对每件事都把正义作为他的内在本质,做每件事都依照礼仪,讲每件事都谦逊,完成每件事都诚信。这么做,他就是一位君子啊!"(15. 18)

【英译】

The Master said,"A superior man takes righteousness as his intrinsic quality for everything, carries everything out according to the Rites of Proprieties, expresses everything humbly, and accomplishes everything faithfully. By doing this, he truly is a superior man!" (15. 18)

子曰:"君子病无能焉,不病人之不己知也。"(15. 19)

【注释】病:担忧。无能:自己没有才能。人:别人。己知:知己,别人了解自己。

【白话译文】

孔子说:"君子担心他的能力不足,但不担心他不被别人理解。"(15. 19)

【英译】

The Master said, "A superior man is anxious about his deficiency of capabilities but is not anxious about his not being understood by others." (15.19)

子曰:"君子矜而不争,群而不党。"(15.22)

【注释】矜(音 jīn 今):庄重。争:争执。群:合群、团结。党:结党营私。

【白话译文】

孔子说:"君子为自尊约束自己,但不与他人争斗;团结别人,但不结党营私。"(15.22)

【英译】

The Master said, "A superior man restrains himself out of self-respect, but does not scramble with others; he unites others but does not gang up with them." (15.22)

子曰:"君子不以言举人,不以人废言。"(15.23)

【注释】以:因为。不以:不因为。言:言论、说话。不以言:不因为他的言论、能说会道。举:举荐、提拔。不以人:不因为这个人。废言:废弃(他有益的)言论。

【白话译文】

孔子说:"君子不仅仅因为一个人能说会道就提拔他,也不仅仅因为他的不利地位而放弃他的有益言论。"(15.23)

【英译】

The Master said, "A superior man neither promotes someone simply because of his eloquence, nor abandons his beneficial propositions simply because of his unfavourable status." (15.23)

子曰:"君子贞而不谅。"(15.37)

【注释】贞:正、正道、正直,坚守正道。而:却、但。谅:(小)诚信,小节。不谅:以坚持正道、正义为前提的辩证灵活性。贞而不谅:既坚持原则,又高度灵活。

【白话译文】

孔子说:"君子在原则问题上坚定不移,但在小是小非上高度灵活。"(15.37)

【英译】

The Master said, "A superior man is firm in a matter of principle but is highly flexible in trifles." (15.37)

子贡曰:"君子亦有恶乎?"子曰:"有恶。恶称人之恶者,恶居下流而讪上者,恶勇而无礼者,恶果敢而窒者。"曰:"赐也亦有恶乎?""恶徼以为知者,恶

【注释】子贡:姓端木名赐,字子贡。恶(音 wù 务):厌恶。乎:吗。称:宣扬。者:的人、事。称人之恶(音 è 饿)者:宣扬别人坏处的人。居:处在。下流:地位低。讪(音 shàn 善):诽谤。上:地位高的。果敢:刚愎自用。窒:阻塞,

不孙以为勇者，恶讦以为直者。”（17.24）

顽固，不通事理。曰：孔子又说。赐：姓端木，名赐，字子贡。也：停顿词。亦：同样，也。徼（音 jiāo 交）：窃取，抄袭。以为：作为。知（音 zhì 治）：智，智慧、聪明。孙（音 xùn 训）：逊，谦让。讦（音 jié 杰）：揭短、揭发他人隐私。直：直率。

【白话译文】

子贡问："君子也憎恶什么事吗？"孔子说："有的。憎恶公开宣传他人的缺点，憎恶下级讥讽上级，憎恶侠义的人不守礼节，憎恶勇敢的人头脑简单。"孔子说："赐，你也憎恶什么事吗？""憎恶剽窃却自认有知识的人，憎恶没有礼貌却认为是勇敢的人，憎恶揭露别人隐私却认为是正直的人。"（17.24）

【英译】

Zigong(1) asked, "Does a superior man also have any detestations?" The Master said, "Yes, he does. He detests a person who publicizes demerits of others; he detests an inferior who slanders his superiors; he detests a chivalrous person who does not observe the Rites; and he detests a courageous person who is simple-minded." The Master said, "Ci(2), do you have any detestations too?" "I detest the one who plagiarize others and thinks himself knowledgeable; I detest the one who abandons courtesy as a kind of bravery; and I detest the one who reveals other's privacy as being righteous." (17.24)

【英译注】(1) Zigong: Surname Duanmu and first name Ci, style name Zigong, Confucius's disciple. (2) Ci: The first name of Zigong.

子夏曰:"君子有三变:望之俨然,即之也温,听其言也厉。"(19.09)

【注释】子夏:姓卜名商,字子夏。三:三种。变:形态。望:远看。俨(音 yǎn 眼):庄严、恭敬。即:接近。温:温和可亲。言:说话。厉:严肃,严厉。

【白话译文】

子夏说:"在别人看来,君子有三种不同的感觉:看起来,他很庄重;接近他时,他很和蔼可亲;听他说话,很严厉。"(19.09)

【英译】

Zixia(1) said, "A superior man has three different appearances as seen by others: he is stately by looking at him, amiable by approaching him, and severe by listening to him." (19.09)

【英译注】(1) Zixia: Confucius's disciple, surname Bu, first name Shang, style name Zixia.

08

女 Women

邦君之妻,君称之曰夫人,夫人自称曰小童,邦人称之曰君夫人,称诸异邦曰寡小君,异邦人称之亦曰君夫人。(16.14)

【注释】邦:国家。君:国君。之:的。妻:妻子。称:称呼。曰:说。称之曰:称呼她为。童:僮仆、奴仆。邦人:本国人。诸:之于。异邦:外国。称诸异邦:对于外国人称呼她。异邦人:外国人。

【白话译文】

对于一个邦君的妻子，君主称她为"夫人"，夫人自称她"女仆"。她的国人称她为"君夫人"。对于其他国家，称她为"第一夫人"。其他国家的人，也称她为"君夫人"。(16.14)

【英译】

For the wife of a state sovereign, the sovereign calls her "Lady" and she calls herself "A Girl Attendant". The people of her state call her "Sovereign Lady". To other states, she is called "First Lady" and the people from other states also call her "Sovereign Lady." (16.14)

子曰："唯女子与小人为难养也，近之则不孙，远之则怨。"(17.25)

【白话译文】

孔子说："只有与年轻女子和小人很难长久相处。如果离他们近了，他们就无礼；如果离他们远了，他们就怨恨。"(17.25)

【注释】唯：只有。女子：专指未婚少女，不泛指妇女，已婚女称为"妇"。《诗经·邶风·泉水》等有"女子"二字，指要出嫁的少女。孔子时，女子婚龄约为十五岁[J03]，此处"女子"非"妇"，当低于婚龄，是十来岁的小女孩。为：是。难：费劲、不易。养：教育、生养、教养、相处。也：呀。为难养也：与未婚少女相处好，难啊；换言之，青春少女让人多操心啊。女子十来岁，正处青春期的初期，即今天所谓的"叛逆期"。"难养"指其天真、淘气、害羞、胆怯、孤独，渴望关爱，同时出于自我保护、安全感缺乏、青春期焦虑等，她又娇气任

【英译】

The Master said, "It is difficult to get on only with a young girl(1) or an inferior man for long. If you get close to them, they are rude to you; and if you keep a distance from them, they are resentful to you." (17.25)

性,独立谨慎,异常警觉,需要微妙关注爱护。面对今天竞争压力加大,吸毒、诈骗等社会问题复杂的情况,此句的现实意义可引起注意。近:亲近。之:他、她。则:就。孙(音 xùn 训):逊,谦让。远:疏远。怨:抱怨。

【英译注】(1) a young girl: Refers to an unmarried girl shown in a song named *Spring Water Under North Wind* of *Poems and Odes*, currently named *Book of Poetry* that sings "a young girl (maiden) is to be married in a foreign country far away from their parents and brothers." The age for marriage was about 15 years old at the time of Confucius[J03], so the young girl was a teenager below 15.

09

民 Common People

哀公问曰:"何为则民服?"孔子对曰:"举直错诸枉,则民服;举枉错诸直,则民不服。"(02.19)

【注释】鲁哀公十一年(公元前484年),孔子68岁周游列国回鲁,答鲁哀公问。哀公:姓姬名蒋,谥(音 shì 是)号哀,鲁国国君,公元前494至公元前468年在位。何:如何。为:做。民:百姓。服:

【白话译文】

哀公问道:“我做什么才会让人民服从我?”孔夫子敬答:“如果你提拔正直的人,让他们的位置高于不诚实的人,那么百姓就会服从;如果你提拔不诚实的人,让他们的位置高于正直的人,那么百姓就不会服从。”(02.19)

服从。对曰:敬答,答国君或上位者问,以示敬。举:选用,提拔。直:正直(者)。错(音cuò挫):同措,弃置。枉:不正、邪佞(者)。

【英译】

Duke Ai(1) asked: “What shall I do so that the people obey me?” Confucius replied respectfully, “They will obey you if you promote righteous people to the positions higher than those held by the dishonest. They will not obey you if you promote the dishonest to positions higher than those held by the righteous.” (02.19)

【英译注】(1) Duke Ai: A Duke of the State of Lu, surname Ji, first name Jiang, posthumous title Ai, ruling from 494 BC to 468 BC. He talked with Confucius on this in 484 BC after Confucius returned to the State of Lu.

子曰:“民可使由之,不可使知之。”(08.09)

【白话译文】

孔子说:“有能力让老百姓服从一件事,没有能力让他们明白为什么要服从它。”(08.09)

【注释】民:百姓。可:能够。使:让(他们)。由:遵从。之:道理、领导的意志。知:懂得。不可使知之:不能够让他们懂得为什么要这样做。有的句读为:“民,可,使由之。不可,使知之。”用意可以理解,但古代无此句法。

【英译】

The Master said, "The common people can be made to obey something but cannot be made to understand why they should obey it." (08.09)

子适卫，冉有仆。子曰："庶矣哉!"冉有曰："既庶矣，又何加焉?"曰："富之。"曰："既富矣，又何加焉?"曰："教之。"(13.09)

【注释】孔子周游列国期间，分别于鲁定公十四年(公元前496年)、鲁定公十五年、鲁哀公二年、鲁哀公七年(公元前488年)，分别到卫国，推测此对话发生于孔子第一次到卫国时，因为首次见常会感叹，多次见则习以为然。适:前往。卫:卫国。冉有:姓冉名求，字子有。仆:驾车。庶:人丁兴旺。既:已经。何:如何。加:增益。富:脱贫致富，施舍薄敛，授之以渔，使其衣食富足。之:民。教:教化、教育。

【白话译文】

孔子访问卫国，冉有为他驾车。孔子说:"这里人丁兴旺啊!"冉有问:"既然此处人丁兴旺了，下一步应当给他们增加什么呢?"孔子说:"让他们致富。"他问:"既然富了，下一步应当给他们增加什么呢?"孔子说:"给他们教育。"(13.09)

【英译】

The Master visited the State of Wei(1) and Ran You(2) drove a carriage for him. The Master said, "How populous is it here!" Ran You said, "What should be added next as the population is big here?" The Master said, "Enrich them." He asked, "What should be added next when they are rich?" The Master said, "Educate them." (13.09)

【英译注】(1) the State of Wei: A state of the Zhou Dynasty granted to Ji Kangshu, the youngest brother of King Wu, located around Qi River at the north of Yellow River, currently Weihui City of Henan Province. (2) Ran You: Surname Ran, first name Qiu, style name Ziyou, Confucius's disciple from the State of Wu.

子曰："古者民有三疾，今也或是之亡也。古之狂也肆，今之狂也荡；古之矜也廉，今之矜也忿戾；古之愚也直，今之愚也诈而已矣。"（17.16）

【白话译文】

孔子说："古代的老百姓有三个毛病，今天或许不存在了。古代的狂人粗野，放肆直言，今天的狂人放荡、越礼。古代自负的聪明人威严逼人，不可触犯，而今天的自负的聪明人凶暴，无理取闹。古代的愚人直来直去，而今天的愚人自欺欺人。"（17.16）

【英译】

The Master said, "In the ancient times, the common people had three faults that may possibly disappear today. The madmen were wild and unbridled in their speech in the ancient times, but the madmen are presumptuous and ignorant in the Rites today. The conceited but clever men were dignified and inviolable in the ancient times, while the conceited but clever men are truculent and unreasonable today. And the foolish men were straightforward in the ancient times, but the foolish men are cheating and self-deceiving today." (17.16)

【注释】古者：古代。民：人、百姓。三疾：三个毛病。今：今天。也：停顿词。或：或许。是：这。亡（音 wú 吴）：无、不存在。今也或是之亡也：今天这些毛病或许没有了。狂：狂妄自大。肆：放肆无礼。荡：放荡不羁。矜（音 jīn 金）：骄傲。廉：威严，不可触犯。矜也廉：骄傲自夸的人，端正有威严。忿：怒恨。戾（音 lì 利）：蛮横、凶暴、恼羞成怒。愚：愚笨、愚昧。直：直率。诈：欺诈。愚也诈：愚笨的人，会欺诈。而已矣：罢了。

三

Three

五常和礼乐

Five Constants and Ritual Music

10

仁 Superior Benevolence

樊迟问仁。子曰:“爱人。”问知。子曰:“知人。”樊迟未达。子曰:“举直错诸枉,能使枉者直。”樊迟退,见子夏,曰:“乡也吾见于夫子而问知,子曰:‘举直错诸枉,能使枉者直。’何谓也?”子夏曰:“富哉言乎!舜有天下,选于众,举皋陶,不仁者远矣。汤有天下,选于众,举伊尹,不仁者远矣。”(12.22)

【白话译文】

樊迟请教仁德。孔子说:“热爱人。”请教智慧。孔子说:“理解人。”樊迟没有完全理解。孔子说:“提拔正直的人,让他们的位置高于搞歪门邪道的,这样能够使搞歪门邪道的变为正直的人。”樊迟离开孔子,遇见子夏说:“刚才,我见到我们的老师,向他请教智慧。老师说:‘提拔正直的人,让他们的位置高于搞歪门邪道的,这

【注释】樊迟:名须,字子迟。问:请教。仁:仁德。爱人:对人有深刻的感情、善意。知(音 zhì 治):智,智慧。知(音 zhī 织)人:辨别人的善恶优劣。未达:不明白。举:提拔。直:正直。错:措,搁置。诸:于。枉:邪恶。举直错诸枉:提拔正直的人,罢免邪恶的人。使:让。能使枉者直:能让邪恶的人正直起来。退:出来。子夏:姓卜名商,字子夏。乡(音 xiàng 向):刚才。夫子:孔子。富:寓意丰富。言:言论。选:选拔。举:提拔。皋陶(音 gāo 高 yáo 姚):舜的刑法大臣,姓偃,传说是东夷族的首领,后被禹选为继承人,因早死,未继位。远:疏远。汤:商朝开国帝,名履。伊尹:汤的宰相,出身奴隶,姓伊,尹代表长官。

样能够使搞歪门邪道的变为正直的人。'这是什么意思?"子夏说:"这句话内容多么丰富啊! 舜帝统治天下时,从百姓中选人才,提拔了皋陶,没有仁德的人不见了。商朝汤帝统治天下时,从百姓中选人才,提拔了伊尹,没有仁德的人不见了。"(12.22)

【英译】

Fan Chi(1) asked advice about superior benevolence. The Master said, "Love people." Fan Chi asked advice about wisdom. The Master said, "Understand people." Fan Chi did not fully comprehend it. The Master said, "Upright people are promoted to positions higher than those held by crooked ones, and this may make the crooked people become upright." Departing from Confucius, Fan Chi encountered Zixia(2) and told him, "A moment ago, I saw our Master and asked him advice about wisdom. The Master said, 'Upright people are promoted to positions higher than those held by crooked ones, and this may make crooked people become upright.' What does it mean?" Zixia said, "How rich the speech is! When Emperor Shun(3) ruled the country, he selected talented ones from the common people, and appointed Gaoyao(4) to

【英译注】(1) Fan Chi: Surname Fan, first name Xu, style name Zichi. (2) Zixia: Confucius's disciple, surname Bu, first name Shang, style name Zixia. (3) Emperor Shun: The ancient Chinese legendary saintly emperor, surname Gongsun allegedly, served as the chieftain of Yu's Tribe, and the successor of Emperor Yao. As he once lived at Mt. Chong, currently north Mt. Song of Henan Province, his style name was Chong Bo. (4) Gaoyao: Surname Yan, the senior official of Emperor Shun in charge of criminal administration. (5) Emperor Tang: Surname Zi, first name Li, also named Tianyi, Dayi, Chengtang, and Shang Tang, extinguished the Xia Dynasty around 1600 BC and created the Shang Dynasty and ruled for 13 years. (6) Yi Yin: The prime minister of Emperor Tang in the Shang Dynasty, selected from slaves.

high position, so those without superior benevolence disappeared. When Emperor Tang[(5)] of the Shang Dynasty ruled the country, he selected talented ones from the common people and appointed Yi Yin[(6)] to high position, so those without superior benevolence disappeared." (12.22)

颜渊问仁。子曰:"克己复礼为仁。一日克己复礼,天下归仁焉。为仁由己,而由人乎哉?"颜渊曰:"请问其目。"子曰:"非礼勿视,非礼勿听,非礼勿言,非礼勿动。"颜渊曰:"回虽不敏,请事斯语矣。"(12.01)

【白话译文】

颜渊请教仁德。孔子说:"克制自己,恢复周礼就是仁。一旦克制自己,恢复周礼,天下万物就符合仁德要求了。实行仁德,是由自己。难道这由别人吗?"颜渊说:"请问要做到仁德,具体有多少项?"孔子说:"不符合礼仪的,不看;不符合礼仪的,不听;不符合礼仪的,不说;不符合礼仪的,不做。"颜渊说:"虽然我愚钝,一定按照老师你指示的办。"(12.01)

【注释】颜渊:姓颜名回,字子渊。问:请教。仁:仁道。克:克制。己:自己。复:符合、一致。礼:礼的要求。一日:一旦。归:归顺。为:实行。由:在于。人:别人。为仁由己,而由人乎哉:实行仁爱由自己,难道由别人吗。目:条目,与纲相对。非礼:不符合礼。动:行为、做。回:颜渊,姓颜名回,字子渊。不敏:愚笨。请:让我。事:照办。斯:这些。语:言论。

【英译】

Yan Yuan[1] asked Confucius's advice about superior benevolence. The Master said, "It is to restrain oneself and recover the Rites of Proprieties of the Zhou Dynasty. Once one restrains oneself and recovers the Rites of Proprieties, all the things under heaven will be in compliance with the requirements of superior benevolence. Superior benevolence is practiced by oneself. Is it truly done by others?" Yan Yuan said, "Might I ask how many items are practiced for this specifically?" The Master said, "Never look at what does not conform to the Rites of Proprieties. Never listen to what does not conform to the Rites. Never speak what does not conform to the Rites. And never do what does not conform to the Rites." Yan Yuan said, "Though I am not wise, I must do it according to what you, my Master, instruct." (12.01)

【英译注】(1) Yan Yuan: Surname Yan, first name Hui, style name Ziyuan, Confucius's excellent disciple.

司马牛问仁。子曰:"仁者其言也讱。"曰:"其言也讱,斯谓之仁已乎?"子曰:"为之难,言之得无讱乎?"(12.03)

【注释】司马牛:姓司马名耕,字子牛,传其兄宋国大夫桓魋(音 huán 环 tuí 颓)作乱被追杀,全家出逃。问:请教。仁:仁道。讱(音 rèn 认):说话缓慢,不轻易说。斯:就。谓之:把它叫作。已:了。乎:吗。为:做。之:事。难:困难。得无:能不。

【白话译文】

司马牛向孔子请教仁德。孔子说:"具有仁德的人,说话精练且谨慎。"他说:"如果他说话精练且谨慎,这样就能称之为仁德了吗?"孔子说:"按照仁德完成一件事就难,那么一个人说话能不精练且谨慎吗?"(12.03)

【英译】

Sima Niu(1) asked Confucius's advice about superior benevolence. The Master said, "A man of superior benevolence speaks laconically and deliberately." He said, "If he speaks laconically and deliberately, can this be called superior benevolence?" The Master said, "As it is difficult to accomplish a thing in accordance with superior benevolence, how could one speak but not laconically and deliberately?" (12.03)

【英译注】(1) Sima Niu: Surname Sima, first name Niu, Confucius's disciple. It was said that his brother Huantui, a senior officer of the State of Song, staged an armed rebellion, and was pursued for dead punishment.

子张问仁于孔子。孔子曰:"能行五者于天下,为仁矣。"请问之。曰:"恭、宽、信、敏、惠。恭则不侮,宽则得众,信则人任焉,敏则有功,惠则足以使人。"(17.06)

【注释】子张:姓颛(音 zhuān 砖)孙名师,字子张。行:实行。五者:五种品德。请问:请教。之:它们,五者。恭:庄重。宽:宽厚。信:诚实。敏:勤敏。惠:慈爱,恩惠,给人好处。则:就。侮(音 wǔ 五):轻慢、怠慢,遭受侮辱。得众:得到众人的拥护。人:别人。任:任用,信任,负担。信则人任焉:诚信就会得到别人的信任(任用)

【白话译文】

子张向孔夫子请教仁德。孔夫子说:“如果一个人能够在天下各处实行五个品德,这就是仁德了。”他问其详细内容。孔夫子说:“恭敬、宽厚、诚信、勤奋、恩惠。一个人恭敬,就不会受到侮辱;一个人宽厚,就会得到大众的支持;一个人诚信,就会受到别人的任用;一个人勤奋,就会获得成功;一个人给人们恩惠,就足以领导他们。”(17.06)

啊。有功:取得成绩、成功。使:役使,使人忘其劳而服从。

【英译】Zizhang(1) asked Confucius's advice on superior benevolence. Confucius said, "If one may practice the five virtues everywhere under heaven, this is superior benevolence." He begged to know the details. Confucius said, "They are deference, tolerance, faith, diligence and beneficence. One cannot be humiliated if he is deferential. One can be supported by the masses if he is tolerant. One can be authorized for a task if he is faithful. One can be successful if he is diligent. And one can fully lead people if he is beneficent." (17.06)

【英译注】(1) Zizhang: Surname Zhuansun, first name Shi, and style name Zizhang, Confucius's disciple.

子曰:"刚、毅、木、讷,近仁。"(13.27)

【白话译文】

孔子说:"刚强、果断、质朴、说话精练,是四种接近仁德的品质。"(13.27)

【英译】

The Master said,"Firmness, resoluteness, simplicity, and succinctness are four virtues close to superior benevolence."(13.27)

【注释】刚:刚强,质直寡欲。毅:果敢。木:质朴,朴实。讷(音nè):语言迟钝,不善言辞。近:接近。

子贡曰:"如有博施于民,而能济众,何如?可谓仁乎?"子曰:"何事于仁!必也圣乎!尧舜其犹病诸!夫仁者,己欲立而立人,己欲达而达人。能近取譬,可谓仁之方也已。"(06.30)

【白话译文】

子贡说:"如果有人广泛地将利益给予人民,救助需要帮助的大众,你认为他怎么样?他可以称为有仁德的人吗?"孔子说:"他何止于仅仅是有仁德!他一定是圣人!尧舜大概还担心他们是否能够全部做到这些!什么是有仁德的人呢?如果一个有仁德的人期望自己在社会上站稳,他

【注释】子贡:姓端木名赐,字子贡。博:广泛。施(旧读shì市):施恩。济:周济。众:大众。何事于:何止于。必:一定。圣:圣人。尧:唐尧。舜:虞舜。其:大概。犹:还。病:担忧。诸:这。夫仁:所谓仁。立:站稳。达:通达。近:自身、跟前。取:拿,选,用,得到。譬(音pì媲):打比方,推己及人。能近取譬:能拿身边仁德的人或事作例子,一件一件,一步一步将此实例推广开来。方:方法。仁之方:实践仁的办法。也:了。已:啊。

首先要让别人站稳。如果他要自己成功，首先要让别人成功。如果一个人能够就近取仁德的人或仁德的事件作例子，一个一个地推广开来，这就可以称作为履行仁德的捷径。”(06.30)

【英译】

Zigong[(1)] said, "If someone extensively gives benefits to the people and rescues the masses in need, how do you think about him? Can he be called a benevolent man?" The Master said, "How can he be just benevolent? He must be a sage! Even the Emperor Yao[(2)] and Emperor Shun[(3)] might probably be worried that they could accomplish all this! What is a benevolent person? If a man of superior benevolence desires to establish himself firmly in society, he must first establish others. If he desires to succeed himself, he must first make others succeed. If one can take the cases of the benevolent persons or benevolent events around him as examples and promote them one by one, this can be called a shortcut to practice superior benevolence." (06.30)

【英译注】(1) Zigong: Surname Duanmu and first name Ci, style name Zigong, Confucius's disciple. (2) Emperor Yao: Yao is regarded as the ancient Chinese legendary saintly emperor, name Fangxun. As the head/chieftain of Taotang's Tribe, he united many tribes, good for hydraulic work and agriculture development. (3) Emperor Shun: The ancient Chinese legendary saintly emperor, surname Gongsun allegedly, served as the chieftain of Yu's Tribe, and the successor of Emperor Yao. As he once lived at Mt. Chong, currently north Mt. Song of Henan Province, his style name was Chong Bo.

子夏曰:"博学而笃志,切问而近思,仁在其中矣。"(19.06)

【白话译文】

子夏说:"一个人广博学习,坚定不移坚持自己的理想,同时真诚地提出问题,思考身边发生的事情,因此仁德就在此过程中。"(19.06)

【英译】

Zixia(1) said, "One learns widely and extensively, persists firmly in his ambitions, as well as raises questions sincerely and thinks currently about the issues around him. From this arises superior benevolence." (19.06)

【注释】子夏:姓卜名商,字子夏。博:广泛。笃:牢固、坚实。志:记住;志向。切:恳切。问:请教。近:当前的、现实的问题。思:思考。近思:思考当前、现实相关的事物,否则泛问远思,则劳而无功。

【英译注】(1) Zixia: Surname Bu, first name Shang, and style name Zixia, Confucius's disciple.

子曰:"巧言令色,鲜矣仁。"(01.03)

【白话译文】

孔子说:"仁德是很难在花言巧语和伪善的表情中找到的。"(01.03)

【英译】

The Master said, "The superior benevolence can rarely be found in flattering speech and hypocritical countenance." (01.03)

【注释】巧:虚浮不实。令:伪善。色:面貌。鲜(音 xiǎn 显):少,缺少。

子曰:“巧言令色,鲜矣仁。”(17.17)

【注释】巧:虚浮不实。令:伪善。色:面貌。鲜(音 xiǎn 显):稀少,缺少。矣:语气词,表示感叹。另一句读法:“子曰:‘巧言令色鲜矣,仁。’”不巧言令色,是一种仁德啊。

【白话译文】

孔子说:“仁德是很难在花言巧语和伪善的表情中找到的。”(17.17)

【英译】

The Master said,“Superior benevolence can rarely be found in flattering speech and hypocritical countenance.” (17.17)

子曰:“人而不仁,如礼何?人而不仁,如乐何?”(03.03)

【注释】不仁:无仁爱。如:对于。何:怎么。如礼何:怎么对待礼仪制度。如乐何:怎么对待礼乐。

【白话译文】

孔子说:“如果一个人没有仁德,礼仪能为他做什么?如果一个人没有仁德,音乐能为他做什么?”(03.03)

【英译】

The Master said,“If a person does not possess the virtue of superior benevolence, what do the Rites of Proprieties work for him? If a person does not possess the virtue of superior benevolence, what does Music work for him?” (03.03)

子曰："不仁者不可以久处约，不可以长处乐。仁者安仁，知者利仁。"(04.02)

【注释】久：长久。处（chǔ楚）：处于。约：穷困。不仁者不可以久处约：不仁的人不可以长期穷困。长：长期。乐：安乐。安仁：无论贫贱，安于实行仁道。知（音 zhì治）：智，智慧、聪明。利仁：知仁为美，无私利地实行仁道。

【白话译文】

孔子说："没有仁德的人，既不能够长久忍受贫困，也不能够长久享受富有和快乐。具有仁德的人，安心地实践仁德。智慧的人能够无私利地履行仁德。"(04.02)

【英译】

The Master said, "A person without the virtue of superior benevolence can neither long endure poverty nor long dwell in prosperity and contentment. A benevolent person can peacefully practice superior benevolence. A wise person can carry out superior benevolence selflessly." (04.02)

"克、伐、怨、欲不行焉，可以为仁矣？"子曰："可以为难矣。仁则吾不知也。"(14.02)

【注释】克：好胜。伐：夸耀、自夸。怨：怨恨；抱怨。欲：贪婪。不行：没有，不做。为：算作。难：难得。可以为难矣：可以认为是难得了。则：那么。

【白话译文】

"如果一个人不好胜、不自夸、不怨恨、不贪婪,可以认为他是一个仁人吗?"孔子说:"他这样实在难得。但他是不是一位仁人,我不知道。"(14.02)

【英译】

"If one is free from rivalry, boasting, complaining, and greed, can he be thought as a benevolent person?" The Master said, "It is difficult for him to do so, but I do not know whether he is a benevolent person." (14.02)

或曰:"雍也仁而不佞。"子曰:"焉用佞?御人以口给,屡憎于人。不知其仁,焉用佞?"(05.05)

【注释】或曰:有人说。雍:姓冉名雍,字仲弓。佞(音 nìng 宁):能言善辩。不佞:口才不好。焉:为什么。御:防御,对抗。以:用。给(音 jǐ 挤):富足。口给:嘴快话多。御人以口给:用嘴快话多来反驳别人。屡:常常。憎于人:招致别人的憎恨。不知其仁:(口才好,)不知是否有仁德。

【白话译文】

有人说:"雍是一个具有仁德的人,但口才不好。"孔子说:"为什么他要口才好呢?用利齿快嘴反驳别人,经常让人讨厌。我不知道他是否有仁德,但是为什么他要口才好呢?"(05.05)

【英译】

Someone said, "Yong[1] is a person of superior benevolence but is not eloquent." The Master said, "Why should he be eloquent? It happens that a person who has a glib tongue often makes others dislike him. I do not know whether Yong possesses the virtue of superior benevolence, but why should he have a glib tongue?" (05.05)

【英译注】(1) Yong: Surname Ran, first name Yong, style name Zhonggong, Confucius's disciple.

孟武伯问:"子路仁乎?"子曰:"不知也。"又问。子曰:"由也,千乘之国,可使治其赋也。不知其仁也。""求也何如?"子曰:"求也,千室之邑,百乘之家,可使为之宰也。不知其仁也。""赤也何如?"子曰:"赤也,束带立于朝,可使与宾客言也。不知其仁也。"(05.08)

【注释】孟武伯:孟懿子之子,名彘(音 zhì 至),谥号武。子路:姓仲,名由,字子路,卞(故城在今山东平邑县东北仲村)人。由:子路。乘(音 shèng 胜):辆,量词,配有 4 匹马,3 甲士,72 步卒,25 后勤员。千乘之国:诸侯国。使:任用。治:主持。其:诸侯国。赋:君主向臣属征用的士卒、牛马、兵车及其他军需品。其仁:他的仁德。求:姓冉名求,字子有。何如:怎样。千室:1000 户。邑:城镇。百乘之家:卿大夫的采地。使为:让他当。宰:总管。赤:姓公西名赤,字子华。束带:礼服。朝:朝廷。与宾客言:接待宾客。

【白话译文】

孟武伯问:"子路是有仁德的人吗?"孔子说:"我不知道。"他再次问。孔子说:"由,可以负责千辆战车国家的军政事务。我不知道他是否有仁德。""求,怎么样?"孔子说:"求,可以成为 1000 户城市及百辆战车卿大夫封地的总管。我不知道他是否有仁德。”“赤，怎么样？”孔子说：“赤，可以在朝廷上穿礼服，接待国宾，处理外交事务。但是，我不知道他是否有仁德。”(05.08)

【英译】

Meng Wubo(1) inquired, “Is Zilu(2) a man of superior benevolence?” The Master said, “I don't know.” He inquired it again. The Master said, “You(3) can be in charge of the military administration of a 1000-chariot state. I do not know whether he is benevolent.” “How about Qiu(4)?” The Master said, “Qiu can serve as chief administrator of a 1000-household town and 100-chariot fief land of a senior official. I do not know whether he is benevolent.” “How about Chi(5)?” The Master said, “Chi can stay at the court wearing ceremonial dress, receive state guests and handle diplomatic affairs. I do not know whether he is benevolent.” (05.08)

【英译注】(1) Meng Wubo: First name Zhi, posthumous title Wu, a son of Master Meng Yi who served as a high-rank official of the State of Lu. (2) Zilu: Surname Zhong, first name You, and style name Zilu, Confucius's disciple. (3) You: Zilu. (4) Qiu: Surname Ran, first name Qiu, and style name Ziyou, Confucius's disciple. (5) Chi: Surname Gongxi, first name Chi, and style name Zihua, Confucius's disciple.

子张问曰:“令尹子文三仕为令尹,无喜色。三已之,无愠色。旧令尹之政,必以告新令尹。何如?”子曰:“忠矣。”曰:“仁矣乎?”子曰:“未知,焉得仁?”“崔子弑齐君,陈文子有马十乘,弃而违之。至于他邦,则曰:‘犹吾大夫崔子也。’违之,之一邦,则又曰:‘犹吾大夫崔子也。’违之。何如?”子曰:“清矣。”曰:“仁矣乎?”曰:“未知,焉得仁?”(05.19)

【白话译文】

子张问:“子文三次被任命为楚国宰相,表情上没有露出快乐的脸色。三次解除职务,他没有表露出不高兴的脸色。当他解职后,有关政务和国家规章一定告诉新宰相。他这个人何如?”孔子说:“他忠诚。”他问:“他这个人有仁德吗?”孔子说:“我不知道。这怎么能称得上仁?”

“崔子弑杀了齐君后,陈文子放弃了他的40匹马、10辆车,离开了齐国。当他到另外一个国家时,他说:‘这里的大夫与我们的崔子一样。’他离开这个国家,又到一国,他又说:‘这里的大夫与我们的崔子一样。’又离开了。他怎么样?”孔子说:“他是保持清白的人。”问:“他有仁德吗?”孔子说:“我

【注释】子张:姓颛(音 zhuān 砖)孙名师,字子张。令尹:宰相。子文:姓斗,名谷於菟(gòu 构 wū 乌 tú 徒),字子文,楚国名相。三:多次。仕:担任。已:罢免。之:官职。三已之:多次被罢官。愠(音 yùn 运):内心里的恼怒,怨恨。政:政务。告:交代。何如:怎么样。忠:尽心竭力,不背叛。知:晓得、明了。未知:不晓得。焉:怎么。焉得仁:怎么称得上仁。崔子:崔杼(音 zhù 住),齐国大夫。弑(音 shì 事):杀地位高的人,如子杀父、臣杀君。齐君:齐庄公,齐景公的异母兄,姓姜名光,公元前554年至公元前548年在位,与崔杼妻棠姜淫乱被杀,见《左传·襄公二十五年》。陈文子:姓陈名须无,齐国大夫。马十乘:40匹马。弃:舍弃。犹:类似。犹吾大夫崔子也:像我国崔子一样啊。违:逃离。之:这个国家。违之:逃离这个国家。他邦:他国。之一邦:(又)到一国。清:清高。

不知道。这怎么称得上仁?"(05.19)

【英译】

Zizhang[1] asked, "Ziwen[2] did not show a happy countenance when he was three times[3] appointed as the Premier of the State of Chu. He did not show an irritated countenance when he was three times dismissed from his position. When he was dismissed, he certainly notified his successors of the governmental affairs and regulations of the state. How about him?" The Master said, "He was loyal to the state." He asked, "Was he a man of superior benevolence?" The Master said, "I do not know. How could this be called benevolent?"

"After Master Cui[4] murdered Duke Zhuang[5] of the State of Qi, Master Chen Wen[6] gave up his 10 chariots and 40 horses and fled from the State of Qi. When he came to another state, he said, 'The officials here are similar to our Master Cui.' And then he fled from that state. When he arrived at next state, he again said, 'The officials here are similar to our Master Cui.' Then he fled again. How about him?" The Master said, "He was a man who preserved his purity." "Was he a man of superior benevolence?" "I do not know. How could this be called benevolent?" (05.19)

【英译注】(1) Zizhang: Surname Zhuansun, first name Shi, style name Zizhang, Confucius's disciple. (2) Ziwen: Surname Dou, first name Gouwutu, style name Ziwen, a famous premier of the State of Chu. (3) three times: Many times. (4) Master Cui: Surname Cui, first name Zhu, a senior official of the State of Qi. (5) Duke Zhuang: Surname Jiang, first name Guang, as the Duke of the State of Qi from 554 BC until 548 BC when he was murdered as he had an affair with Master Cui's wife Tang Jiang. (6) Master Chen Wen: Surname Chen, first name Xuwu, a senior official of theState of Qi.

子游曰："吾友张也，为难能也，然而未仁。"(19.15)

【注释】子游：姓言，名偃(音 yǎn 眼)，字子游，吴人。张：姓颛(音 zhuān 砖)孙名师，字子张。为：做。难：难得。为难能：做了难以做到的事。然而：但是。未：没有达到。

【白话译文】

子游说："我的朋友张，做的事难能可贵，然而还没有达到仁德的标准。"(19.15)

【英译】

Ziyou[1] said, "My friend Zhang[2] has done what is difficult of attainment, but he still has not met the standard of superior benevolence yet." (19.15)

【英译注】(1) Ziyou: Surname Yan, first name Yan, style name Ziyou, a disciple of Confucius from the State of Wu. (2) Zhang: Surname Zhuansun, first name Shi, style name Zizhang, Confucius's disciple.

曾子曰："堂堂乎张也，难与并为仁矣。"(19.16)

【注释】曾子：姓曾名参(音 shēn 申)，字子舆，鲁国南武城(今山东平邑)人。堂堂：仪表堂堂。张：姓颛(音 zhuān 砖)孙名师，字子张。难：很难。与：和(他)。并：一道。为：做到。

【白话译文】

曾子说："虽然张的举止堂堂正正，无与伦比，但是他很难带领别人达到仁德的标准。"(19.16)

【英译】

Master Zeng[1] said, "Although the behaviours of Zhang[2] are imposing and exceptional, it is difficult for him to lead

【英译注】(1) Master Zeng: Surname Zeng, first name Shen, style name Ziyu, from Nanwucheng Town (currently Pingyi County, Shandong Province), Confucius's disciple. (2)

others to meet the criteria of superior benevolence." (19.16)

Zhang: Surname Zhuansun, first name Shi, style name Zizhang, Confucius's disciple. It is said that he emphasized external appearance and language more than cultivation mind.

子曰:"唯仁者能好人,能恶人。"(04.03)

【白话译文】

孔子说:"只有仁德的人会爱一个人,又会憎一个人。"(04.03)

【英译】

The Master said, "Only a man of superior benevolence can either love a person or detest a person." (04.03)

【注释】能:会;能够;恰当地去做。好(音 hào 号):喜爱、赞扬等。能好人:恰当地爱一个人;相反者则是溺爱、娇生惯养等。恶(wù 务):憎恶、批评、惩罚等。能恶人:能够恰当批评、惩罚一个人;相反者则是,体罚虐待,甚至一棍子把人打死。

子曰:"苟志于仁矣,无恶也。"(04.04)

【白话译文】

孔子说:"一个人致力于履行仁德,就不会有邪恶的念头,也不会做出任何邪恶的行为。"(04.04)

【注释】苟(音 gǒu 狗):假若。志:立志。于:在。苟志于仁矣:若志在实行仁德啊。无:没有,不会。恶(音 è 饿):(做)坏事、行恶。

【英译】

The Master said, "A person resolved to carry out the superior benevolence will neither have a wicked intention nor do any evils." (04.04)

子曰:"我未见好仁者恶不仁者。好仁者,无以尚之;恶不仁者,其为仁矣,不使不仁者加乎其身。有能一日用力于仁矣乎? 我未见力不足者。盖有之矣,我未之见也。"(04.06)

【注释】好(音 hào 号):喜爱。仁者:有仁德的人。恶(音 wù 务):憎恶、厌恶。不仁者:缺乏、没有仁德的人或事。无以:无法。尚:超越。为仁:实行仁德。加:影响、惹。其:他的。身:自身。不使不仁者加乎其身:不要让恶人对自己有伤害(坏影响)。有能:有人能够。盖:可能。有之:有这样的人。未之见:未见之,未见到他。

【白话译文】

孔子说:"我没有看到过一个真正喜爱仁德的人却厌恶任何没有仁德的人。没有任何事比追求仁德更高尚了。一个讨厌没有仁德品性的人,当他履行仁德时,不要使这种没有仁德的品性影响到自己的身上。谁能全天一直致力在实行仁德上呢? 我没有看见过哪个人是力量不足的。也许有这样的人,但我还没有见过。"(04.06)

【英译】

The Master said, "I have not seen that a person who truly loves superior benevolence detests anyone who does not possess superior benevolence. There is nothing more lofty than pursuit of superior benevolence. The one who detests a person without superior benevolence should take care not to let the person influence himself when he carries superior benevolence out. Who can ever put all his strength into practising superior benevolence throughout a single day? I have never seen such a person who has no sufficient strength. Perhaps there is such a person, but I have never seen him yet."(04.06)

子曰:"志士仁人,无求生以害仁,有杀身以成仁。"(15.09)

【白话译文】

孔子说:"有理想或者有仁德的人,从来不会为了生存,放弃仁德,相反他可以牺牲自己的生命来成全仁德。"(15.09)

【英译】

The Master said,"A person of ideals or of superior benevolence never forsakes the virtue of superior benevolence in order to survive. On the other hand, he can sacrifice his life to achieve superior benevolence."(15.09)

【注释】志:有理想。士:读书人、有某种品质或技能的人。无:没有。求生:贪生怕死。害:损害。无求生以害仁:没有贪生怕死而损害仁德的。有:只有。杀身:牺牲自己的性命。以:用来。成:成全。

微子去之,箕子为之奴,比干谏而死。孔子曰:"殷有三仁焉。"(18.01)

【白话译文】

微子逃离了纣帝,箕子降为奴隶,比干因为直言劝谏纣帝被杀。孔夫子说:"殷朝有三位仁人。"(18.01)

【注释】微子:殷纣王的异母兄长,劝止纣王不听。去:逃离。之:纣王,商代亡国之君,暴君,姓姒,名辛,谥(音 shì 是)号纣,约公元前 1060 年至公元前 1027 年在位。箕(音 jī 鸡)子:纣王的叔父,劝纣王不听,披发装疯。奴:被降为奴隶。比干:纣王的叔父,屡次强谏,被挖心。殷:商代。三仁:三位仁人。

【英译】

Weizi(1) fled from Emperor Zou(2), Jizi(3) was enslaved, and Bigan(4) was killed due to his criticism against the Emperor. Confucius said, "There were three people of superior benevolence in the Yin Dynasty." (18.01)

【英译注】(1) Weizi: Emperor Zou's elder brother whose advice was not accepted by the Emperor. (2) Emperor Zou: Tyrant emperor from 1060 BC to 1027 BC in The Shang Dynasty, also called The Yin Dynasty, surname Si, first name Xin and posthumous name Zou. (3) Jizi: An uncle of Emperor Zou. His advice against the Emperor was not accepted and he was dismissed as a slave after he had played mad with his hair overcast his shoulder. (4) Bigan: An uncle of Emperor Zou who frequently strongly remonstrated against the Emperor and was killed by cutting his chest open to observe his heart alive.

子曰："回也，其心三月不违仁，其余则日月至焉而已矣。"(06.07)

【注释】回：姓颜名回，字子渊，鲁国人，今山东人。其：他的。三月：长久。违：离开、背离。其余：其他弟子。日月：或一日或一月。至：而已。矣：罢了。

【白话译文】

孔子说："回呀！很长时间，他的心不违背仁德，而我的其他弟子仅仅偶尔达到仁德要求而已。"(06.07)

【英译】

The Master said, "Alas Hui(1)! For a long time, his heart did not lapse from superior benevolence, while my other disciples can only occasionally meet the demands of superior benevolence." (06.07)

【英译注】(1) Hui: Surname Yan, first name Hui, and style name Ziyuan, a disciple of Confucius from the State of Lu.

子曰："仁远乎哉？我欲仁，斯仁至矣。"(07.30)

【注释】远：离得很远。欲：想得到。斯：此。至：到。

【白话译文】

孔子说："仁德离我远吗？我渴望仁德，仁德就来到我身边，变成我的行为。"(07.30)

【英译】

The Master said, "Is superior

benevolence far from me? If I desire superior benevolence, it comes to me and becomes my behaviour."(07.30)

宰我问曰:"仁者虽告之曰:'井有仁焉。'其从之也?"子曰:"何为其然也?君子可逝也,不可陷也;可欺也,不可罔也。"(06.26)

【注释】宰我:姓宰名予,字子我。仁:仁德。告之:告诉他。井:水井。有仁:有仁德仁义。焉:呀。其:他。从:跟从(跳入井中)。也:吗,语气词,表示疑问。何:为何。为:做。然:如此。何为其然也:为什么要这样做呢。逝:离开不再回来。也:语气词,在句中或句末。陷:陷害。欺:(被)欺骗、欺负。罔(音 wǎng 往):蒙蔽、骗。不可罔也:不会被蒙骗,指良知、正义、真理等是不可骗的。可参考《孟子·万章上》:子产让人把鱼放生池塘,那人把鱼吃了,编造放生过程及鱼生活情况。子产信了,但对实情那人是心知肚明的、蒙不过自己的,这是说良知不可罔也。

【白话译文】

宰我问:"如果告诉一位有仁德的人说:'仁德在井里',他跳到井里去跟随它吗?"孔子说:"为什么他要这么做呢?可以让一名君子永远离开不再回来,但不可陷害他;他可以受欺负,但正义不可以被欺骗。"(06.26)

【英译】

Zai Wo(1) asked, "If a benevolent man is told that 'the virtue of superior benevolence is inside a well', does he jump into the well to follow it?" The Master said, "Why should he do so? A superior man can be asked to go away forever, but cannot be lured into a trap; he can be bullied, but justice(2) cannot be cheated."(06.26)

【英译注】(1) Zai Wo: Surname Zai, first name Yu, style name Ziwo, Confucius's disciple. (2) justice: Justice exists in everyone's heart. On this Mencius told a story. A pond-keeper was assigned to free live fish into a pond, but he cooked it. He successfully lied to his superior, but he could not lie to himself as his heart witnessed the truth.

子曰:"君子而不仁者有矣夫,未有小人而仁者也。"(14.07)

【注释】而:却。不仁者:不仁德的行为。有矣夫:是有的。君子而不仁者有矣夫:高尚的君子偶尔也会做不仁德的事。未有:没有。未有小人而仁者也:卑鄙的小人从来不会做仁德的事。

【白话译文】

孔子说:"会有君子偶尔做出不符合仁德的事,但是小人从来不会做出符合仁德的事。"(14.07)

【英译】

The Master said, "There may be a superior man who occasionally does a thing not consistent with superior benevolence, but an inferior man may never do a thing of superior benevolence." (14.07)

子曰:"民之于仁也,甚于水火。水火,吾见蹈而死者矣,未见蹈仁而死者也。"(15.35)

【注释】民:百姓。于:对于。民之于仁:百姓对仁(的需求)。甚:超过。见:看到。蹈:踏踩、实行。死者:死了人的情况。

【白话译文】

孔子说:"百姓对于仁德的需求,超过了对水火的需求。对于水火,我看到有人踩在上面而死的,但我没有看到哪一个走了仁德之路而死的。"(15.35)

【英译】

The Master said, "The necessity of superior benevolence in common man surpasses the necessity of water or fire. For water or fire, I have seen men die for treading on fire or water, but I have never seen anyone die for treading the path of superior benevolence." (15.35)

11

义 Righteousness

子曰:"孰谓微生高直?或乞醯焉,乞诸其邻而与之。"(05.24)

【注释】孰:谁。谓:说。微生高:姓微生名高,鲁国人,今山东人。直:直率。或:有人。乞:讨。醯(音 xī 西):醋。诸:之于。邻:邻居。乞诸其邻:向他的邻居讨醋。而:进而、且。与:给。之:讨醋的人。

【白话译文】

孔子说:"谁说微生高直率?有人向他讨醋,他向邻居讨了,然后给人。"(05.24)

【英译】

The Master said, "Who says that Weisheng Gao(1) is straightforward?

【英译注】(1) Weisheng Gao: Surname Weisheng, first name Gao, a man from the State of Lu, currently in Shandong Province.

Someone begged some vinegar from him, but he begged it from his neighbor and gave it to him." (05.24)

子华使于齐,冉子为其母请粟。子曰:"与之釜。"请益。曰:"与之庾。"冉子与其粟五秉。子曰:"赤之适齐也,乘肥马,衣轻裘。吾闻之也,君子周急不继富。"(06.04)

【注释】子华:姓公西,名赤,字子华。使:出使。齐:齐国。冉子:姓冉名有,字子有。其:他的(子华的)。请:请求(补助)。粟:谷、小米。与:给。之:她。釜(音fǔ 斧):6 斗 4 升。益:增加。庾(音 yǔ 雨):16 斗。秉:10 庾、16 斛(音 hú 胡),160 斗。五秉:800 斗。赤:姓公西,名赤,字子华。适:往。乘:车子。肥马:肥马拉车。衣:穿。轻裘:皮袍。周:救济。急:急需者。继:接济,帮助,续有余。富:富人。

【白话译文】

子华出发,出使齐国。冉子向孔子请求帮助,给子华的母亲一些小米。孔子说:"给她一釜(6 斗 4 升)。"他请求多些。孔子说:"给她一庾(16 斗)。"冉子给她的小米是五秉(5×160=800 斗)。孔子说:"赤出使齐国,坐的是肥马拉的车,穿的是轻质的皮袍。我听说,一名君子帮助的是有需求的穷人,而不是给富人增加财富。"(06.04)

【英译】

Zihua(1) departed as an envoy to the State of Qi. Master Ran(2) was seeking Confucius's help for millet for Zihua's mother. The Master said, "Give her one *fu* (6.4 decalitres) of millet." He asked for

【英译注】(1) Zihua: Surname Gongxi, first name Chi, style name Zihua, Confucius's disciple. (2) Master Ran: Surname Ran, first name You, style name Ziyou, Confucius's disciple. (3) Chi: Zihua. His first name was Chi.

more. The Master said, "Give her one *yu* (16 decalitres) of millet." Master Ran gave her 5 *bing*'s (5 × 160 = 800 decalitres) of millet. The Master said, "As Chi(3) comes to the State of Qi, he drives a chariot drawn by fat horses and wears on a light and warm furred robe. I have heard that a superior man only helps the poor in need, and does not add riches to the rich." (06.04)

原思为之宰,与之粟九百,辞。子曰:"毋,以与尔邻里乡党乎?"(06.05)

【注释】原思:姓原名宪,字子思。为:担任,是。之:他(孔子)的。宰:管家。与:给。之:原思。粟:谷、小米。九百:900(斗)。辞:推辞。毋(音 wú 无):别推辞,别客气。以:用来,用以。与:给。尔:你。邻:5 家。里:25 家。乡:12500 家。党:500 家。乎:吗。以与尔邻里乡党乎:用来给你乡亲们吗。

【白话译文】

原思当孔子的总管家,孔子给他 900 斗小米,他推辞不要。孔子说:"不要客气,米拿走吧。如果你有富余,你不可以给你乡亲、邻居有需要的人一些吗?"(06.05)

【英译】

Yuan Si(1) served as a chief manager for Confucius's home and was given 900 decalitres of millet, but he declined them. The Master said, "Don't be so polite! Take the millet. If you have a surplus, cannot you give some to your neighbors or someone in need at your town?" (06.05)

【英译注】(1) Yuan Si: Surname Yuan, first name Xian, style name Zisi, Confucius's disciple.

朋友死，无所归，曰：“于我殡。”（10.22）

【注释】无所归：没有亲属殓埋。于：由。殡：停放灵柩和埋葬。

【白话译文】

当孔子的朋友去世，没有亲戚料理他的后事时，孔子说：“让我买棺安葬他吧。”（10.22）

【英译】

When a friend of Confucius's died and had no relatives to take care of his burial, the Master said, "Let me buy a coffin to bury him." (10.22)

12

礼 Rites of Proprieties

有子曰：“礼之用，和为贵。先王之道，斯为美。小大由之，有所不行。知和而和，不以礼节之，亦不可行也。”(01.12)

【注释】有子：姓有，名若，字子有，孔子弟子。礼：礼仪制度。之：的。用：运用。和：恰当、和谐。先王：禹、汤、周文王、周武王。斯：此，这。美：好。小大：小事大事。由：按照。有所：有些事。行：通行。小大由之，有所不行：大小事都按此办，有时就行不通。而：却，就。知和而和：知道和之贵就一味求和。节：约束。亦：也是。

【白话译文】

有子说：“当履行礼仪的时候，极为珍贵的是将所有事情完成得和谐。以前圣帝统治这个国家时,他们在这一点上做得特别出色。如果大小事,都这么做,有时是行不通的。如果不用礼仪来约束,为了和谐的美好,盲目地追求和谐,这是不可行的。”(01.12)

【英译】

Master You[1] said, "When the Rites of Proprieties are practiced, it is extremely valuable to get everything done in harmony. When the previous sage emperors ruled the country, they did excellently on this point. It may not work sometimes if all the things major or minor are done this way. If it is not regulated by the Rites of Proprieties, it is not workable to blindly seek harmony only for the goodness of harmony." (01.12)

【英译注】(1) Master You: You Ruo, Confucius's disciple.

林放问礼之本。子曰:“大哉问!礼,与其奢也,宁俭,与其易也,宁戚。”(03.04)

【注释】林放:鲁国人,今山东人。本:根本。大哉问:你问得意义重大;你问得好啊。奢:奢侈。宁:宁可。俭:节俭。易:礼节仪式周全。戚:心中悲哀。

【白话译文】

林放问礼仪的本质。孔子说:“你的问题太好了!礼仪,与其铺张浪费,宁可节俭。对于葬礼,与其所有礼节面面俱到,宁可心中悲伤。”(03.04)

【英译】

Lin Fang[1] asked the essences of the Rites of Proprieties. The Master said, "How great is your question! For the Rites of Proprieties, it is better to be frugal than extravagant and wasteful. For funerals, it is better to be sorrowful than strict observance of the protocols." (03.04)

【英译注】(1) Lin Fang: A person from the State of Lu, currently in Shangdong Province, and his life is unknown.

子曰:"夏礼吾能言之,杞不足徵也;殷礼吾能言之,宋不足徵也。文献不足故也。足,则吾能徵之矣。"(03.09)

【注释】夏:夏朝。礼:礼仪制度。言:说出。杞:杞国,夏禹的后裔,今河南杞县。足:够用,充分。徵(音 zhēng 征):简化为"征",作证,追问、证明。不足徵:文献证据不充分。殷:商朝。宋:宋国,商汤的后裔,今河南商丘。文:历史典籍、文件。献:贤人。文献:历史文件和贤者。故:缘故。

【白话译文】

孔子说:"我可以讲夏代的礼仪,但杞国的文献不足。我可以讲殷代的礼仪,但宋国的文献不足。问题是,历史文献和贤良的证人不充分。如果充分,我就可以用以考证了。"(03.09)

【英译】

The Master said, "I can speak about the institutions of the Rites of Proprieties of the Xia Dynasty[1], but archives in the State of Qii[2] are not sufficient. I can speak of institutions of the Rites of Proprieties of the

【英译注】(1) the Xia Dynasty: An ancient dynasty from 2100 BC to 1600 BC (2) the State of Qii: A state currently at Yu County of Henan Province, where offsprings of Emperor Yu lived. Double "i" in "Qii" indicates difference from the

Yin (Shang) Dynasty[3], but archives in the State of Song[4] are not sufficient. The question is that documents and able and virtuous witnesses are not sufficient. If they were, I could have done research with them." (03.09)

State of Qi currently at Shandong Province. (3) the Yin (Shang) Dynasty: An ancient dynasty from 1600 BC to 1100 BC. (4) the State of Song: Currently at Shangqiu, Henan Province, where offsprings of Emperor Tang of the Shang Dynasty lived.

子曰:"周监于二代,郁郁乎文哉! 吾从周。"(03.14)

【白话译文】

孔子说:"周朝借鉴夏朝和商朝二代的礼仪制度,形成了自己的体系。周朝的礼仪制度是多么丰富、多么辉煌啊! 我赞成并遵从周朝的礼仪。"(03.14)

【英译】

The Master said, "The Zhou Dynasty has formed its own system by taking examples of the institutions of the Rites of Proprieties from previous Xia and Shang dynasties. How rich and splendid are the system of the Rites of Proprieties of the Zhou Dynasty! I stand for and follow the Rites of the Zhou Dynasty." (03.14)

【注释】鲁昭公二十四年(前518年),孔子34岁到东周首都洛邑,学礼、学乐,拜见老子,收获极大,讲此言。周:周朝。监(音jiàn鉴):借鉴、取长补短。二代:夏代、商代。郁郁:茂盛、浓郁,文采盛貌。文:礼仪制度。郁郁乎文哉:(周朝的)礼仪制度,真是丰富多彩啊。吾:我。从:赞成、遵从。

子入太庙,每事问。或曰:"孰谓鄹人之子知礼乎?入太庙,每事问。"子闻之曰:"是礼也。"(03.15)

【注释】入:来到。太庙:君主的祖庙;鲁国太庙祭祀周公旦。问:请教。或:有人。孰:谁。鄹(音 zōu 邹):鲁国地名,今山东曲阜附近。鄹人之子:孔子。是礼也:这正是礼呀。

【白话译文】

孔子进入太庙,他每件事都向别人请教。有人说:"谁说鄹人的儿子知礼呀?他进入太庙,每件事都请教别人。"听到这,孔子说:"这正是礼呀!"(03.15)

【英译】

The Master entered the Great Ancestral Temple(1), and he sought advice for everything from others. Someone said, "Who says that the son of Zou Town(2) knows the Rites of Proprieties? As he comes to the Great Ancestral Temple, he consults others for everything." Hearing this, the Master said, "Exactly this is the Rite." (03.15)

【英译注】(1) the Great Ancestral Temple: The temple to pray for Duke Dan, the ancestor of the State of Lu, the feudal lord who established the Rites of Proprieties of the Zhou Dynasty. (2) Zou Town: Confucius's hometown, at the State of Lu, currently at Qufu, Shandong Province. The son refers to Confucius.

子贡欲去告朔之饩羊。子曰:"赐也,尔爱其羊,我爱其礼。"(03.17)

【注释】子贡:姓端木,名赐,字子贡。去:提议去掉。告朔:秋冬,天子颁发第二年的历书,初一举行祭祀。朔:农历每月初一。饩(音 xì 戏):送人的谷物、牲口。饩羊:祭祀用的活羊。赐:子贡,姓端木,名赐。爱:爱惜。其:那。

【白话译文】

子贡想放弃宣告新月开始的祷告仪式,其中每月的第一天杀一只活羊做祭祀。

孔子说:"赐,你珍惜这只羊,我珍惜这个礼。"(03.17)

【英译】

Zigong[(1)] desired to abandon a prayer ritual ceremony to inaugurate a new month that sacrificed a living goat on the first day of each month. The Master said, "Ah Ci[(2)]! You treasure the goat, but I treasure the Rites of Proprieties." (03.17)

【英译注】(1) Zigong: Surname Duanmu, first name Ci, style name Zigong, Confucius's disciple. (2) Ci: First name of Zigong.

子曰:"能以礼让为国乎,何有?不能以礼让为国,如礼何?"(04.13)

【注释】以:用。礼让:按礼谦让。为国:治国。何有:何难之有,岂有其难。如礼何:怎么实行礼?怎么对待礼仪?

【白话译文】

孔子说:"如果一个国家按照礼仪和谦让思想来治理,怎么会有困难?如果不能按照礼仪和谦让思想治理,那么如何对待礼仪?"(04.13)

【英译】

The Master said, "If a country is ruled according to the Rites of Proprieties and thoughts of compliance, how can it be difficult? If a country is ruled not according to the Rites of Proprieties and thoughts of compliance, how are the Rites of Proprieties treated?" (04.13)

子曰："恭而无礼则劳，慎而无礼则葸，勇而无礼则乱，直而无礼则绞。君子笃于亲，则民兴于仁；故旧不遗，则民不偷。"(08.02)

【白话译文】

孔子说："如果一个人恭顺而不受礼仪的约束，他会劳而无功。如果一个人谨慎而不受礼仪约束，他会过于胆小。如果一个人勇敢而不受礼仪约束，他会无法无天。如果一个人直率而不受礼仪约束，他会非常刻薄。如果一名君子全心合意对待他的亲眷，仁德就会在百姓中兴起。如果一名君子不放弃老朋友，百姓之间就不会相互冷淡。"(08.02)

【英译】

The Master said, "If one is deferential but is not bound by the Rites of Proprieties, he will labor fruitlessly. If one is cautious but is not bound by the Rites, he will become cowardly. If one is courageous but is not bound by the Rites, he will be absolutely lawless. If one is upright but is not bound by the Rites, he will be sarcastic. If a superior man serves his relatives wholeheartedly, superior benevolence will prevail among the people. If a superior man does not forsake his old friends, the people will not be indifferent toward one another." (08.02)

【注释】恭：恭敬。而：却。无礼：不以礼指导、节制。则：就会。劳：辛劳，劳而无功，如《庄子·天运》中"推舟于陆也，劳而无功"；疲劳、劳累。慎：谨慎。葸（音 xǐ 洗）：拘谨。乱：叛乱，作乱，不太平。直：耿直。绞：尖刻。笃（音 dǔ 堵）：忠厚。于：对于。亲：亲属。民：百姓。兴：盛行。君子：地位高的人。笃于亲，则民兴于仁：厚待自己的亲属，那么百姓中就会兴起仁德风气。故旧：老友。遗：抛弃。偷：刻薄、不厚道。故旧不遗，则民不偷：不遗弃故友，那么百姓对人就不会冷淡。

子曰:"麻冕,礼也。今也纯,俭,吾从众。拜下,礼也。今拜乎上,泰也。虽违众,吾从下。"(09.03)

【注释】麻:麻布,要用2400经线,细密难成,费时费工。冕:礼帽。纯:黑丝绸,丝质细,易织,省工。俭:俭省。从:遵从、赞成。众:大家。从众:赞同大家的做法,跟随多数人去做。拜下:臣见君礼,先堂下跪拜,后堂上跪拜。拜乎上:仅堂上跪拜。泰:傲慢。违:违背。违众:背离多数人,不追随多数人。下:先堂下跪拜。

【白话译文】

孔子说:"礼帽用麻纤维做的,这是礼仪。今天礼帽用丝做的,节俭一些,我认同大家的做法。臣拜见国君,在大厅内、外都要向他磕头,这是礼仪。今天,多数大臣都只在大厅内磕头,这是一种傲慢的行为。我依然在大厅内、外都磕头,尽管我与大家不同。"(09.03)

【英译】

The Master said, "It is the Rites of Proprieties that a ritual cap is made of hemp fibre(1). Today the ritual cap is made of silk for the sake of thrift, so I agree on it with the masses. It is the Rites of Proprieties that officials kowtou(2) to their sovereign both outside and inside the hall when they meet with him. Today most officials kowtou to his sovereign inside the hall only, which is arrogant conduct. I still kowtou both outside and inside the hall, although I am against the masses." (09.03)

【英译注】(1) The ritual cap was made of helm fibre with 2400 longitudinal threads and the process was difficult and labor-cost, while silk cap was made of black silk easily embroidered. (2) Kowtou: To touch forehead to the ground while kneeling, as an act of worship, reverence in ancient Chinese customs.

入太庙，每事问。（10.21）

【注释】入：来到。太庙：君主的祖庙，鲁国太庙祭祀周公旦。问：请教。

【白话译文】

孔子进入太庙，他每件事都向别人请教。（10.21）

【英译】

The Master entered the Great Ancestral Temple(1), and sought advice for everything from others. (10.21)

【英译注】(1) the Great Ancestral Temple: The temple to pray for Duke Dan, the ancestor of the State of Lu, the feudal lord who established the Rites of the Proprieties of the Zhou Dynasty.

朋友之馈，虽车马，非祭肉，不拜。（10.23）

【注释】之：的。馈：赠送（物）。虽：即使是。非：不是。祭肉：祭祀用的肉。拜：行礼，不拱手弯腰行礼。

【白话译文】

孔子的朋友向他赠礼物，即使是车或马，但是如果不是祭肉，他也不向朋友作揖行礼。（10.23）

【英译】

The Master did not bow to his friend who sent him a gift if it was not sacrificial meat, even if it was a horse or a carriage. (10.23)

子曰："先进于礼乐，野人也；后进于礼乐，君子也。如用之，则吾从先进。"（11.01）

【注释】先进：先学习，后做官。于：在。乐（音 yuè 月）：乐曲乐舞。野人：平民，朴素粗鲁的人。后进：后学习，先做官。君子：卿大夫等贵族的子弟。如：若。用：任用。之：他。从：跟随、赞同。如用之，则吾从先进：若要选用人才，那我就选先学习礼乐的人。

【白话译文】

孔子说："那些在做官之前先学习礼仪和礼乐的，是野人。那些在做官之后再学习礼仪和礼乐的，是贵族（君子）。如果要任用他们，那么我会选择先学习礼仪和音乐的。"（11.01）

【英译】

The Master said, "They are called rustics who learn the Rites of Proprieties and Music before they become officials. They are called the nobles (superior men) who learn the Rites of Proprieties and Music after they become officials. If I am to use them, I shall choose those who learn the Rites of Proprieties and Music in advance." (11.01)

子曰："上好礼，则民易使也。"（14.43）

【注释】上：地位高的。好（音 hào 号）：喜爱。则：那么。民：百姓。易使：容易服从、易受役使。

【白话译文】

孔子说："处在上位的人对于所处理的任何事，都热爱遵守礼仪，那么老百姓就

容易服从他们的命令。"(14.43)

【英译】

The Master said, "People in superior positions love and observe the Rites of Proprieties for everything they handle, and then the common people will find it easy to obey their orders." (14.43)

13

智 Wisdom

子曰:"由,诲女知之乎!知之为知之,不知为不知,是知也。"(02.17)

【白话译文】

孔子说:"由!让我教你知晓一件事物的正确态度吧!如果你知晓它,就说知晓。如果你不知晓它,就说不知晓。这就是真正的智慧。"(02.17)

【注释】由:姓仲名由,字子路。诲(音 huì 会):教育、教诲。女(音 rǔ 辱):汝,你。诲女:一解"告诉你";二解"告诉你的"。知(音 zhī 织):懂、明白。之:这,此,学问,道理。知之:明白、懂得(此、学问等)。乎:吗。诲女知之乎:一解"教诲你怎样正确求知";二解"教你的,你知道了吗"。为:是,就是。知之为知之:懂就说懂,明白就说明白。是知(音 zhì 治)也:这是智慧啊。

据张晓英、吴敏研究,此章应当是"孔子告诫子路君子当具'知人、知言、知时'、'非时不见'的人生智慧"[J04]。从"子路无宿诺"

(12.12,46 法)和孔子因材施教,担心子路"不得其死然"(11.13,28 忧)看,此章讲孔子教诲子路智慧是合情的。特此抛砖引玉,依此意注译如后,供大家参考。

文中所有"知(音 zhì 治)"皆是"智、智慧、理智"意。诲女知之乎:教诲你如何智慧地做事吧。此处"之"是为人、处事的"人、事"等"知(智)"的宾语。知之为知之:天下是智慧的,就按照这一智慧的情况去办事。其中"知之"指天下、社会是智慧、理智的;"之"为语助词,无意义;"为"指做事、行事、行为、处理人际关系等。不知:天下、外部环境"不智"、糊涂、不理智或天下无道。为不知:将计就计,智慧地为人处事。不知为不知:天下不是智慧的,就按照这一不智慧的情况去办事;不妨参考韩信受胯之辱的典故。整句意思是:孔子说:"仲由,让我教你做事的智慧吧!如果天下是智慧的,你智慧地做事。如果天下不是智慧的,你依然智慧地做事。这才是真正的智慧啊。"

【英译】

The Master said, "You(1)! Let me teach you the correct attitude(2) to know a thing! If you do know it, say that you do. If you don't know it, say that you don't. This is the true wisdom." (02.17)

【英译注】(1) You: Surname Zhong, first name You, style name Zilu (542 BC – 480 BC), from the Village of Zhong at the town of Northeastern Bian (currently Pingyi County, Shandong Province), Confucius's disciple, 9 years younger than his master. (2) the correct attitude: Normally this article is interpreted to be a lesson of faith as above, but reasonably it was about how Zilu did a thing wisely based on Zilu's nature and Confucius's individualized education as studied by Prof. Zhang and Ms. Wu Min[J04]. "Zilu never postpones overnight what he promises to do this day" (12.12,46 the Law), but he "is foolhardy" (11.18), "stubborn and unyielding, will not die a natural death (11.13, 28 Anxiety)". Obviously Zilu was faithful, but inflexible or in need of wisdom. The whole passage is thus translated below: *The Master said, "Zhong You! Let me teach you the wisdom to do a thing! If it is wise under heaven, you do it wisely. If it is unwise under heaven, you still do it wisely. This is the true wisdom."*

子曰:"知之者不如好之者,好之者不如乐之者。"(06.20)

【白话译文】

孔子说:"弄懂它不如热爱它,热爱它不如痴迷它。"(06.20)

【注释】知:懂得。之:学问。者:的人。好(音 hào 浩):喜爱。乐(音 lè 勒):快乐,以知此为乐趣。

【英译】

The Master said, "To know it is not better than to love it. And to love it is not better than to be infatuated with it." (06.20)

子曰:"可与共学,未可与适道;可与适道,未可与立;可与立,未可与权。"(09.30)

【注释】与:同,在一起。共:共同。学:学习。未:不、不一定。可:能够。适:到……去,得到,理解,实践。道:真理,社会与自然发展规律。未可与适道:不一定共同理解与实践社会与自然的真理。立:守道不改,坚持真理,常包含"立于礼"之意[2],也译成依礼行事。权:秤锤,制宜,权衡轻重、利弊,辩证灵活地处理问题。可与权:共同因势利导,因时(地、事、人等)制宜,通权达变,辩证科学地处理问题。

【白话译文】

孔子说:"我们可以与某人一起学习,但是不可以与他一起理解社会和自然的规律。我们可以与他一起理解社会和自然规律,但是不可以与他一起在社会上站稳脚跟。我们可以与他一起在社会上站稳脚跟,但是不可以与他一起随机应变灵活地做一件事情。"(09.30)

【英译】

The Master said, "We can learn together with someone, but we cannot understand the laws of nature and society with him. We can understand the laws of nature and society with him, but we cannot establish ourselves with him in the society. And we can establish ourselves with him in the society, but we cannot do a thing with him flexibly according to changing circumstances." (09.30)

子曰:"不曰'如之何,如之何'者,吾末如之何也已矣。"(15.16)

【白话译文】

孔子说:"当一个人遇到问题,他不问自己'如何解决它,如何解决它',我不知道对他如何办了。"(15.16)

【英译】

The Master said, "When someone encounters a problem, if he does not ask himself 'how to solve it', 'how to solve it', I do not know how to deal with him." (15.16)

【注释】不曰:(遇到困难)不说。如之何:怎么办,不深入提出问题、思考问题,不想办法解决问题。者:的人。末(音 mò 墨):无,不知道。已矣:了啊。吾末如之何也已矣:我对他也不知道怎么办了呀。

子曰:"唯上智与下愚不移。"(17.03)

【白话译文】

孔子说:"积极上进是智慧的,自暴自弃与堕落是愚蠢的,唯有这样的结论是不变化的。"(17.03)

【英译】

The Master said[(1)], "Actively making progress is wisdom. Being resigned to one's backwardness is stupidity. It is this kind of conclusion that is unchangeable." (17.03)

【注释】孔子有教无类,故"上"、"下"未解作人的等级。唯:只有。上:上进、追求进步。知(音 zhì 志):智,智慧、明智。下:自暴自弃、自甘堕落、不思进取。愚:愚昧。不移:(这一结论,无论何时何地都)不会改变。

【英译注】(1) Normal translation of this sentence: The Master said, "It is only unchangeable that a man of a superior rank is wise and a man of inferior rank is stupid."

14

信 Faith

子贡问君子。子曰:“先行其言而后从之。”(02.13)

【白话译文】

子贡请教君子是如何做的。孔子说:“他一说话就想清结果,然后说到做到。”(02.13)

【英译】

Zigong[(1)] asked Confucius’ advice about how a superior man did. The Master said, “He begins his words with the end in mind and practices what he preaches .” (02.13)

【注释】子贡:姓端木,名赐,字子贡。行:可执行,使之可行。言:承语、承诺。从:做。之:所言、所承诺的。

【英译注】(1) Zigong: Surname Duanmu, first name Ci, style name Zigong, Confucius's disciple.

子曰:“人而无信,不知其可也。大车无輗,小车无軏,其何以行之哉?”(02.22)

【白话译文】

孔子说:“一个人却没有诚信,不知他如何能够在社会上立身。好比牛车缺少固

【注释】而:却;不能当“如果”讲,古书多有此句法。信:诚信、言语真实。其:他。可:可以(立得住脚,立身处世,被认可)。不知其可也:不知此人怎么能立身处世、得到社会认可。大车:牛车。輗(音 ní 泥):称作“鬲”的辕前横木的活木销子,套牛用。小车:马车。軏(音 yuè 月):称作“衡”的

定套牛用横木的輗(关键),或马车缺少连接马套和横木的軏(活销),车子怎么能够前进呢?"(02.22)

辕前横木的木销,套马用。何:怎么。行:行走。

【英译】

The Master said,"For a person who is not faithful,it is not known how he can stand in society. As an ox cart is without pegs that fasten the horizontal bar to yoke the oxen,or as a horse carriage lacks the pins that connect the harness and horizontal bar to harness the horses,how can they move ahead?" (02.22)

子贡问政。子曰:"足食,足兵,民信之矣。"子贡曰:"必不得已而去,于斯三者何先?"曰:"去兵。"子贡曰:"必不得已而去,于斯二者何先?"曰:"去食。自古皆有死,民无信不立。"(12.07)

【注释】子贡:姓端木名赐,字子贡。问:请教。政:治国。足:充足。食:粮食。兵:军备。民:百姓。信:信任。之:官员。必:一定。不得已:无可奈何。去:去除。斯:这。三者:三项。何:哪个。先:时间、次序在前。去食:放弃粮食,国君不收税赋,以求不失信于民。皆有死:总是要死的。民无信:无民的信任。立:成立,建立,存在。民无信不立:失去人民的信任,统治者就站不住脚。

【白话译文】

子贡请教如何治理一个国家。孔子说:"要有充足的粮食,充足的兵力,百姓对国君充分的信任。"子贡问:"万不得已要去除一项,于这三项中先去除哪个?"孔子说:"去除兵力。"子贡问:"万不得已去除一项,于这二项中先去除哪个?"孔子

说:"去除粮食。自古至今,任何人不免一死,但没有百姓的信任国君就不能在世上站稳。"(12.07)

【英译】

Zigong[1] asked advice about how to rule a country. The Master said,"There must be sufficient grain, sufficient military force, and sufficient trust from the people upon the sovereign." Zigong asked,"If one thing must be removed,which should it be?" The Master said,"Military force is removed." Zigong asked,"If one thing must be removed,which should it be?" The Master said,"Grain is removed. From the ancients to now, death cannot be avoided, but the sovereign cannot be established firmly in the world without trust from the people."(12.07)

【英译注】(1) Zigong: Surname Duanmu, first name Ci, style name Zigong,Confucius's disciple.

子曰:"吾犹及史之阙文也。有马者借人乘之,今亡矣夫!"(15.26)

【注释】犹:还。犹及:还看到。史:史书。阙文:史官记史时,遇到疑问,缺而不记的地方,不敢没有凭据而擅自补缺。有马者:有马的人。借人乘之:将马借给别人骑,因自己不会调教,让人调教好后,归还主人。今:当今。亡(音wú吴):无,没有,无此实事求是的做法。

【白话译文】

孔子说:"我依然能够看到国史官由于缺乏历史资料,在历代历史文献中对于可疑细节留下的空缺。这就好比一个人有

一匹烈马自己不能驯服,就借给技艺娴熟的骑士来乘然后再要回来。这种实事求是的态度,今天再也看不到了。”(15.26)

【英译】

The Master said, “I see times when historians lacked sufficient materials, and that there were blank spaces in the historical because the materials were suspect. This is like one has a fiery horse and by himself he cannot tame it, so he lends it to a skillful equestrian to ride it and then gets it back. This attitude to seek the truth from facts is not seen anymore today.” (15.26)

子夏曰:“君子信而后劳其民,未信则以为厉己也。信而后谏,未信则以为谤己也。”(19.10)

【注释】子夏:姓卜名商,字子夏。信:获得信任。后:之后。劳:役使。民:百姓。则:否则。以为:认为。厉己:虐待他们自己。谏:规劝。谤己:诽谤他们自己。

【白话译文】

子夏说:“君子首先获得百姓的信任,然后给他们劳役。没有信任,他们认为要求他们的任何劳动都是虐待他们。君子首先获得国君的信任,然而向他进谏。没有信任,他会认为任何谏言都在诽谤他。”(19.10)

【英译】

Zixia[1] said, "A superior man first wins trust from the people and then imposes services on them. Without trust, they think that any labour required on them is to mistreat them. A superior man first wins trust from his sovereign and then remonstrates against him. Without trust, he thinks that any remonstration is to slander him." (19.10)

【英译注】(1) Zixia: Surname Bu, first name Shang, style name Zixia, Confucius's disciple.

15

礼乐 Ritual Music

孔子谓季氏:"八佾舞于庭,是可忍也,孰不可忍也?"(03.01)

【白话译文】

孔夫子评论季氏说:"他用8行每行8位舞者在他的家庙奏乐舞蹈。如果他这都可以忍心做,还有什么别的事不可忍心做呢?"(03.01)

【注释】谓:谈到。季氏:很可能是季桓子,姓姬、季孙氏,名斯,谥号桓。他从鲁定公五年(公元前505年)父亲季平子去世至哀公三年(公元前492年)任鲁国正卿。孔子在他手下任大司寇(定公九年至十四年)。若非亲自看到,人是很难感慨的。佾(音yì义):乐舞行列,《周礼》规定一佾8人,天子用八佾,诸侯六佾,卿大夫四佾,士用二佾;季氏是正卿,应用四佾。舞:跳舞,演奏乐舞。于:在。庭:庭院、家庙。是:这。忍:忍心。孰:什么。是忍也,孰不可忍也:像这违礼的事都狠心做,还有什么不能狠心做的呀。

【英译】

Confucius commented on the Ji[1], "He used eight rows[2] of eight dancers a row to perform music and dance at his ancestral temple. If his action could be tolerated, what else could not be tolerated?" (03.01)

【英译注】(1) the Ji: Possibly Master Ji Huan, surname Jisun, first name Si, posthumous title Huan, chief senior official of the State of Lu from 505 BC to 492 BC during Duke Ding to Duke Ai of the State of Lu when Confucius served as Grand Judge and commented on what he saw. (2) eight rows: Eight dancers a row and 64 dancers for eight rows. According to the Rites of Proprieties of the Zhou Dynasty, the emperor used a band of 8 rows, a duke 6 rows, a senior official 4 rows, and home manager 2 rows. Ji's was a senior official and a 4-row band was applicable to him only.

子语鲁大师乐,曰:"乐其可知也:始作,翕如也;从之,纯如也,皦如也,绎如也,以成。"(03.23)

【白话译文】

孔子与鲁国音乐太师讨论音乐,说:"音乐是可以知晓的。开始演奏,所有乐器齐鸣,激烈恢弘。音乐展开,音乐和谐悠扬。之后,音调明朗清晰,节奏优美分明。所有五音相连,平滑如珍珠项链,袅袅不绝,回荡空中。整曲完美,一气呵成。"(03.23)

【注释】鲁国礼乐崩坏,孔子谈正乐之法,五音六律,让人知晓。语(音 yù 玉):和别人一起谈论。鲁:鲁国。大(音 tài 太)师:乐官名。乐(音 yuè 月):乐曲乐舞。其:这是。始:开始。作:演奏。翕(音 xī 西):合奏,五音皆发。翕如:轰鸣繁美。从(音 zòng 纵):放纵、展开。纯:五音相继而发,和谐悠扬委婉。皦(音 jiǎo 佼):音节分明。绎:五音相连如串珠,袅袅不绝。以:而,然后。成:完成,结束。

【英译】

The Master discussed on music with a grand musician of the State of Lu, saying, " Music can be understood. At the beginning, all the instruments play together to construct a symphonic performance loudly and beautifully. When the performance unfolds further, the tones are rising and falling harmoniously. As it proceeds, it becomes clear and graceful melodiously with distinct ryhthms. And then all the five tones(1) are connected smoothly like a pearl necklace and the music lingers long in the air continually. The whole music work is accomplished perfectly without interruption. " (03.23)

【英译注】(1) five tones: Ancient Chinese had the five tones with five notes and a five-tone scale.

子谓《韶》:"尽美矣,又尽善也。"谓《武》:"尽美矣,未尽善也。"(03.25)

【注释】谓:认为,以为。韶:相传歌颂虞舜的乐舞。尽:达到顶点。美:音调、舞蹈的形式上的优美。善:乐舞思想内容的完善。武:相传歌颂周武王的乐舞。

【白话译文】

孔子评论《韶》乐:"它的曲调完全优美,它的内容十分完美。"评论《武》乐:"它的曲调完全优美,它的内容不十分完美。"(03.25)

【英译】

The Master commented on the Music of Shao[1], "Its melody is completely beautiful and its content is completely perfect." On the Music of Wu[2], he said, "Its melody is completely beautiful, but its content is not completely perfect." (03.25)

【英译注】(1) the Music of Shao: It is said that this work was the music and dance to eulogize the Emperor Shun whose throne was given by the first emperor in Chinese history. (2) the Music of Wu: It is said that this work was the music and dance to eulogize the first Emperor Wu of the Zhou Dynasty.

子在齐闻《韶》,三月不知肉味,曰:"不图为乐之至于斯也。"(07.14)

【注释】鲁昭公二十六年(前516年),36岁的孔子到齐国闻《韶》。齐:齐国。韶:歌颂虞舜的舜时古乐曲名。三月:很久。图:想到。为:创作。乐(音 yuè 月):乐曲乐舞。至:达到。斯:此等(美妙、迷人的)地步。不图为乐之至于斯也:未想到古人创作音乐竟达到如此美妙的水平。

【白话译文】

孔子在齐国听到《韶》乐,三个月吃不出来肉味,说:"我没有想到,此乐创作完美到如此美妙的程度。"(07.14)

【英译】

The Master heard the Music of Shao[1] performed at the State of Qi, and he could not notice the taste of meat for three months[2], saying, "I have never thought of that the music was created so perfectly to such a splendid degree!" (07.14)

【英译注】(1) Confucius visited the State of Qi at the age of 36 in the 26th Year (516 BC) of Duke Zhao of the State of Lu and heard the Music of Shao that was to eulogize the saint Emperor Shun. (2) three months: Not exactly 3 months, meaning a long period.

子与人歌而善，必使反之，而后和之。(07.32)

【白话译文】

当孔子赞扬某人唱歌好时，一定要求他再唱，而后与他一起唱。(07.32)

【英译】

When the Master praised someone for his good singing, he certainly asked him to sing it again and then he was singing together with him. (07.32)

【注释】与：通“誉”，赞许、称誉。歌：歌唱。而：如果。善：好、不错。与人歌而善：表扬别人唱得好。必：一定。使：请他。反：再唱。之：此歌。和（音 hè 贺）：（孔子与他）一起唱。

子曰：“师挚之始，《关雎》之乱，洋洋乎盈耳哉！”(08.15)

【白话译文】

孔子说：“乐师长挚演奏序曲。终曲是《关雎》。所有演奏悠扬、优美，气势磅礴，久久回荡在耳边。”(08.15)

【英译】

The Master said, “The Grand Musician Master Zhi(1) performed an overture. The final was *Guanju*(2), a piece of instrumental ensemble music. All the performance is melodious and graceful, full of power and grandeur, and reverberates long in the ears.” (08.15)

【注释】师挚（音 zhì 治）：鲁国太乐师，名挚。之：的。始：乐曲的开端，序曲。关雎（音 jū 居）：乐曲，也是《诗经》首篇。乱：终曲，合奏乐。师挚之始，《关雎》之乱：师挚演奏序曲，《关雎》为终曲。洋洋：丰富而优美。盈：回荡。盈耳：经久回荡在耳边。

【英译注】(1) Zhi: Grand Music Master of the State of Lu, first name Zhi. (2) *Guanju*: The first song of *Poems and Odes*, currently named *Book of Poetry*.

师冕见,及阶,子曰:"阶也。"及席,子曰:"席也。"皆坐,子告之曰:"某在斯,某在斯。"师冕出。子张问曰:"与师言之道与?"子曰:"然。固相师之道也。"(15.42)

【注释】师:乐师,古代乐师通常由盲人担任。冕:人名。见:求见。及:到达。阶:台阶。席:坐席。某:某某人。斯:这。出:走了。子张:姓颛(音 zhuān 砖)孙名师,字子张。与师言:跟乐师说话。道:办法。然:是。固:本来、就是。相:帮助。

【白话译文】

乐师冕被引见给孔子,快到台阶时,孔子说:"这是台阶。"快到坐席时,孔子说:"这是席子。"大家都坐下来,孔子给他介绍说:"某某人在这,某某人在这。"乐师冕离开。子张问道:"这就是与乐师说话的方式吗?"孔子说:"是的。我的一言一行就是帮助乐师的方式。"(15.42)

【英译】

Mian(1), the Music Master was presented to Confucius. Approaching the steps, the Master said, "Here are steps." Reaching a mat, the Master said, "It's a mat." When all people sat down, the Master introduced him by saying, "Someone is here, and someone is here." When Master Mian left, Zizhang(2) asked, "Is this the way to speak with a music master?" The Master said, "Yes. What I say and do is just the way to help a music master." (15.42)

【英译注】(1) Mian: A blind music master of the State of Lu whose name was Mian. In ancient China, music masters were normally blind people. (2) Zizhang: Surname Zhuansun, first name Shi, style name Zizhang, Confucius's disciple.

子曰:"恶紫之夺朱也,恶郑声之乱雅乐也,恶利口之覆家邦者。"(17.18)

【注释】恶(音 wù 务):憎恶。紫:紫色。之:的。夺:取代。朱:红色。郑声:郑国的声乐。乱:扰乱。雅:规范的。乐(音 yuè 月):乐曲乐舞。利口:伶牙俐齿。覆:颠覆。家:卿大夫统治地。邦:诸侯统治地。邦家:国家。

【白话译文】

孔子说:"可恶的是紫色取代了红色的光彩和地位。可恶的是郑声破坏了雅乐。可恶的是伶牙俐齿颠覆了诸侯之国或大夫之家。"(17.18)

【英译】

The Master said, "It is abominable that purple overtakes the splendor and position of red. It is abominable that the music of the State of Zheng(1) undermines graceful music. And it is abominable that a glib tongue undermines a duke's state or a senior official's fief land." (17.18)

【英译注】(1) music of the State of Zheng: The music and ditty, featured at quick and distinct rhythms, lingering melody. It was popular music on love, much different from the formal Music of Shao.

大师挚适齐,亚饭干适楚,三饭缭适蔡,四饭缺适秦,鼓方叔入于河,播鼗武入于汉,少师阳、击磬襄入于海。(18.09)

【注释】大:太。大师:鲁国乐官之长。挚:人名。适(音 shì 市):往、到、逃亡。亚饭、三饭、四饭:乐官名,天子、诸侯每餐奏乐,乐章各异,各有乐师。干、缭、缺:皆是人名。楚:楚国。蔡:蔡国。秦:秦国。鼓:击鼓的乐师。方叔:人名。入:进、来、隐居。于:到。河:黄河边。鼗(音 táo 桃):长把摇鼓。武:人名。汉:汉江边。少师:副乐师。阳:人名。击磬:击磬

【白话译文】

乐师长挚逃亡到了齐国,二餐乐师干逃亡到了楚国,三餐乐师缭逃亡到了蔡国,

四餐乐师缺逃亡到了秦国,鼓手方叔隐居黄河边,长把摇鼓手武隐居汉水边,副乐师长阳、击磬乐师襄隐居海边。(18.09)

的乐师。襄:人名。海:海滨。

【英译】

Zhi(1), the Grand Music Master, escaped to the State of Qi. Gan, musician for the second meal(2), escaped to the State of Chu. Liao, musician for the third meal, escaped to the State of Cai. Que, musician for the fourth meal, escaped to the State of Qin. Fang Shu, the drummer, retreated to the bank of the Yellow River. Wu, the long-handle drum player, retreated to the bank of the Han River. Both Yang, the Deputy Music Master, and Rang, the stone chimes player, retreated to the seacoast. (18.09)

【英译注】(1) Zhi: Grand music master of the State of Lu, first name Zhi, serving as the band leader of the State of Lu. (2) musician for the second meal: The musician who performed at the second meal of an emperor or duke in Confucius's time. The same is for the third or fourth meal musicians. The musicians left the State of Lu where the Music of Rites was greatly undermined.

四
Four

美德
Excellent Morals

16

忠 Loyalty

子曰:“君子不重则不威,学则不固。主忠信。无友不如己者。过则勿惮,改。”(01.08)

【白话译文】

孔子说:“如果一位君子轻浮,他既不会受到别人的尊重,也不能把从师所学的知识与他的行为牢固地结合为一体。他把忠诚和诚信作为他立身社会的核心品质。他不与那些与他没有任何共同点的人交朋友。他不担心犯错,因为改正了就好。”(01.08)

【英译】

The Master said, “If a superior man is frivolous, he neither can be respected by others nor can his knowing from his master be firmly united with his doing. He takes loyalty and faithfulness as his essential qualities to establish himself independently in society. He does not make friends with those who have nothing in common with him. And he does not worry about his mistakes as it is still good to have corrected them.” (01.08)

【注释】重:庄重。则:就、便、那么。威:威严。学:学的知识。固:牢固,所学知识牢固到能产生条件反射的状态,即“把所学所悟之理时时处处落实到人生的实践中,稳固到自己身上,将知行合为一体”。主:为主。忠:尽心竭力。主忠信:以忠、信为主、为本。无:通“毋”,不,不要。友:交友。如:像,等同,人以类聚。不如己:不像自己,与自己志、道等不同。者:的人。过:错。勿:不。惮(音 dàn 蛋):怕、畏。改:改正。

子曰:"主忠信,毋友不如己者,过则勿惮,改。"(09.25)

【注释】主:重视。忠:尽心竭力。主忠信:以忠、信为主、为本。毋:不要。友:交友。如:像,等同。不如己:不像自己,与自己志、道等不同。者:的人。过:错误。勿:不。惮(音 dàn 蛋):怕,畏。改:改正。

【白话译文】

孔子说:"把忠诚和诚信作为你立身社会的核心品质。不与那些与你没有共同点的人交朋友。不担心犯错,因为改了就好。"(09.25)

【英译】

The Master said, "Take loyalty and faithfulness as your essential qualities to establish yourself independently in society. Do not make friends with those sharing nothing in common with you. And do not worry about your mistakes, as it is all right to have them corrected." (09.25)

子张问政。子曰:"居之无倦,行之以忠。"(12.14)

【注释】子张:姓颛(音 zhuān 砖)孙名师,字子张。问:请教。政:治国。居:身居、处在。之:官位。无:不要。倦:懈怠。行:执行。之:政令。忠:不背叛国家,利国利民、无私奉公、尽心竭力。

【白话译文】

子张请教如何成为一位好官员。孔子说:"你一旦身居官位,就要不懈怠地处理政府事务,忠诚地执行政府的法令和政策。"(12.14)

【英译】

Zizhang[1] asked how to be a good official. The Master said, "Once you occupy an official post, manage your governmental affairs untiringly, and carry out governmental orders and policies faithfully." (12.14)

【英译注】(1) Zizhang: Surname Zhuansun, first name Shi, style name Zizhang, Confucius's disciple.

樊迟问仁。子曰:"居处恭,执事敬,与人忠。虽之夷狄,不可弃也。"(13.19)

【注释】樊迟:名须,字子迟。问:请教。居:在家、在住所及周边,邻里。处:闲住,待人接物。恭:规规矩矩。执事:办事。敬:严肃认真。与人:待人。忠:诚实。虽:即使。之:到、去。夷狄:外国、边远地区。不可弃:不要抛弃、忘记。

【白话译文】

樊迟请教仁是什么。孔子说:"当你与邻居相处,对他们要恭顺。为人工作要严肃认真。对待他人要忠诚守信。即使你到边远地区和国外,也不要放弃这些品德。"(13.19)

【英译】

Fan Chi[1] asked what superior benevolence was. The Master said, "Be deferential to your neighbors and get along with them. Work seriously and carefully for others. And treat others loyally and faithfully. Even when you go to remote areas and foreign countries, do not abandon these virtues." (13.19)

【英译注】(1) Fan Chi: Surname Fan, first name Xu, style name Zifan, Confucius's disciple.

子曰:“爱之,能勿劳乎?忠焉,能无诲乎?”(14.08)

【白话译文】

孔子说:“爱一个人,我们能不让他辛苦工作吗?对他忠诚,我们能不真诚地教育和批评他吗?”(14.08)

【英译】

The Master said, “To love a person, can we ask him not to work hard? To be loyal to him, can we not teach and criticize him earnestly?” (14.08)

【注释】爱之:爱一个人。勿:不。劳:为他操劳;让他劳作、辛苦。乎:吗。忠:尽心竭力,不背叛。忠焉:忠诚(于他)呀。诲:教诲、劝告。能无诲乎:能不教诲他吗。

子张问行。子曰:“言忠信,行笃敬,虽蛮貊之邦行矣。言不忠信,行不笃敬,虽州里行乎哉?立则见其参于前也,在舆则见其倚于衡也,夫然后行。”子张书诸绅。(15.06)

【白话译文】

子张问他如何在社会上受欢迎。孔子说:“说话真实,做事敬重,即使你到南方的少数民族地区或者北方的边远地区,你也会受到欢迎。如果你既不能说话真实,

【注释】子张:姓颛(音 zhuān 砖)孙名师,字子张。问:请教。行:行得通,到处受欣赏,俗话说“吃得开”。言:对人说话。忠:尽心竭力,不背叛。信:诚实。行:行为。笃:忠厚。敬:恭敬。蛮:南方民族。貊(音 mò 莫):北方民族。蛮貊:边远地区。之:的。邦:国家。行矣:行得通呀。州:2500家,五党。里:25家,即五邻,5家1邻。州里:近处。立:站着。其:忠信笃敬。参(音 cān 餐):列,显现。于:在。前:面前。立则见其参于前也:站着,就仿佛见“忠信笃敬”显现在面前啊。在舆(音 yú 鱼):坐车。倚:靠、粘、刻。衡:车

又不能做事敬重，即使在你自己的家乡，你能够受到欢迎吗？当你站立时，你想象着这些话出现在你的面前。当你乘车时，你想象着这些话贴在车的前横木条上。你只有这样，才能到处都受欢迎。”子张将孔子的这些话写在他的装饰带子上。（15.06）

辕前的横木。书：写。诸：此在。绅：贵族系在腰间的大带子。

【英译】

Zizhang[(1)] asked how he could be welcome everywhere. The Master said, “Speak truthfully, and behave respectfully, so you can be welcome even if you go to the minority areas in the south or remote areas in the north. If you neither speak truthfully nor behave respectfully, can you be welcome even at your own hometown? When you stand, imagine that these words appear before your face. When you take a carriage, imagine that these words are attached to the front horizontal yoking bar. Only when you do this, can you be welcome everywhere.” Zizhang wrote these words on his girdle. (15.06)

【英译注】（1）Zizhang: Surname Zhuansun, first name Shi, style name Zizhang, Confucius's disciple.

17

孝 Filial Piety

有子曰:"其为人也孝弟而好犯上者,鲜矣。不好犯上而好作乱者,未之有也。君子务本,本立而道生。孝弟也者,其为仁之本与!"(01.02)

【注释】有子:姓有,名若,字子有,孔子弟子,小孔子43岁。《论语》中称"子"的孔子弟子只有四个,他是其一,由此推断他或他的弟子参与了《论语》的编纂。《史记》载他的身材面貌与孔子相似,孔子刚去世时,孔子弟子一致立他为师,对待他如同对待孔子一样。其:他,一个人。为人也:做人呀。孝:尽心奉养和服从父母。弟(音 tì 替):悌,顺从尊敬兄长。犯:抵触、触犯。上:地位高的人。者:的人。鲜(音 xiǎn 显):少,稀少、缺少。乱:叛乱。务:致力、重视。本:根基。立:建立、形成。道:原则。生:有,形成。与:吧。

【白话译文】

有子说:"如果一个人的为人,是孝敬父母和尊重兄长,他喜欢触犯上级的情况是罕见的。如果他不喜欢触犯上级,他喜欢武装叛乱的可能是不存在的。君子致力于打好基础。当基础建成时,人生的原则就形成了。孝敬父母和尊重兄长,就是仁的基础。(01.02)

【英译】

Master You(1) said, "If a gentleman conducts himself filial piety towards his parents, and conducts fraternal respect towards his older brothers, it is most unlikely that he will like offending his superiors. If he does not like offending his superiors, the

【英译注】(1) Master You: Confucius's excellent disciple, surname You, first name Ruo. He was recommended by his classmates to teach them after their Master Confucius passed away. It was deduced that his disciples partially edited *The Analects*.

possibility that he will launch an armed rebellion against his superiors is nonexistent. A superior man devotes himself to establishing a foundation. When the foundation is established, the principles of life are formed. Filial piety and fraternal respect are exactly the foundation of superior benevolence." (01.02)

子曰:"父在,观其志。父没,观其行。三年无改于父之道,可谓孝矣。"(01.11)

【注释】在:在世。观:观察。其:儿子的。志:志向。没:去世。行:行为。三年:父亲去世三年,长期。改:改变。道:规矩、原则。

【白话译文】

孔子说:"父亲活着的时候,观察儿子的理想。父亲去世后,观察儿子的行为。如果父亲去世三年后,他还不改变他父亲的言行原则和风格,可以称他有孝心了。"(01.11)

【英译】

The Master said, "When one's father is alive, a son is observed on his ambitions. When his father passes away, he is observed on his conduct. He can be called filial if he does not change his father's principles and styles of actions and speech in three years(1) after his father passes away." (01.11)

【英译注】(1) three years: Not limited to three years, it could be longer.

孟懿子问孝。子曰:“无违。”樊迟御,子告之曰:“孟孙问孝于我,我对曰‘无违’。”樊迟曰:“何谓也?”子曰:“生,事之以礼;死,葬之以礼,祭之以礼。”(02.05)

【注释】孟懿子:姓仲孙名何忌,谥(音 shì 是)号懿(音 yì 益,品德美、好),鲁国大夫,三家之一。无违:不违背(父母的意愿)。樊迟:名须,字子迟。御:驾车。告:告诉。之:他。孟孙:孟懿子。于:向。对曰:敬答。何谓:怎么讲。生:父母在世。事:侍奉。以:用。

【白话译文】

孟懿子请教孝是什么。孔子说:“不要违礼仪。”樊迟给他驶车,孔子给他说:“孟孙问我孝是什么,我敬答:‘不要违礼仪。’”樊迟问:“这是什么意思?”孔子说:“父母在时,按礼仪服侍他们;父母去世,按礼仪安葬他们,按礼仪祭祀他们。”(02.05)

【英译】

Master Meng Yi(1) asked advice about what filial piety was. The Master said, “Do not defy the Rites of Proprieties.” When Fan Chi(2) drove a carriage for him, the Master told him, “Mengsun(3) consulted me about filial piety and I replied respectfully, ‘Do not defy the Rites of Proprieties.’” Fan Chi said, “What does it mean?” The Master said, “When one's parents live, serve them according to the Rites; when they pass away, bury them according to the Rites and offer sacrifices to them according to the Rites.” (02.05)

【英译注】(1) Master Meng Yi: Surname Zhongsun, first name Heji, posthumous name Yi, a senior official of the State of Lu. (2) Fan Chi: Surname Fan, first name Xu, style name Zichi, Confucius's disciple. (3) Mengsun: Master Meng Yi.

孟武伯问孝。子曰:“父母,唯其疾之忧。”(02.06)

【注释】孟武伯:孟懿(音 yì 意)子之子,名彘(音 zhì 置),谥号武。唯:特别、只是。其:父母的。疾:病。忧:担忧。

【白话译文】

孟武伯请教什么是孝。孔子说:“对于父母,他们的疾病是子女特别担心的。”(02.06)

【英译】

Meng Wubo(1) asked advice about what filial piety was. The Master said, “For one's parents, their sons and daughters are concerned particularly about their illnesses.” (02.06)

【英译注】(1) Meng Wubo: Son of Master Meng Yi, surname Zhongsun, first name Zhi, posthumous name Wu.

子游问孝。子曰:“今之孝者,是谓能养。至于犬马,皆能有养。不敬,何以别乎?”(02.07)

【注释】子游:姓言,名偃(音 yǎn 眼),字子游,吴人。养(旧音 yàng 样):赡养。敬:尊重,真心孝敬。何:如何。别:区别。乎:吗。

【白话译文】

子游请教孝是什么。孔子说:“今天,孝被理解为子女仅仅赡养父母。至于犬马,也能养活。如果没有发自内心的尊敬,孝与它有什么区别呀?”(02.07)

【英译】

Ziyou(1) asked advice about what filial piety was. The Master said, “Today filial

【英译注】(1) Ziyou: Surname Yan, first name Yan, style name Ziyou, Confucius's disciple.

piety is understood to mean that children only have to provide subsistence to their parents. As for a dog or a horse, they also will be fed. But if filial respect is lacking, what is the difference between them?" (02.07)

子夏问孝。子曰:"色难。有事,弟子服其劳,有酒食,先生馔,曾是以为孝乎?"(02.08)

【注释】子夏:姓卜名商,字子夏。色:和颜悦色。难:不易。色难:始终和颜悦色很难。有事:出了问题。弟子:儿女。服:服侍。其:父母。劳:效力。弟子服其劳:儿女替父母出力。先生:长辈或父母。馔(音 zhuàn 赚):吃喝,好吃好喝的。曾:竟然。是:这。以:可以。为:认为。乎:吗。

【白话译文】

子夏请教孝是什么。孔子说:"孩子在父母面前始终和颜悦色,是件难事。有事需要办,年轻人出力去做。有好酒好菜,请年长者先享用。不始终和颜悦色,这些真正被认为是孝了吗?"(02.08)

【英译】

Zixia[(1)] asked advice on what filial piety was. The Master said, "Children should always keep a pleasing countenance in front of their parents. This is difficult. When something needs to be done, the young render a service to them. When there are nice liquors and delicious foods, the elders are invited to enjoy them first. Can these truly be regarded as filial piety without an always pleasing countenance?" (02.08)

【英译注】(1) Zixia: Surname Bu, first name Shang, style name Zixia, Confucius's disciple.

子曰:“事父母几谏。见志不从,又敬不违,劳而不怨。”(04. 18)

【注释】事:侍奉、伺候。几(音 jī 吉):婉转。谏:(若父母有过错)劝说。见志不从:见父母志有不从己谏之色。又:还是。不违:不违抗。劳:替他们操劳、担忧。而:却,但。怨:抱怨、怨恨。

【白话译文】

子曰:“当父母有不对的地方的时候,伺候他们的子女应当温和巧妙地说服他们来改正。如果父母不接受他们的建议,还要对他们尊敬,不违背他们的意愿。子女继续尊敬地伺候他们,不要怨恨父母。”(04. 18)

【英译】

The Master said, “When parents do something wrong, children waiting upon them should mildly and tactfully persuade them to correct it. If their suggestion is not accepted by parents, they are still respectful to them and not go against their will. They continue to reverently attend upon their parents and never hold a grudge against them.” (04. 18)

子曰:“父母在,不远游,游必有方。”(04. 19)

【注释】在:在世。远:遥远。游:离家外出活动。必:一定。有:留下、给出。方:可找到的地址。

【白话译文】

孔子说:"如果父母在家,子女不要远行。如果必须远行,他们必须给父母详细地址。"(04.19)

【英译】

The Master said, "When parents are at home, children do not travel to a distant place. If they have to go out, they must give them the specific address." (04.19)

子曰:"三年无改于父之道,可谓孝矣。"(04.20)

【注释】三年:父亲去世三年,长期。改:改变。不改:继承、不改变。道:规矩、原则。

【白话译文】

孔子说:"如果父亲去世三年后,儿女还不改变他们父亲的言行原则和风格,可以称他们有孝心了。"(04.20)

【英译】

The Master said, "Children can be called filial if they do not change their father's principles and styles of actions and speech for three years(1) after he passes away." (04.20)

【英译注】(1) three years: Not limited to three years, it could be longer.

子曰:“父母之年,不可不知也。一则以喜,一则以惧。”(04.21)

【注释】之:的。年:年纪、年龄。一:一方面。则:就是,副词。以:因此。喜:高兴。一则以喜:一方面因其长寿而高兴。惧:为其衰老而恐惧。

【白话译文】

孔子说:“父母的年龄,子女都必须知道。一方面,他们为父母高寿而欢喜,另一方面他们年事已高令人忧心。”(04.21)

【英译】

The Master said, “Children must know the ages of their parents. On the one hand, they are happy above their parents' long lives; on the other hand, their advanced ages are cause for concern.” (04.21)

子曰:“孝哉闵子骞!人不间于其父母昆弟之言。”(11.05)

【注释】闵子骞(音 qiān 千):闵损,字子骞。间:批评挑剔。昆:哥哥。不间于:对……无可挑剔,无异议。人不间于其父母昆弟之言:对他父母兄弟夸奖他的话,别人没有不同意见。《韩诗外传》载:“子骞早丧母,父娶后妻,生二子,疾恶子骞,以芦花衣之,父察之,欲逐后母。子骞曰:‘母在一子寒,母去三子单。’父善之而止,母悔改之,遂成慈母。”

【白话译文】

孔子说:“闵子骞,孝顺啊!对于他父母、兄弟表扬他的话,任何人都没有异议。”(11.05)

【英译】

The Master said, "How filial Min Ziqian[(1)] is! Anyone does not dispute about the words praised on him by his parents and brothers." (11.05)

【英译注】(1) Min Ziqian: Surname Min, first name Sun, style name Ziqian, Confucius's disciple, famous for his filial piety. It is said that he was hated by his stepmother who bore two boys. In winter, he worn a thick overcoat but still felt cold. His father was unhappy and beat him, but found that she made his coat of un-warm reed flowers. As his father decided to divorce her, Ziqian said, "When my stepmother is home, it is only then I that am cold. When she is gone, however, all three children will be cold." His father changed his mind, and she regretted for her mistake and became a charitable mother.

曾子曰:"吾闻诸夫子:孟庄子之孝也,其他可能也;其不改父之臣,与父之政,是难能也。"(19.18)

【注释】曾子:姓曾名参(音shēn 申),字子舆,鲁国南武城(在今山东平邑)人。诸:之于。夫子:先生、孔子。孟庄子:孟孙速,鲁国大夫。之:的。其他:其他的(孝行、孝心)。可能:(别人)可以做到。其他可能也:其他的孝行,别人能够做到。其:他。改:改变。与:赞同、跟、同。是:这是。难能:(别人)难能做到。

【白话译文】

曾子说:"我听我老师讲:孟庄子的很多孝敬行为是他人可以做到的,但是难以做到的是,他不撤换他父亲的旧臣,也不改变他父亲的政策和建制。"(19.18)

【英译】

Master Zeng[(1)] said, "I heard from my Master that many filial actions of Master Meng Zhuang[(2)] can be done by others, but what is difficult to do is that he neither dismissed his father's old officials nor changed his governmental policies and establishments." (19.18)

【英译注】(1) Master Zeng: Surname Zeng, first name Shen, style name Ziyu, Confucius's disciple, from South Wucheng County of the State of Lu, currently Pingyi County, Shangdong Province. (2) Master Meng Zhuang: Mengsun Su, a senior official of the State of Lu. He died in 550 BC, four years after his father died in 554 BC.

18

勇 Courage

子曰:"好勇疾贫,乱也。人而不仁,疾之已甚,乱也。"(08.10)

【白话译文】

孔子说:"如果一个人喜欢表现勇力且痛恨贫穷,他会给社会带来灾难。人们过分地痛恨一个没有仁德的人,会给社会带来灾难。"(08.10)

【注释】好(音 hào 浩):喜爱。勇:斗勇。疾:憎恨。贫:自己太穷。乱:作乱、叛乱。人:有人。而:却。不仁:没有仁德。疾:憎恨、厌恶。之:贫穷。已:太。甚:过分。人而不仁,疾之已甚,乱也:一解"无仁德的人,过分痛恨贫穷,会引起社会动乱";二解"对无仁德的人,过分痛恨,他会胡作非为"。译文用二解意。

【英译】

The Master said, "One may bring disasters to society if he likes to show off courage and detests poverty. It may bring disasters to society that people extremely detest a person lacking of benevolence." (08.10)

子路曰："君子尚勇乎？"子曰："君子义以为上。君子有勇而无义为乱，小人有勇而无义为盗。"(17.23)

【注释】子路：姓仲，名由，字子路。尚：崇尚、尊重。勇：勇敢、敢作敢当。乎：吗。以为：作为、用作。上：高尚的品德。而：却，但。为：做。乱：叛乱、起事造反。盗：偷盗。

【白话译文】

子路问："君子崇尚勇敢吗？"孔子说："君子崇尚正义作为他的高尚品质。君子有勇气而无正义，可能会叛乱。小人有勇气而无正义，可能成为强盗。"(17.23)

【英译】

Zilu asked, "Does a superior man advocate courage?" The Master said, "A superior man advocates righteousness as his supreme quality. If a superior man is courageous but unrighteous, he may create armed rebellion. If an inferior man is courageous but unrighteous, he may become a robber." (17.23)

【英译注】(1) Zilu: Surname Zhong, first name You, style name Zilu, Confucius's disciple.

19

善 Goodness

子张问善人之道。子曰:“不践迹,亦不入于室。”(11.20)

【白话译文】

子张请教如何完善自己,以达到完美状态。孔子说:“一个人不踩着以往圣人的脚印,即不学习以往的知识和文献,他就不能来到内室,即达不到完美的崇高水准。”(11.20)

【英译】

Zizhang(1) asked advice about how to improve oneself to be perfect. The Master said,“One cannot enter the inner sanctum, i. e. reach a supreme level of perfection if he does not walk in the footprints of previous saints, i. e. he does not study the previous knowledge and documents.”(11.20)

【注释】子张:姓颛(音 zhuān 砖)孙名师,字子张。善人:一解“本质善良但没经过学习的人”;二解“使人达到完善高尚的境界”。践:踩。迹:(前人的)脚印。不践迹:不踩前人的脚印,不向他人学习。亦:也就。入于室:入内室,学问修养精深。不践迹,亦不入于室:不跟着他人读书学习,也不会有高深的境界。

【英译注】(1) Zizhang: Surname Zhuansun, first name Shi, style name Zizhang, Confucius's disciple.

子曰:“‘善人为邦百年,亦可以胜残去杀矣。’诚哉是言也!”(13.11)

【注释】善人:好人。为邦:治国。百年:经过100年。亦:就。胜残:赢得残暴之人,让其不作恶。去:消除。杀:杀戮暴刑。诚:真实。哉:呀。是:此。言:话。

【白话译文】

子曰:“‘如果一个国家由德才兼备的人连续治理一百年,就可以把残暴的人转变为好人,避免杀戮暴刑了。’这句话说得真对啊!”(13.11)

【英译】

The Master said, “‘If a country is ruled by benevolent and capable people continuously over a hundred years, cruel and ferocious persons can be transformed into good ones and massacres and savage acts can be prevented.’ This saying is truly correct!” (13.11)

孔子曰:“见善如不及,见不善如探汤。吾见其人矣,吾闻其语矣。隐居以求其志,行义以达其道。吾闻其语矣,吾未见其人也。”(16.11)

【注释】见:看到。善:好人好事。如:好像。不及:赶快学习,唯恐达不到。不善:邪恶。如:如同。探:掏,摸,伸手取。汤:烫水、开水。如探汤:好像摸到开水一样,立刻缩手,以免烫伤。其人:这样的人。闻:听到。语:言论、话。隐:隐退。居:闲居。求:保全。志:理想。隐居以求其志:通过隐居实现自己的理想。行义:实行礼义。达:贯彻。道:主张、思想。吾未见其人也:我还没见过这种人。

【白话译文】

孔夫子说:“看到好事,一个人立刻学习它,好像不学习就赶不上了。看到坏事,一个人立刻从那里退出来,好像他碰到了开水,立即缩手。我看见过这样的人,我也听到了这样的话。一个人隐居不做官,以便实现自己的理想并保全自己的清高品质,同时自己推行正义,使得天下人都正义。我听到这样的话,但我没有见过这样的人。"(16.11)

【英译】

Confucius said, "Seeing the good, one immediately studies it. It is as if he would never be able to catch up with it if he did not study it quickly. Seeing the bad, one shrinks from it as quickly as if he were withdrawing his hands from touching boiling water. I have seen such a person and have also heard such words. One withdraws from governmental work, and lives in seclusion in order to realize his ideals and to preserve his pure nature. At the same time he pursues righteousness for himself in order that all the people under Heaven will become righteous. I have heard such words, but I have not seen such a person." (16.11)

20

贤 Sage

子曰:“见贤思齐焉,见不贤而内自省也。”(04.17)

【注释】贤:有道德、有才能(的人)。思:考虑。齐:(如何)赶上,与他看齐,取此长处。内:内心。自省:反省自己有无类似的缺点。

【白话译文】

孔子说:“看见一个人有优点,我想到如何赶上他。看到一个人有缺点,我就反省自己,纠正我自身同样的过错。”(04.17)

【英译】

The Master said,“Seeing a person with superior qualities, I think of how to equal him. Seeing a person of inferior qualities, I examine myself and correct the same fault in me.”(04.17)

子曰:“贤哉,回也!一箪食,一瓢饮,在陋巷,人不堪其忧,回也不改其乐。贤哉,回也!”(06.11)

【注释】回:姓颜名回,字子渊,鲁国(今山东)人。一:数词。箪(音 dān 丹):盛饭的圆竹器。食:食物。瓢:由葫芦做的容器。饮:凉水,喝的东西。陋:简陋。堪:忍受。其:他的,这种。忧:困苦。人不堪其忧:他人不能忍受这种困苦。乐:(好学)乐趣。

【白话译文】

孔子说:"贤人啊,回! 一篮粗饭,一瓢凉水,住在简陋的巷子里。别人都忍受不了这样的困苦和贫穷,但在那里回却不改变他内在的快乐。贤人啊,回呀!"(06.11)

【英译】

The Master said, "Ah, what a sage Hui(1) is! A bamboo basket of coarse food, a gourd of cold water, and a shabby lane to live in. While others cannot tolerate such hardship and poverty, Hui does not change his inner happiness there. Ah, what a sage Hui is!" (06.11)

【英译注】(1) Hui: Surname Yan, first name Hui, style name Ziyuan, Confucius's disciple from the State of Lu.

曾子曰:"以能问于不能,以多问于寡;有若无,实若虚,犯而不校。昔者吾友,尝从事于斯矣!"(08.05)

【注释】曾子:姓曾名参(音 shēn 申),字子舆,鲁国南武城人。能:有才者。问:请教。于:向。不能:无才者。多:知识多。寡:知识少。有:有学问。若:却像。无:没学问。实:充实。虚:空虚。犯:受侵犯。校(音 jiào 叫):计较。昔者:以前。吾友:我的朋友,旧注常指颜回。尝:就,曾经。从事:做。于:在。斯:这。

【白话译文】

曾子说:"有才能的人向没有才能的人请教;知识丰富的人向知识贫乏的人请教;大有,好像一无所有;充实,好像空虚;有人冒犯他,他却不计较。以前,我的一位朋友,曾经就是这么做的。"(08.05)

【英译】

Master Zeng[1] said, "A capable man learns from the incapable; a knowledgeable person learns from the ignorant; having, as if not having; full, as if being empty; and he does not seem to mind when others offend him. In the past I had a friend who did behave exactly this way." (08.05)

【英译注】(1) Master Zeng: Surname Zeng, first name Shen, style name Ziyu, Confucius's disciple from Nanwucheng City, the State of Lu. His friend mentioned here is normally interpreted as Yan Hui.

子曰:"不逆诈,不亿不信。抑亦先觉者,是贤乎!"(14.33)

【白话译文】

孔子说:"不要事先怀疑有人会欺诈你,也不要事先猜测有人会对你不诚实。然而,如果你能够事先觉察到它,你实在是个贤人!"(14.33)

【英译】

The Master said, "Neither suspect in advance that somebody may cheat you, nor guess in advance whether someone is unfaithful to you. If you, however, sense it beforehand, you are really a sage!" (14.33)

【注释】逆:预先猜测。诈:别人会欺诈。亿:臆,猜测。不信:别人会不诚实。抑:然而。亦:也(能)。先:及时。觉:觉察。是贤乎:这是贤人呀。

子曰:"贤者辟世,其次辟地,其次辟色,其次辟言。"子曰:"作者七人矣。"(14.39)

【白话译文】

孔子说:"贤人首先逃避混乱且缺少仁德的社会,其次逃避动乱的地方,再次逃避不尊敬的脸色,再次逃避别人的诽谤中伤。"孔子又说:"已经有七人这么做了。"(14.39)

【英译】

The Master said, "A sage first escapes from a chaotic society without superior benevolence; next he escapes from a disorderly place; third he escapes from a person of disrespectful countenance; and fourth he escapes from slanders of others." He said further, "There are seven people who have done this already." (14.39)

【注释】辟(音 bì 闭):避,逃避。世:(动荡的)世间、社会。其次:次一等。地:(动乱的)地方。色:难看的脸色。言:难听的话。作者:这样做的人。七人:不明,有的解释为伯夷、叔齐、虞仲、夷逸、朱张、柳下惠、少连。

21

恕 Forgiveness

子曰:“参乎! 吾道一以贯之。”曾子曰:“唯。”子出,门人问曰:“何谓也?”曾子曰:“夫子之道,忠恕而已矣。”(04.15)

【注释】参:姓曾名参(音shēn申),字子舆,鲁国南武城人。道:原则、规矩。一:一条基本原则、思想。以:用。贯:贯穿。之:道、学说。吾道一以贯之:我讲的道用一个基本思想贯彻始终。唯:是。门人:孔子的弟子。何谓:怎么讲。夫子:孔子。忠:赤诚无私,不背叛。恕:理解原谅。而已:罢了,就这些了。矣:啊。

【白话译文】

孔子说:“参呀! 我的思想体系是始终用一个基本观念贯穿着。”曾子说:“是。”孔子出去后,孔子的其他弟子问:“这是什么意思呢?”曾子说:“我们老师的全部思想体系,就是忠、恕啊!”(04.15)

【英译】

The Master said, “Ah, Shen! I have one basic thought that runs through my ideology.” Master Zeng(1) said, “Yes.” After the Master left, the Master's other disciples asked, “What does it mean?” Master Zeng said, “All the ideology of our Master is just faithfulness and forgiveness!” (04.15)

【英译注】(1) Master Zeng: Surname Zeng, first name Shen, style name Ziyu, Confucius's disciple from Nanwucheng City (currently Pingyi County of Shandong), the State of Lu.

互乡难与言，童子见，门人惑。子曰："与其进也，不与其退也。唯何甚？人洁己以进，与其洁也，不保其往也。"(07. 29)

【白话译文】

互乡的人不好说话。孔子接见了这个乡的一名儿童，门人很不理解。孔子说："我赞成他的进步，不赞成他的退步。为什么要做得太过分呢？如果一个人改正自己的错误以求进步，要赞扬他的洁己行为，不要抓住他过去的错误不放。"(07. 29)

【英译】

The people from Huxiang Town were difficult to talk to. The Master met with a boy from the town, but his disciples did not understand why he did this. He said, "I approve of his progress, but I do not approve of his backsliding. Why should we make too much of this? If someone corrects his errors to make progress, I will praise him for his actions to purify himself. But do not hold onto his past mistakes." (07. 29)

【注释】互乡：地名，今不可考。与言：与他们说话、讲理。互乡难与言：互乡的人很难讲理。童子：互乡的儿童。见：见到孔子。门人：孔子的弟子。惑：不明白。与：赞许。进：进步。退：退步。唯：句首语气词，表示希望。何：何必。甚：太过分。人：他人。洁己：整洁自己，洁身自爱。与：赞扬。保：保守、抓住不放。其：他的。往：过去，过去的错误、缺点。与其洁也，不保其往也：赞扬他洁身进步，不要抓住他过去的缺点不放。

子贡问曰:“有一言而可以终身行之者乎?”子曰:“其恕乎!己所不欲,勿施于人。”(15.24)

【注释】子贡:姓端木名赐,字子贡。一言:一字。而:却。终身:一生。行:奉行。之:言,代词。乎:吗。其:大概。恕:宽恕。己:自己。欲:期望的。勿:不要。施:强加给。于:对,向。人:别人。

【白话译文】

子贡请教道:“有没有一个字可以让人终身奉行的呢?”孔子说:“大概是‘恕’字吧!自己不想让别人施加给自己的,从来不要施加于别人。”(15.24)

【英译】

Zigong(1) asked, “Is there a word that one can apply it all his life?” The Master said, “Probably it is ‘forgiveness’. Never do unto others what you do not want others to do unto you.” (15.24)

【英译注】(1) Zigong: Surname Duanmu, first name Ci, style name Zigong, Confucius's disciple.

五
Five

教育
Education

22

志 Ambition

子曰："吾未见刚者。"或对曰："申枨。"子曰："枨也欲，焉得刚？"(05.11)

【注释】刚：刚强，质直寡欲。或对曰：有人敬答。申枨(音chéng成)：姓申名枨，字周。枨：申枨。欲：欲望多。焉：哪里。

【白话译文】

孔子说："我没有见过刚强不屈的人。"有人敬答："申枨是一位。"孔子说："枨呀欲望多，他哪里能刚强？"(05.11)

【英译】

The Master said, "I have not seen a person who is firm and unyielding." Someone replied respectfully, "Shen Cheng(1) is one." The Master said, "Cheng(2) is full of desire, so how can he be firm and unyielding?" (05.11)

【英译注】(1) Shen Cheng: Surname Shen, first name Cheng, style name Zhou, Confucius's disciple. (2) Cheng: Shen Cheng.

子曰："圣人，吾不得而见之矣；得见君子者，斯可矣。"子曰："善人，吾不得而见之矣；得

【注释】圣人：如尧、舜、禹者。得：能够。见：看到。之：他。斯：就。可：可以。矣：了。善人：善良者，志于仁而无恶。恒：恒心，一心一意，不贰其心。亡(音wú吴)：

见有恒者，斯可矣。亡而为有，虚而为盈，约而为泰，难乎有恒矣。”（07.26）

无，不存在。而：却。为：装作。有：存在。虚：空虚。盈：充实。约：穷困。泰：富足。难：很难、费劲。乎：于。难乎有恒矣：这种人很难有恒心做善事啊。

【白话译文】

孔子说：“看到圣人，对我来说是不可能的，但是能够看到君子，我就满足了。”孔子又说：“看到完全善良的人，对我来说是不可能的，但是能够看到做好事有恒心的人，我就满足了。一个人将没有的视为存在的，空虚视为充盈，贫穷视为富足，这样的人是很难有恒心做好事的。”（07.26）

【英译】

The Master said, “It is impossible for me to see a saint, but I am satisfied to see a superior man.” The Master said further, “It is impossible for me to see a perfectly kind person, but I am satisfied to see a man always persevering in doing a good thing. It is difficult for a man to always persevere in doing a good thing if he takes nothing as existing, regards emptiness as fullness, and sees his poverty as wealth.” (07.26)

子曰：“三军可夺帅也，匹夫不可夺志也。”（09.26）

【注释】三军：一军12500人，三军为左中右军。夺：强取。帅：统帅。三军可夺帅：三军虽众，可

【白话译文】

孔子说:“可以强行夺取三军的统帅,但不能强迫一个普通男人放弃自己的志向。”(09.26)

【英译】

The Master said, “A commander in chief of the three armies can be removed of by force, but a common man cannot be forced to give up his ambition.” (09.26)

用武力灭其统帅。匹夫:平民男子,古代士大夫以上有妾(qiè 窃,非正妻)媵(yìng 映,随嫁者),平民贫贱,仅夫妇相匹配而已,故称匹夫。夺志:强迫改变志向。匹夫不可夺志也:一个平民的志向不可被迫、强行改变呀。

子路、曾皙、冉有、公西华侍坐。子曰:“以吾一日长乎尔,毋吾以也。居则曰:‘不吾知也!’如或知尔,则何以哉?”

子路率尔对曰:“千乘之国,摄乎大国之间,加之以师旅,因之以饥馑,由也为之,比及三年,可使有勇,且知方也。”夫子哂之。

【白话译文】

子路、曾皙、冉有、公西华恭敬地陪同孔子坐着。孔子说:“我比你们年龄都大,不会有人聘用我了。平时,你们说:‘没有人知道我!’如果有人知道你,聘用你,你能做什么呢?”

子路率先敬答:“一个千辆车子的国家,位于大国之间,经常受到它们的侵犯,又遇到饥饿问题。如果我治理它三年,可以让其人

【注释】子路:姓仲,名由,字子路。曾皙(音 xī 西):姓曾名点,字子皙,曾参的父亲。冉有:姓冉名求,字子有。公西华:公西赤,字子华。侍(音 shì 是):恭敬陪同。侍坐:陪同坐着。以:因为。吾:我。一日:年龄。长:年长。乎:于。尔:你。毋:不。以:任用。毋吾以:没人用我。居:平时。吾知:知我。如:如果。或:有人。尔:你。何:怎么。以:做、办。

率尔:率先,带头。对曰:敬答。乘(音 shèng 胜):量词,辆,4 匹马拉的 1 辆车。摄(音 shè 射):夹在。加:施加,他国侵犯。之:它。以:用。师旅:军队。加之以师旅:他国军队侵犯它。因:接着。之:它。饥馑:饥荒。因之以饥馑:接着国内遭遇饥荒。由:姓仲名由,字子路。为:治理。比(音 bì 闭):等。及:到。使:让(民)。且:而且 。知:懂得。方:道义方向。夫子:孔子。哂(音 shě 婶):讥讽地微笑。

民英勇，并且知道道义。”孔子微微地讥笑他。

【英译】

Zilu[(1)], Zeng Xi[(2)], Ran You[(3)], and Gongxi Hua[(4)] were sitting to respectfully attend upon the Master. The Master said, "As I am older than you all, no one hires me anymore. Ordinarily you say, 'No one knows me.' If someone knows you and employs you, what will you do?"

Firstly Zilu replied respectfully, "A state of 1000 carriages is ranked among the large states, suffers from their invasions, and consequently encounters starvation. If I rule it for three years, I can make their people brave and know morality and justice." The Master smiled slightly at him mockingly.

【英译注】(1) Zilu: Surname Zhong, first name You, style name Zilu, Confucius's disciple. (2) Zeng Xi: Surname Zeng, first name Dian, style name Zixi, Confucius's disciple, his son is Master Zeng Shen. (3) Ran You: Surname Ran, first name Qiu, style name Ziyou, Confucius's disciple. (4) Gongxi Hua: Surname Gongxi, first name Chi, style name Zihua.

“求，尔何如？”对曰：“方六七十，如五六十，求也为之，比及三年，可使足民。如其礼乐，以俟君子。”

“赤，尔何如？”对曰：“非曰能之，愿学焉。宗庙之事，如会同，端章甫，愿为小相焉。”

【白话译文】

“求，你怎么样？”冉求敬答：“如果我治理一个边长60里到70里，或50里到60里的地

【注释】求：冉有，姓冉名求，字子有。方六七十：长宽各六七十里之地。如：或者。为之：治理它。比及：等到。足民：百姓丰衣足食。如：至于。其：它的。礼乐：礼乐制度。以：而。俟（音sì四）：等待。

赤：公西华。能：能做。之：事。宗庙：祭祀。如：或者。会同：诸侯会见、古代诸侯朝见天子、帝王。端：礼服名。章甫（音fǔ辅）：礼帽名。如会同，端章甫：在诸侯盟会上，穿礼服，戴礼帽。为：做。

方,用三年时间,可以使这里的人民富足。至于这里的礼乐问题,我等待一位君子来处理。”

“赤,你怎么样?”赤敬答:“我不能说我有能力,但是愿意学习。我愿意穿上礼服,戴上礼帽,成为一个小赞礼,在司仪进行祖庙及贵族盟会的祭祀时给他当助手。”

相:赞礼,赞礼者,“在古代礼书中,‘相’又称为‘赞’,相的职责只有一项,即‘赞礼’,在祭祀或会盟时襄助他人行礼。相分上、中、下三级。”[J06]焉:语气词,呀。

【英译】

“Qiu(1), how about you?” He replied respectfully, “If I can rule a place squared with a side of 60 to 70 *li*(2) or 50 to 60 *li* for three years, I can make its people have a sufficient life. As for its Rites of Proprieties and Music, I will await a superior man for that.”

“Chi(3), how about you?” He replied respectfully, “I cannot say that I am capable, but I am willing to learn. I wish to wear a ritual cap and gown, and serve as a junior assistant to the master as he conducts sacrificial ceremonies at ancestral temples and at meetings among members of the nobility.”

【英译注】(1) Qiu: The first name of Ran You. (2) *li*: Chinese unit of length, currently one *li* equals 0.5 kilometer. (3) Chi: The first name of Gongxi Hua.

“点,尔何如?”鼓瑟希,铿尔,舍瑟而作,对曰:“异乎三子者之撰。”子曰:“何伤乎?亦各言其志也。”

曰:“莫春者,春服既成,冠者五六人,童子六七人,浴乎沂,风乎舞雩,咏而归。”

【注释】点:姓曾名点,字子皙。鼓:弹奏。瑟:25 弦乐器。希:稀,轻声、悠长;[J07]“《老子》‘听而不闻名曰希’,音量小几乎听不到。”[J06]铿(音 kēng 坑):响亮,象声词,弹奏瑟声。铿尔:手指碰到瑟弦发出的声音[J07]。舍:离开。而:并且。作:起立。异乎:不

【白话译文】

“点，你怎么样?”点正在悠长轻轻地弹25弦乐器瑟，只是用手指触击弦索。他离开乐器瑟，站了起来，敬答：“我的选择与三位说的不一样。”孔子说：“这有什么关系？各自说各自的理想而已。”

点说：“春天之末，当春天服装备好，我领着五六个成年人，六七个男童，到沂水河洗澡，之后到舞雩祈雨坛风干，唱着歌归家。”

同于。撰(音 zhuàn 篆)：选择。伤：妨碍。言：说出。

莫(音 mù 木)：暮，晚，将尽。冠者：成年人。童子：儿童。浴：沐浴、洗澡。沂：沂水河。风：兜兜风。舞雩(音 yú 于)：地名，祭天求雨之地，在今山东曲阜。咏：唱歌。归：回家。

【英译】

“Dian(1), how about you?” He was playing a 25-string instrument *Se* slowly and softly, striking the chord with his fingers. Leaving his instrument aside he stood up, and replied respectfully, “My choice is different from what the three have said.” “What does it matter? Each one simply expresses his own ideal.”

Dian said, “At the end of spring when spring coats are done ready, I will lead 5 or 6 young adults and 6 or 7 small boys to bathe at the Yi River, and dry ourselves in the wind at Wuyu Platform of Praying for Rain. And then we come home singing.”

【英译注】(1) Dian: The first name of Zeng Xi.

夫子喟然叹曰：“吾与点也。”

三子者出，曾皙后。曾皙曰：“夫三子者之言何如?”子曰：“亦

【注释】喟(音 kuì 愧)：叹息。然：……的样子。喟然叹曰：长出一口气感叹说。与：赞同。

出：出门。何如：怎么样。为国：治国。唯：难道。则：就。非：

各言其志也已矣。”曰:“夫子何哂由也?”曰:“为国以礼,其言不让,是故哂之。”“唯求则非邦也与?”“安见方六七十如五六十而非邦也者?”“唯赤则非邦也与?”“宗庙会同,非诸侯而何?赤也为之小,孰能为之大!”(11.26)

不是。邦:治国。也:了。与:吗。安:怎么。见:见得。宗庙会同:祭祀、诸侯会见。非诸侯:不是诸侯的事。而何:又是什么。为:做。为之小:做个小赞礼。大:大赞礼。

【白话译文】

孔子长叹一声,说:“我同意点的想法。”

当三人离去,曾皙在后面。曾皙问:“我三位同学说的话怎么样?”孔子说:“他们只是说了他们的理想。”曾皙说:“老师为何微微讥笑由呢?”孔子说:“治国是按礼节,但他说话不谦虚,所以讥笑他。”“求所说的,不是国事吗?”孔子说:“如何说治理一个方形边长60里到70里或50里到60里的地方,不是国事?”“赤所说的,不是国事吗?”孔子说:“如果诸侯祖庙或者诸侯国之间的外交盟会不是国事,那么国事是什么?如果赤只当个小赞礼,那么谁会当大赞礼?”(11.26)

【英译】

The Master sighed with a long breath, “I agree with Dian for his idea!”

When the three left, Zeng Xi was lagging behind. He asked, “How about the words of my three classmates?” The Master

【英译注】(1) You: The first name of Zilu.

said,"They have simply expressed their ideals." "Why did you my Master slightly smile at You[(1)] mockingly?" The Master said, "A state is ruled according to the Rites, but he was not modest in his words, so I smiled at him mockingly." "Isn't it really a state affair as talked about by Qiu?" The Master said,"How can it not be a state affair to rule a place squared with a side of 60 to 70 *li* or 50 to 60 *li*?" "Isn't it really a state affair as talked about by Chi?" The Master said, "If the sacrificial ceremonies at the duke's ancestral temples or diplomatic meetings between states are not the state affairs, what can be a state affair? If Chi serves only as a junior ritual assistant, who can serve as a senior one?" (11.26)

子曰:"南人有言曰:'人而无恒,不可以作巫医。'善夫!""不恒其德,或承之羞。"子曰:"不占而已矣。"(13.22)

【白话译文】

孔子说:"南方人有一句话:'人没有恒心,做不了巫术医生。'此话实在不错!"恒卦说:"如果一个人翻云覆雨,坚持美德三心二意,他有时会受到污辱。"孔子说:"这样的结果,不用问算命先生,就知道了。"(13.22)

【注释】南:南方。言:说法。恒:恒心。巫医:用占卜算卦为人治病的人。善夫:对呀。或:有时。承:蒙受。羞:羞辱。不恒其德,或承之羞(《易经》32 卦恒卦):自己的品德保持不长久,有时会蒙受羞辱。不:不要。占:占卜算卦。不占而已矣:像这样的结果(无恒心的人受辱),不用占卦就已经知道了。

【英译】

The Master said, "Southerners have a saying, 'If one does not persevere, he cannot serve as a shaman doctor.' This saying is right indeed!" The Hexagram Heng[1] says, "If a person blows hot and cold and half-heartedly keeps good morals, he sometimes might be humiliated." The Master said, "Such a result can be known without asking a fortune-teller." (13.22)

【英译注】(1) Heng: The name of 32nd hexagram of the book *I Ching*, or currently called *Book of Changes* and it means perseverance or duration. The book was for fortune telling and philosophy in the ancient China.

子夏曰:"虽小道,必有可观者焉;致远恐泥,是以君子不为也。"(19.04)

【注释】子夏:姓卜名商,字子夏。虽:即使。小道:各种农工商医之类的小技能。必:一定。可观:借鉴。致:达到。远:远方。恐:担心。泥(音 nì 匿):滞陷、难行。是以:所以,因此。为:做。

【白话译文】

子夏说:"即使低级职业的小技艺,一定有一些值得欣赏的优点。如果一个人追求远大的理想,他担心它会成为事业的一种障碍,因此君子是不从事一种小技艺的。"(19.04)

【英译】

Zixia[1] said, "Even a small skill in an inferior job must have some advantages worthy of appreciation. If one pursues a great ambition, he fears that it may become an obstacle to his cause, therefore a superior man is not engaged in a small skill." (19.04)

【英译注】(1) Zixia: Surname Bu, first name Shang, style name Zixia, Confucius's disciple.

23

师 Teacher

子禽问于子贡曰:"夫子至于是邦也,必闻其政。求之与?抑与之与?"子贡曰:"夫子温、良、恭、俭、让以得之。夫子之求之也,其诸异乎人之求之与?"(01. 10)

【注释】子禽:姓陈名亢(音kàng抗),字子禽。于:向。子贡:姓端木名赐,字子贡。夫子:做过大夫的人,指孔子。是:这个,一个。邦:诸侯国。必:一定。闻:知道。政:政情。求:乞求、私下打听。与:呢。抑:还是。与之:主动告诉他。温:温和。良:善良。恭:恭敬。俭:俭朴、节省。让:谦让。得:获得、得到。其诸:大概。异:不同。乎:于。人:他人。

【白话译文】

子禽向子贡打听:"孔夫子到一个国家,一定能够获得这个国家的政情。他是乞求的吗?还是别人自发给他的呀?"子贡答:"孔夫子用温和、善良、恭敬、节俭、谦让的方法获得的。孔夫子获得的方法,大概和别人获得的方法有所不同,不是吗?"(01. 10)

【英译】

Ziqin[(1)] asked Zigong[(2)], "Once Confucius visits a state, he must have obtained the information of its political affairs. Did he plead it? Or was he given it voluntarily?" Zigong said, "Confucius

【英译注】(1) Ziqin: Surname Chen, first name Kang, style name Ziqin, his profession is unknown, and possibly he was not Confucius's disciple. (2) Zigong: Surname Duanmu, first name Ci, style name Zigong.

obtains it through mildness, kindness, deference, thriftiness, and modesty. Probably the methodology of Confucius to acquire it differs from that of others, doesn't it?" (01.10)

子曰:"温故而知新,可以为师矣。"(02.11)

【白话译文】

孔子说:"一个人复习旧的知识,并且获得新的知识,就可以当别人的老师了。"(02.11)

【英译】

The Master said, "One can be a teacher for others if he reviews old knowledge and acquires new knowledge." (02.11)

【注释】温:复习。故:已学的知识。而:并且。知:知晓,学习。新:新的、未知的知识。为:当。师:为人师表。矣:了。

子曰:"自行束脩以上吾,未尝无诲焉。"(07.07)

【白话译文】

孔子说:"只要一个人自愿给我送上10条干肉,尊重我为师,我从来不拒绝教他。"(07.07)

【注释】自:自愿。行:送上。束:10条,1条叫脡(音 tǐng 挺),10脡为束,古代非常微薄的见面礼。脩(音 xiū 休):干肉,又叫脯。束脩:10条干肉的拜师礼。以:用来。上:敬上。吾:我。未:没有。尝(音 cháng 常):曾经。未尝:从来没有。无诲:不教人。

【英译】

The Master said, "I never refuse to teach a person if he honors me as his master by voluntarily submitting to me ten short strips of dried meat." (07.07)

子曰:"不愤不启,不悱不发。举一隅不以三隅反,则不复也。"(07.08)

【注释】愤:苦思仍未领会。启:开导。悱(音 fěi 诽):想说又说不好。发:启发。举:例举,教。隅(音 yú 鱼):角落,一物有四隅。反:推知。复:再教。

【白话译文】

孔子说:"不到一个弟子已经尝试理解一件事但是冥思苦想后还是理解不了,我不帮助他。不到一个弟子尝试说好一件事但是还是说不好,我不启发他。假如教给一个弟子东方,他却不去推出南、北、西方,我就不再重复教他这个内容了。"(07.08)

【英译】

The Master said, "I will not help a disciple until he has tried hard to understand a thing but still cannot after he racks his brains. I will not enlighten a disciple until he has tried to speak well about a thing but still cannot. And if I teach a disciple East, but he cannot deduce North, South and West, then I will not teach him the same material again." (07.08)

子曰:"三人行,必有我师焉。择其善者而从之,其不善者而改之。"(07.22)

【注释】三人:三人或多人。行:一起走;一起行动做事。师:老师、值得学习或借鉴的地方。其:他们二人之中。善:比我更好、更优。比较而言,二人中一定有一人善些,好些,更有长处。者:的人、事。而:就。从:学习。从之:以善者为师,学其长处。不善:与我比较而言,一人差一些,有不足、短处。改:改正。之:此短处、不善。其不善者而改之:以不善者为师,以其做借鉴,改掉自身存在的那种短处、缺点。

【白话译文】

孔子说:"我同三个人一起行走,其中一位一定是我的老师。我研究此人最好的优点,以便学习这些优点。我研究另一人的缺点,以便克服显现在我身上的这些缺点。"(07.22)

【英译】

The Master said, "When walking in a group of three(1), one of them must be my teacher. I study the best points of the one in order to learn from them. And I study the bad points of the other in order to correct them in myself." (07.22)

【英译注】(1) three: Not exactly three. It can be several people over three.

子曰:"二三子以我为隐乎?吾无隐乎尔。吾无行而不与二三子者,是丘也。"(07.24)

【注释】二三子:弟子们。以:认为。为:是。隐乎:隐瞒吧,孔子知广道深,弟子学不会,以为他有所隐匿。乎尔:对你们。行:行为。与:(教)给。者:的人。丘:孔子,姓孔名丘,字仲尼。

【白话译文】

孔子说:“弟子们,你们以为我隐瞒什么不教你们吗? 我对你们什么都没隐藏。弟子们,我对于你们,所有东西都是公开的,这是我丘的为人。”(07.24)

【英译】

The Master said, “Did you my disciples think that I had concealed something not to teach you? I have hidden nothing from you. I have revealed everything to you my disciples, and this is the conduct of Qiu(1) myself.” (07.24)

【英译注】(1) Qiu: Confucius, surname Kong, first name Qiu, style name Zhongni. His disciples could not learn all his profound knowledge and they guessed that he hid something from them.

子以四教:文、行、忠、信。(07.25)

【注释】以:用。四:四科。教:传授。文:先王遗文。行:德行,在心为德,施之为行。忠:心中无隐,不背叛。信:不欺。

【白话译文】

孔子教授四个专业:古代文献、有品德的个人行为、忠诚于人、诚信。(07.25)

【英译】

The Master taught four specialties: ancient doctrines, personal conduct of virtues, loyalty, and faithfulness. (07.25)

颜渊喟然叹曰:"仰之弥高,钻之弥坚,瞻之在前,忽焉在后。夫子循循然善诱人,博我以文,约我以礼,欲罢不能。既竭吾才,如有所立卓尔,遂欲从之,末由也已。"(09.11)

【白话译文】

颜渊长叹一口气说:"我老师的知识和品德是如此高尚和令人敬佩,我不得不仰视他。我越向他学习,我越感到他的知识深刻。好像我快赶上他了,但我一疏忽和懈怠,突然落在他的后边。我老师善于一步一步引导我。他用文化和文献丰富我的知识,用礼节约束我的行为。他的教育内容是如此精彩和令人激动,我无法停止向他学习。尽管我已经竭尽了我的全力和全才去学习,他渊博的知识仍如同一座山耸立在我的面前。我渴望追随他,但我依然在学习的道路上成为最后一名。"(09.11)

【注释】颜渊:姓颜名回,字子渊。喟(音 kuì 愧):叹息。然:……的样子。喟然叹曰:长出一口气感叹说。仰:抬头看,敬慕。之:孔子学问、道德。弥:更加。高:高大。钻:钻研。坚:深奥。瞻:往上往前看。前:孔子跟前。瞻之在前:眼看与他的距离近了。忽:疏忽,懈怠。后:落后。忽焉在后:一懈怠,远远落在他后面。夫子:老师,孔子。循循:一步一步。诱:引导。博:丰富。以:用。文:典籍。约:约束。罢:停止。欲罢不能:他教得太精彩了,我乐在其中,不愿离开。既:已经。竭:用尽。才:才能、力气。立:树立。卓尔:独立的样子。如有所立卓尔:好像可以独立地工作了。遂:于是,就。从:追随。末:一解"无";二解"末端"。由:路径。已:矣,了。末由也已:一解"不知如何进行了";二解"在学习的道路上,我还是最末端一后学者罢了"。

【英译】

Yan Yuan(1) said with a long sigh, "The erudite knowledge and virtues of my Master are so lofty and admirable that I have to raise my head to look up at him. The more I learn from him, the more profound I feel his

【英译注】(1) Yan Yuan: Confucius's excellent disciple, surname Yan, first name Hui, and style name Ziyuan.

knowledge is. It seems that I become closer and closer to him, but suddenly I lag far behind him in a moment of my negligence and relaxation. My Master is good at leading me step by step. He enriches my knowledge with literature and archives, and restrains my desires with the Rites of Proprieties. His teaching is so brilliant and exciting that I cannot stop learning from him. Though I spare no effort and talent to study, his broad and profound knowledge still looks like a mountain towering aloft in front of me. I crave to follow him, but I still fall behind as the last one on the learning road." (09.11)

子曰:"当仁不让于师。"(15.36)

【注释】当:面对。仁:仁德的事。不:不必。让:谦让。于:向、对,介词。师:老师。

【白话译文】

孔子说:"一旦有仁德的事必须办,即使一个人的老师在身边,他也没有必要谦让它。"(15.36)

【英译】

The Master said, "Once a thing of superior benevolence must be undertaken, one does not necessarily decline to do it out of modesty even though his master is present." (15.36)

子曰:“有教无类。”(15.39)

【注释】有:获得、拥有、接受。教:教诲。无:没有。类:宗族、氏族的分门别类,(贵贱)种类。有教无类:不分宗族,每人都可接受教育;不分贵贱,人人都应受到教育。

【白话译文】

孔子说:“所有的人都有平等受教育的权利,无论他们是什么类别。”(15.39)

【英译】

The Master said, “All the people have equal rights to an education, regardless of their classes.” (15.39)

24

学 Learn

子曰:“学而时习之,不亦说乎?有朋自远方来,不亦乐乎?人不知而不愠,不亦君子乎?”(01.01)

【注释】子:孔子。曰:说。时:时时刻刻。习:踏行,演习、复习。亦:也是。不亦:不也是,委婉词。说(音 yuè 月):悦,愉快。朋:志同道合者。乐(音 lè 勒):高兴。知:理解(自己)。愠(音 yùn 运):心怀而未发的恼怒,怨恨。

【白话译文】

孔子说:“学习知识并时时刻刻践习所学知识,不是很快乐吗?远方朋友的到来,不让人很高兴吗?如果别人不理解自己,而自己内心并不恼怒,他不是君子吗?”(01.01)

【英译】

The Master said, "Isn't it a pleasure to study and always be able to use what one has learned? Isn't it delightful to have friends coming from distant places? Isn't a superior man one who is not upset when not understood by others?" (01.01)

子曰:"弟子入则孝,出则弟,谨而信,泛爱众而亲仁,行有余力,则以学文。"(01.06)

【注释】弟子:少年、学子,孔子对其学生谦称为"弟",敬称为"子"。何时晏《论语注疏》:"为人弟与子者,入事父兄则当孝与弟也,出事公卿则当忠与顺也。弟,顺也。"入:进家门。则:就,那么。出:出家门。弟(音 tì 替):悌,顺从兄长,此为忠诚、听话。谨:慎重、小心、寡言少语。而:却,但是。信:诚信。泛:广泛。众:民众。行:做到(以上这些)。余力:多余的精力。以:用来。文:知识。

【白话译文】

孔子说:"一名后生,在家里对父母、兄长要孝敬顺从,在外边对他人要尊重、真诚。他应说话谨慎,行为诚信,广泛热爱别人,接近有仁德的人。以上做好后,还有精力,应当学习文献和知识。"(01.06)

【英译】

The Master said, "A young man should be filial and obedient at home, and respectful and sincere outside his home. He should speak cautiously, behave faithfully, love the people extensively and be close to benevolent people. When he has energy after he has done these, he should learn literature and knowledge." (01.06)

子夏曰:“贤贤易色,事父母能竭其力,事君能致其身,与朋友交,言而有信。虽曰未学,吾必谓之学矣。”(01.07)

【注释】子夏:姓卜名商,字子夏。贤贤:第一个“贤”意为“尊重”;第二个“贤”意为“贤者、他人好的品德”。易:看淡;另解为“轻松自如”。色:女人的美貌;人的表情。易色:一解“看淡女色”;另解“和颜悦色”。事:侍奉、服侍。竭:不保留。致:献出。身:性命。交:交往。言:说话。而:且、就。信:诚信。未:没有。学:从师受教,读书学习。必:一定。谓:称。

【白话译文】

子夏说:“一个人能以快乐的表情尊重德才兼备的贤人,伺候父母能竭尽全力,服侍君主不惜自己的生命,与朋友交往,言而有信。虽然他没有从师学习过,我一定认为他是一个有学问的人。”(01.07)

【英译】

Zixia[(1)] said, “One can respect a sage with a delightful countenance, exhaust all his efforts to attend upon his parents, give up his life to serve his sovereign, and keep one's promises in making friends with others. Though such a man has not learned from a master at school, I must certainly regard him as a learned man.” (01.07)

【英译注】(1) Zixia: Surname Bu, first name Shang, style name Zixia, Confucius's disciple.

子曰:“君子食无求饱,居无求安,敏于事而慎于言,就有道而正焉,可谓好学也已。”(01.14)

【注释】食:饮食。无求:不要求。饱:充足。居:住。安:安逸。敏:勤敏。事:做事。慎:谨慎、小心。言:说话。就:接近,向……看齐。有道:有道德者。正:匡正、端正(自己),一般解为正其是非、判其得失。焉:呀。可谓:可称作。

【白话译文】

孔子说:“君子不把自己的理想定在满足于充足的饮食及安逸的居住条件上。他做事灵活勤快,说话谨慎;他接近有道德的人,并用他们的道德标准来匡正自己。这样,他就可以被称为热爱学习了。”(01.14)

好(音 hào 号):喜爱。学:读书、学习。也:停顿语气词。已:矣,了。

【英译】

The Master said,“A superior man does not set his ambitions at seeking satisfaction of enough to eat and a comfortable home. He works resourcefully and diligently, and speaks cautiously. He is close to people of good morals and rectifies himself by their moral criteria. By this way, he can be said to love learning.”(01.14)

子曰:“吾与回言终日,不违,如愚。退而省其私,亦足以发,回也不愚。”(02.09)

【注释】回:姓颜名回,字子渊。不违:不反对。如:如同,好像。愚:蠢。退:(他)回去。省:(我)观察。其:他的。私:私下言行。亦:也。足以:能够。发:发挥。亦足以发:他对所学的内容,也能发挥应用。

【白话译文】

孔子说:“我与颜回交谈一整天,他不反对我,好像他很笨。他离开课堂后,我私下观察他的言行,发现他能够将所学的知识充分发挥。因此可见,颜回并不笨。”(02.09)

【英译】

The Master said, "I talk with Hui[1] all day, but he does not disagree with me, as if he was a fool. When he leaves the classroom, I observe his speech and conduct in private, and see that he can bring full play of his knowledge learned so far. Therefore it can be seen that Hui is not a fool." (02.09)

【英译注】(1) Hui: Surname Yan, first name Hui, style name Ziyuan, Confucius's excellent disciple.

子曰:"学而不思则罔,思而不学则殆。"(02.15)

【注释】学:从师受教,读书学习。思:思索。则:就。罔(音wǎng往):惘,迷惑无获;受骗,如孟子"尽信书不如无书"。殆:疑惑、缺乏信心、神思枯竭。

【白话译文】

孔子说:"一个人学习但不思考,他就会迷失方向;一个人仅仅思考但不学习,他就会才智枯窘。"(02.15)

【英译】

The Master said, "One will be disorientated if he learns but does not think; and one will be devoid of wisdom and creativeness if he only thinks but does not learn." (02.15)

子张学干禄。子曰:“多闻阙疑,慎言其余,则寡尤。多见阙殆,慎行其余,则寡悔。言寡尤,行寡悔,禄在其中矣。”(02. 18)

【注释】子张:姓颛(音 zhuān 砖)孙名师,字子张。干:求。禄:俸禄。干禄:求官职。多闻:多听。阙:同缺,(暂时)保留。疑:疑问的地方。阙疑:有疑问的地方,加以保留,不做判断,留待考察而定。慎:谨慎。言:讲。其余:有把握的部分。寡:减少。尤:过错。多见:多观察。殆(音 dài 代):危险、有隐患。阙殆:有危险的地方,不实施,进一步考察。行:做。悔:后悔。

【白话译文】

子张向孔子请教如何通过学习求取俸禄。孔子说:“多听,保留存在疑问的部分,此部分既不判断也不做结论,而是留待以后进一步考察。谨慎地说出剩余可靠的部分,这样你说话的错误就会减少。多看,保留存在有危险的部分,此部分既不实施也不做定论,而是进一步观察。认真地执行剩余没有危险的部分,这样行动上就可以减少后悔。因为你言语上减少了错误,行动上减少了后悔,你的俸禄就在其中了。”(02. 18)

【英译】

Zizhang[(1)] asked the Master how to earn an official salary through learning. The Master said, “Listen much and reserve the suspicious part that is neither applied nor concluded immediately but for further investigation. Cautiously speak out the remaining part of certainty and thus you can reduce your faults in speech. Observe much and reserve the dangerous part that is neither applied nor concluded immediately, but for further inspection. Carefully implement the remaining

【英译注】(1) Zizhang: Surname Zhuanshun, first name Shi, style name Zizhang, Confucius's disciple.

part without danger and thus you may reduce regrets in action. Your official salary is therefore inside your speech with reduced faults and your actions with reduced regrets."(02.18)

子谓子贡曰:"女与回也孰愈?"对曰:"赐也何敢望回。回也闻一以知十,赐也闻一以知二。"子曰:"弗如也。吾与女弗如也。"(05.09)

【注释】谓:问。子贡:姓端木名赐,字子贡。女(音 rǔ 辱):汝,你。回:姓颜名回,字子渊。孰:谁。愈:超过、更好。对曰:敬答。赐:子贡,姓端木名赐。何:怎么。敢:冒昧。望:比、视。何敢望回:怎么能冒昧与颜回比。以:可以。弗:不。如:及,比得上。与:同意、赞同。吾与女弗如也:我同意你,你比不上他呀。

【白话译文】

孔子向子贡问:"你与回,谁更优秀一些?"子贡敬答:"我怎么敢与回比? 回,听到一个可以知道十个,而我赐听到一个只能够知道两个。"孔子说:"不如呀。我同意你,你不如他呀。"(05.09)

【英译】

The Master asked Zigong(1), "Who is more excellent between you and Hui(2)?" Zigong replied respectfully, "How can I dare to be compared with Hui? Hui hears one thing and can perceive ten, and I Ci(3) hear one thing and can understand only two." The Master said, "You are not better than him. I agree with you on that you are not better than him." (05.09)

【英译注】(1) Zigong: Surname Duanmu, first name Ci, style name Zigong, Confucius's disciple. (2) Hui: Surname Yan, first name Hui, style name Ziyuan, Confucius's excellent disciple. (3) Ci: Zigong.

子贡曰:“夫子之文章,可得而闻也;夫子之言性与天道,不可得而闻也。”(05.13)

【注释】夫子:孔子。文章:德的外在形式,指礼、乐、诗、书等。闻:凭耳听目视。言:讲、说。性:人的本性,自然化育之性。天道:天命,天理。得而闻:闻而得,听到就理解。不可得而闻也:不能凭耳听目视就理解呀。

【白话译文】

子贡说:“我听老师讲古代文献,就很容易理解,但是我听我老师讲有关人性与天道的言论,就不容易理解了。”(05.13)

【英译】

Zigong[1] said, “I could easily understand it as I heard my Master’s lectures on ancient doctrines[2], but I could not easily understand it when I heard his speech on the nature of human being and the Way of Heaven.” (05.13)

【英译注】(1) Zigong: Surname Duanmu, first name Ci, style name Zigong, Confucius’s disciple. (2) ancient doctrines: The Rites, music, poems, ancient books, etc. that show the external forms of morals.

子路有闻,未之能行,唯恐有闻。(05.14)

【注释】有闻:听到(道理、学问、仁德)。未:没有。之:它。行:做到。未之能行:还没有去实施它。唯:只。恐:害怕、担心。唯恐有闻:只怕再听得新的(道理)而来不及做。

【白话译文】

当子路听到任何知识,但是还没有用上它的时候,他担心进一步听到新的东西。(05.14)

【英译】

When Zilu[1] heard certain knowledge[2] but had not applied it yet, he was afraid of hearing more new things. (05.14)

【英译注】(1) Zilu: Surname Zhong, first name You, style name Zilu, Confucius's disciple. (2) knowledge: It is about morals, superior benevolence, others, and so on.

子贡问曰:"孔文子何以谓之文也?"子曰:"敏而好学,不耻下问,是以谓之文也。"(05.15)

【注释】子贡:姓端木,名赐,字子贡。孔文子:孔圉(音 yǔ 禹),卫国大夫,谥(音 shì 是)号文。何:为什么。以:用来。谓:称。之:他。文:谥号文。敏:勤奋、努力。而:且。好(音 hào 浩)学:喜爱从师读书学习。不耻:不以为耻。下:地位低。不耻下问:向比自己地位、水平低的人请教,并没有耻辱感。是:这。以:可以。是以:所以。

【白话译文】

子贡请教:"为什么孔文子死后授予'文'的谥号?"孔子说:"他勤奋机敏喜爱学习,向下属请教不以为耻。这是给他'文'谥号的原因。"(05.15)

【英译】

Zigong[1] asked, "Why could Master Kong Wen[2] be given posthumous title 'Wen[3]'?" The Master said, "He was resourceful and fond of learning. He did not feel ashamed to ask advice from his subordinates. This is the reason that he was given the posthumous title 'Wen'." (05.15)

【英译注】(1) Zigong: Surname Duanmu, first name Ci, style name Zigong, Confucius's disciple. (2) Master Kong Wen: Surname Kong, first name Yu, posthumous title Wen (meaning "Culture"), a senior official of the State of Wei. (3) Wen: A character representing literary grace and talent.

子曰:“十室之邑,必有忠信如丘者焉,不如丘之好学也。”(05.28)

【注释】十室:十户。邑:小城。必:一定。如:如同。丘:孔子,姓孔名丘,字仲尼。好学:学而不厌。

【白话译文】

孔子说:“在一个有十户人家的小村镇,一定有像我丘一样对人忠心不贰、诚实守信的人,但是没有一个像我丘一样如此热爱学习的人。”(05.28)

【英译】

The Master said, “In a small town of ten households, there must be a person who is as loyal and faithful as I, Qiu(1), but there is no person who so loves learning as I, Qiu.”(05.28)

【英译注】(1) Qiu: Confucius, Surname Kong, first name Qiu, style name Zhongni.

哀公问:“弟子孰为好学?”孔子对曰:“有颜回者好学,不迁怒,不贰过,不幸短命死矣!今也则亡,未闻好学者也。”(06.03)

【注释】哀公:姓姬名蒋,谥(音 shì 是)号哀,鲁国国君,公元前 494 年至公元前 468 年在位。弟子:学生。孰:谁。好(音 hào 浩)学:喜爱从师读书学习。对曰:敬答。颜回(公元前 521—公元前 490):姓颜名回,字子渊,鲁国(今山东)人。迁:转移。怒:怒气。贰:重复。过:错。短命:寿命短,颜回 31 岁去世。今:今天,现在。亡(音 wú 吴):无、不。

【白话译文】

哀公问:“你的弟子中,谁最热爱学习?”孔夫子敬答:“我的弟子中有个名叫颜回的人最热爱学习。他从不将自己的愤怒转嫁给他人,同一错误不犯二次,但是他不幸短命,早逝了!今天再没有这种弟子了,我也没有听说过哪个弟子如此热爱学

习了。”(06.03)

【英译】

Duke Ai[1] asked, “Who can be called the one fondest of learning among your disciples?” The Master replied respectfully, “The one fondest of learning was Yan Hui[2]. He never vented his anger on others and never made the same mistake twice, but unfortunately his life was short and he died young. There is no such a disciple today, and I have not heard any disciple so fond of learning.” (06.03)

【英译注】(1) Duke Ai: Surname Ji, first name Jiang, posthumous title Ai, the Sovereign of the State of Lu from 494 BC to 468 BC. (2) Hui: Surname Yan, first name Hui, style name Ziyuan, Confucius's excellent disciple, dead at 31 years old.

子曰:“三年学不至,于谷不易得也。”(08.12)

【白话译文】

孔子说:“如果一个人学习了三年,但是还没有达到一定学识水平,要想取得俸禄是不容易的。”(08.12)

【注释】三年学:从师学习三年。至:达到。不至:达不到一定水平。于:对于。谷:俸禄,做官。易:容易。得:获得、找到。于谷不易得也:不容易获得官位啊。另一句读法:“子曰:‘三年学,不至于谷,不易得也。’”至:想到。于:到、向,介词。不至于谷:还没有想去做官的念头。不易得:难得。意思是:“一个人学习三年,还没有想去做官的念头,是很难得的。”

【英译】

The Master said[1], “If one has not attained a certain level of learning after three years of study, it is not easy for him to get an official salary.” (08.12)

【英译注】(1) Some scholars translate this sentence as: “The Master said, ‘It is difficult to find one man who has not thought of getting an official salary after he has studied for three years.’”

子曰:“学如不及,犹恐失之。”(08.17)

【白话译文】

孔子说:“学习如同一个人追逐一件跑动的东西,他生怕不能及时抓住。当他抓住它时,他在担心会失去它。”(08.17)

【英译】

The Master said,“Learning is like that one chases a thing that is running. He fears that it cannot be caught in time,but when he catches it, he is worried about that he may lose it.”(08.17)

【注释】学:读书学习。如:像。及:追赶上(前贤)。犹:还。恐:担心。失:忘记。之:学过的知识。

子谓颜渊曰:“惜乎!吾见其进也,未见其止也。”(09.21)

【白话译文】

孔子评价颜渊说:“啊,他的死太可惜啦!我看到他总是在进步,从来没有看到他止步不前。”(09.21)

【英译】

The Master commented on Yan Yuan(1),“Alas! What a pity his death is! I saw that he always made progress, and never saw that he stopped it.”(09.21)

【注释】谓:评论。颜渊:姓颜名回,字子渊。惜:痛惜、哀伤(颜渊之死)。乎:啊。进:进步。止:停止。

【英译注】(1) Yan Yuan: Surname Yan, first name Hui, style name Ziyuan, Confucius's excellent disciple, dead at 31 years of age.

德行:颜渊,闵子骞,冉伯牛,仲弓;言语:宰我,子贡;政事:冉有,季路;文学:子游,子夏。(11.03)

【白话译文】

孔子弟子中,德行优异的:颜渊,闵子骞,冉伯牛,仲弓;言语好,会说话的:宰我,子贡;处理政务好的:冉有,季路;古典文献好的:子游,子夏。(11.03)

【英译】

Among Confucius's disciples, these are excellent in morals and virtues: Yan Yuan[(1)], Min Ziqian[(2)], Ran Boniu[(3)] and Zhonggong[(4)]; these are excellent in eloquence: Zai Wo[(5)] and Zigong[(6)]; these are excellent in governmental affairs: Ran You[(7)] and Jilu[(8)]; and these are excellent in ancient doctrines: Ziyou[(9)] and Zixia[(10)]. (11.03)

【注释】德行:品德行为好,孝悌忠恕好。颜渊:姓颜名回,字子渊。闵子骞(音 qiān 千):姓闵名损,字子骞。冉伯牛:姓冉名耕,字伯牛。仲弓:姓冉,名雍,字仲弓。言语:善于辞令、外交。宰我:姓宰名予,字子我。姓端木,名赐,字子贡。政事:擅长政务。冉有:姓冉名求,字子有。季路:姓仲名由,字子路。文学:通晓古典文献,孔门"文行忠信"四科之一。子游:姓言,名偃(音 yǎn 眼),字子游,吴人。子夏:姓卜名商,字子夏。

【英译注】(1) Yan Yuan: Surname Yan, first name Hui, style name Ziyuan, Confucius's excellent disciple, dead at 31 years of age. (2) Min Ziqian: Surname Min, first name Sun, style name Ziqian, Confucius's disciple, famous for his filial piety. (3) Ran Boniu: Surname Ran, first name Geng, style name Boniu. (4) Zhonggong: Surname Ran, first name Yong, style name Zhonggong. (5) Zai Wo: Surname Zai, first name Yu, style name Ziwo. (6) Zigong: Surname Duanmu, first name Ci, style name Zigong. (7) Ran You: Surname Ran, first name Qiu, style name Ziyou. (8) Jilu: Surname Zhong, first name You, style name Zilu, also Jilu. (9) Ranqiu: Surname Ran, first name Qiu, style name Ziyou. (10) Zixia: Surname Bu, first name Shang, style name Zixia.

季康子问:“弟子孰为好学?”孔子对曰:“有颜回者好学,不幸短命死矣。今也则亡。”(11.07)

【注释】季康子:姓季孙名肥,谥(音 shì 是)号康,鲁哀公时任正卿。孰:谁。好(音 hào 浩)学:喜爱从师读书学习。对曰:敬答。颜回:姓颜名回,字子渊,鲁国(今山东)人。短命:寿命短,颜回公元前 490 年去世,时年 31 岁。今:今天,现在。亡(音 wú 吴):无、不。

【白话译文】

季康子问:“你的弟子中,谁最爱学习?”孔夫子敬答:“我的弟子中有个名叫颜回的人最爱学习。他不幸短命早逝了!今天再没有这样的弟子了。”(11.07)

【英译】

Master Ji Kang(1) asked, “Who can be called the one who is fondest of learning among your disciples?” Confucius replied respectfully, “The one fondest of learning was Yan Hui(2). Unfortunately his life was short and he died young. There is no such a disciple today.” (11.07)

【英译注】(1) Master Ji Kang: Surname Jisun, first name Fei, posthumous title Kang, senior official during the reign of Duke Ai of the State of Lu. (2) Yan Hui: Surname Yan, first name Hui, style name Ziyuan, Confucius's excellent disciple, dead at 31 years of age.

子曰:“由之瑟奚为于丘之门?”门人不敬子路。子曰:“由也升堂矣,未入于室也。”(11.15)

【注释】由:姓仲名由,字子路。之:的。瑟(音 sè 色):弹瑟,瑟是古代弦乐器,25 弦。奚:为何。为:认为。于:出于、属于。丘:孔子,姓孔名丘,字仲尼。门:门下。奚为于丘之门:怎么配得上出自我(孔丘)的门下。门人:弟子。子路:姓仲名由,字子路。升

【白话译文】

孔子说:“仲由弹瑟的水平这么低,怎么认为能够作为我孔丘的门徒?”孔子的弟子于是不尊重子路。孔子说:“仲由弹瑟的水平和对音乐的理解达到了这个水平:他已经入门、进入厅堂,但还没有到达密室。”(11.15)

堂:入正厅、不错了(弹瑟的水平和对音乐的理解)。入:进。室:内室。未入室:未进入内室,不算极端好、最好。

【英译】

The Master said,“How could You[1] be qualified as my disciple as he plays the *Se*[2] at such a low level?” His other disciples thus did not respect Zilu[3]. The Master said, “You[1] has reached such a level that he has stepped into the gate and come into the hall, but has yet not entered the sanctum in both performance of the *Se* and understanding of music.” (11.15)

【英译注】(1) You: Surname Zhong, first name You, style name Zilu. (2) *Se*: A 25-string instrument. (3) Zilu: You or Zhong You.

子贡问:“师与商也孰贤?”子曰:“师也过,商也不及。”曰:“然则师愈与?”子曰:“过犹不及。”(11.16)

【注释】子贡:姓端木,名赐,字子贡。师:姓颛(音 zhuān 砖)孙,名师,字子张。商:姓卜,名商,字子夏。孰:谁。贤:贤良。过:过头。不及:没有达到要求,有欠缺,欠火候。然则:那么。愈:胜过。与:吗。犹:如同。

【白话译文】

子贡问:“师与商谁更优秀一些?”孔子说:“师做事过了头,而商做事还不够。”

子贡说："那么，师更好一些？"孔子说："做过了头，与做得不够是一样的，两者都不当。"（11.16）

【英译】

Zigong[(1)] asked, "Who is superior between Shi[(2)] and Shang[(3)]?" The Master said, "Shi goes too far, but Shang does not go far enough." Zigong said, "Therefore, is Shi superior?" The Master said, "Going too far is the same as not going far enough, both of which are not proper." (11.16)

【英译注】(1) Zigong: Surname Duanmu, first name Ci, style name Zigong, Confucius's disciple. (2) Shi: Surname Zhuansun, first name Shi, style name Zizhang, Confucius's disciple. (3) Shang: Surname Bu, first name Shang, style name Zixia, Confucius's disciple.

柴也愚，参也鲁，师也辟，由也喭。（11.18）

【注释】柴：姓高名柴，字子羔。愚：耿直，笨。参：姓曾名参（音 shēn 申），字子舆，鲁国南武城人。鲁：迟钝。师：姓颛（音 zhuān 砖）孙，名师，字子张。辟（音 pì 僻）：偏激。由：姓仲名由，字子路。喭（音 yàn 艳）：粗鲁，莽撞。

【白话译文】

柴是愚笨的，参是迟钝的，师是偏激的，由是鲁莽的。（11.18）

【英译】

Chai[(1)] is stupid, Shen[(2)] is slow-witted, Shi[(3)] easily goes to the extreme, and You[(4)] is foolhardy. (11.18)

【英译注】(1) Chai: Surname Gao, first name Chai, style name Zigao, Confucius's disciple as others listed below. (2) Shen: Surname Zeng, first name Shen, style name Ziyu. (3) Shi: Surname Zhuansun, first name Shi, style name Zizhang. (4) You: Surname Zhong, first name You, style name Zilu. They were all Confucius's disciples.

子曰:“古之学者为己,今之学者为人。”(14.25)

【注释】古:古代的人。之:的。学:学习。者:……的事或……的人。为己:提高自己。为人:装饰自己、给别人看。

【白话译文】

孔子说:“古代的学者是为了提高自己的道德和知识;今天的学者是为了装饰自己,展示自己,获得别人的认可。”(14.25)

【英译】

The Master said, “The ancient scholars were to improve themselves in morals and knowledge; current scholars are to decorate themselves and show themselves to others for the approbation.” (14.25)

阙党童子将命。或问之曰:“益者与?”子曰:“吾见其居于位也,见其与先生并行也。非求益者也,欲速成者也。”(14.46)

【注释】阙党:阙里,孔子住的地方。童子:一儿童。将命:在宾主之间传话,用此法教育儿童。或问:有人问。益者:上进的孩子。居于位:该童子(大模大样地)与长者同坐。与:同。先生:长辈。并行:并排而行。欲:想。速成者:急于求成的人。

【白话译文】

阙党的一名儿童来为主人孔子和客人传递口信。有人问孔子:“此儿童是一名上进的人吗?”孔子说:“我看到他大模大样地坐在成年人的座位上,看到他与长辈

并排行走。所以,我认为他不是一个求上进的人,而是一个急于求成的人。”(14.46)

【白话译文】

A boy from Quedang[1] came to pass oral messages between host the Master and his guests. Someone asked the Master, “Is this boy a person trying to improve himself?” The Master said, “I watched that he sat on a seat offered to the elders in an ostentatious manner and walked shoulder to shoulder with the elders. So I see him as one not striving to make progress, but as one overanxious for quick results.” (14.46)

【英译注】(1) Quedang: A place name, now called Queli of Qufu City as Confucius's living place.

子曰:“赐也,女以予为多学而识之者与?”对曰:“然。非与?”曰:“非也。予一以贯之。”(15.03)

【注释】鲁哀公六年(公元前489年),孔子63岁离开陈国,经蔡国去楚国,返回陈、蔡,楚国下聘礼,孔子应聘。陈、蔡大夫惊恐,派人围攻孔子7天,弟子抱怨,孔子问子贡。赐:姓端木,名赐,字子贡。女(音rǔ辱):汝,你。以:以为。予:我。为:是。以予为:以为我是。多学:学得多。而:而后、才。识(音zhì志):记住、认识。之:知识、道理。者:……的人。与:吗。对曰:敬答。然:是。非:不是。一以贯之:以一贯之,把一个根本的东西(如忠恕之道)始终贯彻到学说之中。

【白话译文】

孔子说:“赐,你认为我是学习大量知识并牢固记住的人吗?”他敬答:“对呀。这不是真的吗?”孔子说:“不是。我恒常使用一个核心原则,贯穿到我的学习和学说之中。”(15.03)

【英译】

The Master said, "Ci(1), do you think that I am a person who learns much knowledge and firmly memorizes it?" He replied respectfully, "Yes. Isn't that right?" The Master said, "No. I constantly apply one essential principle throughout my learning and doctrines." (15.03)

【英译注】(1) Ci: Surname Duanmu and first name Ci, style name Zigong, Confucius's disciple. This dialogue happened in 489 BC when Confucius was confined for 7 days at the State of Chen and his disciples complained about the hardship.

子曰:"吾尝终日不食,终夜不寝,以思,无益,不如学也。"(15.31)

【注释】吾:我。尝:曾经。终日:整天。食:吃饭。终夜:整夜。寝:睡觉。以:用来。思:思索。益:增多。无益:没有进步。学:读书学习。

【白话译文】

孔子说:"我曾经整天不吃饭,整夜不睡觉,只是思考一件事,但我没有取得进步,这还不如学习。"(15.31)

【英译】

The Master said, "I once neither ate all day nor slept all night to meditate over a thing, but I made no progress. This was not better than learning." (15.31)

陈亢问于伯鱼曰："子亦有异闻乎？"对曰："未也。尝独立，鲤趋而过庭，曰：'学《诗》乎？'对曰：'未也。''不学《诗》，无以言。'鲤退而学《诗》。他日又独立，鲤趋而过庭，曰：'学《礼》乎？'对曰：'未也。''不学《礼》，无以立。'鲤退而学《礼》。闻斯二者。"陈亢退而喜曰："问一得三：闻《诗》，闻《礼》，又闻君子之远其子也。"（16.13）

【注释】陈亢：姓陈，名亢（音kàng抗），字子禽。伯鱼：姓孔，名鲤，字伯鱼，孔子之子，50岁去世。子：你。亦：也。异闻：不同见闻，特殊的教诲内容。未也：没有呀。尝：（孔子）曾经。独：单独。立：站立。鲤：孔鲤，字伯鱼。趋：快步。庭：院子。曰：（孔子）说。诗：《诗经》。对曰：敬答。无以言：就不会说话。退：回去。他日：过几天。无以立：就无法立身处世。斯：这。二者：两句话。远（音yuàn院）：不偏爱。其子：他的儿子。

【白话译文】

陈亢向伯鱼打听："从你父亲那里你听到了特殊化的课了吗？"伯鱼敬答："没有。一天，他一人在院子里站着，我小心快步走过，他问我：'学《诗》了吗？'我敬答：'没有。'他说：'如果不学《诗》，你不会好好与人说话。'我回到房间，学习《诗》。又一天，他独自一人站在院子里，我小心快步走过。他问我：'学《礼》了吗？'我敬答：'没有。'他说：'如果你不学《礼》，你就无法在社会上立身。'我回到房间，学习《礼》。我就听到这两件事。"陈亢离开，高兴地说："我问一个问题，收获三个答案：为什么我应该学《诗》，为什么我应该学

《礼》,还听到君子对自己的儿子也不偏爱。"(16.13)

【英译】

Chen Kang[(1)] asked Boyu[(2)], "Have you enjoyed privileges from your father in learning?" Boyu replied respectfully, "No. One day when he stood alone in the courtyard and I passed by him quickly in small steps, he asked me, 'Did you learn *Poems and Odes*?' I replied respectfully, 'No.' He said, 'You cannot well talk with others if you do not learn *Poems and Odes*.' I returned to my room and learned *Poems and Odes*. Another day when he stood alone in the courtyard and I passed by him quickly in small steps, he asked me, 'Did you learn the *Rites of Proprieties*?' I replied respectfully, 'No.' He said, 'You cannot establish yourself in society if you don't learn the *Rites of Proprieties*.' I returned to my room and learned the *Rites of Proprieties*. I have heard these two things." Chen Kang left and happily said, "I asked one question, but I got three answers: why I should learn the *Poems and Odes*, why I should learn the *Rites of Proprieties*, and how a superior man does not show favoritism to his son." (16.13)

【英译注】(1) Chen Kang: Surname Chen, first name Kang, style name Ziqin, possibly not Confucius's disciple. (2) Boyu: Surname Kong, first name Li (meaning a carp in Chinese), style name Boyu, the son of Confucius.

子曰:“由也,女闻六言六蔽矣乎?”对曰:“未也。”“居,吾语女。好仁不好学,其蔽也愚;好知不好学,其蔽也荡;好信不好学,其蔽也贼;好直不好学,其蔽也绞;好勇不好学,其蔽也乱;好刚不好学,其蔽也狂。”(17.08)

【注释】由:姓仲名由,字子路。女(音 rǔ 辱):汝,你。言:字;后“五言诗”“七言诗”以一字为“言”大概源于此。六言:仁,知,信,直,勇,刚。蔽:弊病。六蔽:愚,荡,贼,绞,乱,狂。对曰:敬答。未也:没有呀。居:坐。语(音 yù 玉):和别人一起谈论。好(音 hào 浩):喜爱。仁:仁德。不好学:不喜爱读书学习。愚:笨、愚昧。知(音 zhì 治):智慧。荡:放荡、无原则根基。信:诚信。贼:害人害己。直:正直、直率。绞(音 jiǎo 狡):说话尖刻。勇:勇敢。乱:作乱。刚:刚强,质直寡欲。狂:狂妄。

【白话译文】

孔子说:“由,你听说过六个词语六个弊端吗?”他敬答:“没有。”“坐下来,我给你讲。如果一个人喜爱仁德但不好学,它的弊端是他愚笨。如果一个人喜爱智慧但不好学,其弊端是他放荡不羁。如果一个人喜爱诚信但不好学,它的弊端是他易受欺骗且害人害己。如果一个人喜爱正直但不好学,它的弊端是他尖酸刻薄。如果一个人喜爱表现勇力但不好学,它的弊端是他不讲秩序,易于造成社会灾难。如果一个人喜爱刚强但不好学,它的弊端是他狂妄自大。”(17.08)

【英译】

The Master said, “You(1), did you hear six phrases and six maladies?” He replied respectfully, “No.” The Master said, “Sit down, and let me tell you. If one loves superior benevolence but does not learn, his

【英译注】(1) You: Surname Zhong, first name You, style name Zilu.

malady is his stupidity. If one loves wisdom but does not learn, his malady is that he is unconventional and unrestrained. If one loves faithfulness but does not learn, his malady is liability for him to be cheated and harm himself and others. If one loves straightforwardness but does not learn, his malady is his impertinence and bitter sarcasm. If one loves bravery but does not learn, his malady is his disorderly behaviour, liable to cause disasters in society. And if one loves fortitude but does not learn, his malady is his madness and arrogance."(17.08)

子夏曰:"日知其所亡,月无忘其所能,可谓好学也已矣。"(19.05)

【注释】子夏:姓卜名商,字子夏。日:每天。知:知道。亡(音 wú 吴):通"无",没有。其所亡:所不知道的东西、新的东西。月:每月。无忘:记住、复习。所能:已学会的东西。可谓:可叫作。好(音 hào 浩)学:喜爱从师读书学习。

【白话译文】

子夏说:"如果一个人每天学习新知识,每月不忘记所学习的内容,这个人可以被称作喜爱学习了。"(19.05)

【英译】

Zixia[1] said,"One can be called a person who loves learning if he learns new knowledge every day and does not forget what he has learned every month."(19.05)

【英译注】(1) Zixia: Surname Bu, first name Shang, style name Zixia, Confucius's disciple.

子游曰:"子夏之门人小子,当洒扫、应对、进退,则可矣。抑末也,本之则无。如之何?"子夏闻之,曰:"噫! 言游过矣! 君子之道,孰先传焉? 孰后倦焉? 譬诸草木,区以别矣。君子之道,焉可诬也? 有始有卒者,其惟圣人乎!"(19.12)

【注释】子游:姓言,名偃(音 yǎn 眼),字子游,吴人。子夏:姓卜名商,字子夏。之:的。门人小子:学生。当:承担。洒:洒水。扫:扫地。应对:应酬、对答。进退:迎进、送出客人。则:那么。可矣:可以了。抑:但是,不过。末:末节小事。本:根本的东西。无:没学到。如之何:怎么能行。言游:姓言名偃,字子游。过:错。君子之道:君子的学说、学术。孰:哪一部分。传:传授。倦:诲人不倦。譬(音 pì 媲):打比方。诸:之于。区:划分门类。别:类别。譬诸草木,区以别矣:大道小道,好比草木,分门别类,学习是有主次的。诬:诬蔑、歪曲。焉可诬也:怎么能被歪曲呢。卒:结尾。有始有卒者:有始有终,循序教育的人。其:大概。惟:只有。

【白话译文】

子游说:"子夏的弟子,洒水、扫地、迎送客人,还是很好的。但是,这些大概都是末节,他们没有学习到根本的东西。这怎么行?"

子夏听到了,说:"噫! 言游错了! 君子的原则,哪一部分先热心传授呢? 哪一部分后诲人无倦呢? 如果取草木做比喻,它们的根、枝和梢是可以区分开的。这些符合君子标准的原则,哪能被曲解呢? 在教授弟子方面,大概只有圣人知道哪些部分放在前面,哪些部分放在后面吧?"(19.12)

【英译】

Ziyou[(1)] said, "The disciples of Zixia[(2)] are only able to spray water on the ground, sweep the floor, receive guests, and see them off home, but all these possibly are trifles and

【英译注】(1) Ziyou: Surname Yan, first name Yan, style name Ziyou, Confucius's disciple from the State of Wu. (2) Zixia: Surname Bu, first name Shang, style name Zixia,

they have learned nothing essential to human principles. How can this be good?"

Upon hearing this, Zixia said, "Alas! Yan You(3) is wrong. Which part of the principles in compliance with criteria of superior benevolence can be passed on with zeal first? And which part of those can be taught tirelessly last? If I take a metaphor of a grass or a tree, their roots, branches, and tops can be separately distinguished. How can these principles in compliance with the standards of a superior man be misrepresented? To teach disciples, probably only the sages can know the order of which parts are put in the front and which parts are put in the rear?" (19.12)

Confucius's disciple. (3) Yan You: Ziyou.

25

言 Speech

子曰:"古者言之不出,耻躬之不逮也。"(04.22)

【注释】古者:古代人。言:主动讲话。之:的。出:说出口。不出:不轻易说话。耻:羞耻。躬:躬身、行动,承诺后的行为。逮(音dài代):及、做到。不逮:做不到。

【白话译文】

孔子说:“古代的人不轻易说话,因为如果他们的行为赶不上他们的承诺,他们会感到耻辱。”(04.22)

【英译】

The Master said, “The ancient people did not speak casually, as they might feel shameful if their actions could not match their promises.”(04.22)

子所雅言,《诗》、《书》、执礼,皆雅言也。(07.18)

【注释】所:所用。雅:正。雅言:标准话,周朝首都在今陕西,以陕西话或中原古音为标准音作周王朝的官话。诗、书:诵读《诗》《书》。执:礼不背文诵,记其揖让周旋,执而行之,故言执。执礼:行礼。

【白话译文】

孔子会使用标准话。他大声朗诵《诗》《书》,主持礼节仪式,都用标准话。(07.18)

【英译】

The Master might use standard pronunciation. He used the standard pronunciation for loudly reciting *Poems and Odes*, *Book of History*, and hosting ritual ceremonies.(07.18)

子罕言利，与命与仁。(09.01)

【白话译文】

孔子很少讲钱和利，而是赞扬天命、赞扬仁德。(09.01)

【英译】

The Master rarely talked about money and profit, but spoke highly of the ordinances of Heaven and superior benevolence. (09.01)

【注释】子：孔子。罕：稀少。言：主动对人说话。利：财利、金钱。罕言利：很少谈钱。与：赞同、赞扬；金人王若虚、清人史绳祖认为"与"为"许"；有注者认为"与"为连词；此处取"赞许"意。与命与仁：赞扬天命、宣扬仁德。

子曰："语之而不惰者，其回也与！"(09.20)

【白话译文】

孔子说："总是不懈怠听我讲话的人，大概就是回吧！"(09.20)

【英译】

The Master said, "It is probably only Hui(1) who always is not lax in listening to my speech!" (09.20)

【注释】语（音 yù 玉）之：给他谈话。惰：懈惰。语之而不惰者：在给他谈话过程中，毫不懈怠的人。其：只有。回：姓颜名回，字子渊。与：吧。

【英译注】(1) Hui: Surname Yan, first name Hui, style name Ziyuan, Confucius's excellent disciple.

子曰:“法语之言,能无从乎?改之为贵。巽与之言,能无说乎?绎之为贵。说而不绎,从而不改,吾末如之何也已矣。”(09.24)

【白话译文】

孔子说:“符合原则、严肃劝诫的话,一个人能不接受吗?但是珍贵的是改正他的错误。听到恭敬和赞许的话,一个人能不高兴吗?但是珍贵的是抽绎话背后的含义。如果一个人盲目高兴而不抽绎恭敬和赞许的话,同时表面接受劝诫但实际不改正他的错误,这种人我不知道如何与他打交道了。”(09.24)

【英译】

The Master said, “Can a person not accept principled and serious words of admonishment? But what is valuable is that he corrects his mistakes. Can a person not be delighted when he hears respectful words of praise? But what is valuable is to unravel the real meaning behind the words. I do not know how to deal with such a person who blindly accepts respectful words of praise, but does not unravel the real meaning behind the words, and such a person who appears to accept admonishment, but does not correct his mistakes.” (09.24)

【注释】法:法令礼仪。语:正言规劝。从:听从(口服心服)。改之:(行动上)改自己的错。巽(音 xùn 训):恭顺。与:赞许。巽与之言:恭顺和赞许的话。说(音 yuè 月):悦。绎(音 yì 忆):抽丝,鉴别。说而不绎:喜悦而不鉴别。末(音 mò 墨):没有。如之何:拿他怎么样。已:了。矣:啊。吾末如之何也已矣:对此人我就没办法对付他了。

子曰："回也，非助我者也。于吾言无所不说。"（11.04）

【注释】回：姓颜名回，字子渊。助：帮助。非助我者也：对我没什么帮助（注：总顺从，不提问，或全明白）。言：言论。说（音 yuè 月）：悦，愉快，心悦诚服。

【白话译文】

孔子说："回，不是对我有帮助的人。他对我说的所有话都很喜悦。"（11.04）

【英译】

The Master said, "Hui[(1)] is not the one who helps me. He is pleased with all my words." (11.04)

【英译注】(1) Hui: Surname Yan, first name Hui, style name Ziyuan, Confucius's excellent disciple. Confucius mentioned this because Hui possibly always understood him and agreed with him.

定公问："一言而可以兴邦，有诸？"孔子对曰："言不可以若是，其几也。人之言曰：'为君难，为臣不易。'如知为君之难也，不几乎一言而兴邦乎？"曰："一言而丧邦，有诸？"孔子对曰："言不可以若是，其几也。人之言曰：'予无乐乎为君，唯其言而莫予违也。'如其善而莫之违也，不亦善乎？如不善而莫之违也，不几乎一言而丧邦乎？"（13.15）

【注释】定公：鲁国君，姓姬名宋，谥（音 shì 是）号定，公元前 509 年至公元前 495 年在位。一言：一句话。兴：兴盛。邦：国家。一言而可以兴邦：一句话就能使国家兴盛。诸：之，这样的事。对曰：敬答。言：言论。若：像。是：这样。其：大概。几（音 jī 鸡）：接近。人：有人。为君：做国君。几（音 jī 鸡）乎：差不多。丧：亡。丧邦：亡国。予：我。无乐：没有快乐。为君：做国君。唯：只有。其言：我的话。莫：没有。予违：违予，违抗我。善：好、正确。如其善：如果话说得对。莫之违：没人违抗它。如不善：如不对。

【白话译文】

定公问:“一句话可以兴盛国家,这样的事存在吗?”孔夫子敬答:“一句话不可能有这么大的效果,但也差不多。人们说:‘做君王难,但做臣子也不容易。’如果知道做君王难(他自然会认真尽职尽责),这不接近于一句话可以兴盛国家吗?”

定公问:“一句话可以丧失国家,这样的事存在吗?”孔夫子敬答:“一句话不可能有这么大的效果,但也差不多。人们说:‘我做君王没有别的快乐,只有我说的话没有违抗。’如果他说得对,没有人违抗,不是很好吗? 如果他说得错,而且没有人违抗,这不是接近于一句话可以丧失国家吗?”(13. 15)

【英译】

Duke Ding(1) asked, "Does it occur that one sentence can make a state prosper?" Confucius replied respectfully, "A sentence cannot be so effective as that, but it almost is so. People say, 'It is difficult to be a sovereign, and it is not easy to be an official either.' If it is known that to be a sovereign is difficult (he naturally performs his duties conscientiously), is this close to that one sentence can make a state prosper?"

Duke Ding asked, "Does it occur that one sentence can destroy a state?" Confucius

【英译注】(1) Duke Ding: A sovereign of the State of Lu, ruling from 509 BC to 495 BC, surname Ji, first name Song, posthumous title Ding.

replied respectfully, "A sentence cannot be so effective as that, but it almost is so. People say, 'I take no pleasure in being a sovereign other than no one disobeys my words.' If he speaks correctly, and no one disobeys, isn't it good? If he speaks wrongly, and no one disobeys, isn't it close to that one sentence can destroy a state?" (13.15)

子曰:"其言之不怍,则为之也难。"(14.21)

【注释】言:主动对人说话。怍(音 zuò 坐):惭愧。其:他。言之不怍:大言不惭,说出话不感到惭愧。为之:实现它。难:困难。

【白话译文】

孔子说:"如果一个人说大话而不感到耻辱,那么他很难兑现它。"(14.21)

【英译】

The Master said, "If one brags big and does not feel ashamed, it is difficult for him to make good on it." (14.21)

子贡方人。子曰:"赐也贤乎哉?夫我则不暇。"(14.31)

【注释】子贡:姓端木名赐,字子贡。方:评论(别人的长短)、诽谤。赐:姓端木,名赐,字子贡。贤:通"闲",闲暇。乎哉:吗。夫我:那我。则:就。不:没有。暇(音 xiá 峡):闲工夫。夫我则不暇:我可没闲工夫(去评论别人)。

【白话译文】

子贡对别人说长道短。孔子说:"赐,

真有大量闲暇时间吗？我可没这工夫。”(14.31)

【英译】

Zigong[1] gossiped about others. The Master said, "Ci[2], do you really have plenty of leisure time? But I do not have the time for that." (14.31)

【英译注】(1) Zigong: Surname Duanmu and first name Ci, style name Zigong, Confucius's disciple. (2) Ci: First name of Zigong.

微生亩谓孔子曰:“丘何为是栖栖者与？无乃为佞乎?”孔子曰:“非敢为佞也,疾固也。”(14.34)

【注释】微生亩:姓微生名亩,鲁国隐士,应是年长者。谓:对……说,告诉。丘:孔子,姓孔名丘,字仲尼。何:为什么。为:成为。是:如此。栖(音 xī 西)栖:忙碌不安、四处奔波、心神不定。与:呢。无乃……乎:岂不是……吗。为:逞、表现。佞(音 nìng 泞):花言巧语,善辩不正。无乃为佞乎:岂不是显示自己的好口才吗。疾:一解“痛恨”;二解“病,毛病”。固:顽固的。疾固也:一解“痛恨思想顽固的人呀”;二解“游说天下,是我一个顽固的毛病”。

【白话译文】

微生亩给孔夫子说:“丘,为什么你总是到处忙碌呢？莫非你是在炫耀你的好口才,不是吗?”孔夫子说:“我岂敢炫耀口才？但这是我顽固的毛病。”(14.34)

【英译】

Weisheng Mu[1] talked to Confucius, "Qiu[2], why are you always bustling about everywhere? You do this to show off your excellent eloquence, don't you?" Confucius said, "How do I dare to show off my eloquence? but it is really my obstinate fault." (14.31)

【英译注】(1) Weisheng Mu: Surname Weisheng, first name Mu, a hermit from the State of Lu. As he called Confucius directly by his name, he might be elder than Confucius. (2) Qiu: Confucius, surname Kong, first name Qiu, style name Zhongni.

子曰:"可与言而不与之言,失人;不可与言而与之言,失言。知者不失人,亦不失言。"(15.08)

【注释】与:同,跟。可与言:可以同他谈的话。与之:给他。失人:丢身份、得罪人或失去朋友。失言:说错的、不该说的话。知(音 zhì 治):智,智慧。

【白话译文】

孔子说:"一个人,如果应当与另一个人说话,但不同他说话,可能失去一位朋友;如果不应当与另一个人说话,却同他说话,可能浪费语言。明智的人,既不失去朋友,也不浪费语言。"(15.08)

【英译】

The Master said, "One may lose a friend if he should talk with a suitable person, but he does not. But one may waste his words if he talks with a person who is not suitable to talk with. A wise man neither loses a friend nor wastes his words." (15.08)

子曰:"吾之于人也,谁毁谁誉?如有所誉者,其有所试矣。斯民也,三代之所以直道而行也。"(15.25)

【注释】之于:对于。人:别人、前人。谁毁:毁谁,诋毁过谁。谁誉:誉谁,赞美过谁。如:如果。誉:赞美。其:此人。试:考验过。其有所试矣:此人是经过考验证实了的贤人。斯:此。民:百姓。斯民也:这样的贤人、这样做人啊。三代:夏、商、周。所以:因此。直道:正道,正直不私。行:发展。斯

【白话译文】

孔子说："对于前人，我批评过谁？我赞扬过谁？如果我赞扬过有些人，他们一定是由我从历史角度考察过的、优秀的人。因为这些优秀的人，夏、商、周三代才沿着正直的道路发展起来。"(15.25)

【英译】

The Master said, "For our predecessors, whom have I criticized? And whom have I praised? If I have praised some people, I must have examined them historically for their excellence. Because of these excellent people, the societies of three dynasties of Xia, Shang and Zhou could be developed along a righteous way." (15.25)

民也，三代之所以直道而行也：正是这些贤人，夏商周三代能按社会规律正常发展下去。

子曰："辞，达而已矣。"(15.41)

【注释】辞：言辞。达：表达意思。而：就。已：可以。矣：了。

【白话译文】

孔子说："一个人的言辞表达了他的意思，就可以了。"(15.41)

【英译】

The Master said, "It is good that what one says conveys what he means." (15.41)

孔子曰："侍于君子有三愆：言未及之而言谓之躁，言及之而不言谓之隐，未见颜色而言谓之瞽。"(16.06)

【注释】侍（音 shì 事）：站立陪同、侍奉。愆（音 qiān 铅）：过失。言未及之：没有问到你。而：却。言：说。谓之：称作。躁：急躁，浮躁。及之：问到你。隐：隐瞒。颜色：脸色。瞽（音 gǔ 鼓）：盲人。

【白话译文】

孔夫子说："侍奉君子时，有三种说话的错误。如果没有让他说话而说话，这叫作浮躁；如果让他说话，他不说，这叫作隐瞒；如果不看对方的脸色而说话，这叫作不长眼。"(16.06)

【英译】

Confucius said, "There are three faults in attending upon a superior man. When he is not asked to speak but he does, he is called impetuous. When he is asked to speak but he does not, he is called evasive. And when one speaks without looking at the other's countenance, it is called blindness." (16.06)

26

诗 Poems and Odes

子曰:“《诗》三百篇,一言以蔽之,曰:‘思无邪’。”(02.02)

【注释】诗:《诗经》。一言:一句话。以:用来。蔽(音 bì 壁):概括。思:思想。无邪:正直。

【白话译文】

孔子说:“《诗》三百篇,用一句话概述,这就是:‘思想纯正。’”(02.02)

【英译】

The Master said,“Three hundred verses of *Poems and Odes*(1) can be summarized in one sentence, which is ‘they all are pure in thought.’” (02.02)

【英译注】(1) *Poems and Odes*: A poetry collection compiled 2500 years ago. It is the earliest anthology of verses and poems in the world, and covers 160 Folksongs sung by the common people, 74 Odes and 31 Epics sung by the nobles at courts or at banquets, 40 Hymns used during sacrifice to the gods and ancestors.

子夏问曰:“‘巧笑倩兮,美目盼兮,素以为绚兮。’何谓也?”子曰:“绘事后素。”曰:“礼后乎?”子曰:“起予者商也!始

【注释】子夏:姓卜名商,字子夏。巧笑倩兮,美目盼兮:出自《诗经·卫风·硕人》。巧:和悦。倩(音 qiàn 欠):靥,酒窝。目:眼睛。盼:眼睛黑白分明。素:洁白。绚(音 xuàn 炫):多彩艳丽。素以为

可以言《诗》已矣。”(03.08)

【白话译文】

子夏请教道:“‘甜蜜微笑的美丽酒窝呀,镶着黑白分明瞳孔的漂亮眼睛呀,在白底上绘上多彩的花卉呀。’这几句诗是什么意思?”孔子说:“先打白底,然后在上面作画。”子夏问:“礼出现在仁之后吗?”孔子说:“启发我的人是商呀!现在我可以开始与你谈论《诗经》了。”(03.08)

【英译】

Zixia(1) asked advice, "'The pretty dimples of the pleasant smiles, black pupils inlaid in white of beautiful eyes(2), and colorful flowers painted on background white.' What do these lines of a poem mean?" The Master said, "The background is whitened first and then painting is done on it." Zixia said, "Do the Rites of Proprieties appear after superior benevolence?" The Master said, "The one who enlightens me is Shang(3)! Now I can start talking with you on *Poems and Odes*." (03.08)

绚:洁白的底上画着花卉。绘:绘画。后:在后。素:白底。绘事后素:先打白底再画画。礼后乎:礼在(仁义)之后吗。起:启发。予:我。商:姓卜名商,字子夏。起予者商也:启发我的人是商呀。始:开始,现在。言:说、讲。诗:《诗经》。矣:了。

【英译注】(1) Zixia: Surname Bu, first name Shang, style name Zixia, Confucius's disciple. (2) These are from *Buxom Lady*, *Songs Collected in Wei*, *Poems and Odes*, currently named *Book of Poetry*. (3) Shang: First name of Zixia.

子曰:“《关雎》,乐而不淫,哀而不伤。”(03.20)

【注释】《关雎》(雎,音 jū 居):《诗经》第一篇。淫:过分而失当。哀:忧愁。伤:过分伤痛。

【白话译文】

孔子说:“诗篇《关雎》,快乐但不放荡,悲哀但不过分悲伤。”(03.20)

【英译】

The Master said, “The poem *Wooing and Wedding*(1) is delightful but not dissolute, and sad but not extremely sorrowful.” (03.20)

【英译注】(1) *Wooing and Wedding*: It is the first verse of *Poems and Odes*, currently named *Book of Poetry*, in chapter *Book of Songs*. Its Chinese title is *Guan Ju*, where Guan means singing of a bird and Ju is the name of a bird that has only one mate in life. Ju is also said to be a turtledove or a fish hawk.

子曰:“诵《诗》三百,授之以政,不达,使于四方,不能专对,虽多,亦奚以为?”(13.05)

【注释】诵(音 sòng 颂):熟读。诗:《诗经》。三百:300 首。授:交给。之:他。以:把。政:政务。达:通晓、胜任。使:出使。四方:外国。专对:独立对答。多:读诗多。亦:又。奚:什么。以:用。为:呢,反问语气词。亦奚以为:又有什么用呢。

【白话译文】

孔子说:“一个人能流利背颂《诗》三百首诗,但他既不能胜任交给他的政治任务,也不能在出访外国时独立妥当处理外交事务。那么,尽管他背颂的诗很多,但对他有什么用处呢?”(13.05)

【英译】

The Master said, “One can fluently recite three hundred verses of *Poems and*

Odes, but he neither can competently handle governmental tasks assigned to him, nor can independently deal properly with diplomatic affairs when dispatched to a foreign state. What does it help him that he recites numerous poems?" (13.05)

子曰:"小子,何莫学夫诗?诗可以兴,可以观,可以群,可以怨。迩之事父,远之事君。多识于鸟兽草木之名。"(17.09)

【注释】小子:弟子。何:为何。莫:不。诗:《诗经》。兴:借物言志,托物兴辞。观:察万物万象。群:和而不同,不人云亦云,增强交际能力。怨:排遣怨愤、抒发感情。迩(音 ěr 耳):近处、浅近的。事:侍奉。迩之事父:近呢,可用诗浅显的道理侍奉父母。远:深远的,远处。远之事君:远呢,可用诗深刻的道理服侍君王。识:认识、知道。

【白话译文】

孔子说:"弟子们!为什么你们不学《诗》呢?《诗》激发你们的想象力,提高你们的观察能力,锻炼你们与人交往的技巧,让你们的讽刺大有说服力。学习《诗》,近处你可以服侍你们的父母,远处可以服务你们的君王,你们还能够大量认识鸟、兽、草、木的名字。"(17.09)

【英译】

The Master said, "Disciples! Why don't you learn *Poems and Odes*[(1)]? *Poems and Odes* can inspire your imagination, increase your observation capacity, temper your skill to communicate with others and make your satire much more convincing. By learning *Poems and Odes*, you can attend upon your parents nearby, serve your sovereign remotely, and can also recognize many names of birds, beasts, grasses, and trees." (17.09)

子谓伯鱼曰："女为《周南》《召南》矣乎？人而不为《周南》《召南》，其犹正墙面而立也与！"(17.10)

【注释】谓：问、告诉。伯鱼：孔鲤，字伯鱼，孔子之子。女(音rǔ辱)：汝，你。为：学习。周南、召南：《诗经·国风》第一组和第二组诗。犹：像。正：正对。墙：墙壁。面：面向。立：站着，无法前行。与：啊，句末语气词，表示感叹或疑问。

【白话译文】

孔子对伯鱼说："你钻研《周南》《召南》了吗？如果一个人不钻研《周南》《召南》，他好像直接面对墙面而站立！"(17.10)

【英译】

The Master told Boyu(1), "Have you studied the *South of the Capital* and the *South of Zhao*(2)? If a person does not study the *South of the Capital* and the *South of Zhao*, he is like standing directly facing a wall(3)." (17.10)

【英译注】(1) Boyu: Surname Kong, first name Li, style name Boyu, the son of Confucius. (2) the *South of the Capital* and the *South of Zhao*: The Song Collection of the South of the Capital of the Zhou Dynasty and the Song Collection of South of Zhao are the first two parts of *Poems and Odes*, currently called *Book of Poetry*. (3) A wall: It means that he cannot see anything else and cannot march forward neither.

六

Six

修身

Self-Cultivation of Morals

27

惑 Perplexity

子路问:"闻斯行诸?"子曰:"有父兄在,如之何闻斯行之?"冉有问:"闻斯行诸?"子曰:"闻斯行之。"公西华曰:"由也问闻斯行诸,子曰,'有父兄在';求也问闻斯行诸,子曰:'闻斯行之。'赤也惑,敢问。"子曰:"求也退,故进之;由也兼人,故退之。"(11.22)

【白话译文】

子路问:"听到应当做的就做吗?"孔子说:"你父兄在跟前,你为什么要听到就做呢?"冉有问:"听到应当做的就做吗?"孔子说:"听到就做。"公西华说:"由问听到就做吗,你说:'你父兄在跟前。'求也问听到就做吗,你说:'听到就做。'我迷惑不解,冒昧请教你。"孔子说:"求通常犹豫不决,所以促进他;由好勇过人,所以约束他。"(11.22)

【注释】子路:姓仲,名由,字子路。闻:听到。斯:就。行:做。诸:"之乎"合音。闻斯行诸:听到就行动。在:健在。如之何:如何。冉有:姓冉名求,字子有。行之:就行动,就这样做。公西华:姓公西名赤,字子华。由:姓仲名由,字子路。求:姓冉,名求,字子有。赤:公西华的名。惑:糊涂。敢问:请问(原因)。进之:促进、鼓励他。兼人:好勇过人。退之:约束他。

【英译】

Zilu[(1)] asked, "Should I do it as soon as I hear it[(2)]?" The Master said, "Why do you do it at once since your father and elder brother are present?" Ran You[(3)] asked, "Should I do it as soon as I hear it?" The Master said, "Do it once you hear it." Gongxi Hua[(4)] said, "You[(5)] asks, 'Should I do it as soon as I hear it?' And you say, 'Your father and elder brother are present.' Qiu[(6)] also asks, 'Should I do it as soon as I hear it?' And you say, 'Do it once you hear it.' I am perplexed about it and venture to ask your advice on it." The Master said, "Qiu normally is hesitant, so I encourage him; but You[(5)] is fond of courage, so I restrain him." (11.22)

【英译注】(1) Zilu: Surname Zhong, first name You, style name Zilu. He and other two below all were Confucius's disciples. (2) it: What is suitable for one to do. (3) Ran You: Surname Ran, first name Qiu, style name Ziyou. (4) Gongxi Hua: Surname Gongxi, first name Chi, style name Zihua. (5) You: First name of Zilu. (6) Qiu: First name of Ran You.

子张问崇德辨惑。子曰:"主忠信,徙义,崇德也。爱之欲其生,恶之欲其死。既欲其生,又欲其死,是惑也。'诚不以富,亦祇以异。'"(12.10)

【白话译文】

子张问如何能提高自己的道德,并能辨析困惑。孔子说:"把忠诚、诚信作为你

【注释】子张:姓颛(音 zhuān 砖)孙名师,字子张。崇:提高。德:道德修养。惑:迷惑。主忠信:以忠信为重。徙:迁移、接近。徙义:向正义靠拢,唯义是从。爱:喜爱。之:一个人。欲:希望。其:这个人。生:长生不老。恶(音 wù 务):憎恶。死:死亡。恶之欲其死:对于同一个人,恨他、不爱他时,希望他马上死。诚:诚然,即使。以:因为。富:益处、好处。亦:也。祇(音 zhī 织):仅仅。异:奇怪。诚不以富,亦祇以异:这样

自己的核心品质，总是按照正义的标准说话、行为，这样你就可以使自己的品德高尚了。当你爱一个人，你盼望他长生不老；当你恨一个人，你盼望他立刻死亡。当你依照自己的标准，对同一个人既盼望他长生，又盼望他死亡，这就是困惑。这像《诗经》中的一个说辞：'诚然他这么做自己得不到好处，但对于别人显得很奇怪了。'"(12.10)

【英译】

Zizhang(1) asked how to make one's morals lofty and resolve perplexities. The Master said: "Take loyalty and faithfulness as your own essential qualities and speak and conduct yourself always as required by the criteria of righteousness. This is how you can make your morals lofty. For the same person, you wish him a long life when you love him and you wish him to die instantly when you hate him. As you wish for the same person either to live a long time or to die now, based on your own criteria, this is a kind of perplexity. This is like a saying in *Poems and Odes*: 'Truly he cannot benefit himself by doing so, but he seems only strange to others(2).'" (12.10)

确实对自己没什么好处，只是让人觉得奇怪罢了（出自《诗经·小雅·我行其野》）。

【英译注】(1) Zizhang: Confucius's disciple, surname Zhuansun, first name Shi, style name Zizhang. (2) This saying is from a poem titled "A Rejected Husband" in *The Third Decade of Odes*, *Poems and Odes*, the first poem collection in the world, currently named *Book of Poetry*.

樊迟从游于舞雩之下，曰："敢问崇德、修慝、辨惑。"子曰："善哉问！先事后得，非崇德与？攻其恶，无攻人之恶，非修慝与？一朝之忿，忘其身以及其亲，非惑与？"(12.21)

【注释】樊迟：名须，字子迟。从：陪着孔子。游：散步。舞雩（音 yú 于）：地名，祭天求雨之地，在今山东曲阜。敢：冒昧。问：请教。崇：提高。德：品德、道德。修：改正。慝（音 tè 特）：邪恶的念头。辨：辨别。惑：迷惑。善哉：好啊。先事：先努力做事。得：收获。与：吗。攻：检讨。其：自己的。恶（音 è 饿）：邪念、错误。攻其恶：检讨自己的邪念、错误。之：的。人之恶：他人的邪念、错误。一朝（音 zhāo 招，早晨）：一时。忿（音 fèn 奋）：愤怒。忘：忘记。其：自己的。其身：自身安危和存在价值。以：以至。及：牵连、连累。亲：亲人。一朝之忿，忘其身以及其亲：因一时的愤怒（采取不理智、过激行为，害人害己），忘了自身价值，并连累自家亲人。

【白话译文】

樊迟陪同孔子在舞雩台下游逛，问道："我能冒昧向你请教如何提高我的品德、如何消除我内心隐藏的邪念、如何辨别什么是糊涂行为吗？"孔子说："你问得太好了！如果你给予做事的优先级别高于获得报酬，这不是一种提高品德的行为吗？如果你对自己的错误进行自我批评，而不批评别人，这不是一种消除自己内心邪念的方式吗？如果因为一次临时的愤怒，你失去理智，采取过激行为，忘记了自身价值并且连累了父母，这不是一种糊涂行为吗？"(12.21)

【英译】

Accompanying the Master strolling about Wuyu rain-praying platform, Fan Chi(1) asked, "May I take liberty to ask your advice about how to make my morals lofty, how to remove my hidden evil thoughts, and how to resolve a perplexity?" The Master

【英译注】(1) Fan Chi: Surname Fan, first name Xu, style name Zifan, Confucius's disciple.

said, "How great your questions are! If you give priority to your good work ahead of any thoughts of reward, doesn't it make your morals lofty? If you only criticize yourself for a mistake and do not criticize others, doesn't it remove your hidden evil thoughts? If in a fit of anger you lose your senses, resort to extreme behavior, forget your own self worth, and involve your parents, isn't this a kind of perplexing behavior?" (12.21)

28

忧 Anxiety

子曰:"不有祝鮀之佞,而有宋朝之美,难乎免于今之世矣。"(06.16)

【白话译文】

孔子说:"如果一个人不能像祝鮀那样很有口才,而仅仅像宋国公子朝一样英俊,在当今时代,他要避免灾难是非常困难的。"(06.16)

【注释】不有:(如果)没有。祝鮀(音 tuó 驼):字子鱼,卫国大夫。佞:好口才。而有:却只有。宋朝:宋国公子朝,美男,淫荡。美:好看的相貌。难:困难。免:避免(有祸害)。于:在。今:当今。世:世道。矣:了。难乎免于今之世矣:在当今社会上避免祸害,就很难了。

【英译】

The Master said, "If a person is not as eloquent as Zhu Tuo(1), but is only as good-looking as Prince's Son Chao of the State of Song (2), it is very difficult for him to avoid disasters in the current era." (06.16)

【英译注】(1) Zhu Tuo: Surname Zhu, first name Tuo, style name Ziyu, a senior official of the State of Wei, good at diplomatic affairs. (2) Prince's Son Chao: A handsome man, first name Chao, a prince's son of the State of Song. He was recorded as loose in morals and lascivious, having caused several disasters out of his handsomeness.

子曰:"德之不修,学之不讲,闻义不能徙,不善不能改,是吾忧也。"(07.03)

【注释】德:品德、道德。之:的。修:修养、提高。学:学问。讲:追求。徙(音 xǐ 喜):迁移,做到。闻义不能徙:听到正义,不去奔赴而实施。不善:过错。改:改正。是:系词,表示解释和分类。吾:我。忧:忧虑。是吾忧也:是我忧虑的。

【白话译文】

孔子说:"一个人不培养良好的道德,不实践或不向别人讲解他学习到的东西,不按听到的正义的标准行事和说话,而且不能改正自己的错误。这是我忧愁的。"(07.03)

【英译】

The Master said, "A person does not cultivate good morals, does not practice and lecture to others what he has learned, does not act and speak according to the standards of righteousness as he hears, and does not correct his mistakes. This is what I am anxious about." (07.03)

子曰："狂而不直，侗而不愿，倥倥而不信，吾不知之矣。"(08.16)

【白话译文】

孔子说："如果一个人狂妄并且不直率，无知并且不实在，没有能力并且不诚信，我不知道这种人会做出什么来。"(08.16)

【英译】

The Master said, "If a person is impetuous and not straightforward, ignorant and not honest, and neither capable nor faithful, I do not know what such a person may do." (08.16)

【注释】狂：急躁、狂妄。而：而且。直：正直。侗（音 tóng 铜）：幼稚无知。愿：谨慎、朴实、诚实。倥（音 kōng 箜）：空，表面上诚恳，实则无能。信：诚信。不知之：不知道他（会怎么样）。矣：呀。

闵子侍侧，訚訚如也；子路，行行如也；冉有、子贡，侃侃如也。子乐。"若由也，不得其死然。"(11.13)

【白话译文】

闵子恭敬地服侍在孔子身边，他是和颜悦色的样子；子路是不屈不挠倔强的样子；冉有、子贡是从容不迫快乐的样子。孔子高兴起来。一会儿，他说："像由这个状态，恐怕他不能活到他的天寿。"(11.13)

【注释】闵子：姓闵名损，字子骞。侍（音 shì 是）：站立陪同。訚（音 yín 银）：和颜悦色。如也：的样子。子路：姓仲，名由，字子路。行（音 hàng 沆）：倔强（jué jiàng 绝酱）固执。冉有：姓冉名求，字子有。子贡：姓端木，名赐，字子贡。侃：理直气壮、从容不迫、和乐、温和而快乐。乐（音 lè 勒）：高兴。若：像，如同。由：姓仲名由，字子路。其死：他的自然寿命、善终。然：的样子。

【英译】

Master Min[1] seemed kind and pleasant on his face when he attended respectfully upon the Master at his side. Zilu[2] seemed stubborn and unyielding, and Ran You[3] and Zigong[4] seemed easy and delightful. The Master was pleased. In a while, he said, "As for the manner of You[5], I am afraid that he will not die a natural death." (11.13)

【英译注】(1) Master Min: Surname Min, first name Sun, style name Ziqian, famous for his filial piety. He and others below all were Confucius's disciples. (2) Zilu: Surname Zhong, first name You, style name Zilu. (3) Ran You: Surname Ran, first name Qiu, style name Ziyou. (4) Zigong: Surname Duanmu, first name Ci, style name Zigong. (5) You: First name of Zilu.

司马牛问君子。子曰:"君子不忧不惧。"曰:"不忧不惧,斯谓之君子已乎?"子曰:"内省不疚,夫何忧何惧?"(12.04)

【注释】司马牛:姓司马名耕,字子牛,传其兄宋国大夫桓魋(音huán环tuí颓)作乱被追杀,全家出逃。问:请教。忧:忧愁。惧:恐惧。曰:(司马牛)问说。斯:就。谓:叫作。之:这。已:矣,了。乎:吗。内省:内心反省。疚:愧。何:为什么。

【白话译文】

司马牛请教君子应做什么。孔子说:"君子既不忧愁,也不恐惧。"司马牛说:"一个人既不忧愁,也不恐惧,就可以称作君子了吗?"孔子说:"如果他内省自己,并且没有罪恶感,那么他为什么会既忧愁又恐惧呢?"(12.04)

【英译】

Sima Niu[1] asked advice about a superior man. The Master said, "A superior man is neither anxious nor fearful." Sima

【英译注】(1) Sima Niu: Surname Sima, first name Niu, Confucius's disciple. It was said that his brother Huantui, a senior officer of the State of Song, staged an armed

Niu said, "Can a man be called a superior man only if he is neither anxious nor fearful?" The Master said, "If he questions in himself and feels no guilt, why should he be anxious and fearful?" (12.04)

rebellion, and was pursued for dead penalty.

子曰:"群居终日,言不及义,好行小慧,难矣哉!"(15.17)

【白话译文】

孔子说:"有些人整天聚在一起,所说的话都远离道德和正理,而且好卖弄小聪明。这些人难有好生活呀!"(15.17)

【英译】

The Master said, "Some people are together all day long, what they talk about is far from morals and principles, and they also like to show off their cleverness. Oh! How difficult it is for them to have a good life!" (15.17)

【注释】群居:聚在一块。终日:整天。言:说话。及:达到。义:道理、道义。言不及义:说不出一句有道理的话。行:行使、卖弄。小慧:小聪明。难:难以教导、难有作为。哉:啊。

29

怨 Complain

子曰:“放于利而行,多怨。”(04.12)

【白话译文】

孔子说:“如果一个人仿照获得他自己私利的标准行事,他会招惹别人大量怨恨。”(04.12)

【英译】

The Master said, “If a person bases his actions on his own personal profit, he will stir up great animosity among others.” (04.12)

【注释】放(音 fǎng 仿):依照、仿效。于:在、从。利:私利。而:顺接、相承连词。行:做事。放于利而行:凭据自私自利去做事。多:增加。怨:怨恨。

仲弓问仁。子曰:“出门如见大宾,使民如承大祭。己所不欲,勿施于人。在邦无怨,在家无怨。”仲弓曰:“雍虽不敏,请事斯语矣。”(12.02)

【注释】仲弓:姓冉,名雍,字仲弓。问:请教。仁:仁道。出门:外出办事。如:如同。见:接待。大宾:贵宾。使:役使。民:百姓。承:进行。祭:祭祀。己:自己。欲:愿意的。施:强加。人:别人。邦:诸侯统治地。无怨:无人怨恨(自己);不抱怨。家:卿大夫统治地。雍:姓冉名雍,字仲弓。不敏:笨。请:让我。事:照办。请事斯语:(一定)按照此话办。矣:呀。

【白话译文】

仲弓问仁是什么。孔子说："当你出门工作时，你认真的态度如同你出门会见贵宾。当你役使百姓时，你严肃的态度如同你主持重大祭祀礼仪。己所不欲，勿施于人。你为诸侯服务时，不抱怨任何人；你为卿大夫服务时，也不抱怨任何别人。"仲弓说："虽然我雍不智慧，但我也要遵循你的话。"（12.02）

【英译】

Zhonggong(1) asked advice about what superior benevolence was. The Master said, "When you go to work, you should behave as if you were receiving a distinguished guest. When using the common people in their corvee duties, you should have a serious attitude as if you were officiating at a grand sacrificial ceremony. Never do unto others what you do not want others to do unto you. Neither hold a grudge when you serve a duke or a prince, nor hold a grudge when you serve a senior official." Zhonggong said, "Though I am not wise, I, Yong(2) will follow your words." (12.02)

【英译注】(1) Zhonggong: Surname Ran, first name Yong, style name Zhonggong. (2) Yong: First name of Zhonggong.

子曰："贫而无怨难，富而无骄易。"（14.11）

【注释】贫：缺钱。而：却，但。怨：怨恨。富：不缺钱、拥有大量财产。骄：骄傲。

【白话译文】

孔子说:"让一个贫穷的人不抱怨,是很难的,但是让一个富足的人不骄傲,是容易的。"(14.11)

【英译】

The Master said, "It is difficult for a man of poverty not to hold a grudge against anyone, but it is easy for a man of wealth not to be arrogant." (14.11)

子曰:"躬自厚而薄责于人,则远怨矣。"(15.15)

【注释】躬自:责备自己。厚:多。而:却,但。薄:少。责:责备。于:对。人:别人。则:那么。远:避免。怨:怨恨。矣:了。

【白话译文】

孔子说:"一个人狠狠批评自己,同时轻轻谴责他人,怨恨就会远远地离开他。"(15.15)

【英译】

The Master said, "If one seriously criticizes himself and slightly blames others, he may keep enmity and resentment away from him." (15.15)

30

过 Mistake

子曰:“人之过也,各于其党。观过,斯知仁矣。”(04.07)

【白话译文】

孔子说:“一个人所犯的错误,是可以分成不同种类的。通过观察他错误的类别,就可以知道他是否具有仁德。”(04.07)

【英译】

The Master said, “The mistakes made by everyone can be sorted into different categories. By observing the category of his mistake, one can know whether this person is benevolent.” (04.07)

【注释】之:的。过:过错。各:分别。于:归于。其:他的。党:类别、集团,君子或小人。观:仔细看。仁:仁德、为人。观过,斯知仁矣:仔细看一个人过错的性质,就可知其有无仁德了。

陈司败问:“昭公知礼乎?”孔子曰:“知礼。”孔子退,揖巫马期而进之,曰:“吾闻君子不党,君子亦党乎?君取于吴为同姓,谓之吴孟子。君而知礼,孰不知礼?”巫马期以告。子曰:“丘也幸,苟有过,人必知之。”(07.31)

【注释】陈司败:一说是官名,陈国司寇,主管司法,姓名不详;二说是姓名。昭公:鲁国君主,姓姬名惆(音 chóu 绸),公元前541年至公元前510年在位,谥(音 shì 是)号昭。乎:吗。退:退出,出去。揖:作揖,拱手礼。巫马期:姓巫马名施,字子期。进:走近。之:他。而进之:(让巫马期)走近他。党:偏袒、包庇。取:娶。于:从。吴:吴国。为:是。同姓:同姓的女子。谓之:称她为。而:如果、却。孰:谁。以:把此。告:转告孔子。丘:孔子,姓孔名丘,字仲尼。幸:幸运。苟:如果。过:错。

【白话译文】

陈国负责司法的官员请教:“鲁国的昭公明白礼仪吗?”孔夫子答:“他明白礼仪。”当孔夫子走后,这位官员给巫马期作揖,走进他说:“我听说,一位君子不偏袒任何人。一位君子真的包庇自己的人,掩盖其错误吗?此鲁国君,娶了一个吴国的女子为妻,此人与他是同姓,改称她为吴孟子。如果此国君真明白礼仪,谁还不明白礼仪?”巫马期把此话转告孔夫子。他说:“我丘很幸运。如果我犯了错误,别人一定会给我指出来。”(07.31)

【英译】

An official(1) in charge of the jurisdiction of the State of Chen asked, “Did Duke Zhao(2) understand the Rites of Proprieties?” Confucius replied, “Yes, he did.” When Confucius was out, the official came close to

【英译注】(1) An official: He could be a juridical minister of the State of Chen. Another saying is that his name was Chen Sibai. (2) Duke Zhao: The sovereign of the State of Lu and he ruled it from 541 BC to 510 BC, surname Ji, first name Chou, posthumous title Zhao. (3)

Wuma Qi(3), made a bow to him and said, "I hear that a superior man does not show partiality to anyone. Does a superior man truly shield his own family members and cover their mistakes? The sovereign of the State of Lu married a girl from the State of Wu(4) who shared the same surname with him, and he renamed her as Wu Mengzi. If the sovereign truly knew the Rites, then who had not known them?" When Wuma Qi forwarded the words to Confucius, he said, "I, Qiu(5), am lucky. If I make a mistake, someone else certainly points it to me." (07.31)

Wuma Qi: Confucius's disciple, surname Wuma, first name Shi, style name Ziqi. (4) the State of Wu: A state in southeastern China with its capital at currently Suzhou, Jiangsu province. Its sovereign had the same surname Ji with that of the State of Lu where no intermarriage rule between members of same surname prevailed. (5) Qiu: The first name of Confucius.

子曰:"如有周公之才之美,使骄且吝,其余不足观也已。"(08.11)

【注释】如:如果。周公:周公旦,圣人。之:的。才:才能。美:完善。如有周公之才之美:如果有人完全具有周公的才能。使:(他的那些才能)让(他)。骄:骄傲。吝:吝啬。其:他的。余:饶足丰富的才能。足:值。观:细看。其余不足观也已:那么这个人拥有再多的才能,也不值得去欣赏啊。

【白话译文】

孔子说:"如果一个人骄傲且吝啬,那么无论他有多么大的才能,即使他具有能够与周公完全相媲美的才能,他也不值得去欣赏了。"(08.11)

【英译】

The Master said, "If a person is arrogant and miserly, he is not worthy of being

【英译注】(1) Duke Zhou: Surname Ji, first name Dan, a saint of the Zhou Dynasty who assisted his

appreciated no matter how greatly talented he is, even though he has the talents that can perfectly be comparable with those of Duke Zhou[(1)]." (08.11)

elder brother King Wu to overthrow the Shang Dynasty and found the Zhou Dynasty. He also assisted King Wu's orphan son to be a child emperor. He was the first duke of the State of Lu. It is said that he created the policy and ritual system of the Zhou Dynasty.

子曰:"过而不改,是谓过矣。"(15.30)

【注释】过:错。而:却、但。改:改正。谓:称作。矣:了。

【白话译文】

孔子说:"如果一个错误没有被改正,它才真正称作错误了。"(15.30)

【英译】

The Master said, "If a mistake is not corrected, it is truly called a mistake." (15.30)

子贡曰:"君子之过也,如日月之食焉:过也,人皆见之;更也,人皆仰之。"(19.21)

【注释】子贡:姓端木名赐,字子贡。之:的。过:错。日月之食:日蚀月蚀。人:他人。皆:都。见:看见。之:它。更:改正。仰:仰望。

【白话译文】

子贡说:"君子的错误,如同日食或月食。当犯错误的时候,每个人都看见它。

当错误改正时，每个人都尊敬景仰他。”(19.21)

【英译】

Zigong[1] said, “The mistake of a superior man is like a solar eclipse or a lunar eclipse. When the mistake is made, it is seen by everyone. When the mistake is corrected, everyone respects and admires him.” (19.21)

【英译注】(1) Zigong: Surname Duanmu, first name Ci, style name Zigong, Confucius's disciple.

31

思 Think

季文子三思而后行。子闻之，曰：“再，斯可矣！”(05.20)

【注释】季文子：季孙行父，鲁成公、襄公时任正卿，谥(音 shì 是)号文，多计较得失，常寡断。三：多次。思：思考。而后：之后。行：行动。再：一解“两次，要果断，不要左思右想，优柔寡断”；二解“反复三思，要沉稳，不要盲目定论”。斯：这样、就。可：可以。矣：了。

【白话译文】

季文子思考一件事三次以后，才开始做这件事。听到此事，孔子说：“他思考它两次，就挺好了！”(05.20)

【英译】

Master Ji Wen[(1)] started to do a thing after thinking over it thrice[(2)]. Having heard of this, the Master said, "It would be fine for him to think over it twice." (05.20)

【英译注】(1) Master Ji Wen: Surname Jisun, first name Xingfu (? –568 BC), the chief senior official of the State of Lu during Duke Cheng and Duke Xiang, posthumous title Wen. He calculated too much on the gains and losses, and was thus often indecisive. (2) Thrice: Many times, not limited to three times.

"唐棣之华,偏其反而。岂不尔思,室是远而。"子曰:"未之思也,夫何远之有?"(09.31)

【注释】唐棣(音 dì 帝):棠棣树,蔷薇科,落叶灌木。华:花。偏(音 piān 篇):翩,轻快飞舞。反:同"翻",摇曳,反常、反向;别的花先合后开,棠棣树先开后合。而:了。岂:怎么。尔思:想念你。室:住处。是:系词,表示解释和分类。远:遥远。室是远而:住室是太远了。未:没有。未之思:不想念。何:怎么。

【白话译文】

古诗说:"唐(棠)棣的花子,翩翩摇曳起舞。怎么能说我不思念你?我的家住得离你实在太远了。"孔子说:"他真正没有思念对方;否则,怎么会远呢?"(09.31)

【英译】

An ancient poem said, "The flowers of the bush cherry trees dance lightly. How could it be said that I do not long for you? My residence is truly too far away." The Master said, "He did not truly long for the other; otherwise how remote could it be?" (09.31)

曾子曰:“君子思不出其位。”(14.28)

【白话译文】

曾子说:“君子不在自己职位及其职权所要求的范围之外动脑筋。”(14.28)

【英译】

Master Zeng said,“A superior man does not let his thoughts beyond what is required by his position and duties.”(14.28)

【注释】思:考虑。出:超过。其:他的。位:职权范围。思不出其位:考虑问题,不超越自己的职权范围(以使君君、臣臣各得其所)。

孔子曰:“君子有九思:视思明,听思聪,色思温,貌思恭,言思忠,事思敬,疑思问,忿思难,见得思义。”(16.10)

【白话译文】

孔夫子曰:“君子认真思虑九件事:看,思虑是否看全面看得懂;听,思虑是否听明白;对于面部表情,思虑是否温厚;对于举止,思虑是否恭顺;说话,思虑是否真实于内心;做事,思虑是否敬业和认真;对于疑惑的事,思虑如何提出问题并解决问题;对于愤怒,思虑由此引起的后续的困难;对于获得的私利,思虑是否符合正义。”(16.10)

【注释】九:九件事。思:慎重考虑、思考。明:明白。聪:清楚。色:脸色。温:温和。貌:外表。恭:恭敬。言:说话。忠:内心诚实,不自欺欺人。事:做事。敬:认真。疑:有疑问。问:请教。忿:发怒。难:后患、后果。得:利益。

【英译】

Confucius said, "A superior man carefully considers nine things: For seeing, consider whether it is thoroughly observed; for listening, consider whether it is clearly understood; for facial expression, consider whether it is gentle and good-natured; for demeanor, consider whether it is deferential and respectful; for speaking, consider whether it is truthful to one's heart; for doing a job, consider whether one is careful and industrious; for a perplexity, consider the questions to be raised and solved; for indignation, consider the difficult consequences it may cause; and for acquisition of private profits and benefits, consider whether it is in conformity with righteousness." (16.10)

32

察 Observe

子曰:"视其所以,观其所由,察其所安,人焉廋哉? 人焉廋哉?"(02.10)

【注释】视:看。其:他的。以:用。所以:所用,所采用的动机。观:细看。由:经,从,途径,方法。所由:所途经、遵从的行为方法和路线。察:仔细看。安:心安

【白话译文】

孔子说："通过看清一个人怀有什么样的行为动机，细观他的行为采取的方法和原则，彻察他心安理得的行为后果，这样他怎么能够隐藏得住呢？他怎么能够隐藏得住呢？（02.10）

【英译】

The Master said, "By looking clearly at what motives one applies for his behavior, seeing carefully what methods and principles he takes for his conduct, and examining thoroughly what makes him feel at ease and how he justifies the consequences of his actions, how can he conceal his true self? How can he conceal his true self?" (02.10)

理得的事，安顿、停在某处，引申为结果。焉：怎么。廋（音 sōu 搜）：隐藏。人焉廋哉：此人还有什么可隐藏的。

子张问明。子曰："浸润之谮，肤受之愬，不行焉，可谓明也已矣。浸润之谮，肤受之愬，不行焉，可谓远也已矣。"（12.06）

【注释】子张：姓颛（音 zhuān 砖）孙名师，字子张。明：明智、明察事理。浸润：点滴渗透，不易觉察。谮（音 zèn 镇）：谗言，说人坏话、诬陷别人。肤：皮肤。受：感觉疼痛。愬（音 sù 素）：（直接的）诬告。肤受之愬：切肤之痛的诬告。不行矣：在自己这里行不通啊。可谓：可称作。远：明之至也，远见，明智的最高境界。

【白话译文】

子张请教他如何才能明察事理。孔子说："对于一滴一滴渐渐渗入头脑的谗言，以及给他人带来切肤之痛的急迫的诬告，你都不受什么影响，这就可以称作你明察事理了。一滴一滴渐渐渗透到头脑的谗言,以及给他人带来切肤之痛的急迫的诬告,对你都不起作用,这可以称作你具有远见了。”(12.06)

【英译】

Zizhang[(1)] asked for advice about how he could thoroughly understand a thing. The Master said,"If you are neither affected by a gradual, drip by drip slander seeping into your mind, nor urgent false accusations against others, which brings as sharp a pain as a cut on the skin, then it can be said that you thoroughly understand a thing. If you are not moved by a gradual, drip by drip slander seeping into your mind, nor urgent false accusations against others, which brings as sharp a pain as a cut on the skin, then it can be said that you have foresight." (12.06)

【英译注】(1) Zizhang: Surname Zhuansun, first name Shi, style name Zizhang, Confucius's disciple.

子曰:“众恶之,必察焉;众好之,必察焉。”(15.28)

【注释】众:大家。恶(音 wù 务):憎恶。之:一个人。必:一定。察:详细看,认真审查,不人云亦云。好(音 hào 号):喜爱。

【白话译文】

孔子说:“所有的人都讨厌的,必须认真考察。所有的人都喜欢的,必须认真考察。”(15.28)

【英译】

The Master said, "What is detested by all the people must carefully be investigated. What is liked by all the people must carefully be investigated." (15.28)

33

耻 Shame

子曰:"士志于道,而耻恶衣恶食者,未足与议也。"(04.09)

【注释】士:最低层贵族,读书人。耻:耻辱感,有耻辱心。耻恶衣恶食:由于穿不好、吃不好而感到耻辱。未足:不值得。与议:与他谈论。

【白话译文】

孔子说:"一位学士将理想设定在探索真理和道义上,却以衣衫简朴和粗茶淡饭为耻,因此与他商议是不值得的。"(04.09)

【英译】

The Master said, "A scholar is not worth talking with if he sets his ambition on seeking truth, morality and justice, but is ashamed to have simple clothes and rough foods." (04.09)

子曰："笃信，好学，守死，善道。危邦不入，乱邦不居。天下有道则见，无道则隐。邦有道，贫且贱焉，耻也；邦无道，富且贵焉，耻也。"(08.13)

【注释】笃：坚定。信：相信，相信天道。笃信：坚定、虔诚地相信天道。好（音 hào 号）：喜爱。学：读书学习。守：守卫。死：誓死。善：完善、改善。道：个人道德、修养；原则、主张、先王之道。危：不稳的。邦：国。入：进入。乱：动乱的。居：住。有道：政治清明。见（音 xiàn 线）：现，做官。无道：政治黑暗。隐：隐居。贫：缺钱。贱：没有官职。富：有钱。耻：（自己的）耻辱。贵：显贵、禄位高。

【白话译文】

孔子说："虔诚相信天道，热心学习天道，至死不渝坚守天道，加强良好的道德修养。不要进入危机四伏的国家，不要居住在叛乱四起的国家。如果政治公平正义，则出来为国家做事。如果政治腐败不公，则隐居，脱离社会。国家公平正义，一个人还贫穷没有地位，是一种耻辱。国家腐败不公，一个人还富足且有荣耀，也是一种耻辱。"(08.13)

【英译】

The Master said, "For the Way of Heaven(1), believe in it piously, learn it zealously, unswervingly hold fast to it ever unto death, and strengthen one's self-cultivation for good morality. Neither enter a state beset with crises, nor live in a state full of armed rebellions. If administration of a government is fair and just, emerge to work for the state. If administration of a government is corrupt and unjust, be a hermit living in

【英译注】(1) the Way of Heaven: It may refer to the laws of nature and/or societies, principles of the ancient saints and doctrines passed on from sages.

seclusion. It is shameful to be poor and without honour in a fair and just state. And it is also shameful to be wealthy and honourable in a corrupt and unjust state." (08.13)

宪问耻。子曰:"邦有道,谷;邦无道,谷,耻也。"(14.01)

【注释】宪:姓原名宪,字子思。问:请教。耻:耻辱。邦:国家。有道:政治清明。谷:(获得)官员俸禄。无道:政治黑暗。

【白话译文】

宪请教什么是耻辱。孔子说:"当公平正义的政治原则在一个国家流行时,一个人领取官俸。当腐败不公的政治原则在一个国家盛行时,一个人还领取官俸,这是一种耻辱。"(14.01)

【英译】

Xian(1) asked advice about shame. The Master said, "One takes an official salary when principles of fair and just government administration prevail in a country. It is a shame for one to take an official salary when principles of corrupt and unjust government administration prevail in a country." (14.01)

【英译注】(1) Xian: Surname Yuan, first name Xian, style name Zisi, Confucius's disciple.

子曰:"君子耻其言而过其行。"(14.29)

【注释】言:(主动对人)说话。过:超过。行:行动。

【白话译文】

孔子说:“一位君子认为说的多做的少是一种耻辱。”(14.29)

【英译】

The Master said, “A superior man considers it a shame to speak more and act less.” (14.29)

34

修身 Moral Cultivation

子曰:“不患人之不己知,患不知人也。”(01.16)

【注释】患:忧虑、怕。人:别人;有教养者。不己知:不了解自己。知人:了解别人。

【白话译文】

孔子说:“我不被别人理解,我并不着急,但我着急的是,我不理解别人。”(01.16)

【英译】

The Master said, “I am not anxious about that I am not understood by the others, but I am anxious about that I do not understand the others.” (01.16)

子曰:“不患无位,患所以立。不患莫己知,求为可知也。”(04.14)

【注释】患:担心。位:官位;古代“位”与“立”通用,“立”便是“位”了。立:能够胜任官位;能在社会站稳。莫:没有(人)。己知:知己、知道自己。求:只求。为:有。可:值得。知:为人所知的。

【白话译文】

孔子说:“我不担心我没有职位,但我担心我是否具有胜任这个职位的能力。我不担心我不被人知道,但我追求获得值得别人知道的能力。”(04.14)

【英译】

The Master said, “I do not worry about that I do not have a position at officialdom, but I do worry about whether I have the capability to be competent for the position. I do not worry about that I am not known by the others, but I strive to acquire the capacities deserving of recognition by others.” (04.14)

子曰:“以约失之者鲜矣。”(04.23)

【注释】以:因为。约:约束,节制自己,使自己得中合礼。失:失误。者:的人、事。鲜(音 xiǎn 显):很少,缺少。以约失之者鲜矣:因为节制自己而犯错的事,是很少的呀。

【白话译文】

孔子说:“如果一个人以礼约束他自己,他很少会犯错误。”(04.23)

【英译】

The Master said,"One may rarely make mistakes if he restrains himself with the Rites of Proprieties."(04.23)

子贡曰:"我不欲人之加诸我也,吾亦欲无加诸人。"子曰:"赐也,非尔所及也。"(05.12)

【注释】子贡:姓端木,名赐,字子贡。人:他人。加:强加,凌驾、凌辱。诸:之于。人之加诸我:别人强加于我的事。亦:也。欲无加诸人:不想(把此事)强加给别人。赐:姓端木,名赐,字子贡。非:不是。尔:你。所及:能做到。

【白话译文】

子贡说:"我不想被别人欺凌,也不想欺凌别人。"孔子说:"哎呀,赐!这不是你能做到的。"(05.12)

【英译】

Zigong[1] said,"I neither want to be trodden upon by others, nor want to tread upon others." The Master said,"Alas, Ci[2]! This is what you cannot achieve."(05.12)

【英译注】(1) Zigong: Surname Duanmu, first name Ci, style name Zigong, Confucius's disciple. (2) Ci: First name of Zigong.

子曰:"譬如为山,未成一篑,止,吾止也。譬如平地,虽覆一篑,进,吾往也。"(09.19)

【注释】(修身由自己)譬(音pì媲):好比。为山:堆土山。成:完成。篑(音kuì愧):土筐。未成一篑:功亏一篑。止:停止。吾止:我自己停下(虽前面功多,半途而废,前功尽弃)。平:平整。平地:平整土地。覆:倒。进:推进。吾

【白话译文】

孔子说:“(高贵品德是由自己修养的。)好比用土堆山,当还差一筐就要完成了,我不想继续了,工作就停止了,我以前的努力全部白费。又比如用土平整坑坑洼洼的地面,虽然开始只倒了第一筐,如果我不停止并取得进步,我最终可以完成它。”(09.19)

【英译】

The Master said,“(The noble character is cultivated by oneself.) Like building a mound with soil, when it is to be accomplished with one basketful of soil, if I do not want to continue it, it stops and all my previous efforts are nullified. Also like leveling a rough surface with soil, though it starts with the first basket to tip, if I do not stop it, I make progress on it and can finally complete it.” (09.19)

往:我(向目标)前进了,功虽未多,积少成多。

子曰:“苟正其身矣,于从政乎何有?不能正其身,如正人何?”(13.13)

【注释】苟:如果。正:端正。其身:自身。于:对于。从政:做官、治国。何有:有什么困难,这是当时的常用语。如:对于。人:别人。何:如何。如正人何:如何端正别人。

【白话译文】

孔子说:“如果一个人能够端正他自己,那么他治理好一个国家还有什么困难?如果一个人不能端正他自己,那么他如何能够端正别人呢?”(13.13)

【英译】

The Master said, "If one can rectify oneself, how can it be difficult for him to administer a state well? If one cannot rectify himself, how can he rectify others?" (13.13)

子曰:"不患人之不己知,患其不能也。"(14.32)

【注释】患:忧虑。人:别人。己知:知道自己。人之不己知:别人不知道自己。其:自己。能:有本事。

【白话译文】

孔子说:"别人不知道我,我并不着急,但我着急的是,我没有才能。"(14.32)

【英译】

The Master said, "I am not anxious about that I am not known by others, but I am anxious that I do not have the talent." (14.32)

子路问君子。子曰:"修己以敬。"曰:"如斯而已乎?"曰:"修己以安人。"曰:"如斯而已乎?"曰:"修己以安百姓。修己以安百姓,尧舜其犹病诸!"(14.44)

【注释】子路:姓仲,名由,字子路。问:请教。修己:修养自己。以:按照。敬:恭敬。修己以敬:以恭敬谦虚的态度,提高自己的修养。如:像。斯:这样。如斯而已乎:像这样就够了吗。安:安定快乐。人:周围的人,有的注释为官吏、上层人物。修己以安人:以让周围的人安定快乐为尺度,进行修身。修己以安百姓:以广大民众安

【白话译文】

子路问一个人如何能够成为君子。孔子说:"修养自己的品德,严肃认真地工作。"子路问:"这样就可以了吗?"孔子说:"修养自己的品德,给官员提供一个稳定幸福的生活。"子路问:"这样就可以了吗?"孔子说:"修养自己的品德,给老百姓提供一个稳定幸福的生活。就修养自己的品德给老百姓提供一个稳定幸福生活这一点,大概尧、舜筋疲力尽,还不能完全做到!"(14.44)

居乐业为目标,进行修身。尧舜:尧帝、舜帝。其:大概。犹:还。病:筋疲力尽。诸:这一点。

【英译】

Zilu[(1)] asked how one could become a superior man. The Master said, "Cultivate one's morals, work solemnly and carefully." Zilu asked, "Is this all good enough?" The Master said, "Cultivate one's morals to bring a stable and happy life to officials." "Is this all good enough?" asked Zilu. The Master said, "Cultivate one's morals to bring a stable and happy life to the common people. Regarding this point that one cultivates his morals to bring a stable and happy life to the common people, probably Yao[(2)] and Shun[(3)] had exhausted themselves and still could not fully complete it." (14.44)

【英译注】(1) Zilu: Surname Zhong, first name You, style name Zilu, Confucius's disciple. (2) Yao: The ancient Chinese legendary saintly emperor, name Fangxun, serving as the chieftain of Taotang's Tribe. He united many tribes, and was good for hydraulic work and agriculture development. (3) Shun: The ancient Chinese legendary saintly emperor, serving as the chieftain of Yu's Tribe, and successor of Emperor Yao. As he once lived at Mt. Chong (at north of Mt. Song currently of Henan Province), his style name was Chong Bo.

七
Seven

君君臣臣
Emperor and Officialdom

35

天子 The Son of Heaven

三家者以《雍》彻。子曰:"'相维辟公,天子穆穆',奚取于三家之堂?"(03.02)

【白话译文】

三家在祭祀仪式结束时,唱着《雍》歌,撤走祭品。孔子说:"此歌有这样的词:'天子严肃庄重地主持祭祀仪式,各国诸侯来相助。'这样的词,怎么能够适用于三家的祖庙呢?"(03.02)

【英译】

The three families[(1)] sang Yong[(2)] when they cleared away the sacrifices to their ancestors at the end of prayer ceremony. The Master said, "This hymn has the words: 'The Son of Heaven solemnly and dignifiedly presides over the sacrificial rites with assistance of the dukes from all states.' How can these words be applicable for the three families' ancestral temple?" (03.02)

【注释】三家:孟孙氏、叔孙氏、季孙氏,皆鲁桓(音 huán 环)公的后代。者:代词,引出判断。以:用。《雍》:《诗经·周颂》一诗,雍意为"和睦"。彻:天子祭宗庙毕,撤去祭品时唱的诗。三家者以《雍》彻:三家撤祭品时使用《雍》诗。相:助祭者。维:是。辟(音 bì 闭)公:诸侯。天子:上天的儿子。穆穆:肃穆,盛美端庄。相维辟公,天子穆穆:诸侯助祭祀,天子肃穆端庄在中央主祭。奚:怎么(能)。取:采用。于:在。之:的。堂:庙堂。

【英译注】(1) three families: The Mengsun, the Shusun, and the Jisun, all the offsprings of Duke Huan, served as the senior officials of the State of Lu. (2) Yong: This is a song named as "The Emperor's Prayer to His Ancestors" in *The Second Decade of Hymns of Zhou* in *Poems and Odes*. It is said that King Wu of the Zhou Dynasty sang it when he presided over a sacrifice rite to his father King Wen.

孔子曰:"天下有道,则礼乐征伐自天子出;天下无道,则礼乐征伐自诸侯出。自诸侯出,盖十世希不失矣;自大夫出,五世希不失矣;陪臣执国命,三世希不失矣。天下有道,则政不在大夫。天下有道,则庶人不议。"(16.02)

【注释】有道:政治清明、政通人和。则:那么。征:出征。伐:讨伐。礼乐:礼乐(音 yuè 月)制度。自:由。天子:上天的儿子。出:决定。无道:政治黑暗。盖:大概。十世:十代。希:很少。失:丧失、垮台。矣:呀。盖十世希不失:政权大概传十代很少不垮台的。陪臣:卿、大夫的家臣。执:掌握。国命:国家命运。在:掌握、控制在。大夫:卿、大夫。政不在大夫:政权不由大夫掌握。庶人:百姓。议:议论。

【白话译文】

孔夫子说:"当公平正义的政治原则流行于天下,那么礼仪、礼乐及征伐的命令,均由天子颁布。当腐败不公的政治原则流行于天下,那么礼仪、礼乐及征伐的命令,均由诸侯颁布。如果这些由诸侯颁布,大概国家权力很难持续到第十代。如果这些由大夫颁布,这种国家权力很难持续到第五代。如果大臣的家臣把持一个国家的权力时,这种专权很难继续到第三代。当公平正义的政治原则流行于天下时,国家的最高权力不是由大夫控制的。如果公平正义的政治原则流行于天下,老百姓就不会对政府议论纷纷。"(16.02)

【英译】

Confucius said, "When just and fair political principles prevail under Heaven, the Son of Heaven promulgates the Rites of Proprieties, Ritual Music, and orders to go on a military expedition. When corrupt and unjust political principles prevail under Heaven, dukes promulgate the Rites of Proprieties, Ritual Music, and orders to go on an expedition. If a duke promulgates these, the state power probably can rarely be continued for ten generations. If a senior official promulgates these, the state power can rarely be continued for five generations. When the power of a state is monopolized by senior officials, the power can rarely be continued for three generations. When just and fair political principles prevail under Heaven, the supreme power of a state is not controlled by a senior official. The common people shall not talk about the government endlessly if just and fair political principles prevail under Heaven." (16.02)

36

帝 Emperor

子曰:“巍巍乎,舜、禹之有天下也,而不与焉。”(08.18)

【注释】巍巍:崇高。乎:啊。舜:舜帝。禹:姓姒(音 sì 四)名文命,夏朝创立者,治水有方。有:得到,获得帝位,舜、禹因功德受禅(音 shàn 善)让。与:参与,相关,

【白话译文】

孔子说："多么崇高啊，舜帝、禹帝！他们拥有天下大权，不由武力争取，而由禅让而来。他们贵为帝王，依然为天下人勤劳地工作，而不图私利和享乐。"(08.18)

舍私有、享乐之意。不与：因功德受禅让，不是武力夺取，大公无私，不以帝位而乐。

【英译】

The Master said, "Alas! How eminent and majestic the Emperor Shun(1) and Emperor Yu(2) are! They possessed power under Heaven not by scrambling militarily but accepted willingly abdication because of their morals and achievements. Although they were distinguished as emperors, they still worked industriously for all the people other than for their own private interest and pleasure." (08.18)

【英译注】(1) Shun: The ancient Chinese legendary saintly emperor, surname Gongsun allegedly, serving as the chieftain of Yu's Tribe, and the successor of Emperor Yao. As he once lived at Mt. Chong, currently north Mt. Song of Henan Province, his style name was Chong Bo. (2) Emperor Yu: Surname Si, first name Wenming, the earliest achievable person for flood prevention in China by regulating rivers and watercourses, also the creator of the Xia Dynasty.

舜有臣五人而天下治。武王曰："予有乱臣十人。"孔子曰："才难，不其然乎？唐虞之际，于斯为盛。有妇人焉，九人而已。三分天下有其二，以服事殷，周之德，其可谓至德也已夫！"(08.20)

【注释】舜：有虞氏部落首领，名重华，因居崇(今河南嵩山北)，号崇伯。五人：禹、稷、契(音 xiè 谢)、皋陶(音 yáo 姚)、伯益。治：太平。武王：周武王。予：我。乱臣：治乱、治国之臣。十人：九男，一女。才：人才。难：难得。其然：这样。乎：吗。唐：尧在位的时代。虞：舜在位的时代。际：期间。于：在。斯：此。盛：最为兴盛。妇人：文王之妻、武王之母，姓姒(音 sì 四)，有莘氏(今陕西合阳一带)之女，才貌双全。以：用以。服事：侍奉。殷：商朝。至：最高。

【白话译文】

舜帝用五位大臣，使得天下大治。武

王说:“我有十位贤臣治理各项事务。”孔夫子说:“获得人才很难啊,不是吗?就在唐尧帝、虞舜帝时代,此处人才济济,非常昌盛。周武王时期,有十位贤臣,其中有一位妇人,实际是九位男士贤才而已。在商朝晚期,周王拥有天下三分之二的土地,却向商朝帝王称臣。大约可以说,周文王、周武王的品德达到了最高境界了吧!”(08.20)

【英译】

Emperor Shun(1) used only five senior officials and brought great order across the land under Heaven. King Wu(2) said, "I have ten excellent senior officials for handling all administration affairs." Confucius said, "It is difficult to get personnel of ability, isn't it? It was in the eras of Tang Yao(3) and Yu Shun(4) that a galaxy of talents appeared here. At the time of King Wu of the Zhou Dynasty, there were ten excellent senior officials, among whom was a lady, so there were only nine excellent men. The King of Zhou occupied two thirds of the land under Heaven at the end of the Shang Dynasty, but still served as a subject of Emperor of the Shang Dynasty(5). It can probably be said that King Wen(6) and King Wu of the Zhou Dynasty reached the supreme realm of virtues." (08.20)

【英译注】(1) Emperor Shun: The ancient Chinese legendary saintly emperor, surname Gongsun allegedly, serving as the chieftain of Yu's Tribe, and the successor of Emperor Yao. As he once lived at Mt. Chong (at north of Mt. Song currently of Henan Province), his style name was Chong Bo. (2) King Wu: Surname Ji, first name Fa, the son of King Wen, the creator of the Zhou Dynasty. In 1027 BC, he launched military action against the last Emperor Zhou of the Shang Dynasty and exterminated it and established the Zhou Dynasty. (3) Yao: Yao is regarded as the ancient Chinese legendary saintly emperor, name Fangxun, serving as the chieftain of Taotang's Tribe. He united many tribes, good for hydraulic work and agriculture development. (4) Yu Shun: Emperor Shun. (5) the Shang Dynasty: A dynasty of China existing from about 1600 BC to 1027 BC. (6) King Wen: Surname Ji, first name Chang, the third son of Ji Li. He served as the King of the Zhou Tribe (currently at Shaanxi Province) for 50 years and laid a strong foundation to take over the Shang Dynasty by his son King Wu.

子曰:"禹,吾无间然矣。菲饮食而致孝乎鬼神,恶衣服而致美乎黻冕,卑宫室而尽力乎沟洫。禹,吾无间然矣!"(08.21)

【白话译文】

孔子说:"对于禹帝,我真是没有什么可挑剔的啊! 他享用着简单的饮食,却准备丰盛的祭祀品去拜他的祖先。他平时穿着次等的衣服,却在祖先祭祀仪式上穿戴华丽的服装和头冠。他居住在简陋的宫室里,而奉献毕生精力,防止水患、治理水路。对于禹帝,我真是没有什么可挑剔的啊!"(08.21)

【英译】

The Master said, "For Emperor Yu(1), I truly cannot find any fault with him! He enjoyed very simple drinks and foods, but prepared plentiful sacrifices to pray to his ancestors. He wore very humble clothes in daily life, but gorgeously dressed and richly ornamented his cap and clothes during ancestry sacrifice ceremonies. He dwelled in a crude palace, but devoted all his energies of a lifetime into flood prevention and regulation of rivers and watercourses. For Emperor Yu, I truly cannot find any fault with him!" (08.21)

【注释】禹:姓姒名文命,夏朝创立者,治水有方。间:空隙,挑剔。矣:了。吾无间然矣:我没有可挑剔的了。菲:菲薄,不丰厚。而:却,但。致:致力。乎:对。鬼:人死后的灵魂、逝去的祖先。神:神灵,或者天地万物的创造者。恶(音 è 鳄):不好。恶衣服:平时穿戴很不好。致美:华美。黻(音 fǔ 府):用于祭祀的礼服。冕(音 miǎn 免):用于祭祀的帽子。卑:低矮。宫室:宫殿。沟洫(音 xù 序):沟渠。

【英译注】(1) Emperor Yu: Surname Si, first name Wenming, the earliest achievable person for flood prevention in China by regulating rivers and watercourses, also the creator of the Xia Dynasty.

子曰:“如有王者,必世而后仁。”(13.12)

【白话译文】

孔子说:“假若有人能接受天命,成为新的帝王,统治这个国家,那么必须花费三十年时间,才会实行仁德的政务治理。”(13.12)

【英译】

The Master said, “If anyone accepts the heavenly mandates to become a new emperor and rule over this country, it must take him thirty years before superior benevolence will prevail in his government administrations.” (13.12)

【注释】如:如果。有:兴起。王者:受天命而成天下王的人。必:一定。世:30年。而后:之后。仁:使仁政大行其道。

南宫适问于孔子曰:“羿善射,奡荡舟,俱不得其死然。禹、稷躬稼,而有天下。”夫子不答。南宫适出,子曰:“君子哉若人!尚德哉若人!”(14.06)

【白话译文】

南宫适向孔夫子请教说:“羿非常会射箭,奡善于打水战,但二人均死于非命。禹帝、稷,亲身作为农夫耕种庄稼,都获得

【注释】南宫适:姓南宫名适(音 kuò 扩),字子容。羿(音 yì 意):夏代有穷国国君,夺夏太康位,被其臣寒浞(音 zhuó 茁)杀。善:擅长。射:射箭。奡(音 ào 奥):寒浞的儿子,力大,善水战,为夏少康所杀。荡舟:擅长水战。俱:都。其死:其自然寿命。然:的样子。禹:夏朝开国君。稷:周朝祖先,谷神。躬:亲自。稼:种植庄稼。有天下:得到天下。夫子:孔子。出:离开。若人:这个人。尚:尊重。德:道德。哉:啊。

了天下。”孔夫子没有回答他。南宫适离开后，孔夫子说：“此人，好一个君子啊！此人，多么崇尚道德啊！”(14.06)

【英译】

Seeking advice from Confucius, Nangong Kuo(1) said, "Yi(2) was adept in archery, and Ao(3) was good at fighting on the water, but both did not die natural deaths. Emperors Yu(4) and Ji(5) toiled themselves as farmhands and won all the country under Heaven." Confucius did not answer him. After Nangong Kuo left, Confucius said, "What a superior man he is! What a man upholding morals he is!" (14.06)

【英译注】(1) Nangong Kuo: Surname Nangong, first name Kuo, style name Zirong, Confucius's disciple. (2) Yi: A famous arrow shooter in the Xia Dynasty. He overthrew the Xia Dynasty, seized the power of Tai Kang. He loved to hunt, was not good at administration and was killed when he was hunting. (3) Ao: Good at fighting by boats, killed because he was not good at ruling the state. His father was Han Zuo, the Chieftain of Dongyi Tribe who usurped the power of the Xia Dynasty from Emperor Yi for 28 years. (4) Emperor Yu: The creator of the Xia Dynasty and the earliest flood preventer and regulator of rivers and watercourses in China. (5) Ji: Allegedly a senior official of Emperor Xuan Yuan in charge of agriculture, currently regarded as God of Crops, the ancestor of the Zhou Dynasty.

子张曰：“《书》云：‘高宗谅阴，三年不言。’何谓也？”子曰：“何必高宗，古之人皆然。君薨，百官总己以听于冢宰三年。”(14.42)

【注释】子张：姓颛(音 zhuān 砖)孙名师，字子张。《书》：《尚书》。云：说。高宗：商高宗武丁，商王小乙之子，开疆拓土，在位的59年是商朝强盛期，任用傅说大治，其妻妇好为战功赫赫的领兵良将。谅阴：天子守丧。不言：不谈政事。何必：怎么一定。然：这样。薨(音 hōng 轰)：诸侯死叫薨，天

【白话译文】

子张问："《尚书》讲：'高宗帝守孝，住在悼念室，三年不轻易谈政务。'这是什么意思？"孔子说："何止高宗帝？古代，每位帝王继承人都如此。老帝王去世三年内，百官各司其职，听从宰相的命令。"(14.42)

子、帝王死叫崩。总：料理、掌握。己：自己的政事。总己：总摄（音shè设）己职，掌握自己的政事。以：而，并且，连词。听：听命。冢宰：宰相。三年：君王死的三年内。

【英译】

Zizhang[(1)] asked, "*Book of History*[(2)] said, 'Emperor Gaozong[(3)] observed filial piety, stayed at a mourning hut and did not lightly speak on governmental affairs for three years.' What does it mean?" The Master said, "How could only Emperor Gaozong do this? Every new emperor successor did so in ancient times. All the officials attended their own duties, and listened to orders of the prime minister for three years after the old emperor passed away." (14.42)

【英译注】(1) Zizhang: Surname Zhuansun, first name Shi, style name Zizhang, Confucius's disciple. (2) *Book of History*: It is a collection of some governmental affairs of the Xia, Shang, Zhou dynasties. (3) Emperor Gaozong: Surname Zi, first name Wuding, ruled the Shang Dynasty for about 59 years and many times defeated the tribes around him, fully strengthening his power.

子曰："无为而治者，其舜也与？夫何为哉？恭己正，南面而已矣。"(15.05)

【注释】无为：仁政德政，顺其自然，不用刑罚。而：却。治：太平。其：大概。舜：舜帝。也与：吧。夫：他。何为：做了什么。恭己正：用认真、恭敬的态度要求自己，端正自己的行为。南面：面南而坐。而已矣：罢了。

【白话译文】

孔子说："如果有谁不做任何违反自然的事，能够把国家治理得无限的好，那么这个人大概就是舜帝吧？那么他做了什么呢？他用正直严肃的态度约束自己并端正自己的行为，因此他不用做任何违反自然的事，面向南正坐在帝家宝位上，就可以让国家大治。”（15.05）

【英译】

The Master said, "If there is one emperor who rules the country perfectly by doing nothing against nature, is he probably the Emperor Shun(1)? And then what did he do? He restrained himself and rectified his behaviours by righteous and serious attitudes, so he could bring the country great order by doing nothing against nature, simply sitting facing south on the throne." (15.05)

【英译注】(1) Emperor Shun: The ancient Chinese legendary saintly emperor, surname Gongsun allegedly, serving as the chieftain of the Yu's Tribe, and the successor of Emperor Yao. As he once lived at Mt. Chong (at north of Mt. Song currently of Henan Province), his style name was Chong Bo.

颜渊问为邦。子曰：“行夏之时，乘殷之辂，服周之冕，乐则《韶》《舞》。放郑声，远佞人。郑声淫，佞人殆。”（15.11）

【注释】颜渊：姓颜名回，字子渊。为：治理。邦：国家。行：用。夏：夏代。之：的。夏之时：夏代历法，益于农业生产。乘：乘坐。殷：商代。辂（音 lù 路）：天子所乘的车，木制，朴实。服：戴。周：周代。冕：帽子。服周之冕：奉行周朝的礼制，含冕冠等。乐（音 yuè 月）：乐曲乐舞。韶舞：舜时的舞乐。舞：同“武”，武王时的音乐。放：禁绝、抛弃。郑声：郑国乐曲。远：远离。佞：花言巧语、善辩。淫：浮靡不正派。殆：危险、搬弄是非。

【白话译文】

颜渊问如何治理一个国家。孔子说：“实行夏朝的历法（有敬天的意思），乘坐商朝的车子（预示遵循商朝的形制），戴上周朝的礼帽（暗示沿袭周朝的礼仪），礼乐采用舜时的《韶》乐、周武王的《舞》乐。抛弃郑国的乐曲，斥退溜须拍马的人。郑国的乐曲是淫秽的，溜须拍马的人是危险

的。”(15.11)

【英译】

Yan Yuan[1] asked how to govern a state. The Master said, “Carry out the calendar of the Xia Dynasty (which means respecting Heaven), ride in carriage of the Shang Dynasty (suggesting that shape and structure of the Shang Dynasty are followed), wear the caps of the Zhou Dynasty (hinting that the Rites of Proprieties of the Zhou Dynasty are carried on), and perform the Shao Music[2] of Emperor Shun and the Wu Music of King Wu of the Zhou Dynasty for ritual music and dance. Discard the music of the State of Zheng and dismiss sycophants from their posts. The music of the State of Zheng is voluptuous and sycophants are dangerous.” (15.11)

【英译注】(1) Yan Yuan: Surname Yan, first name Hui, style name Ziyuan, Confucius's disciple. (2) Shao Music: Music of the ancient Chinese legendary saintly Emperor Shun.

子曰:“知及之,仁不能守之,虽得之,必失之。知及之,仁能守之,不庄以莅之,则民不敬。知及之,仁能守之,庄以莅之,动之不以礼,未善也。”(15.33)

【注释】知(音 zhì 治):智慧。及:取得。之:国家、百姓、职位等,不明孔子所指。守:保持。仁不能守之:不用仁德保持它。必:一定。失:丢掉。庄:严肃态度。莅(音 lì 利):临,对待。则:那么。民:百姓。敬:诚服敬重。动:言行教化。不以礼:不按礼节。善:完美。

【白话译文】

孔子说:“如果用智慧得到了它,而不用仁德守住它,即使得到了它,也一定会失去它。如果用智慧得到了它,且用仁德守住了它,但是不庄重地对待它,人们也不会敬重它。如果用智慧得到了它,用仁德守住了它,也庄重地对待了它,但是动员百姓不符合礼节,那么也是不完善的。”(15.33)

【英译】

The Master said, “If it[(1)] is obtained by wisdom but is not kept by superior benevolence, it will be lost even though it has been already obtained. If it is obtained by wisdom and kept by superior benevolence, but is not treated solemnly, the people will not respect it. If it is obtained by wisdom, kept by superior benevolence, and treated solemnly, but the common people are not mobzlized in compliance with the Rites of Proprieties, it is not perfect.” (15.33)

【英译注】(1) it: It's not clear what the “it” here indicates according to Confucius. It can possibly be explained as the power of a country, the people, a position, wealth and so on.

周公谓鲁公曰:“君子不施其亲,不使大臣怨乎不以。故旧无大故,则不弃也。无求备于一人。”(18.10)

【白话译文】

周公对其儿子鲁国国君说:“君子不要无正当理由给自己的亲戚加官进爵,不要让大臣抱怨没有被任用。如果老臣和旧

【注释】(周公不是帝王,但功德高于诸侯,不亚于帝王,故将此章分类为“帝”。)周公:姓姬名旦,文王子,武王弟,成王叔父,鲁国国君的始祖,传说西周典章制度制定者。鲁公:周公之子伯禽,封于鲁。施:一解“施”(音 chí 迟),弛,怠慢、疏远;二解“施”(音 shī 诗),给予、加官晋爵。亲:亲属。怨:抱怨。不施其亲:一解“不疏远亲戚”;二解“不要无故给亲戚封官”。不以:不任用。故旧:旧友老

友没有犯大错，不要抛弃、贬谪他们。对于任何人，不要求全责备。”(18.10)

臣。大故：大错。弃：抛弃、废弃。求备：求全责备。于：对。

【英译】

Duke Zhou[(1)] addressed his son, the Duke of the State of Lu[(2)]: “A superior man does not promote his own relatives to a position of high rank without a proper reason, and does not make the senior officials complain that they are not being appointed. Do not forsake old friends and relegate old senior officials if they do not make big mistakes. Do not fault-find and demand perfection from anyone.” (18.10)

【英译注】(1) Duke Zhou: Surname Ji, first name Dan, the son of King Wen, and younger brother of King Wu, and uncle of King Cheng, and the ancestor of Dukes of the State of Lu, who allegedly established the rites and laws of the Zhou Dynasty. He was not an emperor, but had equal achievements of an emperor. (2) Duke of the State of Lu: The son of Duke Zhou, first name Boqin, assigned a fief state at the State of Lu, currently in Shandong Province.

子贡曰：“纣之不善，不如是之甚也。是以君子恶居下流，天下之恶皆归焉。”(19.20)

【注释】子贡：姓端木名赐，字子贡。纣：商代亡国之君，暴君，名辛，谥(音 shì 是)号纣，约公元前 1060 年至公元前 1027 年在位，但经略华夏东南方，客观上传播了中原先进文化，有功于中华民族的形成。不善：不好。如：像。是：这样。甚：厉害。是以：所以。恶(音 wù 务)：憎恶。居：处。下流：地形低洼处。恶(音 è 饿)：坏名声。皆：都。归：聚集(此处)。焉：呀，语气词。

【白话译文】

子贡说：“帝王纣，不像传说的那样，是那么极其邪恶。因此，一位君子厌恶自己处于道德的下游。一旦他处于道德的下游，天下所有的坏名声都会落到他的头上。”(19.20)

【英译】

Zigong[(1)] said, “The Emperor Zou[(2)] was not as extremely wicked as it was said a

【英译注】(1) Zigong: Surname Duanmu, first name Ci, style name Zigong, Confucius’s disciple. (2)

bout him. Therefore a superior man hates himself for dwelling at the low reaches of morality. For if he dwells at the low reaches of morality, he will find that he has fallen among all the bad reputations in the world. " (19.20)

Emperor Zou: Surname Zi, first name Xin, a tyrant, last emperor of the Shang Dynasty, staying in power from 1060 BC to 1027 BC when he burned himself under attack of King Wu of the Zhou Dynasty.

尧[(1)]曰:"咨!尔舜!天之历数在尔躬,允执其中。四海困穷,天禄永终。"

舜亦[(2)]以命禹。

【注释】(1)尧:陶唐氏部落首领,名放勋。咨(音 zī 资):好啊。尔:你。舜:有虞氏部落首领,名重华,圣帝。天:上天。之:的。历:排列。数:序数。躬:本身。允:诚实。执:坚持。其:这。中:正确、中正。四海:四方、天下。困穷:困顿贫穷。天禄:上天禄位。终:终止。

(2)亦:也。以:用来。命:告诫。禹:姓姒名文命,夏朝创立者,治水有方。

【白话译文】

尧帝对舜说:"啊!你舜呀!上天的使命已经赋予了你。你一定要按正直的原则公平地执行它。如果四海之内的人民有难且贫穷,你的上天禄位将永远终止。"

舜帝(禅让给禹时)向禹帝也说了类似的话。

【英译】

Emperor Yao[(1)] abdicating his throne to Shun[(2)] said, "Oh! you Shun! The great mission of Heaven has been entrusted to you. You must carry it out fairly based on righteous principles. If people within the four seas suffer from difficulty and poverty, your official position from Heaven will be terminated forever. "

【英译注】(1) Emperor Yao: Yao is regarded as the ancient Chinese legendary saintly emperor, named Fangxun, serving as the chieftain of Taotang's Tribe, and uniting many tribes, good for hydraulic work and agriculture development. (2) Shun: The ancient Chinese legendary saintly emperor, surname Gongsun allegedly, served as the chieftain of Yu's Tribe, and the successor of Emperor Yao. As he once lived at

Emperor Shun also admonished the similar to Emperor Yu(3) (when he abdicated his throne).

Mt. Chong (at north of Mt. Song currently of Henan Province), his style name was Chong Bo. (3) Emperor Yu: Creator of the Xia Dynasty and the earliest flood preventer and regulator of rivers and watercourses in China.

曰:“予小子履,敢用玄牡,敢昭告于皇皇后帝:有罪不敢赦。帝臣不蔽,简在帝心。朕躬有罪,无以万方,万方有罪,罪在朕躬。”

周有大赉,善人是富。“虽有周亲,不如仁人。百姓有过,在予一人。”

【注释】曰:(商汤)说。予:我。履(音 lǚ 吕):商汤的名字。敢:胆敢。玄:黑色。牡:公牛。昭告:祷告。于:向。皇皇:辉煌。后帝:天帝。有罪:犯了罪的人。敢:擅自。赦:赦免。帝臣:天帝的臣仆。蔽:掩盖。不蔽:不掩盖、文饰。简:明白。帝心:天帝内心。朕:我。无以:不要连累。万方:天下。朕躬:我一人。

周:周朝。有:举行。赉(音 lài 赖):赏赐。周有大赉:周朝大封诸侯。善人:善良人。是富:富贵。周亲:至亲。过:错。在予:在我。

【白话译文】

(商朝的汤帝)说:“我小子履,谨用黑公牛做祭品,胆敢毫不含糊地向光明而伟大的天帝坦白:有罪的人,我不敢擅自赦免。作为你的臣仆,我不敢隐瞒我的罪恶和过错,我的所作所为你都清晰地知晓在心里。如果我本人有罪,不要因为我连累天下的百姓。如果各地的百姓有罪,我一个人代表他们接受所有的惩罚。”

周朝大方地给王子和开国功臣分封诸侯,因此很多品德优秀的人都非常富足并有权势。周武王说:“虽然我有非常亲的亲戚，但是我不聘用他们而聘用具有仁德的人。如果百姓犯了罪、犯有错，为此我请求对我进行惩罚。”

【英译】

(Emperor Tang(1) of Shang Dynasty) said, "I, Li(2), a small boy, sincerely use a black bull as a sacrifice and dare unequivocally to confess to you the brilliant and great Emperor of Heaven: A criminal cannot be presumptuously pardoned by me. As your servant, I cannot conceal my sins and faults to you, and all my actions are clearly perceived by you in your heart. If I am sinful myself, please do not bring troubles upon the common people under Heaven because of me. If the common people commit crimes and faults, the guilt is mine alone."

The Zhou Dynasty(3) generously granted hereditary territories and titles of dukes to their princes and those who contributed greatly to founding the Dynasty and thus many people of excellent merits became wealthy and powerful. King Wu(4) said, "Even though I have many close relatives, I would rather not employ them and instead employ the people of superior benevolence. If the common people create crimes and faults, I demand to be punished for them."

【英译注】(1) Emperor Tang: Surname Zi, first name Li, also name Tianyi, Dayi, Chengtang, also Shang Tang, extinguished the Xia Dynasty around 1600 BC and created the Shang Dynasty and ruled for 13 years. (2) Li: First name of Emperor Tang. (3) The Zhou Dynasty: Referred to the first Emperor King Wu of the Zhou Dynasty, who overthrew the Shang Dynasty in 1027 BC. (4) King Wu: Surname Ji, first name Fa, the son of King Wen, the creator of the Zhou Dynasty. In 1027 BC, he launched military action against the last Emperor Zhou of the Shang Dynasty and exterminated it and established the Zhou Dynasty.

谨权量,审法度,修废官,四方之政行焉。兴灭国,继绝世,举逸民,天下之民归心焉。

所重:民、食、丧、祭。宽则得众,信则民任焉,敏则有功,公则说。(20.01)

【白话译文】

谨慎地确定重量和容量,精确地检查长度的测量,让度量衡标准化,恢复被废弃的行政机关,政令就可以畅通无阻地到达各个地方。恢复被消灭了的国家,接续被断绝的世系,提拔上一个朝代幸存者中贤良的人,天下所有的人都会到来并同心同德地追随我们。

如下是被重视的:人民、粮食、丧礼、祭祀仪式。如果你宽厚,你就会得到大众的支持;如果你诚信,你就会被百姓信任;如果你勤奋并且敏锐,你就会取得伟大的成就;如果你公正,你就会被人们完全心悦诚服地接受。(20.01)

【英译】

Carefully determine weights and capacity and precisely examine the measurement of length so as to standardize the system of weights and measures. Restore the administrative departments that were abandoned before, therefore administrative decrees can reach

【注释】谨:认真检查。权:秤锤。量:斗斛。权量:度量衡器。审:周密地审定。法度:礼乐制度。修:修整、恢复。废:弃置。官:官署、衙门。修废官:恢复被废弃的机关工作。四方:东南西北。政:政令。行:通行。四方之政行焉:全国的政令就通行了。兴:恢复。灭国:被灭的国。继:接续。绝世:断绝了的家族。举:提拔。逸民:被遗落的人才,逸民者,节行超逸也。归心:真心归服。

重:重视。民:百姓。食:粮食。丧:丧礼。祭:祭祀。宽:宽厚。得众:受众人拥护。信:诚信。任:任用。敏:勤敏。功:成绩。公:公平。说(音 yuè 月):悦,愉快。

all the places without obstruction. Recover the states that were extinguished, continue the genealogy that was broken, and promote moral and talented persons from those survivors of previous dynasties, therefore the people under Heaven will come and submit to us heart and soul.

Below are things that should be emphasized: the common people, grains, funeral rites, and sacrificial ceremonies. If you are sincere, you can get support from the masses; if you are faithful, you can be trusted by the common people; if you are industrious and sensitive, you can acquire great achievements; and if you are fair, you will be fully accepted happily by the people. (20. 01)

37

君 A Duke

子曰:"夷狄之有君,不如诸夏之亡也。"(03. 05)

【注释】夷:东方部族。狄:北方部族。夷狄:周边地区不开化民族,贬称。君:国君。有君:执行君主的礼仪制度。不如:不像。诸夏:华夏、中国。亡(音 wú 吴):无、不。不如诸夏之亡也:哪像华夏有君主礼仪制度,却无人履行。

【白话译文】

子曰:"甚至在东部和北部的野蛮部落却能执行君主礼仪制度,不像中央之国

的中国有君主礼仪制度却没有人执行。”(03.05)

【英译】

The Master said, “The rude tribes in the east and north still carry out the ritual system of a sovereign, unlike that China, the so-called Central Kingdom, has the ritual system of a sovereign but no one follows it.” (03.05)

定公问:“君使臣,臣事君,如之何?”孔子对曰:“君使臣以礼,臣事君以忠。”(03.19)

【注释】定公:鲁国君,姓姬名宋,谥(音 shì 是)号定,公元前 509 年至公元前 495 年在位。使:使唤。事:侍奉。如之何:(应该)怎么做。对曰:敬答。以:用。忠:尽心竭力,不背叛。

【白话译文】

定公问:“君主如何任用臣子?臣子如何侍奉君主?”孔夫子敬答:“君主应当按礼节任用臣子,而臣子应当全心全意、忠诚地侍奉君主。”(03.19)

【英译】

Duke Ding[(1)] asked, “How should a sovereign employ officials, and how should the officials attend upon the sovereign?” Confucius replied respectfully, “A sovereign should employ his officials according to the Rites of Proprieties, and the officials should

【英译注】(1) Duke Ding: A sovereign of the State of Lu, ruling from 509 BC to 495 BC, surname Ji, first name Song, posthumous title Ding.

attend upon the sovereign faithfully heart and soul."(03.19)

哀公问社于宰我。宰我对曰:"夏后氏以松,殷人以柏,周人以栗,曰:'使民战栗。'"子闻之曰:"成事不说,遂事不谏,既往不咎。"(03.21)

【注释】哀公:姓姬名蒋,谥号哀,鲁国国君,公元前494年至公元前468年在位。社:土地神,指做牌位的木头或庙里种的树。宰我:名予,字子我。对曰:敬答。夏后氏:夏朝人。以:用。松:松树。殷:商代。柏:柏树。周:周代。栗:栗子树。战栗:发抖。使民战栗:让百姓怕得发抖。成:完成的。说(音shuō):评说、陈述、责备。遂:结束的。谏:规劝。既:已经。往:过去。咎:责备、追究。

【白话译文】

哀公问宰我,土地坛的神主牌位应当用什么木头。宰我敬答:"夏朝人用松木,商朝人用柏木,周朝人用栗子树木,说:'栗子树木的意思是,让百姓害怕得战栗。'"孔子听说这话,说:"不要详细解释已经完成的事。不要补救已经了结的事。不要谴责过去已经发生的事。"(03.21)

【英译】

Duke Ai(1) asked Zai Wo(2) what wood should be used for the spirit tablet in the altar praying the god of earth. Zai Wo replied respectfully, "The people of the Xia Dynasty applied pine, the people of the Shang Dynasty applied cypress and the Zhou Dynasty applied chestnut(3), saying 'The meaning of chestnut may make the common people tremble with fear'." Hearing this, the Master said, "Do not

【英译注】(1) Duke Ai: A Duke of the State of Lu, surname Ji, first name Jiang, posthumous title Ai, ruling from 494 BC to 468 BC. He talked with Confucius on this in 484 BC after Confucius returned to the State of Lu. (2) Zai Wo: Surname Zai, first name Yu, style name Ziwo, Confucius's disciple. (3) chestnut: The pronunciation of the character for "chestnut" in Chinese is similar to that for "trembling with fear".

expound on what has been done already. Do not remedy what has been finished. And do not condemn what happened in the past."(03.21)

齐景公问政于孔子。孔子对曰:"君君,臣臣,父父,子子。"公曰:"善哉!信如君不君,臣不臣,父不父,子不子,虽有粟,吾得而食诸?"(12.11)

【注释】鲁昭公二十六年(公元前516年),36岁的孔子到齐国,答齐景公问。齐景公:姓姜名杵臼(音chǔ楚jiù旧),齐国国君,公元前547年至公元前490年在位。问:请教。政:治国。于:向。对曰:敬答。君君:国君做得像国君。臣臣:臣有臣的德。父父:父像父。子子:子像子。善哉:(讲得)好呀。信如:如果。粟:粮食。吾:我。得而食诸:能吃得上吗。

【白话译文】

齐景公向孔夫子请教政治。孔夫子敬答:"国君做国君应当做的,臣做臣应当做的,父亲做父亲应当做的,儿子做儿子应当做的。"齐景公说:"哎呀,太妙了!假如国君不做国君应当做的,臣不做臣应当做的,父亲不做父亲应当做的,儿子不做儿子应当做的,即使有再多的粮食,我怎么能够吃得到呢?"(12.11)

【英译】

Duke Jing(1) of the State of Qi asked Confucius advice about politics. Confucius replied respectfully,"A sovereign be a sovereign, an official be an official, a father be a father, and a son be a son." Duke Jing said, "Alas, Great! If a sovereign not be a sovereign, an official not be an official, a father not

【英译注】(1) Duke Jing: Surname Jiang, first name Chujiu, the Duke of the State of Qi from 547 BC to 490 BC.

be a father, and a son not be a son, even though there is plenty of food to eat, how can I be sure I will be able to eat?" (12.11)

子曰:"晋文公谲而不正,齐桓公正而不谲。"(14.16)

【白话译文】

孔子说:"晋文公诡诈而不正派,齐桓公正派却不诡诈。"(14.16)

【英译】

The Master said, "Duke Wen (1) of the State of Jin was cunning and not righteous and Duke Huan of the State of Qi was righteous and not cunning." (14.16)

【注释】晋文公:姓姬名重耳,春秋霸主,公元前636年至公元前628年在位。谲(音jué决):欺诈、玩弄阴谋。正:正派。齐桓(音huán环)公:姓姜名小白,春秋霸主,公元前685年至公元前643年在位。

【英译注】(1) Duke Wen: Surname Ji, first name Chong-er, the sovereign of the State of Jin (697 BC – 628 BC), one powerful chief of the five princes of the Spring and Autumn Period (770 BC – 476 BC). (2) Duke Huan: Surname Jiang, first name Xiaobai, the sovereign of the State of Qi (685 BC to 643 BC), great leader and reformer, one powerful chief of the five princes of the Spring and Autumn Period (770 BC – 476 BC).

子言卫灵公之无道也,康子曰:"夫如是,奚而不丧?"孔子曰:"仲叔圉治宾客,祝鮀治宗庙,王孙贾治军旅。夫如是,奚其丧?"(14.20)

【注释】言:讲到。卫灵公:姓姬名元,卫国君,公元前536年至公元前493年在位,不善政,宠爱南子。之:的。无道:昏庸、不守礼法。康子:季康子,姓季孙名肥,谥(音shì是)号康,鲁哀公时任正卿。夫:句首语气词。如是:如此。

【白话译文】

孔夫子谈到卫灵公昏庸无能的行为。康子问："既然如此，为什么他还没有让卫国灭亡呢？"孔夫子说："他有仲叔圉处理外交事务，祝鮀负责祖庙祭祀，王孙贾负责军事。既然如此，他怎么能够让卫国灭亡呢？"（14.20）

夫如是：既然这样。奚：为何。丧：灭亡。仲叔圉：孔圉（音 yǔ 雨），卫灵公大夫，谥号文，称孔文子。治宾客：接待宾客。祝鮀（音 tuó 驼）：字子鱼，卫国大夫。治宗庙：管祭祀。王孙贾（音 jiǎ 钾）：姓王孙，名贾，卫灵公的大夫。治军旅：统率军队。

【英译】

Confucius commented on the fatuous and incompetent behaviours of Duke Ling(1) of the State of Wei. Master Kang said, "Now that he was so, why didn't he make the State of Wei be extinguished?" Confucius said, "He had Zhong Shuyu(2) in charge of foreign diplomats, Zhu Tuo(3) in charge of sacrifices at his ancestry temple and Wangsun Jia(4) in charge of military affairs. Since he was in that condition, how could he make the State of Wei be extinguished?" (14.20)

【英译注】(1) Duke Ling: Surname Ji, first name Yuan, sovereign of the State of Wei (536 BC – 493 BC), did not observe the rites of proprieties, not good at ruling of the state. (2) Zhong Shuyu: A Senior official of the State of Wei for Duke Ling. (3) Zhu Tuo: A Senior official of the State of Wei for Duke Ling. (4) Wangsun Jia: Surnane Wangsun, first name Jia, a senior officer in charge of troops of Duke Ling.

陈成子弑简公。孔子沐浴而朝，告于哀公曰："陈恒弑其君，请讨之。"公曰："告夫三子！"孔子曰："以吾从大夫之后，不敢不告也。君曰：'告夫三子者。'"之三子告，不可。孔子曰："以吾从大夫之后，不敢

【注释】陈成子：陈恒，谥号成，"子"是敬称，齐国大夫，又叫田成子，笼络人心，于齐简公四年、鲁哀十四年（公元前 481 年），孔子 71 岁时，弑齐简公篡权，孔子弟子宰予死于此难。弑（音 shì 事）：杀地位高的人。简公：齐简公，姓姜名壬，公元前 484 年至公元前 481 年在位。朝：上朝。告：报告，请示。哀公：姓姬名蒋，谥号哀，鲁国国君，公元前 494 年至公元前 468

不告也。"(14. 22)

年在位。讨:讨伐。三子:季孙、孟孙、叔孙三家。之:前往。三子告:向三子请示。不敢不告也:不敢不向朝廷(而非向三子)报告啊。不可:不同意。以:因为。从大夫之后:曾任大夫。

【白话译文】

陈成子弑齐国的简公。孔夫子沐浴后上朝,把此事报告给哀公说:"陈恒弑他的国君,我乞求你讨伐他。"哀公说:"报告给那三位大臣吧!"孔夫子说:"因为我曾经当过大臣,发生大事,不敢不向朝廷报告。国君说:'报告给那三位大臣吧。'"孔夫子相应地把此事报告给三位大臣,他们拒绝讨伐。孔夫子说:"因为我曾经当过大臣,发生大事,不敢不向朝廷报告。"(14. 22)

【英译】

Master Chen Cheng(1) murdered his sovereign Duke Jian(2) of the State of Qi. After Confucius washed his hair and bathed himself, he went to court and reported it to Duke Ai(3), saying, "Chen Heng(4) has murdered his sovereign. I beg you to send a punitive expedition against him." Duke Ai said, "Report this to the three senior officials(5)!" Confucius said, "Because I once was a senior official, I cannot but report this important matter to the court. The Sovereign said, 'Report this to the three senior officials!'" Confucius accordingly reported this matter to the three senior officials and they refused the punitive expedition. Confucius said, "Because I once was a senior official, I cannot but report this important matter to the court." (14. 22)

【英译注】(1) Master Chen Cheng: Surname Chen, first name Heng, posthumous title Cheng, also called Master Tian Cheng, who usurped the throne of the State of Qi by killing Duke Jian in 481 BC. (2) Duke Jian: Surname Jiang, first name Ren, posthumous title Jian, a Duke of the State of Qi (484 BC – 481 BC) until he was murdered. (3) Duke Ai: Surname Ji, first name Jiang, the Duke of the State of Lu (494 BC – 468 BC), posthumous title Ai. (4) Chen Heng: The name of Master Chen Cheng. (5) three senior officials: The senior officials from Jisun, Mengsun, and Shusun, all of real rulers of the State of Lu under Duke Ai.

孔子曰:“禄之去公室,五世矣。政逮于大夫,四世矣。故夫三桓之子孙,微矣。”(16.03)

【注释】禄:爵禄(政权)。之:的。去:离失。公室:鲁国国君、朝廷。五世:鲁宣公、鲁成公、鲁襄公、鲁昭公、鲁定公。逮(音dài袋):落到、及。四世:季孙氏文子、武子、平子、桓子。故:所以。夫:句首感叹词。三桓(音huán环):鲁桓公子孙,仲孙(后改其氏称孟氏)、叔孙、季孙。微:衰微。

【白话译文】

孔夫子说:“鲁国官员的俸禄,已经五代不直接由鲁国诸侯发放了。国家的统治权,已经四代落入大臣的手中了。因此,桓公的三家子孙,变得极其弱了。”(16.03)

【英译】

Confucius said, “The salaries for officials of the State of Lu have not been paid out directly by the Dukes(1) for five generations. The ruling power of the state has fallen into the hands of the senior officials(2) for four generations. Therefore the sons and grandsons of the three families of Duke Huan(3) have become extremely feeble.” (16.03)

【英译注】(1) the Dukes: Duke Xuan, Duke Cheng, Duke Xiang, Duke Zhao, and Duke Ding of the State of Lu all lost the control of state power. (2) senior officials: Jisun Wenzi, Wuzi, Pingzi and Huanzi, grasped the ruling power of the State of Lu generation by generation. (3) Duke Huan: Surname Ji, first name Yun, the Duke of the State of Lu from 712 BC to 694 BC. When drunk, he was killed by his wife's brother Duke Xiang of the State of Qi.

38

臣 An Official

季康子问:"使民敬、忠以劝,如之何?"子曰:"临之以庄则敬,孝慈则忠,举善而教不能则劝。"(02.20)

【白话译文】

季康子问:"如何让百姓对我真诚敬重,做事忠心耿耿、自觉服从政府命令?"孔子说:"如果你对待百姓的事庄重,他们就会真诚敬重你。如果你鼓励孝敬父母并倡导慈爱幼童,他们就会忠心耿耿。如果你提拔他们中优秀的并且教育能力差的,他们就会自觉服从政令。"(02.20)

【英译】

Master Ji Kang(1) asked, "What should I do so that the common people respect me truly, work loyally heart and soul, and obey governmental orders conscientiously?" The Master said, "They will respect you truly if you treat their matters solemnly. They will work loyally heart and soul if you encourage filial piety to parents and advocate charities to the young. And they will obey governmental

【注释】季康子:姓季孙名肥,谥(音 shì 是)号康,鲁哀公时任正卿,有权势。民:百姓。敬:尊敬。忠:忠诚。以:而且。劝:努力、勤劳。如之何:如何办。临:对待。之:他们。以:用。庄:庄重。则:那么。慈:对民和善。举:选用。善:善良者。教:教育。不能:能力差者。

【英译注】(1) Master Ji Kang: Surname Jisun, first name Fei, posthumous title Kang, the prime minister during Duke Ai of the State of Lu.

orders conscientiously if you promote their excellent ones to high positions and educate the incapable ones." (02.20)

子曰:"事君尽礼,人以为谄也。"(03.18)

【注释】事:侍奉。君:国君。尽:全部用出。人:别人。以为:认为。谄(音 chǎn 产):巴结。

【白话译文】

孔子说:"如果官员完全按照官员的礼节服侍君主,有人就会认为他在巴结君主。"(03.18)

【英译】

The Master said, "If an official attends upon his sovereign completely according to the Rites of Proprieties, someone will think that he curries favour with the sovereign." (03.18)

子曰:"管仲之器小哉!"或曰:"管仲俭乎?"曰:"管氏有三归,官事不摄。焉得俭?""然则管仲知礼乎?"曰:"邦君树塞门,管氏亦树塞门。邦君为两君之好,有反坫,管氏亦有反坫。管氏而知礼,孰不知礼?"(03.22)

【注释】管仲:姓管名夷吾,齐桓公的宰相。器小:肚量小。哉:啊。或:有人。俭:节俭。管氏:管仲。归:返回,女子出嫁。三归:一解"市租之常例之归之管仲,家财丰厚";二解"娶三个姓氏的女子",此处取一解。摄(音 shè 设):兼任、代理、辅助。不摄:专职。焉:怎么。然则:那么、然而。邦君:国君。树:树立。塞门:照壁、屏风墙。为两君之好:与别国国君修好。反坫(音 diàn 店):放置献过酒的空杯子的土台。孰：谁。

【白话译文】

孔子说："管仲的器量小得很啊!"有人说："管仲不是很节俭吗?"孔子说："管仲收市场的税,用以增加他个人丰厚的资产。他手下的管家,一人一职,从不身兼数职。他怎么能够被认为是节俭呢?"那人又说："然而,管仲遵守礼节吧?"孔子说："他的邦君在宫内建了一个照壁墙,管仲在家里也建了照壁墙。他的邦君为了增强与另外一邦的友好关系,在此邦君来访时举行欢迎宴会,为此,他在宫殿两楹柱之间修建放置酒杯的土桌。相应地,管仲在他家里也修建这种土桌。如果认为管仲遵守礼节,那么谁还不遵守礼节呢?"(03.22)

【英译】

The Master said, "How narrow-minded indeed Guan Zhong(1) was!" Someone said, "Guan Zhong was thrifty, wasn't he?" The Master said, "Guan Zhong levied taxes from the markets to increase his plentiful wealth and properties. For the managers at his home, each one took care of only one duty and never took two or more duties concurrently. How could he be considered to be thrifty?" The person said further, "Did Guan Zhong, however, observe the Rites of Proprieties?" The Master said, "His sovereign set up a screen wall inside the palace, and he did the same at home. The sovereign built up

【英译注】(1) Guan Zhong: Surname Guan, first name Yiwu, style name Zhong, the premier of Duke Huan of the State of Qi. He died in 645 BC.

a soil platform between two pillars in the palace to put liquor cups for a greeting banquet to welcome a visiting sovereign of another state for a good relationship between the two states. Accordingly Guan Zhong built up the same platform at home. If Guan Zhong can be regarded as one observing the Rites of Proprieties, who does not observe them?" (03. 22)

子曰:"晏平仲善与人交,久而敬之。"

【注释】晏平仲:晏婴,字仲,齐国贤大夫,谥号平,留传《晏子春秋》。善:擅长。与:同。交:交往。久而敬之:交往越久越敬重他。

【白话译文】

孔子说:"晏平仲擅长与别人交朋友。一个人与他交往越久,对他越尊重。"(05. 17)

【英译】

The Master said, "Yan Pingzhong[1] was good at making friends with others. The longer one associated with him, the more respectful one was to him. "(05. 17)

【英译注】(1) Yan Pingzhong: Surname Yan, first name Ying, style name Pingzhong, posthumous name Ping, a moral and intelligent premier (556 BC to 500 BC) of the State of Qi. He died in 500 BC.

子曰:"臧文仲居蔡,山节藻棁,何如其知也?"(05. 18)

【注释】臧文仲:姓臧孙名辰,谥(音 shì 是)号文,鲁国大夫正卿,历仕鲁庄公、鲁闵公、鲁僖公、鲁文公四君,曾废除关卡,以利通商。居:提供住所给……。蔡:蔡

【白话译文】

孔子说："臧文仲将名为'蔡'用于占卜的乌龟保护在一座豪华的大房子里。房子上，他使用的是帝王祖庙的山梁和屋顶结构，梁上画着山形图案，美丽的屋顶上绘着藻草植物。这种做法，他怎么能够是明智的呢？"(05.18)

国（今河南省新蔡、上蔡）产的大龟（壳），国君用以占卜；蔡国处淮河上游，气候适宜，产龟，故称大龟为蔡。居蔡：盖房子供奉大龟（壳）。山：山形。节：斗拱。藻：雕成水草花纹。棁（音 zhuō 桌）：房梁的短柱。山节藻棁：天子庙堂的结构。何如：如何，怎么样。其：他。知（音 zhì 治）：智，智慧。何如其知也：他怎么明智呢。

【英译】

The Master said, "Zang Wenzhong(1) built a gorgeous grand house to protect a large tortoise named Cai for divination, and made beams and ceiling structure of the house just like that of an emperor's ancestral temple, where patterns of mountains were carved on the beams and duckweed plants were painted on the beautiful ceiling. So, how could he be known as a wise man?" (05.18)

【英译注】(1) Zang Wenzhong: Surname Zangsun, first name Chen, an important chief senior official of the State of Lu, posthumous title Wen. He took some measures to promote state economy.

子曰："宁武子，邦有道，则知，邦无道，则愚。其知可及也，其愚不可及也。"(05.21)

【注释】宁武子：姓宁名俞，卫国大夫，谥号武。邦：国家。有道：政治清明。则：就，那么。知（音 zhì 治）：智，智慧。无道：政治黑暗。愚：装傻。及：做得到。不可及：做不到。

【白话译文】

孔子说："当一个国家公平的政治原则流行时，宁武子则表现得聪明。当一个国家不公平的政治原则流行时，他表现得

愚笨。他的这种聪明,别人是可以赶上的,而他这种愚笨是别人无法赶上的。”(05.21)

【英译注】(1) Master Ning Wu: Surname Ning, first name Yu, a senior official of the State of Wei, posthumous title Wu.

【英译】

The Master said, "Master Ning Wu[1] acted as wise when just and fair political principles prevailed in a state. He acted as if he were stupid when corrupt and unjust political principles prevailed in a state. His such wisdom can be equaled by others, but his such stupidity cannot." (05.21)

子曰:“为命,裨谌草创之,世叔讨论之,行人子羽修饰之,东里子产润色之。”(14.09)

【注释】为:发布,完成。命:一般为外交辞令,非政令,见《左传·襄公三十一年》。裨谌(音 bì 闭 chén 臣):郑国大夫。草:起草。创:首创。之:它。世叔:子太叔,名游吉,郑国大夫。讨:探求、审查。论:研究。行人:官名,掌管朝觐聘问,即外交事务。子羽:郑国大夫公孙挥的字。东里:地名,子产居住地,今河南省郑州市。子产:姓公孙名侨,字子产,郑国贤相,郑穆公之孙。润色:修辞美化。

【白话译文】

孔子说:“郑国编写外交事务的文件时,裨谌先起草它,世叔研究并精心推敲它,作为外交事务官的子羽修改并美化它,最后住在东里的子产润色并完成它。”(14.09)

【英译注】(1) Bi Chen: A senior official of the State of Zheng, currently located at Zhengzhou, Henan Province. (2) Shi Shu: Zi Taishu, first name Youji, a senior official of the State of Zheng. (3) Ziyu: Gongsun Hui, style name Ziyu, a diplomat

【英译】

The Master said, "When a diplomatic document was prepared in the State of Zheng, Bi Chen[1] first drafted it, Shi Shu[2] studied and meticulously improved it,

Ziyu[3], the senior foreign affair official, embellished it, and Zichan[4], who was living at Dongli[5], polished and completed it." (14.09)

of the State of Zheng. (4) Zichan: Surname Gongsun, first name Qiao, style name Zichan, the chief senior official of the State of Zheng, a grandson of Duke Zheng Mu. (5) Dongli: A place name, located at eastern capital of the State of Zheng, currently at Zhengzhou City, Henan Province.

或问子产。子曰:"惠人也。"问子西。曰:"彼哉彼哉。"问管仲。曰:"人也。夺伯氏骈邑三百,饭疏食,没齿,无怨言。"(14.10)

【注释】或:有人。问:询问。子产:姓公孙名侨,字子产,郑国贤相,郑穆公之孙。惠人:施人恩惠者。子西:多人叫子西,此处推测是楚国昭王的令尹(宰相),姓熊名申,字子西,楚平王之子,用人(白公胜)不当而国乱身死。彼哉:他呀,暗含鄙视,不值得评价。管仲:姓管名夷吾,齐桓公的宰相。人也:人才呀。夺:取走。伯氏:齐国大夫。骈(音 pián 蹁)邑:地名,伯氏的采邑。三百:300 家。饭疏食:(使得伯氏)吃粗粮。没齿:终身。无怨言:(伯氏知自己的罪,心服管仲)没怨言。

【白话译文】

有人问孔子,子产是一个什么样的人。孔子说:"他是一个宽厚慈善的人。"被问到子西是什么人,孔子说:"他呀!他呀!"被问到管仲,孔子说:"他是个人才啊。他剥夺了伯氏的三百户的骈邑,尽管伯氏因此只能吃粗粮,而他到死没有怨言。"(14.10)

【英译】

Someone asked Confucius what a figure Zichan[1] was. The Master said, "He was a generous and benevolent person." When asked what Zixi[2] was, the Master said,

【英译注】(1) Zichan: Surname Gongsun, first name Qiao, style name Zichan, the chief senior official of the State of Zheng, a grandson of Duke Zheng Mu. (2) Zixi: One of the three namesakes was possibly the premier

"Oh, he! Oh, he!" When asked about Guan Zhong(3), the Master said, "He was a person of talents. He deprived Bo Shi(4) of his heritable fief of 300 households at Pianyi(5), but Bo Shi until his death did not express a word of complaint though he therefore took coarse foods only." (14.10)

of Duke Zhao of the State of Chu, surname Xiong, first name Shen, style name Zixi. He wrongly appointed an official and resulted in a rebellion and his own death. (3) Guan Zhong: Surname Guan, first name Yiwu, style name Zhong, the premier of Duke Huan of the State of Qi. (4) Bo Shi: A senior official of the State of Qi. Bo was his surname and his first name was unknown. (5) Pianyi: A place of the State of Qi, currently located at Liushan Zhai, Linju County, Shandong Province allegedly.

子曰:"孟公绰为赵、魏老则优,不可以为滕、薛大夫。"(14.12)

【注释】孟公绰(音 chuò 辍):鲁国大夫,属于孟孙氏家族,《左传·襄公二十五年》记载有他。赵魏:晋国的诸卿,赵氏、魏氏。老:大夫的家臣。则:还。优:(才能)有余。不可以:不能。滕:诸侯国,今山东滕县。薛:诸侯国,今山东滕县东南。

【白话译文】

孔子说:"孟公绰作晋国大夫赵、魏的家臣,他的才能是富富有余的,但他的才能却不足以做滕国或薛国的大夫。"(14.12)

【英译】

The Master said, "Meng Gongchuo(1) is talented enough to be chief household manager of the Zhao(2) and the Wei(3), the senior officials of the State of Jin, but his talent is not good enough to be the senior official of either the State of Teng(4) or the State of

【英译注】(1) Meng Gongchuo: Surname Mengsun, first name Chuo, a senior official of the State of Lu. (2) the Zhao: A senior official of the State of Jin. (3) the Wei: A senior official of the State of Jin. (4) Teng: A small state close to the State of Lu, currently located at 7.5 kilometers southwest from Tengxian Coun

Xue[5]." (14.12)

ty, Shandong Province. (5) Xue: A small state close to the State of Lu, currently located at Guanqiao Town of Tengxian County, 22 kilometers south from Tengxian County, Shandong Province.

子曰:"臧武仲以防求为后于鲁,虽曰不要君,吾不信也。"(14.15)

【注释】臧武仲:臧孙纥(音gē哥),鲁国大夫。以:凭借。防:防邑。求:请求(鲁国君)。为后:立他儿子为大夫。于:在。鲁:鲁国。虽曰:虽有人说。要(音yāo腰):要挟。不要君:(他)不是要挟国君。信:相信。

【白话译文】

孔子说:"臧武仲凭借他在防邑的优势,请求他的国君封他的后代为鲁国的大夫。虽有人说,他没有威胁国君这么做,但是我是不相信的。"(14.15)

【英译】

The Master said, "Zang Wuzhong[1] requested his sovereign to appoint his offspring to be senior officials of the State of Lu because of his dominant position in the City of Fang[2]. Though someone said that he did not force his sovereign to do so, I do not believe it." (14.15)

【英译注】(1) Zang Wuzhong: Zang Sunge, posthumously titled Wuzhong, a senior official of the State of Lu and fled to the State of Qi in 550 BC. (2) the City of Fang: The fief land of Zang Wuzhong, close to the boundary of the State of Qi, currently at Huacheng, 30 kilometers north of Feixian County, Shandong Province.

子路曰:"桓公杀公子纠,召忽死之,管仲不死。"曰:"未仁

【注释】子路:姓仲,名由,字子路。桓(音huán环)公:齐桓公,姓姜名小白,春秋霸主,公元前685年至公元前643年在位。公子

乎?"子曰:"桓公九合诸侯,不以兵车,管仲之力也。如其仁,如其仁。"(14.17)

纠:齐桓公之兄,争位失败,借鲁攻齐又败,在鲁被杀。召忽:公子纠的老师,与管仲同为公子纠的家臣。死之:为公子纠自杀殉死。管仲:姓管名夷吾,齐桓公的宰相。曰:问。未仁:不仁。九:九次或很多次。合诸侯:召集诸侯盟会。以:用。兵车:武力。之:的。力:力量、能力。如:如同,相当。其:他的。如其仁:如同他有仁德。

【白话译文】

子路说:"桓公杀死他的哥哥公子纠,召忽因对公子纠的失败而感到耻辱而自杀,但是管仲却不为他的主人而死。"他又说:"管仲没有仁德吗?"孔子说:"桓公九次召集各国诸侯进行联盟,为此各国停止了相互之间的战争,这是管仲的功劳啊。因此,这如同于他具有仁德!这如同于他具有仁德!"(14.17)

【英译】

Zilu(1) said, "Duke Huan(2) of the State of Qi killed his elder brother Prince Jiu(3), and Zhao Hu(4) committed suicide for the shame he felt for his master Prince Jiu's failure, but Guan Zhong(5) on the contrary did not die for his master." He said further, "Wasn't Guan Zhong benevolent?" The Master said, "Duke Huan nine times(6) gathered the dukes of many states together for alliances and thus stopped the wars against each other, and it was to the credit of Guan Zhong. Therefore this is like that he had such superior benevolence! This is like that he had such superior benevolence!" (14.17)

【英译注】(1) Zilu: Surname Zhong, first name You, style name Zilu, Confucius's disciple. (2) Duke Huan: Surname Jiang, first name Xiaobai, the Duke of the State of Qi ruling from 685 BC to 643 BC, one of the five leaders of alliances in the times of Spring and Autumn Period (770 BC – 476 BC). (3) Prince Jiu: Duke Huan's elder brother, with Guan Zhong and Zhao Hu to serve him when he fled to the State of Lu. He failed in rivalry for the throne with his younger brother Duke Huan and was defeated and killed by his younger brother. (4) Zhao Hu: Prince Jiu's chief household manager, and his colleague was Guan Zong. He killed himself in a shame he felt for his master. (5) Guan Zhong: Surname

Guan, first name Yiwu, the premier of Duke Huan of the State of Qi, originally the chief household manager of Prince Jiu. (6) nine times: Many times, not limited to nine, meaning numerous.

子贡曰:"管仲非仁者与?桓公杀公子纠,不能死,又相之。"子曰:"管仲相桓公,霸诸侯,一匡天下,民到于今受其赐。微管仲,吾其被发左衽矣。岂若匹夫匹妇之为谅也,自经于沟渎而莫之知也。"(14.18)

【白话译文】

子贡说:"管仲不是一个仁德的人吧?当齐桓公杀死公子纠时,管仲不仅没有为他主人的失败而死,反而又辅佐他主人的对手,成为宰相。"孔子说:"管仲为宰相,辅助桓公成为所有诸侯的领袖,匡正了天下的一切事物。人民甚至今天还享受着他的恩赐。没有管仲,我大概要披头散发,穿着野蛮民族左边开衽的衣服呀。难道他要像普通贫贱的丈夫妻子那样,为了小信小节吊死在河、沟边上,而没有人知道吗?"(14.18)

【注释】子贡:姓端木名赐,字子贡。管仲:姓管名夷吾,齐桓公的宰相。桓(音 huán 环)公:齐桓公,姓姜名小白,春秋霸主,公元前685年至公元前643年在位。公子纠:齐桓公之兄,争位失败,借鲁攻齐又败,在鲁被杀。死:向公子纠殉死。相:任宰相。霸:称霸。匡:匡正。民:百姓。受:得到。赐:恩赐、好处。微:无,没有。被(音 pī 批):披,散离。左衽:左开衣襟。被发左衽:夷狄之俗。岂:怎么。若:如。匹夫匹妇:平民夫妻,古代士大夫有多位妾(音 qiè 窃,非正妻)媵(音 yìng 映,随嫁者),平民贫贱,仅夫妇相匹配而已,故称匹夫匹妇。为:从事。谅:遵守小信用,小节小信。自经:上吊自杀。沟:水沟。渎(音 dú 独):小渠。莫:没人。之知:知之,知道他们。

【英译】

Zigong[1] said, "Wasn't Guan Zhong[2] a person of superior benevolence? When Duke Huan[3] killed Prince Jiu[4], Guan Zhong not only did not commit suicide for his master's failure, but he also served as the prime minister of his master's rival Duke Huan." The Master said, "Guan Zhong as prime minister assisted Duke Huan to become the leader of all the dukes of the states, and thus rectified all the things under Heaven. The people have been enjoying his kindness and grace even today. Without Guan Zhong I might possibly have become like the rude minorities, with disheveled hair and clothes opened on the left. Would he rather be like a poor and humble husband or wife who, because of a trifling matter, would hang themselves by a river without anyone knowing?" (14.18)

【英译注】(1) Zigong: Surname Duanmu, first name Ci, style name Zigong, Confucius's disciple. (2) Guan Zhong: Surname Guan, first name Yiwu, the premier of Duke Huan of the State of Qi, originally the chief household manager of Prince Jiu. (3) Duke Huan: Surname Jiang, first name Xiaobai, the Duke of the State of Qi ruling from 685 BC to 643 BC, one of the five leaders of alliances in the times of Spring and Autumn Period (770 BC – 476 BC). (4) Prince Jiu: Duke Huan's elder brother, with Guan Zhong and Zhao Hu to serve him when he fled to the State of Lu. He failed in rivalry for the throne with his younger brother Duke Huan and was defeated and killed by his younger brother.

公叔文子之臣大夫僎,与文子同升诸公。子闻之曰:"可以为文矣。"(14.19)

【注释】公叔文子:姓公孙,名拔,卫国大夫,卫献公之孙,谥号文;子为敬称。之:的。臣:家臣。僎(音 xún 勋):公叔文子的家臣。文子:公叔文子(举荐了僎)。同:一同。升:提拔为。诸公:大夫、公一级的高官。为文:给他"文"的谥号。

【白话译文】

公叔文子推荐了大夫僎,此时僎是他的家臣。僎因此被提拔为与他的主人具有相同职位的大夫级别。孔子听到此事说:

“(通过他的行为)公叔文子获得他的谥号‘文’当之无愧。”(14.19)

【英译】

When Master Gongshu Wen[1] hired Xun[2] as his family manager, he recommended him to be promoted to a senior official of the same rank as himself. Hearing of this, the Master said, “Master Gongshu Wen deserved his posthumous title of Wen[3] (by his conduct)!” (14.19)

【英译注】(1) Master Gongshu Wen: Surname Gongsun, first name Ba, style name Gongshu, a senior official of the State of Wei, a grandson of Duke Xian of the State of Wei. Zi was a title of respect. (2) Xun: A family manager of Master Gongshu Wen. (3) Wen: It means civil or civilization, literary talent, as compared to Chinese character “Wu” i. e. military officer or military.

子路问事君。子曰:“勿欺也,而犯之。”(14.23)

【注释】子路:姓仲,名由,字子路。问:请教。事:侍奉。君:国君。勿:不要。欺:欺骗。而:但是。犯:可以犯颜直谏。

【白话译文】

子路问一个人如何侍奉他的国君。孔子说:“他绝不能阳奉阴违地欺骗国君,(但是当坦率提建议时)可以当面冒犯他。”(14.23)

【英译】

Zilu[1] asked how one should serve his sovereign. The Master said, “Never cheat his sovereign by the way of agreeing with him overtly but opposing him covertly, but one may risk offending him (by offering frank advice to him) in person.” (14.23)

【英译注】(1) Zilu: Surname Zhong, first name You, style name Zilu, Confucius's disciple.

子曰："事君，敬其事而后其食。"(15.38)

【白话译文】

孔子说："侍奉国君，一个人把全心全意、恭敬地完成他的职责，放在优先的位置，然后考虑他俸禄的事。"(15.38)

【英译】

The Master said, "To serve his sovereign, one places his first priority on how to reverently discharge his duties heart and soul. Afterwards he considers his official salary." (15.38)

【注释】事君：侍奉国君。敬：尽力。其：自己的。事：事情。而后：然后，放在后面。食：食禄，俸禄。敬其事而后其食：先恭敬地做好自己的事，后考虑俸禄。

39

士 A Scholar

曾子曰："士不可以不弘毅，任重而道远。仁以为己任，不亦重乎？死而后已，不亦远乎？"(08.07)

【白话译文】

曾子说："学者既不可以不刚强，也不

【注释】曾子：姓曾名参(音 shēn 申)，字子舆，鲁国南武城人。士：读书人，学者，有某种品质、技能的人，或低等贵族。弘：大，刚强，心胸宽广；章太炎(炳麟)称，弘，弓声，后人借"强"为之，用为"弓彊"义，即今天的"强"字；有注者认为，"弘"为发扬、光大、扩大。毅：坚定，意志刚强。任：责任。重：重大。乎：吗。道：道路。远：

可以不果决，因为他肩负着重任，而且前面的道路很遥远。他将实现仁德作为自己的责任，这不沉重吗？他至死才停止下来，这不遥远吗？”（08.07）

遥远。以：用、当。为：作。亦：也。死而后已：到死才停下。

【英译】

Master Zeng[(1)] said, “A scholar[(2)] cannot but be firm and resolute, because he shoulders a heavy burden, and the road is long. To attain superior benevolence is his own responsibility. Isn’t that a heavy burden? He will not stop until his death. Isn’t it indeed a long road?” (08.07)

【英译注】（1）Master Zeng: Surname Zeng, first name Shen, style name Ziyu, Confucius’s disciple. (2) A scholar: It is not necessarily only referred to a scholar. It could also be a lower rank of nobility, a superior man or a person with certain special qualities or skills subject to different situations. It is generally translated as a scholar here.

子张问：“士何如斯可谓之达矣。”子曰：“何哉，尔所谓达者？”子张对曰：“在邦必闻，在家必闻。”子曰：“是闻也，非达也。夫达也者，质直而好义，察言而观色，虑以下人。在邦必达，在家必达。夫闻也者，色取仁而行违，居之不疑。在邦必闻，在家必闻。”（12.20）

【注释】子张：姓颛（音 zhuān 砖）孙名师，字子张。何如：怎么样。斯：那么，就。谓：叫作。达：通达。所谓：所称作的。对曰：敬答。邦：诸侯国。必：一定。闻：有名望。家：卿大夫统治地。质：品质。直：正直。察言：善于揣摩别人的话。观：细看。色：脸色表情。虑：着想。以：用以，用来。下：谦恭有礼，位置低于自己者。虑以下人：想到的是对人谦让，站在职位比自己低的人的位置上考虑问题。夫闻也者：所谓闻名。色取仁：外表上装仁。行：行动。违：违背（仁）。居之不疑：以仁人自居而不惭愧。

【白话译文】

子张问：“一位学者如何做，他才能称得上成功呀？”孔子说：“你所说的成功，是什么意思？”子张敬答：“他在诸侯国做官、在大臣的封地做官,都很出名。”孔子说:“这是出名,不是成功。成功的人是什么样呢?他必须具有正直的品质,热爱正义,透过别人说的话理解他们的思想,从表情中识别他们的意思,站在他下属的位置上思考事情。这样的人在诸侯国做官,或者在大臣的封地做官,都必然会成功。所谓出名的人是什么样呢?他表面喜欢仁德,行动上违背仁德,但他自己深信不疑地以仁人自居。这样的人在诸侯国做官,或者在大臣的封地做官,都必然会求名。”(12.20)

【英译】

Zizhang[(1)] asked, "What can a scholar do so that he can be called successful?" The Master said, "What do you mean by being successful?" Zizhang replied respectfully, "He must be well-known when he serves as an official either at the state of a duke or at the fief of a senior official." The Master said, "It is fame other than success. What is it for a person to be successful? He possesses upright qualities, loves righteousness, understands others' thoughts from their words, discerns their thoughts by the expressions on their faces, and thinks of things at the standpoints of his inferiors. This person must succeed when he serves as an official either at the state of his duke or at the fief of a senior official. What is it for a person who pursues

【英译注】(1) Zizhang: Surname Zhuansun, first name Shi, style name Zizhang, Confucius's disciple.

fame? He likes superior benevolence superficially, but behaves contrary to it, and he still poses as a person of superior benevolence. He must pursue fame either at the state of a duke or at the fief of a senior official." (12.20)

子贡问曰:"何如斯可谓之士矣?"子曰:"行己有耻,使于四方,不辱君命,可谓士矣。"曰:"敢问其次。"曰:"宗族称孝焉,乡党称弟焉。"曰:"敢问其次。"曰:"言必信,行必果,硁硁然小人哉!抑亦可以为次矣。"曰:"今之从政者何如?"子曰:"噫!斗筲之人,何足算也。"(13.20)

【白话译文】

子贡问道:"一个人如何做,才能称得上是一个学者呢?"孔子说:"一个人通过保持一颗羞耻的心来约束他的行为,作为国君的使者出使国外,不会让国君交给他的使命落空,这样他就可以称为学者了。"子贡又问:"我冒昧地请教,次一等称得上学者的是什么人?"孔子说:"次一等的是,一个人在宗族中能够被赞扬孝敬父母,在邻里间,能够被赞扬尊敬兄长。"子贡再问:"我冒昧请教,再次一等的是什么人?"

【注释】子贡:姓端木名赐,字子贡。问:请教。何如:怎么。斯:才,就。谓:叫作。之:这、此人。行:做事。己:自己。耻:知耻心。使:出使。四方:外国。辱:玷辱、辜负。君:国君。命:使命。矣:了。敢:冒昧。次:次一等的。宗族:本族的人。称:称赞(他)。孝:孝敬父母。乡党:家乡人。弟(音 tì 替):悌,顺从、尊敬兄长。言:说话。信:守信。果:果断;结果。硁(音 kēng 坑):敲击石头声,喻如石之硬,浅薄固执己见。然:的样子。哉:啊。言必信,行必果,硁硁然小人哉:说话一定守信,办事一定果断(只求贯彻自己言行,不问是非曲直),这不过是浅薄固执己见的小人物罢了。抑:可是。从政者:执政者。噫:唉。筲(音 shāo 烧):竹器,容 5 升,0.5 斗。斗筲之人:按部就班,如同用斗筲称粮者、才识短浅的人。算:算是、算作(学者)、算得了什么。

孔子说："再次一等的，是那些言必信，行必果，说话如石头碰石头，掷地有声的人，虽然他是肤浅、固执的小人物。"子贡最后问："对当今从政的人，您怎么看待？"孔子说："唉！他们仅仅按部就班，如同每天用斗、用筲称量粮食，他们怎么算得上是学者呢？"（13.20）

【英译】

Zigong[(1)] asked, "What does a person do so that he can deserve the title of a scholar?" The Master said, "One can deserve the title of a scholar if he restrains his behaviour by having a sense of shame, and does not fail to accomplish the mission of his sovereign when he is dispatched as an envoy to other states." Zigong said further, "May I venture to ask who is next deserving the title of a scholar?" The Master said, "Next is the one who is praised by his family for his filial piety, and by his fellow villagers for his respectful attitude toward his older brothers." He asked further, "Then who is next?" The Master said, "Next is the one who keeps his words true as the sound of a stone striking another stone, and who must produce observable results, although he may be a shallow and stubborn inferior person." Zigong finally asked, "What do you think about government workers today?" The Master said, "Alas! They are merely bureaucrats, spending

【英译注】(1) Zigong: Surname Duanmu, first name Ci, style name Zigong, Confucius's disciple. (2) liter: Liter is used to represent "Shao", the Chinese weight unit for grains. Shao was made of bamboo, and its volume was 0.5 decaliters.

their days like measuring out grains by the peck and by the liter[(2)]. How could they be considered to be scholars?" (13.20)

子路问曰:"何如斯可谓之士矣?"子曰:"切切、偲偲、怡怡如也,可谓士矣。朋友切切偲偲,兄弟怡怡。"(13.28)

【注释】子路:姓仲,名由,字子路。何如:怎么样。斯:那么,就。谓:叫作。之:这、此人。切(音 qiè 窃)切:恳切、诚恳、深切。偲(音 sī 私)偲:互相督促,相互批评,相互勉励。怡(音 yí 姨)怡:和气、顺从。如也:……的样子。朋友切切偲偲:朋友之间,相互诚恳批评。兄弟怡怡:兄弟和睦相处。

【白话译文】

子路问:"一个人如何做,可以称作学者呀?"孔子说:"他能够真诚地相互勉励、相互批评,以便自我完善,并且能够和睦相处,就可以称为学者了。朋友之间,真诚勉励并相互批评,而兄弟之间,和睦相处。"(13.28)

【英译】

Zilu asked, "What can a person do so that he can be called a scholar?" The Master said, "He can be called a scholar if he can faithfully encourage and constructively criticize each other for self-improvement, and can get along harmoniously with one another. For friends, he faithfully encourages and constructively criticizes each other, while for brothers, he gets along harmoniously with one another." (13.28)

【英译注】(1) Zilu: Surname Zhong, first name You, style name Zilu, Confucius's disciple.

子曰:“士而怀居,不足以为士矣。”(14.03)

【注释】而:若,如果。怀:思念,留恋。居:家居、安逸生活。不足:不够、不配。

【白话译文】

孔子说:“如果一位学者贪图休闲舒适的生活,他就不配这个学者的称号了。”(14.03)

【英译】

The Master said, “A scholar does not deserve the title of a scholar if he seeks a life of leisure and comfort.” (14.03)

周有八士:伯达、伯适、仲突、仲忽、叔夜、叔夏、季随、季騧。(18.11)

【注释】周:周代。八士:八位贤人,其生平都不详,有的说是周宣王或周成王时,一母八同胞,皆名士。适:音 kuò 扩。騧:音 guā 瓜。

【白话译文】

周朝有以下八位名士:伯达、伯适、仲突、仲忽、叔夜、叔夏、季随、季騧。(18.11)

【英译】

There were these eight scholars in the Zhou Dynasty: Boda, Bokuo, Zhongtu, Zhonghu, Shuye, Shuxia, Jisui, and Jigua(1). (18.11)

【英译注】(1) The biographies of these eight people are unknown now. It is guessed that they were celebrities of the Zhou Dynasty during King Cheng (ruling circa 1030 BC) or King Xuan (ruling from 828 BC to 782 BC).

子张曰："士见危致命，见得思义，祭思敬，丧思哀，其可已矣。"(19.01)

【注释】子张：姓颛(音 zhuān 砖)孙名师，字子张。见：遇到。危：危险。致命：献出生命。得：利益。思：想到。祭：祭祀。敬：恭敬。丧：居丧。哀：哀伤。其：这样。可：可以。已矣：完成、结束了。

【白话译文】

子张说："一位学者，见到重大公共利益面临危险，他能够挺身而出，献出自己的生命。当金钱摆在他的面前，他能够思考这是否符合正义。在祭神、祭祖时，他思考严肃和尊敬。在服丧期间，他思考哀痛。这样，他就可以是一位合格的学者了。"(19.01)

【英译】

Zizhang(1) said, "A scholar can stand up and dedicate his life when important public interests are in danger. When he is presented with gold, he thinks of what is right. In offering sacrifices to gods or ancestors, he thinks of respect and solemnity. And during the mourning period for the deceased, he thinks of grief and deep sorrow. Thus, he can be qualified as a scholar. (19.01)

【英译注】(1) Zizhang: Surname Zhuansun, first name Shi, style name Zizhang, Confucius's disciple.

八
Eight

分工
Occupations

40

仕 Officialdom

子使漆雕开仕。对曰:“吾斯之,未能信。”子说。(05.06)

【白话译文】

孔子让漆雕开去当官。他敬答:“如果现在我去当官,我的能力和品德还不足以赢得人们的信任。”听到这,孔子很高兴。(05.06)

【英译】

The Master let Qidiao Kai[1] become an official. He replied respectfully, “If I become an official now, my capacity and my moral character is not good enough to win the trust of the people.” The Master was delighted upon hearing it. (05.06)

【注释】使:让。仕:做官。漆雕开:姓漆雕名开,字子开,一说字子若。对曰:敬答。斯:句中语气词。之:此事,到任从政。信:取信于民。吾斯之,未能信:我呀此时去从政,(品德、修养、能力等还不够)不足以得到百姓的信任。说(音 yuè 月):悦,愉快。

【英译注】(1) Qidiao Kai: Surname Qidiao, first name Kai, style name Zikai or Ziruo, Confucius's disciple.

子曰:“雍也可使南面。”(06.01)

【白话译文】

孔子说:“啊,雍!他可以面南而坐,

【注释】雍:姓冉,名雍,字仲弓。使:让他。南面:做大官,面南而坐,类似公、卿、大夫等。

做一位高级官员。”（06.01）

【英译】

The Master said, “Alas, Yong[1]! He may become a high rank official sitting with face to the south.” (06.01)

【英译注】(1) Yong: Surname Ran, first name Yong, style name Zhonggong, Confucius's disciple.

子谓仲弓曰：“犁牛之子骍且角，虽欲勿用，山川其舍诸？”（06.06）

【注释】仲弓：姓冉，名雍，字仲弓。犁牛：耕牛。之：的。子：犊。犁牛之子：古人祭祀不用耕牛及其犊，因为出身地位低。骍（音xīng星）：赤，红色，周朝以红色为贵。角：牛角端正。骍且角：红毛、牛角正，适合用来祭祀，以此比喻仲弓虽出身差，但人品好，应任为高官。虽：虽然。欲：想。勿：不。用：祭祀用。山：山神。川：河，河神。其：岂、难道。舍：舍弃。诸：之乎，它吗。

【白话译文】

孔子评论仲弓说：“耕牛的犊子，长着红色的毛和端正的角。虽然人不想把它用于祭祀，山神河神如何能够舍弃它呢？”（06.06）

【英译】

The Master spoke of Zhonggong[1], “If the bull calf of an ox used for plowing[2] grows with red coat and developed horns, though men would not want it to be used in a sacrificial rite, would the gods of mountains and rivers give it up?” (06.06)

【英译注】(1) Zhonggong: Surname Ran, first name Yong, style name Zhonggong, Confucius's disciple, extremely capable. (2) Farm cattle were humble and normally not used for sacrifice. This metaphor means that Zhonggong was capable of the heavy duties though his father was of humble origins.

季康子问：“仲由可使从政也与？”子曰：“由也果，于从政

【注释】季康子：姓季孙，名肥，谥（音shì是）号康，鲁哀公时任正卿。仲由：姓仲，名由，字子

乎何有?”曰:“赐也可使从政也与?”曰:“赐也达,于从政乎何有?”曰:“求也可使从政也与?”曰:“求也艺,于从政乎何有?”(06.08)

路。与:吗,语气词。由:姓仲名由,字子路。果:果断。于:对于。从:参与。政:政事。何有:有何困难。于从政乎何有:对于做官从政呀,哪有什么困难。赐:姓端木,名赐,字子贡。达:达理。求:姓冉,名求,字子有。艺:多才多艺。

【白话译文】

季康子问:“仲由这个人,可以让他处理政务吗?”孔子说:“由勇敢、果断,这对他怎么会有困难?”他问:“赐这个人,可以让他处理政务吗?”孔子说:“赐通情达理,这对他怎么会有困难?”他问:“求这个人,可以让他处理政务吗?”孔子说:“求多才多艺,这对他怎么会有困难?”(06.08)

【英译】

Master Ji Kang(1) asked, “As for Zhong You(2), can he be employed to handle government affairs?” The Master said, “You(3) is courageous and resolute. What difficulty can he have with this?” He asked, “As for Ci(4), can he be employed to handle government affairs?” The Master said, “Ci is reasonable. What difficulty can he have with this?” And he asked, “As for Qiu(5), can he be employed to handle government affairs?” The Master said, “Qiu is versatile. What difficulty can he have with this?” (06.08)

【英译注】(1) Master Ji Kang: Surname Ji, first name Fei, posthumously titled Kang, the chief senior official of the State of Lu. (2) Zhong You: Surname Zhong, first name You, style name Zilu, Confucius's disciple. (3) You: The first name of Zhong You. (4) Ci: Surname Duanmu, first name Ci, style name Zigong, Confucius's disciple. (5) Qiu: Surname Ran, first name Qiu, style name Ziyou, Confucius's disciple.

季氏使闵子骞为费宰。闵子骞曰："善为我辞焉。如有复我者，则吾必在汶上矣。"(06.09)

【注释】季氏：鲁国正卿季孙氏，季康子。使：请。闵子骞(音qiān千)：姓闵名损，字子骞。费(旧音bì闭)：今山东费(音fèi废)县。宰：总管。善：婉转，妥当。辞：拒绝。如：如果。复我：再来召我。汶(音wèn问)：大汶河，南岸为鲁，北岸为齐。上：水阳为北，水上即是水北，指齐国。必在汶上矣：一定到汶水以北的齐国了。

【白话译文】

季氏派使臣任命闵子骞为费县县令。闵子骞说："请礼貌地为我谢辞了吧！如果有人再来为此请我，那么我一定逃到汶河北岸去了。"(06.09)

【英译】

Ji[(1)] sent an escort to appoint Min Ziqian[(2)] the magistrate of the County of Bi[(3)]. Min Ziqian said, "Please politely decline it for me! If someone comes to invite me again for that, I must certainly run away to the north bank of the River Wen[(4)]." (06.09)

【英译注】(1) Ji: Master Ji Kang, surname Ji, first name Fei, posthumously titled Kang, the chief senior official of the State of Lu. (2) Min Ziqian: Surname Min, first name Sun, style name Ziqian, Confucius's disciple, famous for his filial piety. (3) County of Bi: A place currently located at Feixian County of Shandong Province. (4) River Wen: A river at the boundary of the State of Lu at the south bank and the State of Qi at the north bank. Min might leave for the State of Qi.

季子然问："仲由、冉求，可谓大臣与？"子曰："吾以子为异之问，曾由与求之问。所谓大臣者，以道事君，不可则止。今由与求也，可谓具臣矣。"曰："然

【注释】季子然：鲁国季氏的同族人。仲由：姓仲，名由，字子路。冉求：姓冉名求，字子有。谓：算是。大臣：大义正直、仁德至高的高官。异：别人。以子为异之问：以为你是问别人。曾：乃，竟然。由：姓仲名由，字子路。求：姓

则从之者与?"子曰:"弑父与君,亦不从也。"(11.24)

冉名求,字子有。曾由与求之问:竟然问的是子路(由)和子有(求)。不可:这样不行。止:辞职。具臣:普通的臣子、办具体事的官。然:但是。则:就。从:听从。之:季氏。与:吗。然则从之者与:但是他们就顺从季氏吗。弑(音 shì 事):子杀父、臣杀君。亦:也就。

【白话译文】

季子然问:"仲由、冉求,可以称作大臣吗?"孔子说:"我以为你在问别人,原来你问的是由与求呀。所谓大臣,是那些按照符合仁德的道德和行为标准,密切服侍其君主的人。如果他们达不到这个标准,他们宁可辞职不干。现在,对于由和求,他们只能称作处理具体政务的人。"季子然问:"那么,他们能够很好地执行上级的命令吗?"孔子说:"对于弑父、弑君的命令,他们是不会服从的。"(11.24)

【英译】

Ji Ziran(1) asked, "Can we call Zhong You(2) and Ran Qiu(3) great ministers?" The Master said, "I was thinking of others whom you might ask. Eventually you will ask about You(4) and Qiu(5). The so-called great ministers are those who closely serve their sovereign with the moral and virtue of superior benevolence as their behaviour standard. If they cannot meet the standard, they would rather resign from their posts. Now for You(4) and Qiu, they can be called the officials who handle concrete governmental affairs." Ji Ziran asked, "Then can they well execute orders from their superiors?" The Master said, "As to the orders of patricide or regicide, they will not obey them." (11.24)

【英译注】(1) Ji Ziran: A family member from the Ji of the State of Lu. (2) Zhong You: Surname Zhong, first name You, style name Zilu, Confucius's disciple. (3) Ran Qiu: Surname Ran, first name Qiu, style name Ziyou, Confucius's disciple. (4) You: The first name of Zhong You. (5) Qiu: The first name of Ran Qiu.

阳货欲见孔子，孔子不见，归孔子豚。孔子时其亡也，而往拜之。遇诸途。谓孔子曰："来，予与尔言。"曰："怀其宝，而迷其邦。可谓仁乎?"曰："不可。好从事而亟失时，可谓知乎?"曰："不可。日月逝矣，岁不我与。"孔子曰："诺。吾将仕矣。"(17.01)

【注释】此事发生在鲁定公五年(公元前505年)六月，孔子47岁。阳货：阳虎，季孙氏的家臣，把持鲁国国政，孔子鄙视他，不见他。欲：想。见：求见。归(音kuì愧)：赠送。豚(音tún屯)：小猪，此为烹熟的。时：伺(音sì四)，等待、窥探。亡(音wú吴)：外出不在家。往：前去。拜：依俗还礼。诸：之于。涂：道路。遇诸涂：在路上遇见他。与尔言：同你说。怀：收藏。宝：宝贝，本领。而：却。迷：(不救)混乱。好(音hào号)：喜爱。从事：从政。亟(音qì气)：屡次。失时：错过机会。知(音zhì治)：智慧、明智。日月：时间。逝：消逝。岁：岁月，时间。与：给、予。不我与：时间不等我。诺：好吧。

【白话译文】

阳货想见孔夫子，但孔夫子没有来见他。他送给孔夫子一头蒸熟的小猪作为礼物。孔夫子依礼答谢，选他不在家的时候，前往还礼。他俩在路上相遇了。阳货对孔夫子说："来！我给你说句话。"他说："如果一个人有让国家大治的方略，但听任这个国家继续混乱，能称这个人有仁德吗?"(孔子没说话。)他继续说："不能！一个人喜爱做官报国，但频繁错过时机，能称这个人有智慧吗?"(孔子还没说话。)他接着说："不能！一天天逝去，一月月逝去，时间不会等待我们啊！"孔夫子说："好吧！我就去做官。"(17.01)

【英译】

Yang Huo(1) wanted to see Confucius, while Confucius did not come to see him.

【英译注】(1) Yang Huo: Surname Yang, first name Huo or Hu, a general manger of Ji Sun who was

He presented Confucius a gift of a steamed piglet. Confucius selected a time when he was not at home to return him a gift according to the rites. They encountered each other on the road. Yang Huo said to Confucius, "Come! Let me chat with you." He said, "If a person has a general plan to bring about great order across a state, but allows the state continuously to be chaotic, can he be said to possess the virtue of superior benevolence?" (Confucius kept silent.) He continued, "No, he can't. And if a person likes to serve the state as an official, but he frequently misses his chances, can he be said to have wisdom?" (Confucius kept silent too.) He again continued, "No, he can't. Oh, time passes away day by day, month by month, never waiting for us!" Confucius said, "All right! I will start my career of officialdom." (17.01)

premier of the State of Lu. This dialogue happened in 505 BC when Confucius was 47 years old.

子夏曰:"仕而优则学,学而优则仕。"(19.13)

【白话译文】

子夏说:"一个人要想做官优秀,就把他的富余时间致力于学习,而一个人在学业上优秀,就致力于仕途。"(19.13)

【注释】子夏:姓卜名商,字子夏。仕:做官。而:如果。优:一解"余力,有额外的精力、时间";二解"优秀"。则:就。学:读书学习。仕而优则学:一解"做官先尽力做好官事,如果还有精力,就读书学习";二解"如果要做好官,就要学习"。学而优则仕:学习达到优秀水平,就去做官。

【英译】

Zixia[1] said, "An official who wants to excel in officialdom dedicates his surplus time to learning, and a scholar excellent in learning devotes his efforts to officialdom." (19. 13)

【英译注】(1) Zixia: Surname Bu, first name Shang, style name Zixia, Confucius's disciple.

41

农 A Farmer

子曰:"苗而不秀者有矣夫!秀而不实者有矣夫!"(09. 22)

【注释】苗:庄稼出了苗。秀:吐穗扬花。有:是有的。实:结果实。

【白话译文】

孔子说:"有这种情况,庄稼能长出苗,但不能开花!也有这种情况,苗能开花,但不能结出种子!"(09. 22)

【英译】

The Master said, "There is a case that plants can become seedlings but cannot grow blossoms! There is also a case that seedlings can produce blossoms but cannot bear seeds!" (09. 22)

樊迟请学稼。子曰:“吾不如老农。”请学为圃。曰:“吾不如老圃。”樊迟出。子曰:“小人哉,樊须也!上好礼,则民莫敢不敬;上好义,则民莫敢不服;上好信,则民莫敢不用情。夫如是,则四方之民襁负其子而至矣,焉用稼?”(13.04)

【注释】樊迟:名须,字子迟。请:请求。稼(音 jià 架):种田。老:年龄大的、经验多的。农:农民。圃(音 pǔ 普):菜地,种菜人。出:退出。樊须:姓樊名须,字子迟。上:地位高的。好(音 hào 号):喜爱、重视。莫:没有谁。敬:敬畏。莫敢不敬:没有谁敢不敬畏。服:服从。信:诚信。情:真心实情。用情:以真心实情来对待。夫:如果。如:像。是:这样。四方:四面八方。民:百姓。襁(音 qiǎng 抢):婴孩背篓。负:背着。至:来投奔。焉:为什么。用稼:(亲自)种庄稼。

【白话译文】

樊迟请教如何种庄稼。孔子说:“我不如老农。”他请教如何种菜。孔子说:“我不如老园丁。”樊迟出去后,孔子说:“小人啊,樊须这个人!统治者喜好礼仪,那么人民不敢表示不尊敬。统治者喜好正义,那么人民不敢表示不服气。统治者喜好诚信,那么人民不敢向他们说谎话。假若做到这些,那么四方的人民,都会背着自己的婴儿,蜂拥而来,为什么需要你们自己种庄稼呢?”(13.04)

【英译】

Fan Chi[(1)] sought advice on how to plant crops. The Master said, “I am not as good as an old farmer.” He sought further advice on how to grow vegetables. The Master said, “I am not as good as an old gardener.” When Fan Chi was out, the Master said, “An inferior man indeed is Fan

【英译注】(1) Fan Chi: Surname Fan, first name Xu, style name Zichi, Confucius's disciple. (2) Fan Xu: Fan Chi. Xu is his first name.

Xu(2)! If the rulers like the Rites of Proprieties, the people dare not to show them irreverence. If the rulers like righteousness, the people dare not to disagree with them. If the rulers like faith, the people dare not to lie to them. If it is done so, the people of the four directions come here carrying their babies on their backs, therefore why need you grow crops yourselves?" (13. 04)

子路从而后,遇丈人,以杖荷蓧。

子路问曰:"子见夫子乎?"丈人曰:"四体不勤,五谷不分,孰为夫子?"植其杖而芸。

子路拱而立。止子路宿,杀鸡为黍而食之,见其二子焉。

【白话译文】

子路作为孔子的随从,落在了孔子的后边。他遇到一个老农夫,肩挑拐杖,上挂草筐。

子路问他说:"您见到我的老师了吗?"老农夫说:"我的四肢还不够用,以致五谷的苗子与杂草分辨不出来了。谁是你的老师呢?"说罢,他把拐杖插到田里,开始除草。

子路在地头拱手,恭敬站着。农夫请

【注释】鲁哀公五年(公元前490年),孔子62岁,从蔡国去楚国,见叶公后返回蔡国途中,子路被纯朴的农夫热情招待,此人为隐者。子路:姓仲,名由,字子路。从:跟随。后:落在后面。遇:遇见。丈人:老先生。以杖:用拐棍。荷:挑。蓧(音diào吊):耘田用的竹器。

子:你。夫子:孔子、老师。四体:手脚。勤:勤劳、勤快。不勤:两种解释,一是"(说孔子)不勤劳、懒惰好逸";二是"(说自己——从他热情款待子路看,说自己是妥当的)忙不过来、四肢不够用,显得不勤快"。五谷:稻、黍、稷、麦、豆。分:辨别,分开。五谷不分:两种解释,一是"(说孔子)不辨五谷";二是"(说自己)手脚一懒,杂草就旺,五谷苗弱草旺,苗与草分不清"。孰:谁。为:是。植:立、竖立。芸:除草。

拱:拱手。立:站着。止:留。宿:住宿。为:做。黍(音shǔ鼠):黏小米(饭)。而:并且。食(音sì

子路在他家过夜,杀鸡,做小米饭给他吃。他让他的两个儿子来见子路。

四):拿食物给人吃。食之:给子路吃饭。其:他的。

【英译】

Zilu[1] served as an attendant of the Master, but lagged far behind him, and encountered an old farmer. The farmer shouldered a walking stick, on which was a basket for weeds. He asked him, "Have you seen my master, sir?" The elder farmer replied, "My four limbs are not nimble enough so that seedlings of five cereals[2] cannot be distinguished from grasses. Who is your master?" After these words, he inserted his stick in the field and started weeding.

Zilu stood respectfully at the edge of the field, cupping one hand in the other before his chest. The farmer invited him to stay overnight at his home, had chickens killed and millet meal cooked to feast him. He presented his two sons to Zilu.

【英译注】(1) Zilu: Surname Zhong, first name You, style name Zilu, Confucius's disciple. (2) five cereals: Five cereals are rice, husked sorghum, broomcorn millet (millet), wheat, and beans. Interpretion of this sentence is based on the friendly behaviour of the old farmer to Zilu. Normally it is interpreted that the old farmer criticized Confucius for his laziness and ignorance of crops. If he had treated Zilu and his Master Confucius as lazy and ignorant people, he would have probably not accommodated him.

明日,子路行以告。子曰:"隐者也。"使子路反见之,至则行矣。

子路曰:"不仕无义。长幼之节,不可废也。君臣之义,如之何其废之?欲洁其身,而乱大伦。君子之仕也,行其义也。道

【注释】明日:第二天。行以告:走来报告(孔子)。隐:隐居、不做官。反:返回(丈人家)。之:老先生。至:(子路)到达。行矣:(丈人)外出、不在家了。

仕:做官。不义:没有道理。节:礼节。废:废弃。君臣之义:君臣的关系、体系。如之何:为何。其废之:要废弃它。欲:想。洁:洁净。其身:自己。乱:破坏。大伦:

之不行,已知之矣。”(18.07)

【白话译文】

第二天,子路向农夫告辞,赶上孔子,把与老者相见的事告诉他。孔子说:“他是一个隐者。”让子路回去,再次见他。当子路回去时,老农夫已经离开家了。

子路说:“放弃进入仕途的机会,是没有道理的。因为长幼的礼节不能废弃,君臣之间的基本关系怎么能够抛弃呢?一个人作为隐士意欲洁身自好,避免邪恶的影响,但实际上毁坏了人类的重大基本伦理。一名君子去做官,就是在实现他的义务。我们的主张不能广泛推行,我是知道的。”(18.07)

【英译】

Next day, Zilu took leave of this farmer and caught up with the Master and reported his meeting with him. The Master said the farmer was a hermit and asked Zilu to come back to visit him for the second time. When Zilu arrived, the farmer had left home already.

Zilu said, “It is no reason to give up the chance to enter officialdom. As the proprieties between the old and the young cannot be abandoned, why can the fundamental relationship between a sovereign and officials be discarded? A person becomes a hermit to keep himself pure and to avoid evil influences. However,

根本伦理。行其义:实行他的道义、义务。道:社会、政治的最好准则。不行:行不通。已:已经。

by doing so, he destroys the most basic part of human relationships. An obligation of a superior man is to becomean official. However, I know that our beliefs cannot be put into practice." (18.07)

42

兵 A Soldier

子曰:"孟之反不伐。奔而殿,将入门,策其马,曰:'非敢后也,马不进也。'"(06.15)

【注释】孟之反:姓孟名侧,字之反,鲁国大夫,贤而有勇。伐(音fá罚):夸耀、显功。不伐:不自我夸奖。奔:败走,公元前484年,鲁国战败给齐国。而:却。殿:殿后掩护。将:快要。门:城门。入门:进城门。策:鞭打。其:他的。非敢后也:不是敢于殿后保护。马不进也:(而是)我的马跑不快啊。

【白话译文】

孔子说:"孟之反不自我夸奖。当部队被打败,逃回家时,他殿后掩护。在进城门的时候,他用鞭打他的马,说:'我不敢殿后保护部队,但是我的马跑不快呀!'"(06.15)

【英译】

The Master said, "Meng Zhifan[(1)] does not praise himself. When the army was defeated[(2)] and retreated home, he shielded the army at the rear. Upon entry into the city gate

【英译注】(1) Meng Zhifan: A senior official of the State of Lu, surname Meng, first name Ce, style name Zhifan. (2) The army of the State of Lu was defeated by the State of Qi in 484 BC.

spurring his horse with whip, he said, 'I dare not to bring up the rear of the army, but my horse does not run fast enough!'" (06. 15)

子谓颜渊曰:"用之则行,舍之则藏,唯我与尔有是夫!"子路曰:"子行三军,则谁与?"子曰:"暴虎冯河,死而无悔者,吾不与也。必也临事而惧,好谋而成者也。"(07. 11)

【注释】谓:告诉、讲给。颜渊:姓颜名回,字子渊。用:任用。之:我。则:就。行:做。舍:舍弃。藏:隐居,辞官。惟:只有。尔:你。有:拥有。是:这个。夫:吧。子路:姓仲,名由,字子路。行三军:统帅三军,12500人一军。谁与:与谁共事。与:在一起。暴:赤手。虎:打老虎。冯(音píng平):凭,徒步。河:过河。悔:悔恨。临:遇到。惧:谨慎、警惕。谋:谋划。成:完成。

【白话译文】

孔子对颜渊说:"如果一个人被任命为官,他则推行他的主张。如果他不被任用,他将藏起他的主张。大概只有我和你能够做到这一点吧!"子路问:"如果任命您去统帅三军,您选择与谁为伴?"孔子说:"徒手打虎、无船赤脚过河,死到临头而不后悔的人,我是不与他为伍的。与我为伍的人,必须是那些关键时刻谨慎完成任务、灵活机智谋划成功的人。"(07. 11)

【英译】

The Master said to Yan Yuan[(1)], "If a person is appointed to officialdom, he will promote his doctrines. If he is not, he will conceal his thoughts. It is possibly only you and I that can do this!" Zilu[(2)] said, "If you

【英译注】(1) Yan Yuan: Surname Yan, first name Hui, style name Ziyuan, Confucius's excellent disciple. (2) Zilu: Surname Zhong, first name You, style name Zilu, Confucius's disciple.

are appointed to command three armies, whom do you choose to accompany you?" The Master said, "I would not take anyone who would attack a tiger with bare hands and cross a river with bare feet, dying without any regret. My associates must be those who cautiously accomplish a task at a crisis and plan strategies for success." (07.11)

子曰:"善人教民七年,亦可以即戎矣。"(13.29)

【白话译文】

孔子说:"如果一位统治者爱护他的人民,他对他们进行七年训练,就可以让他们参加作战。"(13.29)

【英译】

The Master said, "If a ruler loves his people, he trains them for seven years and then they can be engaged to fight in a war." (13.29)

【注释】善:爱惜、关爱,参考《道德经》"善者吾善之,不善者吾亦善之",《孟子》"穷则独善其身,达则兼善天下"。善人:爱护民众。教:教练。民:百姓。亦:也。即:从事、走近。戎:参军打仗。矣:了。亦可以即戎矣:也就可以叫他们去参军打仗了。

子曰:"以不教民战,是谓弃之。"(13.30)

【白话译文】

子曰:"人民在投入战场前,没有受过

【注释】以:用。不教民:未训练的百姓。战:打仗。是:这。谓:叫作、称作。弃:抛弃。之:他们。是谓弃之:这就叫抛弃他们(白白送命)。

训练,就是放弃他们的生命。”(13.30)

【英译】

The Master said, “People’s lives will be thrown away if they receive no training before going to war.” (13.30)

季氏将伐颛臾。冉有、季路见于孔子曰:“季氏将有事于颛臾。”

孔子曰:“求!无乃尔是过与?夫颛臾,昔者先王以为东蒙主,且在邦域之中矣,是社稷之臣也。何以伐为?”

冉有曰:“夫子欲之,吾二臣者,皆不欲也。”

【白话译文】

季氏策划进攻鲁国的附属国颛臾。冉有、季路拜见孔夫子说:“季氏将对颛臾用兵作战。”

孔夫子说:“求!难道不应当责备你吗?以前几个君王曾经授权颛臾主祭东蒙山,而且它在国家之中,是对国家有功劳的臣属国,为什么要伐它呢?”

冉有说:“是我家主人愿意这么做,我们俩作为臣属都不愿意。”

【注释】季氏:季孙氏,季康子,名肥。将:快要、将要。伐:攻打。颛臾(音 zhuān 砖 yú 鱼):鲁国的附属国,今山东费县西。冉有:姓冉名求,字子有。季路:仲由,字子路。见于:拜见。有事:军事征伐。

求:姓冉,名求,字子有。无乃:岂不。尔:你、你们。是:这。过:错,当受责备。与:吗。无乃尔是过与:岂不是你们的过错吗;难道不该责备你们吗。昔者:从前。先王:周朝先王。以为:用作。东蒙:蒙山,在东部,称东蒙。主:主祭祀人。昔者先王以为东蒙主:从前周天子始封颛臾为附庸之君,使他主祭蒙山。邦:鲁国。域:国域。社:土神。稷:谷神。社稷:国家,指鲁国。臣:臣属。为:呢,反问语气词。何以伐为:怎么能去攻打呢。

夫子:季氏。欲:想要。之:这样。

【英译】

The Ji Clan[(1)] plotted to attack Zhuanyu[(2)], a small dependent state of the State of Lu. Ran You[(3)] and Jilu[(4)] reported it to Confucius, "The Ji Clan is going to start military operations against Zhuanyu."

Confucius said, "Qiu[(5)]! Really shouldn't you be blamed? Zhuanyu once was authorized by the previous kings to preside over the sacrificial ceremonies in the Dongmengshan Mountains, and it is inside our state for which it serves as a meritorious sub-state, why do you attack it?"

Ran You said, "It is our master who desires it, but we two as inferior officials do not."

【英译注】(1) The Ji Clan: Master Ji Kang, surname Jisun, first name Fei, posthumous title Kang, the chief senior official of the State of Lu. (2) Zhuanyu: A small state subordinate to the State of Lu, currently located at Western Feixian County, Shandong Province. (3) Ran You: Surname Ran, first name Qiu, style name Ziyou, Confucius's disciple. (4) Jilu: Surname Zhong, first name You, style name Zilu, another style name Jilu, Confucius's disciple. (5) Qiu: First name of Ran You.

孔子曰:"求!周任有言曰:'陈力就列,不能者止。'危而不持,颠而不扶,则将焉用彼相矣?且尔言过矣。虎兕出于柙,龟玉毁于椟中,是谁之过与?"

冉有曰:"今夫颛臾,固而近于费,今不取,后世必为子孙忧。"

【注释】周任:人名,周代史官。陈力:发挥能力。就列:按才干任职。不能者:不能胜任者。止:辞职。危:危险。持:支撑。颠:跌倒。扶:扶起。将:又。焉:怎么。用:任用。彼:你们。相:搀扶盲人的人叫相,辅助。兕(音 sì 四):雌性犀牛。出:出来。于:从。柙(音 xiá 匣):木笼。龟:龟甲。玉:美玉。毁:毁坏。椟(音 dú 独):匣子。谁:疑问人称代词,主人或助手。

固:城郭坚固。近:接近。费(旧音 bì 闭):今山东费(音 fèi 废)县,季氏的采邑。取:攻下。后世:将来。子孙忧:子孙的忧患。

【白话译文】

孔夫子说:“求! 周任有言说:‘如果一个人能够贡献能力时,他居于官位。否则,就从官位上辞退下来。’如果你们既不能让主人避开危险,在他跌倒时又不能扶起来,那么为什么要任命你们为他的助手呢? 而且你的话是错的。如果老虎、雌犀牛从其笼子中逃出来,神圣的龟壳及漂亮的玉石在其匣子中损毁了,是谁(是主人还是他的助手)对这一过错负责呢?”

冉有说:“今天,颛臾的城墙很坚固,而且离季氏的属地费城很近。如果今天不攻占它,将来它必定成为对(季氏)子孙的严重忧患。”

【英译】

Confucius said, "Qiu! Zhou Ren(1) once said, 'If one is able to contribute his capabilities, he takes a position in officialdom. Otherwise, he resigns from it.' You neither can keep your master from danger, nor can hold him up when he falls down, so why have you been appointed as his assistants? Further more your words are wrong. If a tiger and a female rhinoceros flee from their cages, and sacred tortoise shells and beautiful jade are destroyed in their caskets, who (the master or his assistant) is responsible for these mistakes?"

Ran You said, "Today, Zhuanyu has strong city walls, and is very close to the Bi(2)

【英译注】(1) Zhou Ren: The name of a historical official of the Zhou Dynasty. (2) Bi Fief: The land granted to Master Ji Kang, currently located at Feixian County of Shandong Province.

Fief of the Ji Clan. If it is not attacked and occupied today, it must become a serious worry of the sons and grandsons (of the Ji Clan) in the future."

孔子曰:"求!君子疾夫舍曰'欲之',而必为之辞。丘也闻有国有家者,不患寡而患不均,不患贫而患不安。盖均无贫,和无寡,安无倾。夫如是,故远人不服,则修文德以来之。既来之,则安之。今由与求也,相夫子,远人不服而不能来也,邦分崩离析而不能守也,而谋动干戈于邦内。吾恐季孙之忧,不在颛臾,而在萧墙之内也。"(16.01)

【白话译文】

孔夫子说:"求!一个人不说'我贪得它',而一定给它找个借口,这是君子所厌恶的态度。孔丘我听说过,拥有国的诸侯或拥属地的大夫,不怕财产不丰富,但怕在相关人员中分配不公平;不怕他们的人口少,而怕他们的人民生活不安定。如果财产分配公平,就没有贫穷。如果保障了和谐,就不会有人口少的感觉。如果安定维

【注释】疾:讨厌。夫:那种。舍曰:撇开不谈。欲之:贪得它。为之辞:给它借口。有:治理。国:诸侯国。家:大夫封地。患:担心。寡:贫困、财物少。均:公平。贫:人少。安:安定。盖:因为。均无贫:公平才没有贫穷。和无寡:和睦才不觉人少。安无倾:安定才无倾覆的危险。夫如是:像这样,这样做了。故:若、如果。远人:远方的人。服:归服。则:就。修文德:修治仁、义、礼、乐。来之:招徕他们。既:已经。安之:安定他们。既来之,则安之:已经来了,就让他们安心住下去。由:姓仲名由,字子路。相:辅助。分:分裂。崩:崩溃。离:离去。析:析散。谋:策划。动:动用。干:盾牌。戈:长把兵器。恐:害怕。季孙:鲁国正卿季孙氏,季康子。萧墙:照壁,季氏家使用的屏风[J08,J09],指季康子自己。

护好,就没有被推翻的危险。如果这些都做到了,远方的人对我们还是不顺服,那我们就修养我们的文化品德以吸引他们。当他们来到这里,我们就给他们提供适当的生活和工作条件,让他们安全安心。今天,由、求你们俩协助你们的主人季氏,但不能吸引远方的人民顺服、到来,而且你们不能守住国家以免分裂破碎,相反,你们谋划国内战争。我担心季孙氏的忧患,不在颛臾,而在他自家的屏风墙以内。"(16.01)

【英译】

Confucius said,"Qiu! A superior man detests the attitude that one does not say 'I covet it', but he must find an execuse for it. I Kong Qiu[(1)] have heard that for those dukes or senior officials who possess a state or a fief, they do not fear that they do not have sufficient wealth, but they do fear that wealth is not fairly distributed among the persons. They do not fear that they have small population, but do fear that their people's lives are not stable. If wealth is distributed fairly, there is no poverty. If harmony is guaranteed, there is no small population. If stability is maintained, there is no danger of being overthrown. If all these have been done, the people of distant quarters do not submit and come to us, we will cultivate our cultural virtues[(2)] in order to attract them. When they come here, we offer them suitable conditions

【英译注】(1) Kong Qiu: Confucius, surname Kong, first name Qiu. (2) cultural virtues: The Rites of Proprieties, Ritual music, morals, political virtues and so on. (3) You: First name of Jilu.

to live and work in security and contentment. Today You[3] and Qiu you two assist your master, but you can neither attract people of distant quarters to submit and come, nor keep the state from fragmenting. But on the contrary, you are plotting a war inside the state. I am afraid for that the worries of the Jisun Clan do not come from Zhuanyu, but come from inside the screen walls of his own clan." (16. 01)

43

工 A Workman

子贡问为仁。子曰:"工欲善其事,必先利其器。居是邦也,事其大夫之贤者,友其士之仁者。"(15. 10)

【注释】子贡:姓端木名赐,字子贡。为:实行。仁:仁德。工:做工的人。欲:想。善:做好。其:他的。事:工作。必:一定。利:锋利、完善。器:工具。居:住。是邦:这个国。事:侍奉。友:交结。

【白话译文】

子贡请教如何培养一个人的仁德。孔子说:"工匠想把工作做好,他必须先让他的工具锋利起来。一个人住在一个国家,他侍奉大臣中贤明的人,结交那些具有仁德品质的学者。"(15. 10)

【英译】

Zigong[1] asked advice on how to cultivate one's virtue of superior benevolence. The Master said, "If a workman wishes to get his work done well, he must first have his tools sharpened. When one lives at a state, he serves the sages of senior officials, and makes friends with benevolent scholars." (15.10)

【英译注】(1) Zigong: Surname Duanmu, first name Ci, style name Zigong, Confucius's excellent disciple.

子夏曰:"百工居肆以成其事,君子学以致其道。"(19.07)

【注释】子夏:姓卜名商,字子夏。百工:各行各业的工匠。居:处,在。肆:制作物品的作坊。以:用来。成:完成。其:他的。事:工作。学:学堂、学校,在校学习。致:掌握、达到。

【白话译文】

子夏说:"百行百业的工人守在作坊来完善他们的业务。一名君子通过在校学习来完善他的思想体系。"(19.07)

【英译】

Zixia[1] said, "Workmen from one hundred professions work in the workshops to perfect their crafts. A superior man perfects his understanding through learning at school." (19.07)

【英译注】(1) Zixia: Surname Bu, first name Shang, style name Zixia, Confucius's excellent disciple.

44

商 A Merchant

子贡曰:“有美玉于斯,韫椟而藏诸? 求善贾而沽诸?”子曰:“沽之哉! 沽之哉! 我待贾者也。”(09. 13)

【白话译文】

子贡说:“如果此处有一块漂亮的玉石,我们是包裹它、藏在柜子里呢,还是求一个好价钱卖了呢?”孔子说:“卖了吧! 卖了吧! 我会等待识货的买家。”(09. 13)

【英译】

Zigong(1) said, “If there is a piece of beautiful gem here, should we wrap it and hide it in a cabinet or should we sell it at a good price?” The Master said, “Oh, sell it! Sell it! I would wait for an expert buyer.”(09. 13)

【注释】子贡:姓端木,名赐。于:在。斯:此。韫椟(音 yùn 运 dú 独):(使用)藏物柜。而:进而。藏:收藏。诸:它。韫椟而藏诸:放在柜里收藏它。求:找。善:好的。贾(音 gǔ 古):一解“价钱”,而孔子在等商人上门,因为《周礼》注曰“行曰商,处曰贾”;二解“坐商”,孔子或弟子找上门。沽:卖掉。之:它。哉:啊。待:等待。

【英译注】(1) Zigong: Surname Duanmu, first name Ci, style name Zigong, Confucius's excellent disciple.

子曰:“回也其庶乎,屡空。赐不受命,而货殖焉,亿则屡中。”(11. 19)

【注释】回:姓颜名回,字子渊。其:大概。庶:庶几,相近(道德完善)。屡:多次。空:贫困、匮乏。赐:姓端木,名赐,字子贡。

受:得到。命:一解“天命、命运”;二解“官府授权”。而:并且。货殖:做买卖、囤积居奇。亿:臆,猜测。则:就、便。中(音 zhòng 众):对、准确。

【白话译文】

孔子说:“回啊!他的品德和学问大概接近完美了,但他经常穷得几乎没法活。赐不相信命运,所以他囤积居奇,投机买卖,而且经常猜中价格。”(11.19)

【英译】

The Master said,“Ah Hui(1)! He possibly has nearly perfect virtues and learning, but he is frequently so poor that he often has almost nothing for his life. Ci(2) does not believe in fate, so he hoards and corners supplies for speculation, and frequently guesses right for the prices.”(11.19)

【英译注】(1) Hui: Surname Yan, first name Hui, style name Ziyuan, Confucius's excellent disciple. (2) Ci: Zigong, Surname Duanmu, first name Ci, style name Zigong, Confucius's excellent disciple.

九
Nine

政法
Politics and Laws

45

政 Politics

子曰:“道千乘之国,敬事而信,节用而爱人,使民以时。”(01.05)

【注释】道(音 dǎo 岛):导,引导、治理。乘(音 shèng 胜):辆,量词,指一辆兵车,配有4匹马,3甲士,72步卒,25后勤员。之:的。敬:认真。而:并且。信:诚信。敬事而信:严肃认真处理政务,且诚实无欺。节:节约。用:费用、经费。人:官吏。使:役使。民:百姓。以:按照。时:耕种时节。

【白话译文】

孔子说:“治理好拥有千辆兵车的国家,统治者必须严肃地处理政务,坚决讲究诚信,认真节省财政收入,亲切爱护官吏,依照利于农业生产的农时役使百姓。”(01.05)

【英译】

The Master said, “To well administer a state of 1000 chariots, the ruler must earnestly handle government affairs, resolutely keep the faith, frugally handle financial matters, treat his officials with kindness, and use the common people in agriculture according to the season.” (01.05)

子曰:“为政以德,譬如北辰,居其所,而众星共之。”(02.01)

【注释】为:从事。政:(当官)治国。以:用。譬(音 pì 媲):打比方。譬如:好比。北辰:北极星。居:安居。其:它的。所:位置。而:就、便。共:拱,围绕。

【白话译文】

孔子说:“按照道德标准统治一个国家,统治者可以比作北斗星,处在中心位置,群星环绕。”(02.01)

【英译】

The Master said, “To rule a state according to moral standards, the ruler is compared to the Big Dipper that stays at the centre encircled by many other stars revolving around it.” (02.01)

或谓孔子曰:“子奚不为政?”子曰:“《书》云:‘孝乎惟孝,友于兄弟,施于有政。’是亦为政,奚其为为政?”(02.21)

【注释】或:有人。谓:对……说。奚(音 xī 希):为什么。为:从事。政:(当官)治国。书:《尚书》。乎:啊。惟孝:只有孝顺(的人)。友:(才能)友爱。施(音 yì 义):蔓延。于:到。有政:治国。是:这。亦:也。为为政:算是当官治国。

【白话译文】

有人对孔夫子说:“你为什么不参政?”孔夫子说:“《尚书》有这样的话:‘啊,孝顺!要孝顺你的父母!要友爱你的兄弟!你的这些品德可以延续到政府治理上。’这也是一种参政。为什么我非要做官,才被认为是参政呢?”(02.21)

【英译】

Someone said to Confucius, “Why don't you participate in government?” Confucius said, “*Book of History*(1) says, ‘Ah, filial

【英译注】(1) *Book of History*: A historical book about ancient China and it records important affairs having occurred mainly in the Xia, Shang, and Zhou dynasties.

piety! Be filial to your parents! Show fraternal love toward your brothers! By extension, this moral quality can be extended to government administration.' This is also a kind of participation in government. Why do I have to be an official to be regarded as participating in government?" (02.21)

仲弓问子桑伯子。子曰:"可也,简。"仲弓曰:"居敬而行简,以临其民,不亦可乎?居简而行简,无乃大简乎?"子曰:"雍之言然。"(06.02)

【注释】仲弓:姓冉,名雍,字仲弓。问:向孔子询问。子桑伯子:生平遗失,伯子似乎是卿大夫。可:尚可。简:简要,不烦琐。居:处、保留。而:而且。行:办事、治理。居敬而行简:安心恭敬,抓大放小,办事简单。临:面对,治理。民:百姓。居简而行简:居心潦草,只图省事,办事简单。无乃:岂不是。大:太。乎:吗。雍:姓冉名雍,字仲弓。之:的。言:话。然:是。

【白话译文】

仲弓请教子桑伯子工作得怎么样。孔子说:"他可以,处理事务非常简单。"仲弓说:"如果他存心工作认真,简单高效地处理日常工作,依照抓大体、放烦琐的作风领导百姓,岂不是没什么不好?如果他存心工作粗心,处理日常事务疏忽,岂不是太简单了吗?"孔子说:"雍,你的话很对。"(06.02)

【英译】

Zhonggong(1) asked about Master Sang Bozi(2)'s work. The Master said, "Not bad. He deals with matter very simply." Zhonggong said, "If he works conscientious

【英译注】(1) Zhonggong: Surname Ran, first name Yong, style name Zhonggong, Confucius's disciple. (2) Master Sang Bozi: A person unknown now. He served as a senior official as his name Bozi represented

ly, deals with day-to-day work simply, and leads the common people by grasping the basic principles and eliminating tedious formalities, what is wrong with that? But if he does his work carelessly, and is negligent in handling daily affairs, isn't he rather too simple?" The Master said, "Yong(3), your words are right."

a title of a senior official. Sang is possibly his surname. (3) Yong: First name of Zhonggong.

子游为武城宰。子曰:"女得人焉耳乎?"曰:"有澹台灭明者,行不由径,非公事,未尝至于偃之室也。"(06.14)

【注释】子游:姓言,名偃(音 yǎn 眼),字子游,吴人。武城:今山东费县。宰:总管。女(音 rǔ 辱):汝,你。得:得到。人:人才。焉:啦。耳:了。乎:吗。有:名词前置词。澹台灭明:姓澹(音 tán 谈)台,名灭明,字子羽,武城人。行:走路。由:自、从,介词。径:小路,邪路。尝:从来。至:到。偃:姓言名偃,字子游。之:的。室:房室。

【白话译文】

子游做武城市的总管。孔子问:"你那里发现了什么人才了吗?"他说:"有一位叫澹台灭明的人,走路不走斜插道,除非有公事,从来不到我的房子里来。"(06.14)

【英译】

Ziyou(1) was magistrate of Wucheng City(2). The Master asked, "Have you found any talented people here around you?" He replied, "There is one named Tantai Mieming(3). He does not walk along an oblique road, and never comes into my room except for public duties." (06.14)

【英译注】(1) Ziyou: Surname Ran, first name Qiu, style name Ziyou, Confucius's disciple. (2) Wucheng City: A city of the State of Lu, currently at Southwestern Feixian County of Shandong Province. (3) Tantai Mieming: Surname Tantai, first name Mieming, style name Ziyu, later becoming Confucius's disciple.

子曰:“不在其位,不谋其政。”(08. 14)

【注释】其:那个。位:职位。谋:图谋、干涉、插手。政:事务。不谋其政:不得干涉(插手)此位上的事。

【白话译文】

孔子说:“一个人不占居那个职位,就不干涉那个职位的政务。”(08. 14)

【英译】

The Master said,“If one does not occupy that position, he does not interfere with the administration affairs of the position.”(08. 14)

季康子问政于孔子。孔子对曰:“政者,正也。子帅以正,孰敢不正?”(12. 17)

【注释】季康子:姓季孙名肥,谥(音 shì 是)号康,鲁哀公时任正卿。问:请教。政:治国、行政、政治。对曰:敬答。者:的事。正:正道。子:你。帅:带头。以正:走正路。孰:谁。

【白话译文】

季康子向孔夫子请教政治。孔夫子敬答:“政治就是正直的意思。如果你带头正直,谁敢不正直?”(12. 17)

【英译】

Master Ji Kang (1) asked Confucius advice about politics. Confucius replied respectfully,“The meaning of politics is righteousness. If you are righteous first, who dares not be righteous?”(12. 17)

【英译注】(1) Master Ji Kang: Surname Ji, first name Fei, posthumous title Kang, chief senior official of the State of Lu from 492 BC to 468 BC.

季康子问政于孔子曰:"如杀无道,以就有道,何如?"孔子对曰:"子为政,焉用杀?子欲善,而民善矣。君子之德,风;小人之德,草。草上之风,必偃。"(12.19)

【白话译文】

季康子向孔夫子请教政府管理:"如果我们杀掉所有坏人,以便引导老百姓按照道德要求做事,你看怎么样?"孔夫子敬答:"你要做好行政,为什么非要用杀戮的方式?如果你真追求善良,那么老百姓就会善良。君子的道德就像风,老百姓的道德就像草。风吹到草上,草就倒到风的方向。"(12.19)

【英译】

Master Ji Kang asked Confucius about government administration, "What would you think if we were to kill all the evildoers in order to guide the common people to behave according to dictates of morality?" Confucius replied respectfully, "If you have a good administration, why would you resort to slaughter? If you truly desire the goodness, the goodness will prevail among the common people. The morality of a ruler is

【注释】问:请教。政:政务、行政、治国、政治。于:向。如:如果。杀:杀戮。无道:坏人、无道的人。以:用来。就:亲近。有道:好人、有道者。对曰:敬答。子:你。为政:治理政事。焉:哪里。欲:想。民善:百姓跟着行善。君子:领导、执政者。之:的。德:品德、行为。风:(好比)刮风。小人:百姓。草:(像)草。君子之德,风;小人之德,草:领导的德行好比风,百姓的德行像草。上:加,吹。之:这,此。必:一定。偃(音 yǎn 眼):倒下,卧倒。草上之风,必偃:风向哪儿吹,草一定向哪儿倒。

like the wind, and that of the common people is like grass. When the wind blows, the grass will bend in the direction of wind." (12.19)

子路问政。子曰:"先之,劳之。"请益。子曰:"无倦。"(13.01)

【注释】子路:姓仲,名由,字子路。先:先导,教化。之:百姓。劳之:使百姓勤劳。先之劳之:给百姓做榜样,教化他们,使百姓勤劳。请:请求。益:增多、多讲些。倦:厌倦,松懈。无倦:自己不松懈。

【白话译文】

子路请教行政问题。孔子说:"你先给老百姓做好表率,然后让他们勤奋干活。"他请多建议些。孔子说:"你永远不要倦怠。"(13.01)

【英译】

Zilu(1) asked advice about governmental administration. The Master said, "You set a good example first for the common people and then ask them to work diligently." He asked more advices. The Master said, "You must never be sluggish." (13.01)

【英译注】(1) Zilu: Surname Zhong, first name You, style name Zilu, Confucius's disciple.

仲弓为季氏宰,问政。子曰:"先有司,赦小过,举贤才。"曰:"焉知贤才而举之?"曰:"举尔所知。尔所不知,人其舍

【注释】仲弓:姓冉,名雍,字仲弓。季氏:季康子,名肥。宰:总管。先:做表率。有司:办事人员,下级官吏。先有司:给下级官吏做表率。赦:赦免。过:错。举:选拔。贤:贤良。才:人才。焉:如

诸?”(13.02)

何。所知:知道的。人:别人。舍:舍弃、埋没。诸:他。人其舍诸:别人难道会埋没他吗。

【白话译文】

仲弓做了季氏的总管,向孔子请教行政问题。孔子说:“给下属先做好表率,赦免他们的小错误,提拔具有优秀品质和卓越才能的人。”他问:“怎么识别谁具有优秀品质和卓越才能去提拔呢?”孔子说:“提拔你所识别的。对于那些你没有把握的,难道别人会埋没他们的才能吗?”(13.02)

【英译】

Zhonggong(1) served as the chief manager of the Ji Clan(2) and asked the Master advice about administration issues. The Master said, “Set a good example before your subordinates, forgive their trivial errors and promote people with excellent qualities and outstanding talents.” Zhonggong asked, “How would I recognize one who has excellent qualities and outstanding talents for promotion?” The Master said, “Promote those whom you can recognize. For those whom you are not sure about, would other people stifle their talents?” (13.02)

【英译注】(1) Zhonggong: Surname Ran, first name Yong, style name Zhonggong, Confucius's disciple. (2) the Ji Clan: Master Ji Kang, surname Jisun, first name Fei, posthumous title Kang, the chief senior official of the State of Lu.

子曰:“其身正,不令而行;其身不正,虽令不从。”(13.06)

【注释】其:自己,领导,执政者。身:本身。正:正直。令:命令。而:就,也会。行:执行。从:服从。

【白话译文】

孔子说:“统治者自身行为正直,不用发布命令,老百姓也会跟随他。如果他本身行为不正直,即使三令五申,老百姓也不会跟随他。”(13.06)

【英译】

The Master said, “If a ruler conducts himself righteously, the common people will follow him without issuing orders. If he himself does not conduct righteously, the common people will not follow him even though he issues repeated orders.” (13.06)

冉子退朝。子曰:“何晏也?”对曰:“有政。”子曰:“其事也?如有政,虽不吾以,吾其与闻之。”(13.14)

【注释】冉子:冉有,字子有。退朝:从朝廷归来。何:怎么。晏(音 yàn 艳):迟,晚。对曰:敬答。政:国君改更匡正之大事,在君为政,在臣为事。事:日常事务。如:如果。以:任用。不吾以:不任用我。其:大概。与:给予。闻:见闻、知晓。

【白话译文】

冉子从朝廷回来。孔子问:“你怎么回来晚了?”他敬答:“有国家大事。”孔子说:“大概是日常事务吧?假如有国家大事,虽然我没有被任用,大概会通知我的。”(13.14)

【英译】

Master Ran(1) returned from the court.

【英译注】(1) Master Ran: Surname Ran, first name Qiu, style name Ziyou, Confucius's disciple.

The Master asked him, "Why are you returning so late?" He replied respectfully, "There are important state affairs." The Master said, "Are they probably common daily affairs? If there had been important state affairs, I might possibly have been notified of them, even though I am not employed by the court." (13. 14)

叶公问政。子曰:"近者说,远者来。"(13. 16)

【注释】鲁哀公五年(公元前490年),孔子62岁,从蔡国去楚国叶城,见楚国贤人叶公,答叶公问。叶(音 shè 社)公:姓沈名诸梁,楚国大夫,封地在叶城(今河南叶县南)。近者:近处的人。说(音 yuè 月):悦,愉快。远者:远处的人。来:归附。

【白话译文】

叶公请教行政问题。孔子说:"让国内的人民都幸福,吸引国外人民的到来。"(13. 16)

【英译】

Senior Official She[(1)] asked advice about government administration. The Master said, "Make the people inside the state happy and attract people outside the state to come." (13. 16)

【英译注】(1) Senior Official She: Surname Shen, first name Zhuliang, senior official of the State of Chu and his fief was given at She City, currently Ye County, Henan Province.

子夏为莒父宰,问政。子曰:"无欲速,无见小利。欲速,则不达;见小利,则大事不成。"(13. 17)

【注释】子夏:姓卜名商,字子夏。莒(音 jǔ 举)父:鲁国城邑,今山东莒县。宰:总管。欲:求。速:过快。达:到达。见:贪求。利:利益。大事:重要的事情。不成:做不成。

【白话译文】

子夏当了莒父县的县宰，请教行政问题。孔子说："不要图快，不要盯住手头小的好处。图快达不到远大的目的，欲速则不达。盯住手头小的好处，那就办不成大事。"（13.17）

【英译】

Zixia[(1)] was the magistrate of Jufu County[(2)] and asked advice about government administration. The Master said, "Neither pursue haste and nor fix your eyes on the minor benefits beforehand. To pursue haste, you cannot realize your long-range goal as haste makes waste. To fix your eyes on minor benefits beforehand, you cannot accomplish important affairs."（13.17）

【英译注】(1) Zixia: Surname Bu, first name Shang, style name Zixia, Confucius's disciple. (2) Jufu County: A city of the State of Lu, currently Juxian County of Shandong Province.

子曰："不在其位，不谋其政。"（14.27）

【注释】（依朱熹注分章）其：那个。位：职位。谋：图谋、干涉、插手。政：事务。不谋其政：不得干涉（插手）此位上的事。

【白话译文】

孔子说："一个人不占居那个职位，就不干涉那个职位的政务。"（14.27）

【英译】

The Master said, "If one does not occupy that position, he does not interfere with the administration affairs of the position."（14.27）

子张问于孔子曰："何如斯可以从政矣？"

子曰："尊五美，屏四恶，斯可以从政矣。"

子张曰："何谓五美？"子曰："君子惠而不费，劳而不怨，欲而不贪，泰而不骄，威而不猛。"

【注释】子张：姓颛（音 zhuān 砖）孙名师，字子张。何如：怎么样。斯：才，就。从政：治理政事。

尊：尊重。五美：五种美德。屏（音 bǐng 丙）：排除。恶（音 è 饿）：坏事、恶行。矣：了。

何谓：什么是。惠：恩惠。而：却，但是。费：耗费。惠而不费：给百姓好处，自己却不耗费。劳：使百姓劳作。怨：怨恨。欲：追求（仁德）。贪：贪图财利。泰：庄重。骄：傲慢。威：威严。猛：凶猛。

【白话译文】

子张向孔子请教："一个人怎么做，他才有资格从事行政工作呢？"

孔子说："他遵守五种美德，排除四种恶行，他就有资格从事行政工作了。"

子张问："什么是五种美德？"

孔子说："君子给人利益，但他不花费太多；役用人民但他们不怨恨他；他追求仁德但不贪得无厌；他泰然自若但不骄傲；他很有威严但不凶猛。"

【英译】

Zizhang[(1)] asked the Master, "What does one do so that he is qualified to undertake government administration?"

The Master said, "He respects the five morals and removes the four bad deeds, and then he is qualified to undertake government administration."

Zizhang asked, "What are the five morals?"

【英译注】(1) Zizhang: Surname Zhuansun, first name Shi, style name Zizhang, Confucius's disciple.

The Master said, "A superior man gives benefits to the people, but it does not cost him much; he uses the common people but they do not complain about him; he pursues superior benevolence but he is not avaricious; he is composed but not arrogant; and he is awe-inspiring but not fierce."

子张曰:"何谓惠而不费?"子曰:"因民之所利而利之,斯不亦惠而不费乎?择可劳而劳之,又谁怨?欲仁得仁,又焉贪?君子无众寡,无小大,无敢慢,斯不亦泰而不骄乎?君子正其衣冠,尊其瞻视,俨然人望而畏之,斯不亦威而不猛乎?"

【注释】因:根据。所利:有利的事。利:给予好处。因民之所利而利之:凡是百姓能得到的好处,便让他们得好处。斯:这。不亦:不就是。乎:吗。择:选择。可劳:可以役使的事。焉:怎么,哪里。无:不分。众:人多。寡:人少。小大:势力大小。无敢:不敢。慢:怠慢。正:整齐。尊:端正、自重自尊。其:自己的。瞻视:目光。俨(音 yǎn 眼):庄严、恭敬。人:别人。望:看见。畏:敬畏。尊其瞻视,俨然人望而畏之:目不邪视,非常庄重,使人敬畏。

【白话译文】

子张问:"给人利益,但他不花费太多,是什么意思?"

孔子说:"君子通过让人民做有利于他们的事,来给他们利益,不是他给人民好处但并不花费他太多吗?如果他选择适当的任务,让合适的人去完成,谁会怨恨他呢?他期望仁德并获得了仁德,那他为什么要贪得无厌呢?无论任何人,不论他们人多还是人少,权势是大还是小,他都不敢怠慢,此君子不是泰然自若而不骄傲吗?如果他衣着得体,目不斜视,非常严肃,让人产生敬畏之心,此君子不是威风但不凶猛吗?"

【英译】

Zizhang asked,"What does it mean that he gives benefits to the people but it does not cost him much?"

The Master said,"A superior man benefits the common people by allowing them to do what is beneficial to themselves, isn't it that he gives benefits to the people but it does not cost him much? If he selects a proper task for the right people to do it, who can complain about him? If he desires superior benevolence and then gets it, why is he avaricious? Isn't a superior man composed but not arrogant if he dares not to ignore any people no matter whether they are many or few or powerful or powerless? Is a superior man awe-inspiring but not fierce if he addresses himself immaculately, does not look sideways, he is so dignified that others hold him in awe and venerate him?"

子张曰:"何谓四恶?"子曰:"不教而杀谓之虐;不戒视成谓之暴;慢令致期谓之贼;犹之与人也,出纳之吝,谓之有司。"(20.02)

【注释】不教:不经教育、教化。杀:杀戮。不教而杀:不经教育就杀戮。谓之:称它为。虐:残暴。不戒:告诫。视:要求。成:成功。不戒视成:不告诫就要求成功。暴:粗暴。慢令:缓慢颁布命令。致期:限期完成。贼:害人。

【白话译文】

子张问:“什么是四种恶行?”

孔子说:“一个官员对一个人没有教育,就判他死刑,就是酷虐。一个官员不告诫一个人,放任他造成不可避免的灾难,然后严厉惩罚,就是残暴。一个官员渎职,延迟颁布命令,突然设置期限来完成一项任务,就是害人。一个人必须支付别人,但吝啬给人钱财,就是下层官员的小家子气。”(20.02)

【英译】

Zizhang asked,“What are the four bad deeds?”

The Master said,“It is tyranny when one official pronounces the death penalty on someone without instructing him on what is right. It is ferocity that one official does not warn a person in advance,leaves him open to inevitable disasters and then strictly punishes him for the consequence. It is a great harm when an official neglects his duty, delays promulgation of an order, but suddenly requires a deadline of a task. And it is niggardliness of a petty official that he pays someone a pittance for his labors.”(20.02)

犹:仍然。与:给予。犹之与人:同样给人财物。出:支出。纳:纳入。吝:吝啬、小气。有司:古代管理事务者,卑微的下等管家,喻为小家子气。

46

法 The Law

子曰:"道之以政,齐之以刑,民免而无耻;道之以德,齐之以礼,有耻且格。"(02.03)

【白话译文】

孔子说:"如果用政府命令来引导老百姓,用刑律来整顿(惩罚)他们,他们会暂时免于处罚但是没有廉耻之心。如果用优异的道德来引导人民,用礼仪来整顿他们,他们会有廉耻之心并且归附政府当局。"(02.03)

【英译】

The Master said, "If the common people are guided by government orders and rectified (punished) according to criminal laws, they may avoid punishment temporarily but do not have sense of shame. If they are guided by the excellent morals and rectified according to the Rites of Proprieties, they may have the sense of shame and submit to the governmental authorities." (02.03)

【注释】道(音 dǎo 岛):导,引导、治理。之:百姓。以:用。政:政令、政法。齐:约束。刑:法度、法制惩罚。民:百姓。免:避免(犯罪受罚)。而:却、但是。无:没有。耻:羞耻之心。免而无耻:避免受罚却没有羞耻心。格:规矩。

子曰:“君子怀德,小人怀土;君子怀刑,小人怀惠。”(04.11)

【注释】怀:思念、关注、心里想的是。土:乡土。刑:法度、法制惩罚。惠:小恩小惠、利益。

【白话译文】

孔子说:“君子关注如何培养品德,小人关注如何耕好土地种好庄稼。君子关心法度,小人关心物质利益。”(04.11)

【英译】

The Master said, “A superior man yearns how to cultivate his morals, while the inferior man yearns how to plant fields for good crops. And a superior man is concerned about laws and regulations, while the inferior man is concerned about material benefits.” (04.11)

子曰:“片言可以折狱者,其由也与。子路无宿诺。”(12.12)

【注释】片言:片面之词,诉讼双方中一方的言辞。折:判断。狱:案件。其:大概(只有)。由:姓仲名由,字子路。与:吧。子路:由,姓仲名由。宿:隔夜。诺:诺言。

【白话译文】

孔子说:“如果有谁仅凭单方面的观点就可以断案的话,这个人大概就是由了。子路从来不把承诺这天办的事拖延到隔夜去办。”(12.12)

【英译】

The Master said, "If someone can settle a lawsuit based on one-sided views, this man probably is You[1]. Zilu[2] never postpones overnight what he promises to do this day." (12.12)

【英译注】(1) You: Surname Zhong, first name You, style name Zilu, Confucius's disciple. (2) Zilu: You, surname Zhong, first name You, style name Zilu.

子路曰:"卫君待子而为政,子将奚先?"

子曰:"必也正名乎!"

子路曰:"有是哉,子之迂也!奚其正?"

【注释】鲁哀公七年(公元前488年),孔子64岁,在楚国未被重用,从楚国到卫国,卫君欲得孔子为政,而子路问。子路:姓仲名由,字子路。卫君:卫出公,姓姬名蒯(音 kuǎi 㧟)辄(音 zhé 哲),卫灵公之孙,因其父聩(音 kuì 愧)暗杀南子未遂被逐而立为君,后父子争位。待:等候。子:你。而:用以、用来。为政:治理政事。待子而为政:等待你去治国。奚(音 xī 息):什么。先:优先。

必:一定。正:端正。名:名分,百事之名。正名:端正名分,明确职责。

有是哉:有这样做的吗。迂:绕远、不实际。

【白话译文】

子路问:"如果卫国的君主请你治理他的国家,老师你首先将做什么?"

孔子说:"那一定是端正名分!"

子路说:"啊,原来如此!我实在认为老师你绕弯路了!为什么是端正名分?"

【英译】

Zilu[1] said, "If the sovereign of the State of Wei invites you to administer his state, what will you, my Master, do first?"

The Master said, "It must certainly be rectification of names!"

Zilu said, "Oh, so it is. I do think that you, my Master, are making a detour. Why is it rectification of names?"

【英译注】(1) Zilu: Surname Zhong, first name You, style name Zilu, Confucius's disciple.

子曰："野哉，由也！君子于其所不知，盖阙如也。名不正，则言不顺；言不顺，则事不成；事不成，则礼乐不兴；礼乐不兴，则刑罚不中；刑罚不中，则民无所措手足。故君子名之必可言也，言之必可行也。君子于其言，无所苟而已矣。"（13.03）

【注释】野：郊外为野，野人、普通百姓（的思想）。由：仲由，子路。于其：对于他。盖：一般。阙：缺，存疑，不做结论。如也：的样子。阙如：存疑，暂不下定论，留待考查判断。言：说法，用来解释名词，说明意义。不顺：无顺序、不顺理。事不成：办不成事。礼乐：礼乐（音 yuè 月）制度。兴：建立。刑罚：刑罚典章。中（音 zhòng 众）：得当。民：百姓。措：放置。名之必可言也：对一事的命名，必须能够准确地讲出。可：能够。行：可行，可执行。言之必可行也：说一事，一定能够执行。苟：苟且，马马虎虎。而已矣：罢了。

【白话译文】

孔子说："由啊，你这种观点，非常接近远郊田野里的普通村民了！君子对于他所不理解的，一般保留意见，不急忙做结论。如果一件事的名称不正确，那么对它的言辞就不能按顺序表达出来。如果对它的言辞不能按顺序表达出来，那么一件事就不能很好地办成。如果一件事不能很好地办成，那么礼仪和礼乐就不能兴办起来。如果礼仪和礼乐不能兴办起来，那么刑罚就不能刚好合适。如果刑罚不能刚好合适，那么老百姓就不知道把手脚放在哪里。因此，君子对于一件事情的命名，必须能够用清晰的语言表达出来。当他表达清晰的时候，他的语言才能够正确地、不走样地执行下去。君子对于他的言语，一定不能有一丝马虎。"（13.03）

【英译】

The Master said, "Your view is close to

【英译注】(1) You: First name of Zilu.

that of a common villager in remote rural areas, You[1]! A superior man normally holds reservations and does not casually jump to conclusions on what he does not understand. If a name is not correct for a thing, the words on it cannot be expressed in order. If the words on it are not expressed in order, a thing cannot be accomplished. If a thing is not accomplished, the systems of the Rites of Proprieties and Ritual Music cannot be established. If the systems of the Rites of Proprieties and Ritual Music are not established, punishments cannot be executed correctly. If punishments are not executed correctly, the common people do not know where to put their hands and feet. Therefore, when a superior man names a thing, he must clearly express it in words. When he expresses it clearly, his words can be applied correctly without distortion. A superior man must not be the least negligent about his language." (13. 03)

孟氏使阳肤为士师,问于曾子。曾子曰:"上失其道,民散久矣。如得其情,则哀矜而勿喜。"(19. 19)

【白话译文】

孟氏任命阳肤为法官,阳肤向曾子请

【注释】孟氏:鲁国大夫。使:任命。阳肤:曾子的学生。士师:典狱官。问:请教。于:向。曾子:姓曾名参(音 shēn 申),字子舆,鲁国南武城人,在今山东平邑县内。上:当权者。失:偏离。道:正道。民:百姓。散:离心离德。久:很久。如:如果。得:获得。其:犯人的。情:实情。哀:伤心、悲伤

教。曾子说:"现在高官不守规矩,人民与他们离心离德很久了。如果你在审讯中得到不利于某人的证据,你应当为他悲哀和怜悯,不能因此而沾沾自喜。"(19.19)

(失道、民散)。矜(音 jīn 今):怜悯同情(犯人不该犯法)。喜:自鸣得意。

【英译】

Meng Shi(1) appointed Yang Fu(2) a judge. Yang Fu asked advice from Master Zeng(3). Master Zeng said, "High officials are not obeying the laws now, and for a long time, the common people have been disaffected. If you find evidence against someone during interrogation, you should feel sad and sympathetic for the person, and should not feel complacent about it." (19.19)

【英译注】(1) Meng Shi: A senior official of the State of Lu. (2) Yang Fu: A disciple of Master Zeng. (3) Master Zeng: Confucius's disciple, surname Zeng, first name Shen, style name Ziyu, from Wucheng of the State of Lu, currently Pingyi County of Shandong Province.

47

讼 A Lawsuit

子曰:"已矣乎!吾未见能见其过而内自讼者也。"(05.27)

【注释】已:停止、完毕。矣乎:啊。已矣乎:到现在为止啊。其:他人的。过:错误。内:内心。自:自己。讼(音 sòng 宋):责备。自讼:反省、自责、自我批评。见其过而内自讼者:看到他人的错误,却能真心反省自己的人。

【白话译文】

孔子说:"到目前为止,我从来没有看

到这样的人，当他意识到别人犯的错误，却从内心责备自己。”（05.27）

【英译】

The Master said, “So far, I have never seen a person who blames himself when he recognizes a mistake(1) made by someone else.” (05.27)

【英译注】(1) a mistake: It is common that one may blame himself when he perceives his own mistake. Confucius might suggest that one could learn from others' mistakes.

子曰：“听讼，吾犹人也。必也使无讼乎！”(12.13)

【注释】讼（音 sòng 宋）：争辩是非，为人辩冤。听讼：审理诉讼案，听人辩冤。犹：同、像。吾犹人也：我的情感同别人一样呀；“人同此心，心同此理，我自不能例外。”[J10] 必：必须，重要的是。使无讼乎：让诉讼的事，根本不发生啊。

【白话译文】

孔子说：“审理案件，我的心情与别人差不多。但是，重要的是，我必须完全避免诉讼案的发生！”（12.13）

【英译】

The Master said, “My feeling to try a case is similar to that of others. But the most important thing is that I must completely prevent a lawsuit from occurring.” (12.13)

48

税 Taxes

季氏富于周公,而求也为之聚敛而附益之。子曰:“非吾徒也。小子鸣鼓而攻之可也。”(11.17)

【注释】季氏:鲁国正卿季孙氏,季康子,姓季孙,名肥,谥号康。周公:周朝的公侯。而:然而,但是。求:姓冉、名求,字子有。为之:为他。聚:积聚。敛:搜刮(钱财)。附:附着、增益。益:增加。非:不是。徒:弟子。小子:弟子们。鸣鼓:大张旗鼓。攻:批驳、声讨。之:姓冉,名求,字子有。可:适当、适宜。鸣鼓而攻之可也:可以大张旗鼓地声讨他。

【白话译文】

季氏的家族比鲁国的朝廷都富有,而求仍然(通过对人民收重税)帮助他们大量搜刮财富,进一步增加他们的钱财。孔子说:“冉求已经失去了作为我弟子的资格了! 弟子们,你们可以大张旗鼓地声讨他!”(11.17)

【英译】

The Ji family[(1)] were richer than the court of the State of Lu[(2)] and Qiu[(3)] still assisted them to further amass more money and properties (by extorting large wealth and levying heavy taxes on the people). The Master said[(4)]:“Qiu no longer qualifies as my disciple! You, my disciples, may denounce him on a grand scale!” (11.17)

【英译注】(1) The Ji family: Master Ji Kang, the head of the Ji family, surname Jisun, first name Fei, posthumous title Kang, senior officer during Duke Ai who ruled from 494 BC to 468 BC. (2) the State of Lu: The sovereign of the State of Lu was offspring of Duke Zhou Dan of the Zhou Dynasty. (3) Qiu: Surname Ran, first name Qiu, style name Ziyou, Confucius's disciple. (4) Background: Confucius thus spoke this to express his view for the Ji Family not to levy heavy taxes on people. Confucius was experiencing one of the most important tax system transformations in China, called "Initial Tax on Land per *Mu*" (*Mu* is a unit of land, 667 square meters currently) that started at the State of Lu in 594 BC. Before this, China adopted "the nine squares" tax system by dividing a plot of land into nine squares. The serfs first cultivated the central square for public and then eight outer squares for themselves. Due to agricultural productivity increment by extensively applying oxen and iron farm tools, the senior officials opened up wasteland to avoid taxes, so the nine square tax system nearly disappeared except in name. The heads of the Ji Family served as the prime ministers of the State of Lu and launched tax reformation by levying farm products other than contribution of labour to the public, and thus they were greatly rich when Ran Qiu served as general manager of the Ji family.

哀公问于有若曰:"年饥,用不足,如之何?"有若对曰:"盍彻乎?"曰:"二,吾犹不足,如之何其彻也?"对曰:"百姓足,君孰与不足?百姓不足,君孰与足?"(12.09)

【注释】哀公:姓姬名蒋,谥(音 shì 是)号哀,鲁国国君,公元前 494 年至公元前 468 年在位。问:咨询、请教。于:向。有若:姓有名若,孔子弟子,比孔子小 43 岁。年:年景。饥:饥荒。用:开支。足:充足,够用。如之何:如何办。对曰:敬答。盍(音 hé 河):何不。彻(音 chè 撤):周代的田税制度,十分抽一的税率。盍彻乎:何不用彻税法呢。二:十分之二的税。犹:还是。如之何:怎么。其:(用)那。孰与:怎么会。

【白话译文】

哀公问有若:"今年是欠年,我们的财政收入不足,我们怎么办?"有若敬答:"为什么我们不收取十分抽一的税?"哀公说:"用十分抽二的税,我还没有足够的收入用于开支,为什么要采用十分抽一的税?"有若敬答:"如果老百姓富足了,君主怎么会不富足呢?如果老百姓没有富足,君主怎么能够富足呢?"(12.09)

【英译】

Duke Ai[(1)] asked You Ruo[(2)], "This is a lean year, and our financial revenue is insufficient for the state. What should we do?" You Ruo replied respectfully, "Why don't we levy a tithe?" Duke Ai said, "With two tenths I still cannot have enough revenue to meet expenditures. Why is tithe to be adopted?" You Ruo replied respectfully, "If the common people are rich, how cannot a sovereign be rich? If the common people are not rich, how can a sovereign be rich?" (12.09)

【英译注】(1) Duke Ai: the Duke of the State of Lu, surname Ji, first name Jiang, posthumous title Ai, ruling from 494 BC to 468 BC. When Confucius returned home after 484 BC, Duke Ai talked about this with You Ruo. (2) You Ruo: Surname You, first name Ruo, style name Ziyou, Confucius's disciple.

49

贫富 Poverty and Wealth

子贡曰："贫而无谄，富而无骄。何如?"子曰："可也。未若贫而乐，富而好礼者也。"子贡曰："《诗》云：'如切如磋，如琢如磨。'其斯之谓与?"子曰："赐也，始可与言《诗》已矣！告诸往而知来者。"(01.15)

【注释】子贡：姓端木名赐，字子贡。贫：缺钱。而：却，但是。谄(音 chè 撤)：巴结。富：有钱。骄：自满、自大。何如：怎么样。可：尚可，可以。未若：不如。乐(音 lè 勒)：高兴。好(音 hào 号)：(公正)喜爱。诗：《诗经·卫风·淇奥》。云：说。如：像。切：切削。磋(音 cuò 蹉)：锉。如切如磋：像制骨器一样，切削陶锉。琢：雕刻。磨：打磨。如琢如磨：像制玉器一样，雕刻打磨，精益求精。其：大概。斯：此。赐：姓端木名赐，字子贡。始：开始，现在。与：和(他)一起。言：说、讲。矣：了。告：告诉。诸：他。往：过去。来：未来。

【白话译文】

子贡问："一个人贫穷时不巴结奉承别人，富有时不骄傲自满。你认为他怎么样?"孔子说："那挺好了。但是，不如他在贫穷时幸福地追求正确的原则，富有时谦虚地热爱礼仪。"子贡说："《诗》说：'就像一根骨头或象牙一样，它被切削陶锉成骨器或象牙器；就像一块玉石一样，精雕、细磨成玉器。'这大体可以解释你的意思吗?"孔子说："赐啊！我可以开始与你讨论《诗》了！告诉你过去的事，你能知道未来的事了。"(01.15)

【英译】

Zigong(1) asked, "What do you think a

【英译注】(1) Zigong: Surname Duanmu, first name Ci, style name

bout a person if he does not fawn on others when he is poor and he is not arrogant when he is rich?" The Master said, " That is good. But it is better for him to either happily pursue the right doctrine in poverty or modestly love the Rites of Proprieties in wealth. " Zigong said, " *Poems and Odes*(2) tells: ' As if it is a piece of bone or ivory, it is cut and filed into a beautiful article; as if it is a piece of jade, it is engraved precisely and polished cautiously into a masterpiece. ' Can that probably be interpreted for what you mean?" The Master said, "Ah Ci(3)! Now I can start talking with you about *Poems and Odes*, as I talk to you about the things of past and then you can know things of future. " (01. 15)

Zigong, Confucius's disciple. (2) This sentence originated from a song titled " Duke Wu of Wei" in *Songs Collected in Wei*, *Poems and Odes*, currently named *Book of Poetry*. (3) Ci: First name of Zigong.

子曰:"富而可求也,虽执鞭之士,吾亦为之。如不可求,从吾所好。"(07. 12)

【白话译文】

孔子说:"如果财富可以用正义的方式获得,即使职位低到一个拿皮鞭的人(给官员开道或者在市场维持秩序),我依然要获得它。如果财富不可以用正义的方式获得,我将做我喜爱的事。"(07. 12)

【注释】富:财富,发财,富有。而:如果。可求:合礼遵道地谋求。富而可求也:如果财富可以合礼遵道地谋求。执鞭:贱职,为帝、君、臣出入而执皮鞭开路。亦:也。为:做。从:依据。所好:我的爱好。从吾所好:依据我的爱好行事。

【英译】

The Master said, "If wealth can be obtained righteously, I would like to take it even though the job is as low as a leather whip holder (who clears the way for an official or maintains order at a market). If wealth cannot be obtained righteously, I would do what I love." (07. 12)

子曰:"奢则不孙,俭则固。与其不孙也,宁固。"(07. 36)

【注释】奢:奢侈。则:就、便。孙(音 xùn 训):逊,谦让、恭顺。不孙:不顺从,越礼。俭:节俭。固:简陋,寒酸。宁:宁可。

【白话译文】

孔子说:"如果奢侈豪华让人骄傲蛮横,节俭朴素让人简陋卑微,我宁可简陋卑微,而不要骄傲蛮横。"(07. 36)

【英译】

The Master said, "If luxury and extravagance may make a person arrogant and unreasonable, and thriftiness and simpleness may make a person shabby and humble, I would be shabby and humble rather than arrogant and unreasonable." (07. 36)

50

盗 Robbery

季康子患盗，问于孔子。孔子对曰："苟子之不欲，虽赏之不窃。"（12.18）

【注释】鲁哀公十一年（公元前484年），孔子68岁周游列国回鲁，答季康子问。季康子：姓季孙名肥，谥（音shì是）号康，鲁哀公时任正卿。患：担忧。盗：偷盗。于：向。对曰：敬答。苟：假如。子：你。欲：贪图财利。虽：即使。赏：奖励。之：偷盗。虽赏之不窃：即使对偷盗进行奖励，（由于知耻）百姓不会偷。

【白话译文】

季康子苦于出现的盗贼太多了，向孔夫子请教如何办。孔夫子敬答："假如你不贪婪大量财富，即使你奖励盗窃行为，他们也不会偷盗的。"（12.18）

【英译】

Master Ji Kang[1] was vexed about too many thieves and robbers appearing and asked advice from Confucius about how to handle it. Confucius replied respectfully, "If you did not covet wealth and riches, they would not steal and rob, even if you offered a reward for doing so." (12.18)

【英译注】（1）Master Ji Kang: Surname Jisun, first name Fei, posthumous title Kang, chief senior official during Duke Ai.

叶公语孔子曰："吾党有直躬者，其父攘羊，而子证之。"孔子曰："吾党之直者异于是。父

【注释】鲁哀公五年（公元前490年），孔子62岁在蔡国，从蔡国去楚国，见贤大夫叶公，当讲此语，但《史记》未记此事。叶（shè

为子隐，子为父隐，直在其中矣。”(13.18)

社)公:姓沈名诸梁,楚国大夫,封地在叶城(今河南叶县南)。语(音 yù 玉):和别人一起谈论。党:500户一党。直:正直、法直、理直。躬:自身。者:的人。直躬者:正直理直的人。父:父亲。攘(音 rǎng 壤):侵夺,偷盗。子:儿子。证:告发。异:不同。是:这。异于是:与这不一样。为:替。隐:隐瞒。直在其中矣:正直在里面了,此处的“直”为合乎人情,为情直,而非叶公的“理直、法直”。

【白话译文】

大臣叶公与孔夫子讨论说:“我家乡有一位直率的人,他父亲偷了别人的羊,他向官府举报此事。”孔夫子说:“我家乡直率的人不同于你们的。父亲为儿子隐瞒过错,儿子为父亲隐瞒过错,他们的直率就在这行为中。”(13.18)

【英译】

Senior Official She(1) discussed with Confucius, “There is one straightforward person at my hometown. His father stole a goat and he reported it to the authorities.” Confucius said, “The straightforward person at my hometown is different from yours. The father conceals an offense for his son and the son conceals it for his father. Their straightforwardness is inside the conduct.” (13.18)

【英译注】(1) Senior Official She: Surname Shen, first name Zhuliang, senior official of the State of Chu and his fief was given at She City, currently Ye County, Henan Province. His straightforwardness is reasonable by the laws. Confucius mentioned the natural and normal human feelings.

十
Ten

生活
Daily Life

51

衣 Clothes

子曰:"衣敝缊袍,与衣狐貉者立,而不耻者,其由也与?'不忮不求,何用不臧?'"子路终身诵之。子曰:"是道也,何足以臧?"(09.27)

【注释】衣:穿戴。敝:坏。缊(音 yùn 运):新旧混合的丝绵絮。与:同,一起。狐:狐皮。貉:貉(音 hé 河)皮。者:的人。立:站。与衣狐貉者立:与穿狐皮、貉皮衣的人站在一起。耻:有耻辱感。其:大概。由:姓仲名由,字子路。与:吗。忮(音 zhì 志):嫉妒。求:贪求。何用:为什么。臧(音 zāng 脏):好。不忮不求,何用不臧(《诗经·邶风·雄雉》):不嫉不贪,为什么不好。诵:朗诵。道:人起码的道理。何足:怎么够得上。是道也,何足以臧:仅仅这样做,怎么能够好得起来。

【白话译文】

孔子说:"一个人穿着磨破了的外衣,里边填着翻新的旧丝绵絮,与穿着狐皮、貉皮大衣的人并排站立而没有耻辱感的人,大概只有由一个人吧?《诗》说:'如果一个人不嫉妒又不贪婪,他怎么能不完美呢?'"子路终身朗诵这首诗。孔子说:"这么做很平常。仅仅这样做,你怎么能达到完美呢?"(09.27)

【英译】

The Master said, "Is probably only You[(1)] who does not feel ashamed standing together with those dressed in fox fur or raccoon dog fur while he is dressed in a worn-out overcoat filled with old silk floss? *Poems and Odes*[(2)] says, 'How can one not become

【英译注】(1) You: Surname Zhong, first name You, style name Zilu, Confucius's disciple. (2) *Poems and Odes*: It is selected from the poem named "My Man In Service", from the part *Songs Collected in Bei* of *Poems and Odes*. (3) Zilu: First name You, surname Zhong, style name Zilu.

perfect if he is neither jealous nor greedy?'" Hearing this, Zilu(3) recited this poem all his life. The Master said, "It is common to do this. How can you reach perfection if you have only done this?" (09.27)

君子不以绀緅饰,红紫不以为亵服。

当暑,袗絺绤,必表而出之。

缁衣,羔裘;素衣,麑裘;黄衣,狐裘。亵裘长,短右袂。

【注释】以:用。绀(音 gàn 赣):深青透红,斋戒服色。緅(音 zōu 邹):黑中透红,丧服色。饰:服饰。亵服:居家便服。

暑:夏天。袗(音 zhěn 诊):单衣。絺(音 chī 痴):细葛布。绤(音 xì 细):粗葛布。袗絺绤:细麻布衣。必:一定。表:作外衣穿。表而出之:套在外面,显露它。

缁:黑色。羔裘:黑羔羊皮衣,毛向外。素:白。麑(音 ní 尼):小鹿,白色。亵(音 xiè 谢):内衣,亲近,熟悉。亵裘:便服皮袍。长:长些。袂(音 mèi):袖子。短右袂:右袖短些。

【白话译文】

君子不用青色或铁灰色做衣服的饰边,不用浅红或紫色作为居家平时的衣服。

在炎热的夏天,他穿着由粗麻或细麻织的单衣,在其外必须套一件衬衣。

黑衣配羊羔皮衣,白色衣服配小鹿皮衣,黄色皮衣配狐皮衣。平时的裘皮衣要足够长,但右袖子要短一些。

【英译】

A superior man neither dresses in blue or grey colours for the trim on his clothes, nor uses light red or purple colours for clothes in daily life.

In the hot summer, he wears a light coat woven by rough or thin hemp fabrics and

【英译注】(1) Black was then an auspicious colour.

must put on an extra shirt outside it.

A black coat matches a lamb fur coat, a white coat matches a deer fur coat, and a yellow coat matches a fox fur coat. The everyday fur coat is long enough, but its right sleeve must be a little shorter.

必有寝衣,长一身有半。狐貉之厚以居。去丧无所不佩。

非帷裳,必杀之。羔裘玄冠不以吊。吉月,必朝服而朝。(10.06)

【注释】寝衣:睡衣;当时的被子。身:上身。一身有半:上身的一倍半长。狐:狐皮。貉(音 hé 河):貉皮。之厚:毛厚。居:坐垫。狐貉之厚以居:狐皮貉皮的毛厚,做成坐席垫。去丧:度过丧期。无:没有。佩:佩戴。

帷(音 wéi 维)裳:礼服,用整幅布制作。杀(音 shài 晒):裁剪。杀之:剪去布边,布边可做褶裙。玄冠:黑礼帽。吊:吊丧。羔裘玄冠不以吊:穿着黑羔羊皮衣,戴着黑帽(都是黑色的,当时是吉祥的服装颜色),不去吊丧。吉月:每月初一;大年初一。朝:朝拜国君,朝贺。

【白话译文】

睡觉一定有睡衣,其长度是一人上身长的一倍半。狐皮、貉皮毛厚的部分,用作坐垫。丧期满后,什么都可以用作饰物。

除非衣服用整块布做,这种衣服通常是礼服或者丧服,这整块布一定事先适当裁去一部分。一个人去吊丧时,不穿黑羔羊皮袍,不戴黑色礼帽。每年正月初一朝拜时,必须穿朝服上朝。(10.06)

【英译】

The pajamas must be used for sleep and their length is one and a half of the trunk of a person. A seat cushion is made of thickest part of fox or raccoon dog fur. When the mourning period is over, anything can be used for clothing decorations.

Unless a whole piece of cloth is used to make clothing that normally is for ceremonial dress or mourning clothes, a suitable part of the whole piece must be cut off in advance. A lamb fur gown and black[1] ceremonial hat are not worn when a person visits the bereaved to offer his condolences. Court clothes must be worn when one pays respects to the court on the first day of January each year. (10.06)

52

食 Foods

子食于有丧者之侧,未尝饱也。(07.09)

【注释】食:吃饭。于:在。有丧:有丧事。未尝:不曾。

【白话译文】

孔子在办丧事的人旁边吃饭,从来不吃饱。(07.09)

【英译】

The Master never ate his fill when he took a meal beside someone who was in mourning. (07.09)

齐,必有明衣,布。齐必变食,居必迁坐。(10.07)

【注释】齐(音 zhāi 摘):斋,斋戒。明衣:沐浴后穿的浴衣。布:布做的,古时没有今天的棉花,布为丝麻台葛、麻布。变食:不同于平常的饮食,无酒、葱、蒜等。居:居住。迁:迁出。坐:卧室。迁坐:搬出卧室住。

【白话译文】

孔子斋戒时,一定换上干净的衣服,衣服的布是用麻织的。斋戒时,孔子一定改变饮食,一定从平时的卧室搬出,睡在外室。(10.07)

【英译】

When the Master practiced the fast, he certainly changed to clean clothes woven of hemp fabrics. Making a fast, the Master changed his food and drink and surely moved from his normal bedroom and slept in the outer room. (10.07)

食不厌精,脍不厌细。食饐而餲,鱼馁而肉败,不食。色恶,不食。臭恶,不食。失饪,不食。不时,不食。割不正,不食。不得其酱,不食。肉虽多,不使胜食气。惟酒无量,不及乱。沽酒市脯,不食。不撤姜食。不多食。(10.08)

【注释】食:粮食。厌:嫌。精:舂得干净。脍(音 kuài 快):切细的鱼、肉。饐(音 yì 忆):陈旧、陈化。餲(音 ài 爱):变味。馁(音 něi):鱼腐烂。而:并且。败:肉腐烂。不食:不吃。色:颜色。恶(音 è 鳄):不好。臭(音 xiù 秀):气味。失饪:烹调不当。时:应时。割:切割。正:符合规矩。酱:佐料。胜:超过。气(音 xì 戏):饩,米面粮。食(音 sì 四)气:饭量,主食。惟:只有。无量:不限量。及:至、达到。乱:酒醉。不及乱:不至于醉。沽:买。市:市场买的。脯(音 fǔ 府):熟肉干。撤:移走。多食:过饱。

【白话译文】

不反对吃舂得干净的粮食,也不反对

精细烹饪的薄片鱼或肉。霉变发臭的粮食,不吃。腐烂的鱼、腐败的肉,不吃。颜色变坏的食物,不吃。气味不对的食物,不吃。烹饪不当的食物,不吃。没有到适当的吃饭时间,不吃饭。切割得不符合规范的食物,不吃。食物没有配上合适的酱,不吃。即使有大量的鱼肉,也不吃得超过粮食食物的量。对酒不限量,但不让自己喝醉。市场上购买回来的酒和肉干,不吃。吃饭时,姜不撤掉。不过量饮食。(10.08)

【英译】

Neither oppose husking the grains cleanly nor oppose meticulously cooked meat or fish slices. Neither eat grains that mildew and stink nor eat putrid fish and rotten meat. Do not eat foods that are badly discolored. Do not eat foods that smell badly. Do not eat foods that are improperly prepared and cooked. Do not eat when it is not the right meal time. Do not eat foods that are not cut according to proper criteria. Do not eat foods that are served without suitable sauces. Though there may be a large quantity of meat or fish available, eat them no more than grains. Only do not set bounds on liquor, but do not allow oneself to drink too much. Neither drink liquor sold on markets nor eat dried meat bought from markets. Don't take ginger off the table when eating. And do not overeat. (10.08)

祭于公，不宿肉。祭肉，不出三日，出三日，不食之矣。(10.09)

【注释】祭：祭祀。于：在。公：朝庙。宿：过夜。不宿肉：祭祀分得的肉不过夜。祭肉：祭祀用的肉。出：超过。食：吃。之：它。

【白话译文】

孔子参加国家祭祀典礼，分配一些祭肉，他立刻处理，不让它过夜不处理。家族祭祀的肉，留存不超过三天。三天后，这肉就不再吃了。(10.09)

【英译】

When the Master was allotted some sacrificial meat at a state sacrifice ceremony, he cleared it instantly and did not let it keep overnight. The meat from a home sacrifice was kept not more than three days; and after three days, the meat was not eaten anymore. (10.09)

虽疏食菜羹，瓜祭，必齐如也。(10.11)

【注释】疏：粗糙。食：粮食。菜羹：菜汤。瓜祭：吃饭前，取出少许席上各食物，放在食具之间祭祖。必：一定。齐(音 zhāi 摘)：斋，斋戒。如：一样。

【白话译文】

虽然孔子只有粗粮、菜汤，他也取出一部分祭祀祖先，非常虔诚、庄重，如正式斋戒一样。(10.11)

【英译】

Though the Master only had coarse food grains and vegetable soup, he piously and solemnly took some of them as a sacrifice to his ancestors, much like a formal fast. (10. 11)

君赐食,必正席先尝之。君赐腥,必熟而荐之。君赐生,必畜之。侍食于君,君祭,先饭。(10. 18)

【注释】君:国君。赐:赐给。食:熟食。必:一定。正席:端正坐在席上。尝:试吃。腥:生肉。熟:煮熟。荐:供奉祖宗。生:活物。畜:饲养。侍(音 shì 是):一旁陪伴,伺候。侍食:陪同吃饭。君祭:国君饭前祭礼。先饭:先替国君尝一尝。

【白话译文】

当君主赐给孔子熟食时,他一定把座位放妥、端正坐好,恭敬地尝一点。君主赐给他新鲜的生肉,他一定是烹饪好,吃前用它先敬祖先。君主赐给他活牲畜,他一定是把它们养起来。孔子伺候君主吃饭,当君主举行祭祀仪式时,他先尝一点以示敬意。(10. 18)

【英译】

When the sovereign granted some cooked foods to the Master, he arranged his seat properly, sat upright, and tried the foods with an attitude of respect. When the sovereign granted fresh meat to him, he cooked it and worshiped his ancestors with it before eating. When the sovereign granted living livestock to him, he raised them. And when he attended upon the sovereign at meals during sacrificial ceremonies, the Master tried the foods first to show respect. (10. 18)

53

住 Residence

子曰:"里仁为美。择不处仁,焉得知?"(04. 01)

【白话译文】

孔子说:"一个人居住的地方具有仁德,是美妙的事。如果一个人选择住处,但这个住处没有仁德,他怎么能够智慧呢?"(04. 01)

【英译】

The Master said, "It is beautiful that one dwells in the place where superior benevolence prevails. If one selects a residence without superior benevolence, how can he be wise?" (04. 01)

【注释】里:住处,居住。仁:仁德风气、仁爱风俗。为美:才好。处(音 chǔ 础):居住。择不处仁:选择住处,没有仁德风气。焉:怎么。得:算得。知(音 zhì 治):智,智慧。焉得知:怎么算是智慧。

子欲居九夷。或曰："陋，如之何？"子曰："君子居之，何陋之有？"(09.14)

【注释】欲：想，打算。居：(搬家)居住。九夷：东方少数民族。或曰：有人说。陋：鄙野，落后，不开化。何陋之有：有什么简陋、鄙陋的呢？

【白话译文】

孔子意欲搬到东方少数民族部落住。有人说："那个地方鄙陋，你怎么能在那里住下？"孔子说："如果一名君子住在那里，那里怎么会鄙陋呢？"(09.14)

【英译】

The Master desired to settle among the minority tribes of the east. Someone said, "The place is mean and crude. How can you dwell there?" The Master said, "If a superior man dwells there, how can it be mean and crude?" (09.14)

子谓卫公子荆："善居室。始有，曰：'苟合矣。'少有，曰：'苟完矣。'富有，曰：'苟美矣。'"(13.08)

【注释】谓：谈论。卫公子荆：卫国大夫，字南楚，卫献公之子。善：会管理。居室：居家过日子。始：初。有：有家业。苟：差不多。合：足够。少：稍微。完：完备。富有：大富。美：完美。

【白话译文】

孔子评论卫国的公子荆说："他擅长家业管理。当他日子开始好起来时，他说：'这差不多凑合了！'当他的家产积蓄多一点时，他说：'这差不多过好生活心满意足

了！'当他财富多起来时，他说：'这差不多完美无缺了！'"（13.08）

【英译】

The Master commented on Jing[1], a son of the Duke of the State of Wei, "He is good at management of the family properties. When conditions began to improve, he said, 'Now it is more or less pretty good.' When the family properties had expanded a little, he said, 'It is more or less sufficient for a good life!' When the family's wealth had increased further, he said, 'It is more or less perfect for us!'" (13.08)

【英译注】(1) Jing: A senior official of the State of Wei, his first name Jing, style name Nanchu, a son of Duke Xian.

54

行 Travel

达巷党人曰："大哉孔子！博学而无所成名。"子闻之，谓门弟子曰："吾何执？执御乎？执射乎？吾执御矣。"（09.02）

【注释】达巷：党名，1 党 500 家。大：伟大。博：渊博。学：学问。无所成名：在一门技术上成名。谓：告诉。门：门下。执：掌握（技艺）。何：什么。何执：执何，掌握什么技艺。御：驾车。射：射箭。矣：吧。

【白话译文】

达巷社区的一个人说："孔子真伟大啊！他学识渊博，可惜没有一个专长能够

树立名声。”孔子听到后，对他的弟子说：“我掌握哪个专长？我驾车吗？我掌握箭术？我还是驾车吧。”（09.02）

【英译】

A person from Daxiang Community said,“How great the Master is! He is erudite, but has not established his reputation in one specialty.” Hearing this, the Master said to his disciples,“What specialty should I master? Do I drive a carriage? Do I master archery? I would better drive a carriage.”（09.02）

君命召，不俟驾行矣。（10.20）

【注释】君：国君。命召：召见。俟（音 sì 四）：等待。驾：驾好马车。行：步行。

【白话译文】

当君主召见孔子时，他不等到车子准备好，就先步行出发了。（10.20）

【英译】

When the Master was called in by his sovereign, he set off on foot immediately, not awaiting the carriage to be prepared for him.（10.20）

升车，必正立，执绥。车中，不内顾，不疾言，不亲指。(10.26)

【白话译文】

孔子上车时，一定站立端正，手持登车带。他在车中，不左顾右盼，不大声说话，也不用手指这指那。(10.26)

【英译】

When the Master mounted a carriage, he stood upright and held the support belt. When he was in a carriage, he did not glance right and left, neither spoke loudly nor pointed to this or that with his fingers. (10.26)

【注释】升：上。升车：孔子上车时。必：一定。正立：端正地站立。执：扶持。绥：上车手扶的索带。内顾：回头看。疾：急剧而猛烈。疾言：大声说话。亲指：手指比划。

55

起居 Daily Behaviors

子之燕居，申申如也，夭夭如也。(07.04)

【白话译文】

孔子在家闲居，穿戴整齐舒适，表情舒

【注释】之：的。燕：安逸、安闲。居：家居。子之燕居：孔子在家闲住。申：整齐、舒展。如也：的样子。申申如也：穿戴整齐舒适。夭(音 yāo 妖)：舒服、和悦。夭夭如也：神色和悦。

展和悦。(07. 04)

【英译】

When the Master stayed at home idly, he dressed neatly and comfortably, and his countenance was easy and kind. (07. 04)

食不语,寝不言。(10. 10)

【白话译文】

吃饭时,不相互答话。睡觉时,不主动给人说话。(10. 10)

【英译】

Do not talk with each other when taking meals and do not speak to anyone when sleeping in bed. (10. 10)

【注释】食:吃饭时。语(音 yù 玉):和别人一起谈论,答话。寝:睡觉时。言:主动对人说话。

席不正,不坐。(10. 12)

【白话译文】

除非座席(按礼节)摆正了,孔子不坐下。(10. 12)

【英译】

The Master did not sit down unless the seat was straight (according to the Rites). (10. 12)

【注释】席:席子,当时无桌椅,铺席子,坐在地面上。正:排位、位置、方向等符合礼节。

寝不尸，居不容。（10.24）

【白话译文】

睡觉时，不仰卧如僵尸一般双手放在两侧。在家时，不像作客一样严肃。（10.24）

【英译】

Do not lie supinely like a corpse rigidly putting both hands to his sides when sleeping. Do not be as serious as a guest when staying at home. (10.24)

【注释】寝：睡觉。尸：僵直仰卧，布展手足。居：在家。容：如作客或待客一样严肃。

子曰："饱食终日，无所用心，难矣哉！不有博弈者乎？为之，犹贤乎已。"（17.22）

【白话译文】

孔子说："一个人饱食终日，无所用心，会特别难受呀！不是有投骰子游戏和围棋吗？做这，也比闲着强。"（17.22）

【英译】

The Master said, "One is sated with meals and remains idle all day. It may be extremely difficult for him to feel good! Aren't there a dice game and *Weiqi*(1) available now? To do that is better than to remain idle." (17.22)

【注释】饱食：吃饱。终日：整天。难：日子不好过。不有：不是有。博：赌输赢的游戏。弈：下棋，比如下围棋。为：做。之：代词，指代上文的"博弈"。犹：还是。贤：更好。犹贤乎已：还是比闲着好的呀。

【英译注】(1) *Weiqi*: Go, a game played with black and white pieces on a board of 361 (19 × 19) crosses.

56

梦 Dream

子曰:"甚矣,吾衰也!久矣,吾不复梦见周公。"(07.05)

【白话译文】

孔子说:"哎呀,我衰老得多么厉害呀!很久了,我再也没有梦见周公了。"(07.05)

【英译】

The Master said, "Alas! I am old and feeble! I have not dreamed of Duke Zhou(1) for a long time now." (07.05)

【注释】甚矣:非常啊,厉害啊。衰:衰老。甚矣,吾衰也:我衰老得非常厉害啊。久矣:很久呀。复:再。周公:姓姬名旦,周文王子,周武王弟,周成王叔父,鲁国国君的始祖,相传为西周典章制度的制定者。

【英译注】(1) Duke Zhou: Duke Dan of the Zhou Dynasty, surname Ji, first name Dan, the son of King Wen, and younger brother of King Wu, and uncle of King Cheng of the Zhou Dynasty, and the ancestor of Dukes of the State of Lu, allegedly who established the rites and laws of the Zhou Dynasty.

57

器 Utensils

子曰:"君子不器。"(02.12)

【白话译文】

孔子说:"一名君子不是一件器物。"(02.12)

【英译】

The Master said, "A superior man is not a utensil(1)." (02.12)

【注释】器:《周易·系辞上》言:"形而上者谓之道,形而下者谓之器。"道是抽象的,精神的;器是具体的,物质的。就性质而言,道是主动的,积极的,独立的;相反,器是被动的,消极的,从属的。除非被人所利用,器是不会发挥作用的。

【英译注】(1) utensil: *Book of Changes* (*Yi Jing*) states, "The Dao is metaphysical, transcending form and shape, while a 'utensil' is concrete and has shape and form." By its nature the Dao is abstract and spiritual, active, positive, and independent. A "utensil", on the other hand, is passive, negative, and dependent. If man does not use it, it has no role to play.

子贡问曰:"赐也何如?"子曰:"女,器也。"曰:"何器也?"曰:"瑚琏也。"(05.04)

【白话译文】

子贡问:"我是一个什么样的人?"孔

【注释】子贡:姓端木,名赐,字子贡。赐:子贡。何如:怎么样。女(音 rǔ 辱):汝,你。器:器具。何:什么。瑚琏:祭祀时盛粮食用的器具。

子说:“你,可以比作一件器物。”子贡又问:“是什么器物?”孔子说:“瑚琏(一种在朝廷祖庙里盛粮食的珍贵器件)。”(05.04)

【英译】

Zigong[1] asked, “What do you think about me?” The Master said, “You can be compared to a utensil.” He asked, “What utensil is it?” The Master said, “Hulian[2].” (05.04)

【英译注】(1) Zigong: Surname Duanmu, first name Ci, style name Zigong, Confucius's disciple. (2) Hulian: A precious sacrificial vessel containing grains, such as millet, sorghum, etc. at ancestral temple of the court.

子曰:“觚不觚,觚哉! 觚哉!”(06.25)

【注释】觚(音 gū 姑):酒礼器,上圆下方,有棱;1 升曰爵,2 升曰觚。不:变样、不再像。觚哉:算是觚吗。

【白话译文】

孔子说:“觚(方酒器)不是原来的那个觚了。觚啊! 觚啊!”(06.25)

【英译】

The Master said, “The drinking vessel *Gu*[1] is not the original *Gu*. Alas, *Gu*! Alas, *Gu*!” (06.25)

【英译注】(1) *Gu*: An alcoholic drink vessel of 2 litres in the ancient time and its Chinese phonetic name is “*Gu*”, circular at the mouth and square at the belly and bottom, with 4 angular corners. It was changed into a round one but still called *Gu*. So Confucius doubted: Could it be still called a *Gu*?

十一
Eleven

社会活动
Social Activities

58

射 Archery

子曰:“君子无所争。必也射乎!揖让而升,下而饮,其争也君子。”(03.07)

【白话译文】

孔子说:“君子之间没有什么可力争的。如果非要以力相争,那就通过射箭的方式来解决吧!射箭开始时,他们相互作揖,之后登堂。射箭结束,他们下堂,开始饮酒。他们争端的解决方式,依然很有礼貌,具有君子风范。”(03.07)

【英译】

The Master said, “There is no strife by strength among superior men. If they have to vie by strength, it is then settled by an archery contest! When the archery contest starts, they bow to each other with hands folded in front and then step up to the archery hall. When their archery is finished, they leave the archery hall and drink. Their strife settlement is very polite, much in a style of a superior man.” (03.07)

【注释】争:以力相争,以手身之力“引之使归于己”[J14],使用力量——包括暴力——等手段,争强好胜、争权夺利,以求己利。所争:可与别人以力相争的事。必:(如果)一定有所以力相争的话。射:射箭,射箭礼。揖(音 yī 衣):作揖,拱手礼。让:谦让。而:便、就。升:上场。下:退场。饮:敬酒。其:他们的。

子曰:"射不主皮,为力不同科,古之道也。"(03.16)

【注释】射:比赛射箭。主:在于。皮:兽皮靶子。主皮:穿透靶子。为:因为。力:力气。同:相同的。科:等级。古:古时。之:的。道:规矩。

【白话译文】

孔子说:"射箭比赛中,穿透兽皮靶心不是目的,因为各人的力气等级不一样,这是古代传下来的规矩。"(03.16)

【英译】

The Master said, "It is not the purpose to penetrate the leather target in an archery contest, because the shooters have different levels of strength. This is a rule passed down from ancient times." (03.16)

59

钓 Fishing

子钓而不纲,弋不射宿。(07.27)

【注释】钓:钓鱼。而:却,但。纲:大绳,大网,横断流水,下系钓钩。不纲:不用这种网。弋(音 yì 意):用带绳的箭射鸟。宿:在巢穴中歇宿的鸟,通常白天宿巢的鸟是孵卵的母鸟。

【白话译文】

孔子钓鱼,但不用大绳系上很多钓钩来钓鱼。他弋鸟,但不射杀卧在巢穴的鸟。(07.27)

【英译】

The Master fished but never used hooks on a headrope[(1)] on which many hooks attached. He shot birds with a retrievable arrow but never shot a bird in its nest[(2)]. (07. 27)

【英译注】(1) headrope: A large rope was put into water across a river. (2) a bird in its nest: This bird is normally a hen bird hatching eggs at nest in the day time. If it is shot, the whole nest of birds will be finished.

60

友 Make Friends

问人于他邦,再拜而送之。(10. 15)

【注释】问:问候,致送礼物。人:朋友。于:在,到。他邦:其他诸侯国。再:两次。拜:拜别。而:用以、用来。之:受托者。问人于他邦:托人向外国友人问好送礼。

【白话译文】

当孔子托人向外国朋友问好送礼时,他向受托人拱手鞠躬两次并送行。(10. 15)

【英译】

When the Master entrusted someone to give a gift to a friend in a foreign state, he twice bowed with hands folded in front to the entrusted and saw him off on his way. (10. 15)

子贡问友。子曰:"忠告而善道之,不可则止,毋自辱焉。"(12.23)

【白话译文】

子贡请教如何对待朋友。孔子说:"忠诚地劝告他,恰当地引导他。如果他不接受,不可强求。你不要自取羞辱。"(12.23)

【英译】

Zigong[1] asked advice on how to treat a friend. The Master said, "Advise him sincerely and guide him properly. If he does not accept it, do not force him. You should not invite humiliation on yourself." (12.23)

【注释】子贡:姓端木名赐,字子贡。问:请教。友:对待朋友。而:而且。善:恰当。道(音 dǎo 岛):导,引导。之:友。可:听从。则:就,便。止:罢。毋:不要。自辱:自取羞辱。

【英译注】(1) Zigong: Surname Duanmu, first name Ci, style name Zigong.

曾子曰:"君子以文会友,以友辅仁。"(12.24)

【白话译文】

曾子说:"君子用学问和文章结交朋友,用朋友帮助天下人培养仁德。"(12.24)

【英译】

Master Zeng[1] said, "A superior man makes friends through learning and writing,

【注释】曾子:姓曾名参(音 shēn 申),字子舆,鲁国南武城人。以:用。文:学问。会:结交。友:朋友。辅仁:帮助天下培养、实行仁德。

【英译注】(1) Master Zeng: Confucius's disciple (505 BC – 436 BC), surname Zeng, first name Shen, style name Ziyu, a person from

and with the friends assists the people under Heaven to cultivate superior benevolence."(12.24)

Nanwucheng, the State of Lu, current Pingyi County, Shandong Province.

孔子曰:"益者三友,损者三友。友直,友谅,友多闻,益矣。友便辟,友善柔,友便佞,损矣。"(16.04)

【注释】益:有益。三:三种。友:朋友。损:有害。直:正直。谅:诚信。便(音 pián 骈):能说会道。辟(音 pì 媲):不正。便辟:逢迎谄媚。善柔:善于当面奉承,背后诽谤。便佞(音 pián 骈 nìng 泞):花言巧语。

【白话译文】

孔夫子说:"三种朋友是有益的,三种朋友是有害的。朋友正直、真诚和见多识广,是有益的。朋友逢迎谄媚、当面赞同背后诽谤、甜言蜜语夸夸其谈,是有害的。"(16.04)

【英译】

Confucius said, "Three types of friends are beneficial and three types of friends are injurious. The friends of righteousness, faith and knowledge are beneficial. The injurious friends are those who flatter and toady, agree when speaking face to face, but slander behind his back, and are boastful and indulge in honeyed words and sweet phrases."(16.04)

子夏之门人问交于子张。子张曰:“子夏云何?”对曰:“子夏曰:‘可者与之,其不可者拒之。’”子张曰:“异乎吾所闻:君子尊贤而容众,嘉善而矜不能。我之大贤与,于人何所不容?我之不贤与,人将拒我,如之何其拒人也?”(19.03)

【注释】子夏:姓卜名商,字子夏。门人:学生。交:交友。于:向。子张:姓颛(音 zhuān 砖)孙名师,字子张。云:说。对曰:敬答。可者:可以相交的。与之:和他交往。拒:拒绝。异:不同。乎:于。吾所闻:我听到的。尊:尊敬、尊重。贤:贤人。容:容纳。众:众人。嘉:赞美。善:善的、优秀的人。矜(音 jīn 今):同情。不能:能力差的。之:如果是。我之:我如果是。大贤:十分贤良的人。与:呢。何所不容:有什么不能容纳的。人:人家。将:会。其:我。如之何:怎么能。

【白话译文】

子夏的徒弟向子张请教如何结交朋友。子张说:“子夏怎么说的?”他们敬答:“子夏说:‘如果一个人值得交往,就与他做朋友;如果他不值得,就拒绝他。’”子张说:“我听说的,与这不同。一名君子敬重德才贤良的人,宽容普通的人,褒奖有能力的人,同情没有能力的人。如果我很贤明,什么人我不能宽容?我不贤明,别人会拒绝我,我有什么资格拒绝别人?”(19.03)

【英译】

The disciples of Zixia(1) asked Zizhang(2) advice about how to make friends. Zizhang said, “What has Zixia said?” They replied respectfully, “If one is worthy to associate with, make friends with him; if he is not worthy, refuse him.” Zizhang said, “This is different from what I have heard. A superior man respects sages and tolerates the

【英译注】(1) Zixia: Surname Bu, first name Shang, style name Zixia, Confucius's disciple. (2) Zizhang: Surname Zhuansun, first name Shi, style name Zizhang, Confucius's disciple.

common people, praises the good and sympathizes with the incapable. If I am sagacious, who can I not tolerate? If I am not sagacious, others may refuse me and what qualifications do I have to refuse others?" (19.03)

61

嫁 Marriage

子谓公冶长:"可妻也。虽在缧绁之中,非其罪也。"以其子妻之。(05.01)

【注释】谓:评论。公冶长:姓公冶名长,字子长,鲁国(今山东)人。妻(音 qì 器):嫁女于人。缧绁(音 léi 雷 xiè 泄):捆绑犯人的绳索,象征犯人身份。非:不是。其:他的。罪:罪过。以:把。子:女儿。之:他。

【白话译文】

孔子评论公冶长说:"我把女儿嫁给他,是值得的。虽然他曾是犯人,被绳索捆绑着,他是无辜的。"他将自己的女儿嫁给了他。(05.01)

【英译】

The Master commented on Gongye Chang(1), "It is worthwhile to marry my daughter to him. Even though he was imprisoned, bound and tied, he was not guilty." He married his daughter to him. (05.01)

【英译注】(1) Gongye Chang: Surname Gongye, first name Chang, style name Zichang, Confucius's disciple.

子谓南容:"邦有道,不废;邦无道,免于刑戮。"以其兄之子妻之。(05.02)

【注释】谓:评论。南容:姓南宫名适(音 kuò 扩),字子容。废:废置,不做官。刑:刑罚。戮:杀头。以:把。其:他的。兄:孔子的哥哥,孔孟皮。之子:的女儿。妻(音 qì 器):嫁女于人。之:他。

【白话译文】

孔子评论南容说:"如果一个国家公平正义,他不放弃做官的机会。如果国家腐败不公,他尽自己做大努力避免刑罚和杀戮。"他把他哥哥的女儿嫁给了他。(05.02)

【英译】

The Master commented on Nan Rong(1), "He would not pass up the opportunity to serve as an official if the state were just and fair. If the state were corrupt and unfair, he would do his best to avoid instances of punishments and massacres." He married him to the daughter of his elder brother. (05.02)

【英译注】(1) Nan Rong: Surname Nangong, first name Kuo, style name Zirong, Confucius's disciple and son-in-law of Confucius's elder brother Kong Mengpi.

南容三复白圭,孔子以其兄之子妻之。(11.06)

【注释】南容:姓南宫名适(音 kuò 扩),字子容。三:多次。复:复习诵读。圭(音 guī 归):上圆下方的玉器。白圭:《诗经·大雅·抑》诗句,其中有"白圭之玷(污点),尚可磨也;斯言之玷,不可为也"。以:让。兄:孔子的哥,孔孟皮。之子:的女儿。妻(音 qì 器):以女嫁人。之:他。

【白话译文】

南容三次诵读"白圭"诗篇。孔夫子将他哥哥的女儿嫁给了他。(11.06)

【英译】

Nan Rong(1) loudly recited "the White Jade Tablet"(2) poem three times(3). Confucius married him to the daughter of his elder brother. (11.06)

【英译注】(1) Nan Rong: Surname Nangong, first name Kuo, style name Zirong, Confucius's disciple and son-in-law of Confucius's elder brother Kong Mengpi. (2) "White Jade Tablet": It is from *Poems and Odes*, currently named *Book of Poetry* and it contains the sentences "The flaw of white jade tablet can possibly be ground away, but a flaw of one's language cannot be removed from his speech." (3) three times: Many times.

62

酒 Drink Liquor

子曰:"出则事公卿,入则事父兄,丧事不敢不勉,不为酒困,何有于我哉?"(09.16)

【注释】出:在外。则:就、便。事:侍奉。公卿:王公大臣。入:在家。勉:尽力。为:被。困:迷惑。不为酒困:不贪酒。何有:有何困难。于:对。哉:啊。

【白话译文】

孔子说:"我外出侍奉王公贵族,在家服侍父兄。我办丧事不由自主竭尽全力,喝酒不误事。对于这些,我都做好了什么?"(09.16)

【英译】

The Master said, "I serve the nobility when I am out of my home, and wait upon my father and elder brother at home. I cannot help but exert all my efforts when managing a funeral. I drink but not so much that it affects my work. Of all of these, have I done them very well?" (09. 16)

乡人饮酒,杖者出,斯出矣。(10. 13)

【注释】乡:本乡。饮酒:饮酒礼仪,以年龄大小排序。杖者:拿拐杖者,老年人。出:离席。斯:这才。矣:呀。

【白话译文】

当孔子与家乡的人饮酒,他在拄拐杖的人离席之后才离席。(10. 13)

【英译】

When the Master drank liquor with the people at his hometown, he left his seat only after the elder people with canes left. (10. 13)

63

火灾 Fire Disaster

厩焚。子退朝，曰："伤人乎?"不问马。(10.17)

【白话译文】

孔子的一个马棚被焚毁了。他从朝廷回来问："火灾中有人员受伤吗?"他没问马的情况。(10.17)

【英译】

A stable of the Master was destroyed by fire. When he came back from the court, he asked, "Has anyone been injured in the fire?" He did not ask about the horses. (10.17)

【注释】厩：马棚。焚：失火烧坏。退：归来。朝：臣见君，朝拜国君。

64

翻修 Reconstruction

鲁人为长府。闵子骞曰："仍旧贯,如之何?何必改作?"子曰："夫人不言,言必有中。"(11.14)

【注释】鲁:鲁国。人:官吏。为:改建。府:仓库,藏财货、兵器等。长府:国库名。闵子骞(音qiān千):闵损,字子骞。仍:依然。旧:以前的。贯:事,例。仍旧贯:仍按老样。如之何:怎么样。改作:改建。夫(音fú扶):这。言:主动对人说话。中:正中要害。言必有中:一说话就说到点上。

【白话译文】

鲁国的官员翻修长府国家金库。闵子骞说:"我们依然按老样子,你们看怎么样?为什么必须改建成其他风格呢?"孔子说:"这个人平时不说。一旦说话,他一定言中要害。"(11.14)

【英译】

The officials of the State of Lu rebuilt the Changfu State Treasury. Min Ziqian(1) said, "What do you think about following the original patterns? Why must it be rebuilt into a different style?" The Master said, "This person normally does not talk. Once he talks, he always hits the crucial point." (11.14)

【英译注】(1) Min Ziqian: Surname Min, first name Sun, style name Ziqian, Confucius's disciple, famous for his filial piety.

十二
Twelve

人生百态
Life Kaleidoscope

65

笑 Laugh

子曰:“道不行,乘桴浮于海。从我者,其由与?”子路闻之喜。子曰:“由也好勇过我,无所取材。”(05.07)

【注释】道:(孔子的)主张、道义。不行:行不通。桴(音 fú 俘):木筏子。浮:漂浮。于:在。从:跟随。其:大概。由:姓仲名由,字子路。子路:姓仲名由,字子路。之:这、它。好(音 hǎo 郝):令人满意的。勇:勇气。好勇:好的勇气,勇敢精神。过:超过。无:没有。所取:可采用的,能获取的。材:木材,木料;“是指树木中直的部分,包括主干和枝条,只要直挺就是材。这是‘材’的本义。”[J11] 无所取材:没地方获取木材,来做木筏。

【白话译文】

孔子说:“如果我的学说行不通,我将乘木筏漂浮到海外去。能够跟我一起到那儿的,大概是由吧?”子路听到这,非常高兴。孔子说:“噢!由呀,你的勇气大大超过了我,但是我们没地方获取能做木筏的木材。”(05.07)

【英译】

The Master said, “If my doctrines cannot prevail, I might float out to sea on a raft. Probably is it only You(1) who can follow me there?” Hearing this, Zilu(2) was delighted. The Master said, “Oh, your courage surpasses me greatly, but nowhere can we obtain the wood to make the raft.” (05.07)

【英译注】(1) You: Surname Zhong, first name You, style name Zilu, Confucius's disciple. (2) Zilu: You, his style name is Zilu.

子问公叔文子于公明贾曰:"信乎夫子不言、不笑、不取乎?"公明贾对曰:"以告者过也。夫子时然后言,人不厌其言;乐然后笑,人不厌其笑;义然后取,人不厌其取。"子曰:"其然?岂其然乎?"(14.14)

【注释】问:询问。公叔文子:卫国大夫公孙拔,谥(音 shì 是)号文,卫献公之子,《檀弓》载有他的故事。于:向。公明贾:姓公明字贾(音 jiǎ 钾),卫国人。信乎:可信吗。夫子:公叔文子。言:主动对人讲话。取:取钱财。对曰:敬答。以:此、这(是)。告:告诉。过:错。以告者过也:这是告诉您的人错了。时:恰当时候。然后:而后。人:别人。其:他。乐:快乐。义:符合道义。其然:原来这样。岂:难道。岂其然乎:难道真是这样吗。

【白话译文】

孔子向公明贾询问公叔文子的情况说:"你的主人不说、不笑、不取人钱财,你信吗?"公明贾敬答:"说话的人言过其实了。我的主人该说话则说话,别人就不厌烦他说。他心里快乐然后笑,别人就不厌烦他笑。他取人钱财符合正义,别人就不厌烦他取。"孔子说:"是这样吗?难道真是这样吗?"(14.14)

【英译】

The Master asked Gongming Jia(1) about Master Gongshu Wen(2), "Can you believe that your master neither speaks, laughs, or takes money from others?" Gongming Jia replied respectfully, "The speaker exaggerates. My master speaks when it is opportune, so others never tire of his speaking. He laughs when he is happy at heart, so they never tire of his laughing. He takes money from others when it is righteous, so they never tire of his

【英译注】(1) Gongming Jia: Surname Gongming, first name Jia, an official of the State of Wei. (2) Master Gongshu Wen: Senior official of the State of Wei, surname Gongsun, first name Ba, posthumous title Wen, a grandson of Duke Xian of the State of Wei.

taking." The Master said, "Is it so? Is it truly so indeed?" (14.14)

孔子曰:"益者三乐,损者三乐。乐节礼乐,乐道人之善,乐多贤友,益矣。乐骄乐,乐佚游,乐晏乐,损矣。"(16.05)

【白话译文】

孔夫子说:"有三种有益的爱好,有三种有害的爱好。爱用礼乐节制自己,爱宣扬别人的优点,爱多结交德才兼备的朋友是有益的。爱骄奢淫逸,爱放荡闲逛,爱沉醉酒宴享乐,是有害的。"(16.05)

【英译】

Confucius said, "There are three beneficial pleasures and there are three injurious pleasures. It is beneficial to enjoy restraining oneself with the Ritual Music, to enjoy singing the praises of others and to enjoy making friends with many moral and talented people. It is injurious to enjoy wallowing in luxury and pleasure, to enjoy idleness and sauntering and to enjoy indulging in magnificent banquets." (16.05)

【注释】益:有益。三:三种。乐(音 lè 勒,旧音 yào 耀):高兴、快乐。益者三乐:有益的快乐有三种。损:有害。节礼乐(音 yuè 月):用礼乐来节制自己。道:宣扬。多:众多。乐骄乐:以骄傲放肆为乐。佚:逸,安逸。游:游玩。晏:大吃大喝。晏乐:沉溺吃喝、宴饮。

子之武城，闻弦歌之声。夫子莞尔而笑曰："割鸡焉用牛刀。"子游对曰："昔者偃也闻诸夫子曰：'君子学道则爱人，小人学道则易使也。'"子曰："二三子！偃之言是也。前言戏之耳。"(17.04)

【注释】子：孔子。之：到。武城：鲁国小城，今山东费县，子游为城宰。弦：弹奏琴瑟。歌：唱。夫子：孔子。莞（音 wǎn 晚）尔：微微地笑。莞尔而笑：微微笑着。割鸡：杀鸡。焉：何必。牛刀：屠宰牛的刀。子游：姓言名偃（音 yǎn 眼），字子游。昔者：以前。偃：子游。闻：听。诸：之于。则：就，那么。易使：易于役使。二三子：弟子们。前言：前边说的话。戏之：给他开玩笑。耳：呀。

【白话译文】

孔子到武城，听到歌声和弦乐的演奏声音。孔子微微地笑着说："杀鸡怎么用得上杀牛刀？"子游敬答："以前我从老师你那里听到：'君子学习礼乐，就具有仁爱的心，关爱人民。小人学习礼乐，容易听从指挥，更好工作。'"孔子说："弟子们！偃的话是对的。我刚才是在给他开玩笑。"(17.04)

【英译】

When the Master came to Wucheng City(1), he heard the sound of singing and playing of stringed-instruments. With a slight smile, he said, "How can a chicken be slaughtered with a meat-cleaver?" Ziyou(2) replied respectfully, "I heard from a saying previously from you my Master that, 'A superior man(3) can have a heart of superior benevolence and love the people if he learns the Rites and Music. And an inferior man may

【英译注】(1) Wucheng City: A small city of the State of Lu close to its capital, currently at Feixian County of Shandong Province, where Confucius thus commented it because it was small. (2) Ziyou: Surname Yan, first name Yan, style name Ziyou, Confucius's disciple. (3) A superior man: He could be an official, an educated man, or a member from the noble family, while an inferior man could be working people or the common people. (4) Yan: First name of Ziyou.

easily obey an instruction to work well if he learns the Rites and Music.'" The Master said, "My disciples, the words of Yan(4) are correct. I was joking with him a moment ago." (17.04)

66

气 Enrage

子曰:"居上不宽,为礼不敬,临丧不哀,吾何以观之哉!"(03.26)

【白话译文】

孔子说:"处在上层地位的人不宽厚大度,有的人在礼仪仪式上不恭敬,在葬礼上不悲伤。这些行为,我怎么能够看得下去啊?"(03.26)

【英译】

The Master said, "People in high positions are not generous. People are not respectful at a ritual ceremony, or are not sorrowful at a funeral. How can I bear seeing such behaviors?" (03.26)

【注释】居:处在一个职位或地方。上:地位高的,执政者。宽:宽厚待人。居上不宽:执政者(当领导)不宽宏大量。为:举行。礼:礼仪。敬:严肃认真。临:参加。丧:丧葬礼。哀:悲伤。吾:我。何以:怎么。观:看下去。之:他、此。哉:啊。

孺悲欲见孔子，孔子辞以疾。将命者出户，取瑟而歌，使之闻之。(17.20)

【注释】孺悲：鲁国(今山东)人，鲁哀公曾派他向孔子学礼。欲：想。辞：推辞。以：用。疾：有病。将命者：传话的人。户：门。而：进而。取瑟而歌：取出瑟来弹奏并且唱歌。之：他，孺悲。闻之：听到孔子弹唱。

【白话译文】

孺悲来，想见孔夫子一面，但是孔夫子以自己生病为由谢绝了他。传话的人一出房门，孔夫子就开始弹瑟并唱歌，声音之大，故意让孺悲听到。(17.20)

【英译】

Ru Bei[(1)] came and desired to meet with Confucius, but Confucius declined it by an excuse of being ill. As soon as the messenger stepped out of his door, Confucius started playing the *Se*[(2)] and singing songs loudly because he deliberately wanted Ru Bei to hear it. (17.20)

【英译注】(1) Ru Bei: A person of the State of Lu, currently at Shandong Province. Duke Ai once sent him to learn rites from Confucius. (2) the *Se*: A twenty-five-stringed plucked instrument, somewhat similar to the zither.

长沮、桀溺耦而耕，孔子过之，使子路问津焉。

长沮曰："夫执舆者为谁？"子路曰："为孔丘。"曰："是鲁孔丘与？"曰："是也。"曰："是知津矣。"

【注释】鲁哀公五年(公元前490年)，孔子62岁，从蔡国去楚国，见叶公后返回蔡国途中，迷路问津。长沮(音 jù 剧)、桀溺(音 jié 杰 nì 匿)：两位隐士，身世不详。耦(音 ǒu 偶)：二耜(音 sì 四)为耦，耜为耕犁具。耕：耕作。耦而耕：并排犁地，或一起干农活。过：路过。之：他们。使：派。子路：姓仲，名由，字子路。问：打听。津：渡口。

【白话译文】

长沮、桀溺并排耕地,孔夫子路过,派子路向他们打听哪里有渡口。长沮问:“那位驾车的是谁?”子路答:“是孔丘。”长沮问:“他是鲁国的那位孔丘吗?”子路答:“是的。”长沮说:“他已经知道渡口了。”

执舆:驾车,拿着马缰绳,子路问路时,孔子代其驾车。者:的人。为:是。鲁:鲁国。与:吗。矣:了。是知津矣:此人早就知道渡口的位置了。

【英译】

When Changju and Jieni(1) were ploughing side by side, Confucius passed by them and sent Zilu(2) to ask them directions to a ford.

Changju asked Zilu, “Who is the driver on the carriage there?”

Zilu said, “He is Kong Qiu(3).”

“Is he the Kong Qiu from the State of Lu?”

“Yes,” replied Zilu.

【英译注】(1) Changju and Jieni: Two hermits and their true names are unknown. (2) Zilu: Surname Zhong, first name You, style name Zilu, Confucius's disciple. (3) Kong Qiu: Confucius (551 BC – 479 BC), surname Kong, first name Qiu, style name Zhongni, a great thinker and educator of the State of Lu of the Zhou Dynasty.

问于桀溺。桀溺曰:“子为谁?”曰:“为仲由。”曰:“是鲁孔丘之徒与?”对曰:“然。”曰:“滔滔者天下皆是也,而谁以易之?且而与其从辟人之士也,岂若从辟世之士哉?”耰而不辍。

子路行以告。夫子怃然曰:“鸟兽不可与同群,吾非斯人之徒与而谁与?天下有道,丘不与

【注释】于:向。子:你。仲由:姓仲名由,字子路。徒:弟子。对曰:敬答。然:是。滔滔:洪水滔天。而:却,但是。谁以:与谁一起。易:改变。之:它,现状。而谁以易之:但是,你们能与谁一道改变这一局面呢。且:而且。而:你。与其:连词,表示比较,后接宁可、不若等。从:跟随。辟:避。辟人:躲避坏人。士:人。且而与其从辟人之士也:而且你与其跟随躲避坏人的人呀。岂若:难道比得上。辟世:躲避乱世。哉:吗。耰(音yōu

易也。”(18.06)

【白话译文】

子路向桀溺打听。桀溺说:“你是谁?”子路说:“是仲由。”他问:“是鲁国孔丘的徒弟吗?”子路敬答:“是。”桀溺说:“天下邪恶的事,像滔滔洪水到处都是,但是谁能改变它们?然而,你与其跟随逃避坏人的人士(如孔夫子),还不如跟随逃避坏社会的人士(如我们)呢?”他说完,继续干他的农活,用土盖住种子。

子路回来向孔夫子汇报。孔夫子失望地说:“鸟兽不能成为我们生活中相处的伙伴。如果我不与人打交道,那我与谁打交道?如果天下公平正义,我丘也不参与改变它了。”(18.06)

【英译】

“He already knows where the ford is,” said Changju.

He asked Jieni for the directions.

“Who are you, sir?” asked Jieni.

“I am Zhong You(1),” answered he.

“Are you a disciple of Kong Qiu from the State of Lu?”

“Yes, I am,” Zilu replied respectfully.

Jieni said, “Evil is like torrential flood everywhere under Heaven, but who can change it? Would you rather follow those (like Confucius) who are fleeing from evil

优):用土覆盖种子。辍(音 chuò 绰):中止。

行:走来。以:用此。告:报告,汇报。怃(音 wǔ 武)然:失意、怅然。与同群:合群共处。斯人:世人。徒:相处。非斯人之徒与:不同世上的人群打交道。谁与:与谁,同谁。有道:(如果)政治清明、太平。与:参与。易:改变。

【英译注】(1) Zhong You: Zilu. (2) Qiu: First name of Confucius, Kong Qiu.

people, or would you rather withdraw (like us) from the evils of this world altogether?"

After that, he continued working by covering seeds with soil.

Zilu came back and reported this to Confucius. Confucius said disappointedly, "Birds and beasts cannot be our companions in life. If I do not associate with people in the world, whom can I communicate with? If the world was just and fair, I, Qiu[2] would not take part in the reforming on it." (18.06)

67

骂 Scold

宰予昼寝。子曰:"朽木,不可雕也,粪土之墙,不可圬也。于予与何诛?"子曰:"始吾于人也,听其言而信其行;今吾于人也,听其言而观其行。于予与改是。"(05.10)

【白话译文】

宰予大白天睡大觉。孔子说:"腐朽

【注释】宰予:姓宰名予,字子我,鲁国(今山东)人。昼:白天。寝:睡觉。朽:腐朽的。雕:雕刻。粪土:脏土。圬(音 wū 乌):瓦工抹子,粉饰。于:对于。予:姓宰名予,字子我。与:啊,语气词。何:当何。诛:责备。始:当初。其:他的。言:说话。而:就。信:相信。行:行为。观:观察。而观其行:却要观察他的行为。于予:在宰予这里。改:改变。是:此(看法)。于予与改是:从宰予这事起,我就改变了看人的方法。

的木头是不能雕刻的，粪肥泥土构成的墙，是不能抹饰的。对于予啊，为何谴责他呢?”孔子继续说:“当初我对于一个人，相信他说的就是他做的。今天，我对于一个人，听他说的，观察他做的。是予这件事，让我改变了看待一个人的观点。”(05.10)

【英译】

Zai Yu[1] slept in the daytime. The Master said, "Rotten wood cannot be carved and a manure wall cannot be decorated with a trowel. For Yu[2], why has he been condemned?" The Master continued, "About a person, originally I believed that what he said was what he did. Today about a person, I listen to what he says and then watch what he does. It is from the instance of Yu that I have changed my view of how I see a person." (05.10)

【英译注】(1) Zai Yu: Surname Zai, first name Yu, style name Ziwo, a person from the State of Lu, currently Shandong Province. (2) Yu: Zai Yu.

子路使子羔为费宰。子曰:“贼夫人之子。”子路曰:“有民人焉，有社稷焉。何必读书，然后为学?”子曰:“是故恶夫佞者。”(11.25)

【注释】子路:姓仲名由，字子路。使:让。子羔:姓高名柴，字子羔，为人好，但学业未成。费(旧音bì闭):今山东费(音fèi废)县。宰:总管。贼:害。夫:语气词。人之子:人家的子弟，指子羔，学不足，当官会慢神、虐民，对人有害。有:存在。民:百姓。人:官吏。有民人焉:跟着老百姓、官员啊(也算学习)。社:土地神。稷:谷神。有社稷焉:祭祀，也算学习啊。然后:之后。为:算是。何必读书，然后

【白话译文】

子路任命子羔为费城的长官。孔子说:“你是在误人子弟。”子路说:“那里有

老百姓啊,也有管理土地神和谷神祭祀的官员。为什么只有拜师学习才被认为是学习呢?”孔子说:“这就是我讨厌油嘴滑舌的人的原因。”(11.25)

为学:为什么从师读书才算学习。是故:所以。恶(音 wù 务):憎恶。夫:那。佞:花言巧语。是故恶夫佞者:所以(我)憎恶狡辩的人。

【英译】

Zilu[1] appointed Zigao[2] as the magistrate of Bi City. The Master said, “You are leading a family's young child astray.” Zilu said, “There are the common people and there are also officials taking care of sacrifices to the God of the Land and the God of Grain. Why is it that one can only be regarded as learned if he has studied with a Master?” The Master said, “This is why I hate someone who has a glib tongue.” (11.25)

【英译注】(1) Zilu: Surname Zhong, first name You, and style name Zilu, Confucius's disciple. (2) Zigao: Surname Gao, first name Chai, style name Zigao, Confucius's disciple. He was a good guy but has not accomplished learning when he was appointed as an official.

原壤夷俟。子曰:“幼而不孙弟,长而无述焉,老而不死,是为贼。”以杖叩其胫。(14.45)

【白话译文】

原壤坐在地上,双腿叉开,等待孔子。孔子骂道:“你幼年不谦逊、不尊重兄长。你长大,没有什么优秀品质和成就可以传述。你年龄大了,该死不死,空吃粮食,没有用,很像吃庄稼的害虫。”孔子用拐杖轻敲他的小腿。(14.45)

【注释】原壤:鲁国(今山东)人,孔子的老友,《礼记》载他母亲去世,他站在棺材上唱歌。夷:双腿分开而坐。俟(音 sì 寺):等待。幼:孩童。而:就。孙(音 xùn 训):逊,谦让。弟(音 tì 替):悌,顺从、尊敬兄长。长:长大成人。无述:没有可述说的仁、义、功德等。是:这、此。为:当作、是。贼:虫子,食根曰螟,食节曰贼。是为贼:像个空吃庄稼粮食的害虫。以:用。杖:手杖。叩:轻敲。其:他的。胫:小腿。

【英译】

Yuan Rang[1] sat on the ground with both his legs stretching out, waiting for the Master. The Master sternly criticized him, "When you were a child, you did not respect your elders. As an adult, you have no accomplishments worth passing on. When you become a useless old man, with no reason to keep living, just eating your fill, you will be just like a pest eating the crops." The Master tapped him lightly on his shank with his walking stick. (14.45)

【英译注】(1) Yuan Rang: An old friend of Confucius from the State of Lu. It was said that he sang on his mother's coffin when she died.

子曰:"色厉而内荏,譬诸小人,其犹穿窬之盗也与?"(17.12)

【注释】色:外表。厉:威严。而:却,但是。内:内心。荏(音 rěn 忍):虚弱。譬:比喻。诸:之于,他为。譬诸小人:比喻他为小人。其:大概。犹:像。窬(音 yú 余):洞。与:吗。

【白话译文】

孔子说:"如果一个人外表坚强,但内心虚弱,他就像一个卑鄙的小偷,翻墙头或在墙上打洞入室抢掠。"(17.12)

【英译】

The Master said, "If a person has a fierce appearance, but is inwardly weak, he is like a mean and petty thief who climbs over a wall or who cuts a hole in it to burglarize a house." (17.12)

子曰："鄙夫可与事君也与哉？其未得之也，患得之。既得之，患失之。苟患失之，无所不至矣。"（17.15）

【注释】鄙：品德恶劣卑鄙的。夫：人。可与：可以一起。事：侍奉。君：君主。与哉：吗。其：他。未：没有。得：得到。之：官位。患：担心。其未得之也，患得之：他没当官呀，害怕当不上官。既：已经。失：失掉。苟：如果。至：做。无所不至：什么事都干得出来。

【白话译文】

孔子说："一个卑鄙邪恶的人怎么能与他人一起侍奉君主？这样的人没有得到职位的时候，担心得不到。当他已经得职位时，他又担心失去它。如果他担心失去它，他无所不用其极，什么手段都会使出来。"（17.15）

【英译】

The Master said, "How can a wicked and disgusting man serve a sovereign with others? When he does not get a position in officialdom, he is worried about whether he can get it. When he does get it, he is also worried about whether he may lose it. If he is worried about losing it, he may resort to every conceivable means." (17.15)

68

攻 Condemn

子曰:“攻乎异端,斯害也已。”(02.16)

【白话译文】

孔子说:“攻击与自己不同的观点,是一种有害行为啊。”(02.16)

【英译】

The Master said,“Alas,it is harmful behaviour to condemn opinions different from one's own.”(02.16)

【注释】攻:攻击。异端:一解“不正确的言论”;二解“不同的学术观点或学说”。斯:代词,这。害:一解“祸害”;二解“有害的”。也:呀。已:一解“停止、完毕”;二解,叹词,啊。整句:一解“攻击不正确的言论,其祸害就可消除了”。二解“攻击与己不同的学说,是一种有害的做法”。此处取二解。

69

忌 Taboo

子不语:怪、力、乱、神。(07.21)

【注释】语(音 yù 玉):答话,和别人一起谈论。怪:怪异。力:暴力。乱:叛乱。神:鬼神。

【白话译文】

孔子与别人不谈论：怪异、暴力、叛乱、鬼神。(07.21)

【英译】

The Master did not talk with others about monsters, violence, armed rebellion, and ghosts and gods. (07.21)

子绝四：毋意、毋必、毋固、毋我。(09.04)

【注释】绝：断绝，彻底没有。四：四种弊病。子绝四：孔子彻底没有这四种毛病。毋：不，没有。意(音 yì 臆)：猜疑，主观臆断，凭空揣测。必：绝对肯定。固：固执己见，拘泥固执。我：唯我独是，自以为是。

【白话译文】

孔子彻底没有这四种毛病：从来不凭空臆测，从来不绝对肯定，从来不固执己见，从来不以自我为中心。(09.04)

【英译】

The Master did entirely not have the four faults below: never conjecture groundlessly, never affirm absolutely, never adhere to his opinions stubbornly and never be an egoist. (09.04)

十三
Thirteen

高士和孔子
Eminent People and Confucius

70

高士 Eminent People

子曰:“伯夷、叔齐,不念旧恶,怨是用希。”(05.23)

【白话译文】

孔子说:“伯夷、叔齐,宽恕别人过去的错误,很少招惹别人的怨恨。”(05.23)

【英译】

The Master said, “Boyi and Shuqi[(1)] forgave others' old grievances, so they rarely provoked grudges and hatred from them.” (05.23)

【注释】伯夷、叔齐:北方小国孤竹国君两子;伯夷:姓墨,名允,字公信;叔齐:姓墨,名致,字公达。念:惦记。旧恶:以往的仇怨。怨:怨恨。是:助词,无意义。用:招惹。希:稀。怨是用稀:很少招惹他人怨恨。

【英译注】(1) Boyi and Shuqi: Boyi was the elder son of a monarch of the State of Guzhu in the Shang Dynasty, and Shuqi was his younger brother. Their father appointed Shuqi as his successor. After their father died, Shuqi gave the throne to Boyi, while Boyi respected their father and refused it. They all fled to the State of Zhou. Later they remonstrated with the King of Zhou not to overthrow the last emperor of the Shang Dynasty. When the Zhou Dynasty succeeded, they sadly ran into Shouyang Mountains and refused the foods from the Zhou Dynasty and died from hunger.

子曰："巧言、令色、足恭，左丘明耻之，丘亦耻之。匿怨而友其人，左丘明耻之，丘亦耻之。"(05.25)

【注释】巧：虚浮不实。令：伪善。色：面貌。足恭：过分恭敬。左丘明：姓左丘名明，鲁太史，《左传》作者。耻：耻恶。之：此人、此行。丘：孔子，名丘，字仲尼。亦：也。匿怨：心藏怨恨。而：却，但是。友：表面友好。

【白话译文】

孔子说："谄媚的话、虚伪的面孔、过分的顺从，是左丘明所羞耻的，也是我丘所羞耻的。内心隐藏着对某人的怨恨但是表面上显示出对他友好的态度，是左丘明所羞耻的，也是我丘羞耻的。"(05.25)

【英译】

The Master said, "The flattering speech, hypocritical countenance and excessive deference are what Zuo Qiuming(1) found shameful, and so am I, Qiu(2). The attitude of concealing one's hatred of someone but showing friendliness to him is what Zuo Qiuming found shameful, and so am I, Qiu." (05.25)

【英译注】(1) Zuo Qiuming: Surname Zuo, first name Ming, the state history official of the State of Lu, the author of *The Zuo's Comments*, a historical book of comments on Confucius's *History of Spring and Autumn*. (2) Qiu: The first name of Confucius, surname Kong, the Master.

子曰："直哉史鱼！邦有道，如矢；邦无道，如矢。君子哉蘧伯玉！邦有道，则仕；邦无道，则可卷而怀之。"(15.07)

【注释】直：正直。哉：啊。史鱼：名鰌(音 qiū 秋)，字子鱼，卫国大夫，推荐过蘧伯玉。邦：国。有道：政治清明。如：像、同。矢：箭，直。无道：政治黑暗。蘧伯玉：姓蘧(音 qú 渠)名瑗，卫国大夫，孔子曾住其家。则：就，便。仕：做官。卷：收藏，辞官。而：并且。

【白话译文】

孔子说:“真刚直啊,史鱼! 国家政治公平正义,他像箭一样的直。国家政治腐败不正,他也像箭一样的直。蘧伯玉,真是一名君子啊! 国家政治公平正义,他就出来做官。国家政治腐败不公,他就把他的能力隐藏在心里。”(15.07)

怀:放在心里。之:主张、本领。则可卷而怀之:就辞官,不显露自己的才能。

【英译】

The Master said, “Oh, how upright and outspoken Shi Yu(1) is! When the state is just and fair, he is straight like an arrow; when it is corrupt and unjust, he is still straight like an arrow. What a superior man Qu Boyu(2) is! When the state is just and fair, he emerges to be an official in the government. When it is corrupt and unjust, he conceals his abilities in his heart.” (15.07)

【英译注】(1) Shi Yu: Surname Shi, first name You, style name Ziyu, a senior official of the State of Wei. (2) Qu Boyu: Surname Qu, first name Yuan, a senior official of the State of Wei. Confucius once stayed at his home during his trips to the State of Wei.

子曰:“臧文仲其窃位者与? 知柳下惠之贤,而不与立也。”(15.14)

【注释】臧文仲:姓臧孙名辰,鲁国大夫,谥号文,据说他不守周礼。其:大概。窃位:身居官位而不称职。与:吗。知:知道。柳下惠:姓展名获,又名禽,封地是柳下,私谥号惠,鲁国大夫,成语“坐怀不乱”出自此人。而:却,但是。不与:不授予、不给予。立:举荐为官。

【白话译文】

孔子说:“臧文仲大概渎职吧? 他明知柳下惠德才兼备,却不给他官位。”(15.14)

【英译】

The Master said, "Was Zang Wenzhong(1) probably delinquent in his duty? He clearly knew the good morals and talents of Liuxia Hui(2), but did not give him a post in officialdom." (15.14)

【英译注】(1) Zang Wenzhong: Surname Zangsun, first name Chen, a senior official of the State of Lu, his posthumous name was Wen, and it was said that he did not observe the Rites of Proprieties. (2) Liuxia Hui: Surname Zhan, first name Huo, also Mingqin or Zhan Ji, a talented moral official of the State of Lu, famous for being not disturbed when a young girl sat in his lap to be warmed outside the city wall in a cold winter. His fief was at Liuxia, and he was given a posthumous name Hui as advocated by his wife.

柳下惠为士师，三黜。人曰："子未可以去乎?"曰："直道而事人，焉往而不三黜? 枉道而事人，何必去父母之邦?"(18.02)

【注释】士师：典狱官，管刑狱。黜（音 chù 触）：罢免不用。人：有人。子：你。未：不。去：离开（鲁国）。乎：吗。直道：正道。事：侍奉。直道而事人：按正义去侍奉国君。焉：哪里。往：去。枉：曲邪。父母之邦：祖国。

【白话译文】

柳下惠当法官，三次被罢免。有人问："先生你就不能去别的国家?"他答："如果我服务别人正直不偏，我到哪里不被三次罢免呢? 如果服务别人歪曲事实不正直，何必要离开自己的祖国?"(18.02)

【英译】

Liuxia Hui(1), as a judge, was dismissed three times(2), so someone asked him, "Can

【英译注】(1) Liuxia Hui: See remarks on pervious passage (15.14, 70 Eminent People). (2) three times: Many times, not limited to

not you leave for another state, sir?" He replied, "If I serve others righteously without any bias, where can I not be dismissed three times? If I serve others dishonestly by distorting the truth, why should I leave my motherland?" (18.02)

three times.

逸民伯夷、叔齐、虞仲、夷逸、朱张、柳下惠、少连。子曰:"不降其志,不辱其身,伯夷、叔齐与?"谓柳下惠、少连:"降志辱身矣。言中伦,行中虑,其斯而已矣。"谓虞仲、夷逸:"隐居放言,身中清,废中权。""我则异于是,无可无不可。"(18.08)

【白话译文】

被遗落的人才有伯夷、叔齐、虞仲、夷逸、朱张、柳下惠、少连。孔子说:"既不降低其志向标准,又不屈辱自己人格的那些人,是伯夷、叔齐吧?"他继续说:"柳下惠、少连降低了志向水平、屈辱了自己人格,但是他们的言论合乎道德标准,他们的行为是深思熟虑的。他们就这样了。"他进一步说:"虞仲、夷逸,逃离社会,隐居、放肆直言,行为清廉。他们所放弃的,是认真权衡和考虑的。对上述每个人,我的看法是多种多样的:他们有些值得赞扬,有些不值

【注释】逸:佚,散失、遗弃。逸民:节行超逸之人。伯夷:姓墨,名允字公信。叔齐:姓墨,名致字公达。虞仲:身份待定;《左传·僖公五年》假道伐虢及《史记·周本纪》载虞仲为古公亶(音 dǎn 胆)次子,周文王二伯父,与泰伯一起逃到蛮,创立吴国。夷逸、朱张、少连:身世不详,似乎是没落贵族。谓:评论。降:降低。志:志向、理想。辱:屈辱。身:身份。与:句末语气词,表示疑问或感叹。言:说话。中(音 zhòng 众):中正,符合、正好。伦:伦理。行:行为。虑:人心。其:他们。斯:如此。其斯而已矣:他们只是如此罢了。放:放置。放言:放肆直言。身:自身。清:清廉。身中清:自身保持清廉。废:弃权、辞官。权:权宜、适宜。废中(音 zhòng 众)权:辞官合乎权宜之计。异:不同的(认识、评价)。于:和、对。是:这。我则异于是:我则对这些人有不同的评价。无:没有。可:赞同、赞许。无可无不可:有值得赞许的,也有不值得赞许的。

得赞扬。”（18.08）

【英译】

The forgotten talented persons were Boyi, Shuqi[1], Yu Zhong, Yi Yi, Zhu Zhang[2], Liuxia Hui[3], Shao Lian[4]. The Master said, "Were Boyi and Shuqi people who neither lowered their standards of ambition nor brought disgrace upon themselves?" He continued, "Liuxia Hui and Shao Lian lowered their standards of ambition and humiliated their personalities, but their words were in conformity with the moral standards, and their actions were done after serious consideration. That is all to be said about them." He said further, "Yu Zhong and Yi Yi, escaped from society and lived in seclusion, speaking unbridledly. They behaved honestly and uprightly. They carefully balanced and considered what they gave up. My view is diverse on the behaviours for each person above: some are worthy praising and some not." (18.08)

【英译注】(1) Boyi and Shuqi: Boyi was the elder son of a monarch of the State of Guzhu in the Shang Dynasty, and Shuiqi was his younger brother. Refer to Chapter 05.23 or above for their story. (2) Yu Zhong, Yi Yi, Zhu Zhang: Their lives are unknown. (3) Liuxia Hui: Famous for his story that he was not disturbed by beauties. See remarks on Chapter 15.14, 70 Eminent People. (4) Shao Lian: His life is unknown.

71

孔子 Confucius

子曰："述而不作，信而好古，窃比于我老彭。"(07.01)

【白话译文】

孔子说："我传述古代典籍但不创编新作。我相信而且喜爱古代文化。我私自向我祖上贤人老彭看齐。"(07.01)

【英译】

The Master said, "I pass on the ancient doctrines and do not fabricate new works. I believe and love the ancient culture, quietly keeping abreast with my moral and talented ancestor Lao Peng(1)." (07.01)

【注释】述：传述。而：却。作：创造、创作。述而不作：传述却不创作，以保持所传内容完整、不失真。信：相信。好古：喜爱古籍。窃：私自。比于：(我的做法)与……相比较、看齐。我老彭：孔子为殷商微子的后人，老彭是商代贤大夫，或指老子、彭祖，信古而传述者，故言我老彭，即我祖上的老彭。

【英译注】(1) Lao Peng: Unidentified by now. It may be referred to one person closely related with Confucius. Another saying is that it is referred to two persons named Lao and Peng respectively.

子曰："默而识之，学而不厌，诲人不倦，何有于我哉？"(07.02)

【白话译文】

孔子说："我默默记住我所学习和遇到的知识和道理，学习上有不满足的欲望，

【注释】默：默默地。识(音 zhì 志)之：一解"识，记住"；之，所见所闻、所学的知识、道理。二解"识，通'志'，标志、标准"；之：学而不厌、诲人不倦两项；识之，制定实现这两项的标准。学：读书学习。厌：厌烦。诲：教诲。倦：疲倦。何有：古代常用语，不同场合意思不同；此为孔子谦虚词，"有什么"。

教育他人上有孜孜不倦的热情。对于上述这些,我做好了什么?”(07.02)

【英译】

The Master said,“I silently bear in mind the knowledge and principles that I have learned and encountered, have an insatiable desire to learn, and have tireless zeal to teach others. With all the above, have I accomplished them well?”(07.02)

子之所慎:齐,战,疾。(07.13)

【注释】慎:小心对待。齐(音zhāi 摘):斋,斋戒。战:战争。疾:疾病。

【白话译文】

孔子小心翼翼对待如下的事情:斋戒、战争、疾病。(07.13)

【英译】

The Master approached the following things with great caution: a fast, a war, and a disease. (07.13)

子曰:“饭疏食,饮水,曲肱而枕之,乐亦在其中矣。不义而富且贵,于我如浮云。”(07.16)

【注释】鲁定公五年(公元前505年)六月,孔子47岁,讲此言,拒见季孙氏的家臣阳货。饭:吃。疏食:粗粮、菜食。水:凉水,热水为汤。曲:弯。肱(音gōng 公):胳膊。而:就。枕:枕头。枕之:枕着胳膊。而:却。于我:对于我。如:同、像。

【白话译文】

孔子说:“就是吃粗粮,喝凉水,弯曲上臂枕着睡觉,我也十分幸福。如果巨大财富和高官优越地位不用正义方式获得,它们对我来说就如同飘浮的云彩。”(07.16)

【英译】

The Master said,“I also find great pleasure in taking coarse food, drinking cold water and sleeping on my upper arm bent as a pillow. Great wealth and superior privilege of senior officialdom are like flying clouds for me if they are not obtained righteously.” (07.16)

子曰:“盖有不知而作之者,我无是也。多闻,择其善者而从之,多见而识之,知之次也。”(07.28)

【注释】盖:大概。知:懂。而:就。作:创作,穿凿妄作成篇章。无:没有。是:这样。我无是也:我不这样(孔子述而不作)。闻:听。择:选择。从:跟着学。见:看。识(音 zhì 志):记住。知:生而知之的上智。之:的。次:次一等;次第,依次。知之次也:仅次于生而知之呀;知识渐次形成的啊。

【白话译文】

孔子说:“大概有不懂装懂、编造作品的人。但是,我不是这样的人。我宽泛地多听,选择接受优秀的加以学习。我广泛地多观察,牢固记在心间。因此,我的知识一步一步循序渐进增长了。”(07.28)

【英译】

The Master said, "There probably is someone who really does not understand a thing and pretends to understand it, and also fabricates his works. I am not that person. I listen much and select the best to follow after. I observe much extensively to firmly bear it in mind. Therefore my knowledge advances gradually step by step in an orderly way." (07. 28)

子曰:"文,莫吾犹人也。躬行君子,则吾未之有得。"(07. 33)

【注释】文:文献的掌握,我的学问。莫:没有。犹:如同。人:他人。莫吾犹人也:在文献掌握上,我没有达到别人的深度。躬行君子:(做)身体力行的君子。则:那么。未:没有。有得:做到。吾未之有得:我在这方面还没做到。

【白话译文】

孔子说:"在掌握古代典籍方面,我还没有接近其他人达到的程度。而且,我还没有成功地做一名知行合一的君子,来踏踏实实做好我日常所倡导的事。"(07. 33)

【英译】

The Master said, "In aspect of mastery of ancient doctrines and records, I have not approached the level which others have reached. Neither have I successfully become a superior man in earnestly practicing what I advocate in daily life." (07. 33)

子曰:“若圣与仁,则吾岂敢?抑为之不厌,诲人不倦,则可谓云尔已矣。”公西华曰:“正唯弟子不能学也。”(07.34)

【注释】若:如果说(我是)。圣:圣人。与:和。仁:仁人。则:那么。岂敢:怎么敢当。抑:只不过。为:做。之:圣与仁。厌:厌烦。诲:教育。倦:疲倦。则:就、那么。可谓:可以说。云尔:这样说。已矣:罢了。则可谓云尔已矣:还可以这样说罢了。公西华:姓公西名赤,字子华。正:恰好。唯:是。不能:没有能力。学:学会。

【白话译文】

孔子说:“如果评价我为圣人和仁人,我岂敢担当?大约说我学习与工作有不能满足的欲望,教诲别人有不知疲倦的热情。仅这样评论我,还是可以的。”公西华说:“这正是我们弟子不能跟你学到的。”(07.34)

【英译】

The Master said, “If I am evaluated as a sage and a benevolent man, how could I deserve such an honour? It can probably be said about me that I have an insatiable desire to learn and work, and tireless zeal to teach others. That is all that can be talked about me.” Gongxi Hua[1] said, “This is exactly what we your disciples cannot be able to learn from you.” (07.34)

【英译注】(1) Gongxi Hua: Surname Gongxi, first name Chi, style name Zihua, Confucius's disciple.

子温而厉,威而不猛,恭而安。(07.38)

【注释】子:孔子。温:温和。而:却,但是。厉:严厉。威:威严。猛:凶猛。恭:庄重。安:安详。

【白话译文】

孔子温厚而且严厉,很威风而且不凶猛,恭顺而且安详。(07.38)

【英译】

The Master was good-natured and serious, awe-inspiring and not fierce, and deferential and composed. (07.38)

太宰问于子贡曰:"夫子圣者与?何其多能也?"子贡曰:"固天纵之将圣,又多能也。"子闻之,曰:"太宰知我乎?吾少也贱,故多能鄙事。君子多乎哉?不多也。"(09.06)

【注释】太宰:宫廷事务的总管。子贡:姓端木名赐,字子贡。夫子:孔子。圣:圣人。与:吗。何:为什么。其:他。多能:多才多艺。天:上天。纵:让。之:他,孔子。将:成为。圣:圣人。多:增多。闻之:听到这。贱:贫贱,地位低。鄙事:卑贱的事情,具体的技能。君子:一解"卿、大夫等贵族的子弟"。二解"品德高尚、多能的人"。君子多乎哉,不多也:一解"贵族子弟(称君子)能会这么多的技艺吗?没这么多呀"。二解"按照君子的要求,我的技能还算多吗?不算多呀"。

【白话译文】

太宰向子贡打听说:"你老师是圣人吗?为什么他那么多才多艺?"子贡说:"上天本来要让他成为圣人,所以给他更多的才干。"孔子听到后说:"太宰知道我的身世吗?我小时候很穷很卑微,因此我掌握了很多低贱的能力。如果按照君子的标准,我的能力足够多吗?不够多呀!"(09.06)

【英译】

The chief director of the court asked Zigong(1), "Is your Master a sage? Why is

【英译注】(1) Zigong: Surname Duanmu, first name Ci, style name Zigong, Confucius's disciple.

he so versatile?" Zigong said, "Heaven naturally made him become a sage, therefore it gave him much ability." Hearing it, the Master said, "Did the chief director know my life? I was humble and poor in childhood, so I have mastered many humble capacities. Are my capacities enough if I am to be judged according to the standards of a superior man? Oh no, they are not!" (09.06)

牢曰:"子云:'吾不试,故艺。'"(09.07)

【注释】牢:子牢,孔子弟子。试:被任用,做官。故:因此。艺:会许多技艺。

【白话译文】

牢说:"孔子说过:'我过去没有被任用为官,所以我才有机会掌握一些技艺。'"(09.07)

【英译】

Lao(1) said, "The Master mentioned: 'I was not appointed as an official, so I had the chance to master some skills(2).'" (09.07)

【英译注】(1) Lao: Surname Qin, first name Lao, style name Zikai, from the State of Wei. It is doubted that he was Confucius's disciple. (2) skills: The Rites of Proprieties, Music, archery, carriage driving, *Book of History* and mathematics.

子曰:"吾有知乎哉?无知也。有鄙夫问于我,空空如也。我叩其两端而竭焉。"(09.08)

【注释】知:知识。鄙夫:乡下人。问:询问。于:向。空空:说不清楚。如也:的样子。叩:推敲。两端:(从)对立的两方面,如本末、上下、正反等。竭:穷尽追究。

【白话译文】

孔子说:"噢,我是一个有知识的人吗? 不,我不是的。有一次,一个没有文化的人向我请教,我对此问题,不知道如何回答。我从首尾两端探究,竭尽全力才回答了他。"(09.08)

【英译】

The Master said,"Oh, am I a knowledgeable person indeed? No, I am not. Once I was asked a question by an ignorant fellow, I did not know how to answer it. I made a thorough inquiry from head to tail and answered him after exhausting all my efforts."(09.08)

我叩其两端而竭焉:我从正反两个方面推敲,竭尽所知答复了他。

子见齐衰者、冕衣裳者与瞽者,见之,虽少,必作;过之,必趋。(09.10)

【注释】齐衰(音 zī 资 cuī 崔):麻布丧服。冕:官帽,指贵族。衣:上衣。裳:下服,相当于现代的裙子。衣裳者:穿官服的人。与:和、同。瞽(音 gǔ 鼓):盲。者:的人。虽:虽然。少:比自己年轻。作:站起。过:走过。之:他们。趋:小步快走。

【白话译文】

孔子遇到穿丧服的人、戴礼帽穿礼服的人和失明的人的时候,即使他们比他年轻,他一定站起来。路过他们时,他一定小步子快走。(09.10)

【英译】

When the Master encountered the people in mourning clothes, the people wearing ceremonial caps and ceremonial robes, or blind persons, he stood up even though their ages might be younger than him. When he passed by them, he walked quickly with small and fast steps. (09.10)

孔子于乡党,恂恂如也,似不能言者。其在宗庙朝廷,便便言,唯谨尔。(10.01)

【注释】于:在。乡党:家乡。恂(音 xù 旭):温和恭顺。如也:的样子。似:好像。言:说话。其:他。便:辩,健谈。唯:只,只有。谨:谨慎。尔:耳,而已,罢了。

【白话译文】

孔夫子在家乡,非常随和恭敬,如同讲不好话似的。他在朝廷和君主的祖庙上,清晰流利地表达他想说的话,只是谨慎、话少而精而已。(10.01)

【英译】

Confucius was gentle and deferential at his hometown. It was as if he could not speak. When he was at court and at the ancestral temple of the sovereign, he distinctly and fluently expressed what he wanted to say, cautiously and laconically. (10.01)

朝,与下大夫言,侃侃如也;与上大夫言,訚訚如也。君在,踧踖如也,与与如也。(10.02)

【注释】朝:在朝廷上。言:说话。侃(音 kǎn 砍):理直气壮,不卑不亢,温和快乐。如也:的样子。訚(音 yín 银):和颜悦色而直言争辩。君:国君。在:在场。踧踖(音

cù促 jí 吉):恭敬而不安。与与:小心谨慎。

【白话译文】

孔子上朝,等候君主到来时,耿直快乐地与下大夫说话,正直尊敬地与上大夫说话。在君主面前,敬重紧张,安详,保持适度威仪。(10.02)

【英译】

When the Master was at court waiting for the sovereign to come, he talked with the lower ranking officials frankly and cheerfully and talked with higher ranking officials respectfully and honestly. When the sovereign came, he was respectful but tense, serene with an appropriately dignified manner. (10.02)

君召使摈,色勃如也,足躩如也。揖所与立,左右手,衣前后,襜如也。趋进,翼如也。宾退,必复命,曰:"宾不顾矣。"(10.03)

【注释】君:国君。召:召唤。使:派。摈(音 bìn 鬓):出迎宾客。色:脸色。勃:庄重。如也:的样子。足:脚步。躩(音 jué 决):快。揖:作揖。与:和他人在一起。揖所与立:向站在一起的人作揖。左右手:向左、向右拱手。衣:衣服。前后:一俯一仰。襜(音 chān 搀):整齐,衣袖摇动的样子。趋:快走。翼:飞鸟展翅。退:走了、离开。复命:汇报。顾:回头张望。

【白话译文】

孔子被君主召见去接待国宾,他举止矜持,神态庄重。他快步走向前面站立的宾客,向他们作揖。他再向左边、右边的宾客作揖。当他前俯后仰时,他的衣服整齐地飘动。当他小步子快走时,他的衣袖飘洒如鸟翅飞翔。宾客辞别后,他一定向君主汇报说:"宾客已经走远了,不回头张望了。"(10.03)

【英译】

When the Master was called in by his sovereign to receive state guests, he kept a reserved manner and solemn countenance. He swiftly walked to the guests standing at front and bowed to them with his hands folded in front. He bowed to the guests on the left and also on the right. His clothes floated quite neatly as he bent forwards and backwards. He walked swiftly in small steps, with his sleeves floating like bird wings soaring. After the guests bid farewell, he reported to his sovereign, "The guests have gone away and have not turned their heads looking back." (10. 03)

入公门,鞠躬如也,如不容。立不中门,行不履阈。过位,色勃如也,足躩如也,其言似不足者。摄齐升堂,鞠躬如也,屏气似不息者。出,降一等,逞颜色,怡怡如也。没阶,趋进,翼如也。复其位,踧踖如也。(10. 04)

【白话译文】

在孔子进入朝廷的大门以后,他一直谨慎恭敬,好像没有他的容身之地。他站立的时候,不站在门口中央;他行走的时候,不踩踏门槛。他路过君主的座位时,保持矜持和严肃的表情,加快他行走的步伐,

【注释】入:进入。公门:朝廷大门。鞠:不能当曲讲,与"躬"构成双音词,形容谨慎恭敬的样子。躬:身体。如也:的样子;《论语》中所有"……如也"的词(形容词、副词的全称)都不用动词结构,表示如同什么状态、样子。如:像,如同。容:容身。立:站。立不中门:不站在门中间。履:踩。阈(音 yù 玉):门槛。过:经过。位:国君座位;有注为古代宫廷,中庭左右两侧叫位。色:脸色。勃:庄重。足:脚步。躩(音 jué 决):快。不足:力气不足、不充分。摄(音 shè 设):提起。齐(音 zī 资):衣服下摆。升:走上。堂:朝堂。屏:憋住。气:出气,呼气。似:如同。息:呼吸。出:退堂。降:走下。一等:一级台阶。逞(音 chěng 骋):

说话简约，声调柔和。当他进入主厅时，极其谨慎恭敬，提起衣服的下摆，屏住气，好像没有呼吸一样。当他走出大厅，走下一级台阶时，表情放松，怡然自得。当他走完台阶时，小步子快走，衣袖飘动如同鸟飞翔的翅膀。当他回到大厅他原来的座位时，紧张恭敬，聚精会神。（10.04）

【英译】

After the Master entered the gate of the court, he always was prudent and respectful as if there had been no room to shelter himself. When he stood, he did not stand at the middle of the gate. When he walked, he did not tread on the threshold. When he passed by the seat of his sovereign, he kept a reserved manner and solemn countenance, speeded up his paces. His speech was concise and his tone became placid. When he entered the main hall, very cautiously and respectfully, he pinched the lower hem of his gown with his fingers, and held his breath as if he were not breathing. When he left the main hall and walked down one step, he had a relaxed countenance and became calm and cheerful. When he walked down all the steps, he walked swiftly in small steps, with his sleeves floating like bird wings soaring. When he returned to his original position in the main hall, he was tense and respectful with an air of concentration. (10.04)

舒展。颜色：面容。怡：和悦。没阶：走完台阶。趋：快走。翼：鸟翅。复：回到。踧踖（音 cù 促 jí 吉）：恭敬而不安。

执圭，鞠躬如也，如不胜。上如揖，下如授，勃如战色，足蹜蹜，如有循。享礼，有容色。私觌，愉愉如也。(10.05)

【注释】执：持。圭(音 guī 归)：上圆下方的玉器。鞠：与"躬"构成双音词，表示谨慎恭敬。躬：身体。如也：的样子。如：如同，类似。不胜：举不动。上：上举。揖：作揖。下：放下。授：传递。勃：庄重。战：战栗。色：面色。足：脚步。蹜(音 sù 速)：小步快走，细心畏怯。循：沿着线。享：呈献。礼：礼物。容：和悦。私：私人。觌(音 dí 笛)：会见。私觌：与外国君主以私礼相见。愉：愉快。

【白话译文】

当孔子手持玉圭时，他表情矜持恭敬，好像玉圭重得拿不动。他向上举起玉圭好像作揖。他向下放下玉圭好像传递给别人。他矜持严肃，如同有颤抖的表情。他小步快速行走，好像沿着一条直线。当各国客人开始呈献陈列礼物时，他表情和气喜悦。他与别国君主和大臣以私人名义相见时，显得轻松快乐。(10.05)

【英译】

When the Master carried a jade tablet(1) in his hands, he was prudent and respectful, as if it was so heavy that he could not carry it. He lifted it as if he was bowing with hands folded in front. He put it down as if he was handing it over to someone. He was reserved and solemn as if he had a countenance of shivering. He walked quickly in small paces as if he followed a straight line. When gifts from the guests of various states were presented and displayed, his countenance became amiable. He was easy and delightful when he met with the sovereign and officials of other states in his own name. (10.05)

【英译注】(1) a jade tablet: A tablet was square shaped at bottom and round or pointed at the top, made of jade. It described hereby what Confucius did when he carried a jade tablet at a grand ceremony in his state, a ceremony visiting another state or a ceremony of acceptance of an appointment. Gift presentation described hereby was done after the ceremony of an appointment acceptance.

见齐衰者,虽狎,必变。见冕者与瞽者,虽亵,必以貌。凶服者式之。式负版者。有盛馔,必变色而作。迅雷风烈,必变。(10.25)

【注释】见:看到。齐衰(音 zī 资 cuī 崔):麻布丧服。狎(音 xiá 霞):亲近。变:变得严肃。冕:官帽,指贵族。瞽(音 gǔ 鼓):盲,指乐师。亵(音 xiè 谢):熟悉。以:用。貌:礼貌。必以貌:一定以礼貌相待。凶服:丧服、囚服。式:轼,车前横木,指尊敬或同情礼节,身子向前微俯,伏在横木上。负:背负。版:木版图籍。盛:丰盛。馔(音 zhuàn 啭):饮食。变色:表情改变,脸色庄重。而:且。作:食用。迅雷:急雷电。变:表情变严肃。

【白话译文】

孔子遇见穿丧服的人,即使与他们很亲近,他也一定表情变得严肃。他遇见穿礼服、戴礼帽的人或者失明的人,即使与他们很熟悉,也一定向他们表示敬意。遇到穿丧服或者送丧服的人,他在车里坐着,一定站起来,双手扶车前横木,身体前倾,低一下头,以示同情。遇到背着国家地图或统计图的人,他在车里也做同样的动作。当有丰盛的菜肴筵席呈上,他用餐前一定改变表情。当有迅雷、烈风、暴雨时,他的表情一定变得严肃。(10.25)

【英译】

The Master always adopted a solemn expression when he encountered people in mourning clothes even if he was close with them. He always showed respect when he met people wearing ceremonial caps and ceremonial robes or blind persons even if he was familiar with them. When he encountered people in mourning clothes or carrying mourning clothes, he stood up in his carriage, held the front horizontal bar with both hands, slightly tilted his body forward and bowed his head, to sympathize with them. He also did the same in his carriage if he ran into someone who carried the map of territory and the census register of the state. When a grand feast of sumptuous dishes was laid out, he always changed his expression before he took it. He always adopted a serious expression whenever there was the sound of thunder, or a windstorm, or a violent rain storm. (10. 25)

子路宿于石门,晨门曰:"奚自?"子路曰:"自孔氏。"曰:"是知其不可而为之者与?"(14. 40)

【注释】子路:姓仲,名由,字子路。宿:住。石门:鲁国都城的外门。晨门:早上守城门的人。奚:哪里。自:来。孔氏:孔子。知:明白。其:他。而:却,但是。不可而为之:明知做不到却还要去做。者:的人。与:吗。

【白话译文】

子路在鲁国都城的外门石门过了一夜。第二天,守门人问他:"你从谁那儿来的?"子路说:"从孔家来。"守门人说:"是那位明知自己完成不了,却偏偏还坚持不懈做下去的人吗?"(14. 40)

【英译】

Zilu(1) passed a night outside the external gate at Shimen of the capital of the State of Lu. As he entered the gate next morning, the door keeper asked him, "Where are you

【英译注】(1) Zilu: Surname Zhong, first name You, style name Zilu, Confucius's disciple. (2) the Kong: Surname of Confucius or the family of Confucius. It was here referred to Confucius.

from?" Zilu replied, "From the Kong[2]." He said, "Is he the person who just persists on doing what he cannot accomplish as he clearly knows?" (14. 40)

公山弗扰以费畔,召,子欲往。子路不说,曰:"末之也已,何必公山氏之之也!"子曰:"夫召我者岂徒哉?如有用我者,吾其为东周乎?"(17. 05)

【注释】此事有疑。《左传》有鲁定公五年(公元前 505 年)、八年、十二年,或鲁哀公八年的公山弗扰,均没有召见孔子的事。鲁定公十二年公山弗扰反叛,孔子任司冠,派人打败了他。有人言,不该信《左传》而疑《论语》《史记》。鲁定公八年(公元前 502 年),孔子 50 岁,发生此事。公山弗扰:公山不狃(音 niǔ 扭),字子洩(音 xiè 谢),季氏的家臣。以:用。费(旧音 bì 闭):今山东费(音 fèi 废)县。畔:叛乱。召:请去做官。子:孔子。往:前往。子路:姓仲,名由,字子路。说(音 yuè 月):悦,愉快。末:无。之:到。末之:无处去。末之也已:无处去也就罢了。何必:为什么一定。之之:去该处。公山氏之之也:去公山弗扰那里呢。岂:难道。徒:徒然。其:就。为:建设、做。东周:东方的周王朝。

【白话译文】

公山弗扰在他盘踞的费邑发动叛乱,召见孔子去做官。孔子打算前往接受,但子路不高兴,说:"如果你走投无路了,这对你还可以。你为什么要去公山氏那里呢!"孔子说:"召见我的人,难道白白召我吗?如果适当任用我,我大概能使周文王、周武王的制度在东方复兴吧?"(17. 05)

【英译】

Gongshan Furao[1] launched an armed rebellion from the city of Bi where he entrenched. He invited the Master to come and offered him an official position. The Master wanted to accept it. Not happy with that, Zi

【英译注】(1) Gongshan Furao: Gongshan Buniu, style name Zixie, the manager of the Ji Clan. His armed rebellion was recorded inconsistently in the *Zuo's Commentary*. One of which occurred in Year 12 of Duke Ding of the State of Lu; he did not invite Confucius to come, but on

lu[2] said, "It would be alright if you are nowhere else to go. Why must you go over to Gongshan?" The Master said, "Did he invite me for nothing? If he wants to offer me a proper appointment, could I not help him recreate the systems of the Zhou Dynasty's King Wen and King Wu in the east?" (17.05)

the other hand, Confucius ordered the army to fight him as he was the State Senior Judge of the State of Lu. (2) Zilu: Surname Zhong, first name You, style name Zilu, Confucius's disciple.

卫公孙朝问于子贡曰:"仲尼焉学?"子贡曰:"文武之道,未坠于地,在人。贤者识其大者,不贤者识其小者,莫不有文武之道焉。夫子焉不学?而亦何常师之有?"(19.22)

【注释】卫公孙朝:公孙朝,卫国大夫。子贡:姓端木名赐,字子贡。仲尼:孔子的字。焉:何处。学:学到。文武之道:周文王、周武王之道。未:没有。坠(音 zhuǐ 赘):掉下。于:在。地:地里。在人:留在人间。贤者:贤能的人。识:懂得。其大者:它的根本。小者:末节。莫:没有(地方)。不有:不存在。夫子:孔子。焉:哪里。而:然而,那么。亦:也。何:何必。常师:固定的老师。

【白话译文】

卫公孙朝问子贡说:"仲尼是跟谁学习的?"子贡说:"周文王、周武王的理论体系没有掉到地下而失传,而是继续保留在人间。贤明的人抓住其主要部分,而不贤明的人抓住其末节。没有一个地方是没有周文王、周武王的理论体系的。我的老师向谁不能学习?为什么他必须专门有固定的老师去学习呢?"(19.22)

【英译】

Gongsun Chao[1] of the State of Wei asked Zigong[2], "From whom does Zhong

【英译注】(1) Gongsun Chao: A senior official of the State of Wei. (2) Zigong: Surname Duanmu, first

ni[3] learn?" Zigong replied, "The doctrines of King Wen and King Wu of the Zhou Dynasty have not dropped into the earth being lost, but continue to be handed down in the world. Sagacious people grasp the principal part, and the unsagacious people grasp the minor part. It is no place where the doctrines of King Wen and King Wu of the Zhou Dynasty are not available. Therefore from whomever can't my Master learn? And why must he specially have a fixed teacher to learn from?" (19. 22)

name Ci, style name Zigong. (3) Zhongni: Confucius's style name.

叔孙武叔语大夫于朝,曰:"子贡贤于仲尼。"子服景伯以告子贡。子贡曰:"譬之宫墙,赐之墙也及肩,窥见室家之好。夫子之墙数仞,不得其门而入,不见宗庙之美,百官之富。得其门者或寡矣。夫子之云,不亦宜乎!"(19. 23)

【白话译文】

叔孙武叔在朝廷上同高官们说:"子贡比他老师仲尼贤明。"子服景伯把此话告诉了子贡。子贡说:"让我拿院子的围墙做个比喻。我家的围墙只有肩膀那么高,任何人站在墙外都能窥视家里家具装

【注释】叔孙武叔:名州仇,谥(音 shì 是)号武,鲁国大夫,三桓(音 huán 环)之一。语(音 yù 玉):和别人一起谈论。于朝:在朝廷上。子贡:姓端木名赐,字子贡。贤:贤良、强。于:比。仲尼:孔子。贤于仲尼:比孔子更贤良。子服景伯:鲁国大夫。以:用以。告:告诉。譬(音 pì 媲):打比方。之:这。宫墙:宫廷围墙。赐:子贡,姓端木名赐。及:到。肩:肩膀。窥:从缝隙观察。室家之好:房屋里的宝贝。夫子:孔子。数:几。仞(音 rèn 认):7 尺为 1 仞。入:进入。宗庙:祖宗庙堂。宗庙之美:庙堂、宫殿的绚丽辉煌和祭祀的庄严隆重。富:富丽堂皇。得其门者:能够找到门进去的人。或:或许。寡:少。夫子:先生,叔孙武叔。云:说法。亦:也。宜:当然,不怪。夫子之云,不亦宜乎:叔孙武叔的

饰的优雅。我老师的围墙有很多人(仞)那么高。一个人不找到门、进不去,就看不见宗庙华美的祭祀仪式以及丰富的建筑和房屋宫殿的多姿多彩。大约只有很少的人能够找到大门。因此,叔孙老先生的话很正常,不是吗?”(19.23)

说法,也不奇怪呀。

【英译】

Shusun Wushu[(1)] talked to the senior officials at the court, “Zigong[(2)] is more sagacious than his master Zhongni[(3)].” Zifu Jing Bo[(4)] mentioned this to Zigong. Zigong said, “Let us take a wall around a house as an illustration. My wall is only shoulder height, so anyone standing outside can peep over it and see the elegance of the furniture and decorations of my house. My Master's wall is many times of the height of a man. If someone does not find the gate in order to get in, he will not see the resplendent sacrificial ceremony at the ancestral temple and the rich architecture and various styles of houses and palaces. Probably very few people will be able to find the gate. So it was no surprise that Shusun Wushu spoke as he did, wasn't it?” (19.23)

【英译注】(1) Shusun Wushu: Surname Shusun, first name Zhouqiu, posthumous name Wu, from one of the three Huan families. (2) Zigong: Surname Duanmu, first name Ci, style name Zigong, Confucius's disciple. (3) Zhongni: The style name of Confucius. (4) Zifu Jing Bo: Surname Zifu, first name Bo, posthumous title Jing, a senior official of the State of Lu.

叔孙武叔毁仲尼。子贡曰:“无以为也!仲尼不可毁也。

【注释】毁:诽谤。仲尼:孔子,名丘,字仲尼。以:这样,如此,副词。无以为也:不要这样做了。

他人之贤者，丘陵也，犹可逾也；仲尼，日月也，无得而逾焉。人虽欲自绝，其何伤于日月乎？多见其不知量也。”(19.24)

之：的。贤：贤德。犹：还。逾：超越。日月：太阳和月亮。无得：不可能。无得而逾焉：不可能超越啊。自绝：自己绝命，自己拒绝与日月之光的接触。何：怎么。伤：损害。于：对。乎：吗。多：只是、仅仅。见：表明。其：他。不知量：不自量力。

【白话译文】

叔孙武叔诽谤仲尼。子贡说：“啊，不要这样做！仲尼是不可以诽谤的。他人的贤明好比丘陵，还是可以超越的，但是仲尼的贤明就像太阳和月亮，是无法超越的。一个人虽然可能拒绝接受日月的光辉，但他怎么能够对太阳、月亮有损害呢？这只能显示他不自量力而已。”(19.24)

【英译】

Shusun Wushu(1) defamed Zhongni(2). Zigong(3) said, “Do not do that! Zhongni cannot be defamed. The sagacity of other people is like a hill that can be surmounted, but Zhongni is like the sun and the moon that cannot be surmounted. Someone might refuse to accept the light of the sun and the moon, but how could the sun and the moon be harmed by him? This only shows that he overrates his own abilities.” (19.24)

【英译注】(1) Shusun Wushu: Surname Shusun, first name Zhouqiu, posthumous name Wu, from one of the three Huan families. (2) Zhongni: The style name of Confucius. (3) Zigong: Surname Duanmu, first name Ci, style name Zigong, Confucius's disciple.

陈子禽谓子贡曰：“子为恭也，仲尼岂贤于子乎？”子贡曰：

【注释】陈子禽：姓陈名亢(音kàng抗)，字子禽。子：你。为：是。恭：恭敬。子为恭也：你是太

"君子一言以为知,一言以为不知,言不可不慎也。夫子之不可及也,犹天之不可阶而升也。夫子之得邦家者,所谓立之斯立,道之斯行,绥之斯来,动之斯和。其生也荣,其死也哀。如之何其可及也?"(19.25)

恭敬了吧。岂:怎么。贤:贤良。于:比、超过。一言:一句话。以为:表现为。知(音 zhì 治):智慧。不知:没有智慧。言:说话。慎:谨慎。夫子:孔子。及:赶上。犹:像。天:苍天。阶:梯子。升:攀登。犹天之不可阶而升也:如同不可爬着梯子上天一样。邦:诸侯封国。家:卿大夫治地。得邦家者:如果孔子成为诸侯或大夫。所谓:他所说的。立:树立,立身。之:百姓。斯:就会。所谓立之斯立:他要求百姓自立则百姓就会自立。道(音 dǎo 岛):导,引导、治理。行:行动,跟着前进。绥(音 suí 随):安抚。来:归顺。动:役使。和:齐心协力。其:他。生:活着。荣:(是)国家的荣耀。哀:(是)国家的哀痛。

【白话译文】

陈子禽对子贡说:"你是太谦虚、恭敬了吧?仲尼难道真的比你还贤良吗?"子贡说:"对于一名君子,他的一句话可以揭示他的智慧,他的一句话也显示他的愚昧。因此,一个人说话不可不慎重呀。我的老师不可以超越,如同苍天不可以用一架梯子登上去。如果我的老师被授予一个邦为诸侯,或者一块封地为卿大夫,如同我们常说的,他让百姓自立于社会,那么他们就自立于社会;他引导百姓,那么他们就跟随他;他要安定社会、保持秩序,百姓就从远方来,遵守法令;他动员百姓,他们就积极响应,同心协力。他活着,是国家的荣耀;他死了,是国家的哀伤。因此,我们如何达到他那么崇高的境界啊?"(19.25)

【英译】

Chen Ziqin(1) said to Zigong(2), "Are you too modest and deferential? How is Zhongni(3) truly more sagacious than you?"

【英译注】(1)Chen Ziqin: Surname Chen, first name Kang, style name Ziqin, from the State of Lu. He was possibly not Confucius's disciple. (2)Zigong: Surname Duanmu,

Zigong said, "For a superior man, his one sentence may reveal his wisdom or his one sentence may reveal his ignorance. So he cannot be careless in his words. My Master cannot be equaled just as the Heavens cannot be climbed with a ladder. If my Master were granted a state as a duke or offered a senior official with a great family fiefdom, as we usually call it, he would ask the common people to establish themselves in society, and then they would establish themselves independently. He would lead the common people, and they would follow him. He would bring peace and maintain order in society; then they would come to him from distant quarters, and would obey orders and laws. He would mobilize the common people, and they would actively respond to his call and work together with one heart. When he lives, he is glory of the state; when he dies, the state will be grieved and mourn him. How can we attain such lofty realm as him?" (19. 25)

first name Ci, style name Zigong, Confucius's disciple. (3) Zhongni: Confucius's style name.

十四

Fourteen

周游列国

Travel Through All the States

72

周游 Interstate Travel

齐景公待孔子，曰："若季氏则吾不能，以季、孟之间待之。"曰："吾老矣，不能用也。"孔子行。(18.03)

【白话译文】

齐景公谈到如何给孔夫子俸禄和恰当待遇，说："对他像鲁国君主对待季氏那样，我办不到，但是对他可以比季氏低一些、比孟氏高一些。"接下来，他又说："我太老了，不会有什么作为了。"孔夫子离开了齐国。(18.03)

【英译】

Duke Jing(1) of the State of Qi talked about how to give Confucius an official salary and proper treatment, saying, "I cannot afford to give Confucius terms as high as the Sovereign of the State of Lu gives the head of the Ji(2) family, but I can offer him something lower than that of the Ji and higher than that of the chief of the Meng(3)." Afterwards, he said, "I am so old that I cannot accomplish

【注释】鲁昭公二十五年(公元前517年)，鲁昭公被季氏击败奔齐国，孔子35岁，避鲁乱去齐国，住1年多，不受重用，37岁回鲁国。孔子周游列国为20年后的事，不包括此次去齐国。齐景公：姓姜名杵臼(音chǔ楚jiù旧)，齐国国君，公元前547年至公元前490年在位。待：(谈到)对待。若：像。季氏：季平子(季孙意如)，鲁昭公十二年至鲁定公五年为上卿。以：按。孟：孟孙氏，鲁国下卿。之：孔子。曰：齐景公又说。老：衰老。矣：了。用：作为、用处。不能用也：没有作为了。行：离开(齐国)。

【英译注】(1) Duke Jing: Surname Jiang, first name Chujiu, the sovereign of the State of Qi (from 547 BC to 490 BC). This trip was not included in Confucius's travel through all the states, which started his 19 years later in 496 BC. (2) the Ji: Surname Ji, first name Ruyi, posthumous title Ping, normally called Master Ji Ping, the prime minister of the State of Lu from 530 BC to 505 BC. (3) the Meng: The senior official of the State of Lu.

anything." Confucius departed from the State of Qi. (18.03)

齐人归女乐，季桓子受之，三日不朝。孔子行。(18.04)

【注释】鲁定公十四年（公元前496年），孔子56岁，齐国给鲁国君送美女80人，皆穿文衣而舞康乐，季桓子受之，孔子辞职，开始周游列国。归：馈，赠送。季桓（音 huán 环）子：季孙氏，鲁国宰相。女乐（音 yuè 月）：舞女歌姬。三日：多日。朝：上朝听政。行：辞官离去。

【白话译文】

齐国送给鲁国一群漂亮的歌姬舞女。季桓子接受了她们，三日不上朝治理政务。孔夫子辞职，离开了朝廷。(18.04)

【英译】

The State of Qi presented a big group of beautiful singing and dancing girls to the State of Lu. Master Ji Huan[1] accepted them and did not go to the court for three days[2] to take care of state affairs. Confucius resigned from his position and left the court[3]. (18.04)

【英译注】(1) Master Ji Huan: Surname Jisun, first name Si, prime minister of the State of Lu. (2) three days: Many days, not exact three days. (3) (Confucius) left the court: He started his interstate travel to many states in about 14 years from this year, the Year 14 of Duke Ding of the State of Lu (496 BC).

子畏于匡，曰："文王既没，文不在兹乎？天之将丧斯文也，后死者不得与于斯文也；天之未丧斯文也，匡人其如予何！"(09.05)

【注释】鲁定公十四年（公元前496年）十月，孔子56岁，从卫国到陈国，路过匡地，因貌似匡人的仇人阳虎，被拘留5天，弟子恐惧，故孔子讲此言。畏：被囚禁。于：在。匡：地名，今河南长垣县西南。文王：周文王，姓姬名昌。既：已经。没：死了。文：礼乐文化。兹：一解"我这里"；二解"匡地这里"。乎：吗。文不在兹乎：一解

【白话译文】

孔子被匡地的人拘留。他说:"周文王辞世以后,在这里不也是存在周代的文化遗产吗?如果苍天要消灭这种文化,我们这些后来人也不会掌握这种文化了。如果苍天不消灭这种文化,匡地的人在这种文化影响下对我还能怎样?"(09.05)

【英译】

When the Master was being detained by the people of the town of Kuang (1), he said, "After King Wen(2) of the Zhou Dynasty passed away, doesn't the cultural heritance of the Zhou Dynasty still exist here? If Heaven wants to extinguish this culture, we who have come after will no longer be able to grasp it. If Heaven does not want to extinguish it, what can the people of Kuang under influence of this culture do to me?" (09.05)

"礼乐文化不是在我这里吗";二解"礼乐文化不是传播到匡地这里吗"。天:上天。丧:消灭。斯:这。后死者:后来人。与:举,给予,掌握。于:对于。后死者不得与于斯文也:后来人(我)就不能掌握这种文化了。未丧:不消灭。匡人:匡地的人。其:语气词。予:我。如予何:能把我怎么样。

【英译注】(1) Kuang: A place close to the State of Wei, possibly currently at Kuangcheng Town of 7.5 kilometers southwestern from Changyuan County of Henan Province. Confucius was on his way to the State of Chen in 496 BC and he was confined due to his resembling to Yang Huo, an enemy of Kuang. (2) King Wen: Surname Ji, first name Chang, the third son of Ji Li. He served as the king of the Zhou Tribe (currently at Shaanxi Province) for 50 years and laid a strong foundation to take over the Shang Dynasty by his son King Wu.

子畏于匡,颜渊后。子曰:"吾以女为死矣。"曰:"子在,回何敢死?"(11.23)

【白话译文】

当孔子被匡地的人拘留时,颜渊落在后边。当他们相见时,孔子说:"我以为你

【注释】畏:公元前496年,鲁定公十四年,孔子56岁,由卫国经匡地去陈国,被囚禁5天。于:在。颜渊:姓颜名回,字子渊。后:落在后面。以:以为。女(音 rǔ 辱):汝,你。死:拼死、与人拼命。矣:了。子:老师。回:姓颜名回,字子渊。敢:冒昧。

与那些人拼死去了。”他答:“你还活着,我怎么敢拼死?”(11.23)

【英译】

When the Master was detained by the people of the town of Kuang(1), Yan Yuan(2) lagged behind. When they met, the Master said, "I thought you were fighting to the death with those people." He said, "How can I dare to fight to the death when you are alive." (11.23)

【英译注】(1) Kuang: A place close to the State of Wei, possibly currently at Kuangcheng Town of 7.5 Kilometers southwestern from Changyuan County of Henan Province. Confucius was on his way to the State of Chen in 496 BC and he was confined due to his resembling to Yang Huo, an enemy of Kuang. (2) Yan Yuan: Surname Yan, first name Hui, style name Ziyuan, Confucius's disciple.

子见南子,子路不说。夫子矢之曰:“予所否者,天厌之!天厌之!”(06.28)

【白话译文】

孔子晋见了南子,子路对此很不高兴。孔子纠正他说:“对于我所不认可的事,上天是厌弃的,上天是厌弃的。”(06.28)

【注释】鲁定公十五年(公元前495年),孔子57岁,从匡地回卫国。月余,卫灵公夫人南子派使者求见,孔子辞谢,不得已而见。夫人面南而坐,薄纱垂帘,孔子北面稽首,夫人还礼,环佩玉声有闻。子:孔子。见:晋见、会见。南子:卫国灵公夫人,把持国政,名声不好。子路:姓仲名由,字子路,孔子弟子。说(音 yuè 月):悦,愉快。夫子:孔子。矢:箭,引申为纠正、改正,意为直、正、正直,如“直哉,史鱼!邦有道,如矢。邦无道,如矢。”(15.07,70 高士)通常将“矢”注为“誓”。对此,何晏注称“行道既非妇人之事,而弟子不说,与之咒誓,义可疑焉”。孔安国认为“先儒旧说,不近人情,故疑其义也”。[11]6.28之:子路,子路的态度。矢之:纠正子路;徐前师注“‘矢’

有'直'义,'矢之'之'矢'训直或正,纠正的意思。孔子既然'与门弟子语',不必指天发誓"。[J12] 曰:说。予:我。所:助词,表示结构,与动词相结合组成名词性词组。否:不然,否定,不同意,不认可,与"然"相对。者:的事。予所否者:我所不认可、不同意的事,此为名词性词组,指见南子的事,也是后边"天厌之"的宾语"之"。天:上天、天君。厌:厌恶、厌弃。之:第三人称代词,它,代"予所否者"。天厌之:上天厌恶它,上天厌恶孔子所不同意的事,换言之,孔子与上天的意见是一致的,孔子所做符合天意。

【英译】

The Master called on Nanzi(1). Zilu(2) was not happy about the visit. The Master corrected(3) him, saying, "That which I find disagreeable(4), is (also) that which Heaven detests and rejects, which Heaven detests and rejects." (06.28)

【英译注】(1) Nanzi: Confucius visited Duke Ling of the State of Wei in 495 BC, hoping to get a position as the Duke's adviser. Confucius did not want to call on Nanzi, the Duke's wife, because she was said to be a woman of questionable virtue. But she sent a messenger for Confucius to visit her. He had no choice because it was required by the Rites of Proprieties. He didn't like it, but sometimes one has to do unpleasant things, even if those things are "detested and rejected by Heaven". (2) Zilu: Surname Zhong, first name You, style name Zilu, Confucius's disciple. (3) "Correct" corresponds to a Chinese character meaning "an arrow". Normally it is interpreted as its homophonic character of "vow or swear". Mr. Xu Qianshi points out that "vow" to Heaven between a master and his disciple was not in compliance with the Rites and it should be "correct"[J12]. His opinion is adopted here. (4) "Disagreeable" is for a Chinese character that means "deny" and commonly interpreted as "wrong". This passage was initially translated in this book as: "The Master paid a visit to Nanzi, and Zilu looked unhappy. Confucius vowed, 'If I have done anything wrong, let Heaven detest and reject me! Let Heaven detest and reject me!'"

子曰:"吾未见好德如好色者也。"(09.18)

【注释】鲁定公十五年(公元前495年)十月,孔子57岁,卫国卫灵公与夫人南子同车而行,招摇过市,孔子乘车随后,以为耻。未见:没有看到。好(音 hào 号):喜爱。德:道德、好品行,把道贯彻到心中而不失掉者。如:如同。色(音 sè 涩):女人的美貌,女有姿色,故经传之文通谓女人为色。者:的人。

【白话译文】

孔子说:"我没有见过一个像喜爱美女一样去喜爱道德的人。"(09.18)

【英译】

The Master said(1), "I have never seen a man who loves morals the same as he loves beauties." (09.18)

【英译注】(1) Confucius said this when he saw Duke Ling and his wife Nanzi were in one carriage on the street in 495 BC.

子曰:"已矣乎!吾未见好德如好色者也。"(15.13)

【白话译文】

孔子说:"哎呀!到目前为止,我没有见过一个像喜爱美女一样去崇尚道德的人。"(15.13)

【英译】

The Master said[1], "Alas! Up until now, I have never seen a man who loves morals the same as he loves beauties." (15.13)

【注释】鲁定公十五年(前495年)十月,孔子57岁,卫国卫灵公与夫人南子同车而行,招摇过市,孔子乘车随后,以为耻而感叹。多人闻此言,而重复记录。已矣乎:完了啊,到现在为止,"已"指过去。未见:没有看到。好(音hào号):喜爱。德:道德、好品行,把道贯彻到心中而不失掉者。如:如同。色(音sè涩):女人的美貌。者:的人。

【英译注】(1) Confucius said this when he saw Duke Ling of the State of Wei and his wife Nanzi were in one carriage swaggering through the streets in 495 BC. Confucius was in a carriage behind them then.

子曰:"天生德于予,桓魋其如予何?"(07.23)

【白话译文】

孔子说:"因为上天赋予了我美德,桓魋能把我怎么样?"(07.23)

【英译】

The Master said, "As I have been endowed with excellent virtues by Heaven, what can Huantui[1] do unto me?" (07.23)

【注释】鲁定公十五年(前495年),孔子57岁,孔子离开卫国,经曹国去宋国,与弟子在大树下习礼,宋司马桓魋欲杀孔子,拔树,弟子催孔子快走。天:上天。生:赋予。德:圣德。于:给。予:我。桓魋(音huán环tuí颓):宋桓公后代,宋国司马,管军事。其:句中语气词,能,将。如:对于。何:怎样。如予何:拿我能怎么样。

【英译注】(1) Huantui: One offspring of Duke Huan of the State of Song, in charge of military affairs of the State. He detested Confucius who once blamed him. This happened when Confucius left the State of Wei and passed by the State of Song in 495 BC.

子曰:"苟有用我者,期月而已可也,三年有成。"(13.10)

【白话译文】

孔子说:"如果某个国家任用我主持国事,我一年可以做出一个好样子来,三年可以取得显著成效。"(13.10)

【英译】

The Master said, "If I were to be appointed to manage the affairs of a state, I could get it in fairly good shape within a year's time, and I would achieve remarkable success within three year's time." (13.10)

【注释】鲁哀公二年(公元前493年),孔子59岁,由陈国又到卫国,卫灵公出郊欢迎孔子,但灵公衰老,怠政,不用孔子,孔子出此言。苟:如果。用:任用。者:的人。苟有用我者:如果有人任用我主持国政。期(音 jī 机)月:一整年。可:可以实行政教,搞出个样子。成:大有成效。

卫灵公问陈于孔子。孔子对曰:"俎豆之事,则尝闻之矣。军旅之事,未之学也。"明日遂行。(15.01)

【白话译文】

卫灵公向孔夫子请教军队阵列部署。孔夫子敬答:"有关祭祀器具和礼仪方面的事,我曾经听说过。但是,军事和作战部署的事,我从来没有学习过。"第二天,他离开了卫国。(15.01)

【注释】鲁哀公二年(公元前493年),孔子59岁,卫灵公向他请教军事,仰见飞雁,心不在孔子,孔子决定离开卫国到陈国。卫灵公:姓姬名元,卫国君,公元前536年至公元前493年在位,不善政,宠爱南子。陈(音 zhèn 镇):阵,作战布列。于:向。对曰:敬答。俎(音 zǔ 祖):放祭祀品的礼器皿。豆:盛食物礼器,像高脚盘,汉代后为豆类作物的总称。则:那么。尝:曾经。闻:听说。之:它。军旅:打仗。未:没有。之学:学之,学它。明日:第二天。遂:便、就。行:离开。

【英译】

Duke Ling[(1)] of the State of Wei asked Confucius about battle formations and deployment of military formations. Confucius replied respectfully, "I have ever heard something about sacrificial vessels and the Rites of Proprieties, but I have never learned about military formations and deployment of troops in war." He departed from the State of Wei the next day. (15. 01)

【英译注】(1) Duke Ling: Surname Ji, first name Yuan, the sovereign of the State of Wei (from 536 BC to 493 BC), not good at administration of state affairs. He asked this question in 493 BC and was not interested in hiring Confucius (aged 59).

蘧伯玉使人于孔子。孔子与之坐而问焉,曰:"夫子何为?"对曰:"夫子欲寡其过而未能也。"使者出。子曰:"使乎!使乎!"(14. 26)

【注释】此言时间不详,估计应为孔子离开卫国前所讲。鲁哀公二年(前493年),孔子59岁,卫灵公不用孔子,向他请教军事,孔子决定离开卫国到陈国。鲁哀公十一年(前484年),孔子68岁,从卫国回鲁国。蘧(音qú渠)伯玉:名瑗,卫国大夫,孔子曾住其家。使:派使者。于:至。之:使者。夫子:蘧伯玉。何:什么。为:做。夫子何为:他老先生做些什么。对曰:敬答。寡:减少。其:他的。过:错。而:然而、却。未能:没做到。出:走出,出去。使乎:(好)使者啊。

【白话译文】

蘧伯玉派代表拜见孔夫子。孔夫子请他一起坐下,问道:"你家主人在做什么?"他敬答:"我家主人想减少他的过错,但还没有做到呢。"当他离开后,孔夫子说:"他是多好的一位代表啊!他是多好的一位代表啊!"(14. 26)

【英译】

Qu Boyu[(1)] sent his representative to visit Confucius. Confucius offered him a

【英译注】(1) Qu Boyu: Surname Qu, first name Yuan, a senior official of the State of Wei and once accommodated Confucius at his home when Confucius came to the State of

seat, sat with him, and asked, "What is your master doing?" He replied respectfully, "My master desires to reduce his mistakes but has not succeeded yet." When he was gone, Confucius said, "Oh, what a good representative he is! What a good representative he is!" (14.26)

Wei. This dialogue was unknown for its date.

佛肸召,子欲往。子路曰:"昔者由也闻诸夫子曰:'亲于其身为不善者,君子不入也。'佛肸以中牟畔,子之往也,如之何?"子曰:"然。有是言也。不曰坚乎,磨而不磷?不曰白乎,涅而不缁?吾其匏瓜也哉?焉能系而不食。"(17.07)

【白话译文】

佛肸召见孔子给一个职位,孔子想去。子路说:"以前,我从我的老师你那里听说:'一名君子不会到亲自做不道德事的人的身边。'佛肸盘踞中牟,发动武装叛乱。你要去他那里,这如何说得过去?"孔子说:"对,我是说过这话。我们不是说,最坚硬的东西,磨也磨不薄吗?我们不是说,最洁白的东西,放在涅黑液体里也染不黑吗?我难道是苦瓢葫芦,只能系在那里当瓢不能吃吗?"(17.07)

【注释】此事发生在鲁哀公二年(公元前493年),孔子59岁。佛肸(音bì闭xī西):晋国大夫范氏家臣,中牟城长官。召:请去做官。往:去。子路:姓仲,名由,字子路。昔者:以前。由:子路,姓仲名由。闻:听。诸:之于。夫子:老师,孔子。亲:亲自。于:在。其:他。身:本身。为:做、行。亲于其身为不善者:亲自做坏事的人(那里)。入:前往。中牟:晋国地名,今河北邢台与邯郸间。畔:叛乱。如之何:这是为什么,怎么回事。然:是。是言:这话。不曰:(我)不是说过。坚:坚硬的东西。乎:吗。磨:磨擦。而:却。磷:损伤。白:白东西。涅:矿物质,作染料。缁(音zī资):黑色。匏(音páo袍):瓢葫芦,味苦。系(音jì季):拴、结。食:吃。

【英译】

Bi Xi[(1)] summoned Confucius to offer him a position, and Confucius wanted to go. Zilu[(2)] said, "Once I heard from you my Master, 'A superior man does not go to a man who has personally done immoral things.' Now that Bi Xi launched an armed rebellion and occupied Zhongmou[(3)], you, my Master, insist on going there. How can this be explained away?" The Master said, "Yes. I have said such words. But don't we say that the hardest things cannot be worn thin? Don't we say that the whitest things do not become black as they are soaked in black dye? Am I to be a bitter melon gourd to be hanged up for a ladle, but not suitable for eating?" (17.07)

【英译注】(1) Bi Xi: A manager of senior official Fan Family of the State of Jin and magistrate of Zhongmou City. (2) Zilu: Surname Zhong, first name You, style name Zilu, Confucius's disciple. (3) Zhongmou: A place of the State of Jin, currently located between Xingtai City and Handan City, Hebei Province.

子击磬于卫。有荷蒉而过孔氏之门者,曰:"有心哉,击磬乎!"既而曰:"鄙哉,硁硁乎!莫己知也,斯己而已矣。深则厉,浅则揭。"子曰:"果哉!末之难矣。"(14.41)

【白话译文】

一天,孔子在卫国敲击石磬为乐。恰

【注释】鲁哀公二年(公元前493年),孔子59岁,晋国大夫范氏家臣佛肸(bì闭 xī西),在中牟城叛乱。佛肸召,孔子欲往,子路谏,未成行。击磬在此前后。磬(音 qìng 庆):石、玉打击乐器。于:在。卫:卫国。荷:肩扛。蒉(音 kuì 愧):草筐。过:路过。孔氏:孔子。之:的。者:的人。心:心志,心事重重,有深意。有心哉:有心人啊。击:敲击。乎:呀。既:完了。而:又。鄙:鄙俗。鄙哉:真鄙俗呀。硁(音 kēng 坑)硁:磬

巧有一个肩挑草筐的人路过孔子的门口说："啊，心事重重哟，这个击磬的人！"过一会儿又说："乐音多鄙俗啊！多么浅陋、固执啊！好像在说'没有人理解我'。如果没有人理解你，你自己理解你自己就可以了。《诗经》说：'当水深的时候，穿着衣服过河。当水浅的时候，撩起衣服过河。'"孔子说："他好坚决啊！没有什么责问他了。"（14.41）

声，浅陋而固执。莫：没人。己：自己。己知：知己，了解自己。已：止、息。斯：就。矣：了。斯己而已矣：就坚守己志算了。深：（好比过河）水深（《诗经·邶风·匏有苦叶》）。厉：穿着衣服涉水。浅：水浅。揭：提起衣襟涉水。果哉！末之难矣：一解"好果断啊，没什么可责难他的了；果：果敢、果断；末：没有；之：他；难：责问"。二解"卫国人果然不理解我，末了我在卫国越来越难了；果：果然；末：末了、末尾；之：卫国；难：艰难"。

【英译】

The Master was playing music by striking a chime stone one day in the State of Wei. A man carrying a basket for holding grass happened to pass by his door, and said, "Oh, how laden with anxiety is the man striking chime stone!" After a while, he said, "How vulgar and philistine the sound is! Oh, how shallow and stubborn it is! It sounds like that 'no one understands me'. If no one understands you, it is all right for you to understand yourself. *Poems and Odes*(1) says, 'When a river is deep, ford across it with clothes on; when a stream is shallow, hold clothes up and wade across it.'" The Master said, "Oh, how resolute he is! It is nothing to blame him at all." (14.41)

【英译注】（1）*Poems and Odes*: Currently called *Book of Poetry*. These two sentences are from a poem named "Waiting for Her Fiance", *Songs Collected in Bei*, *Book of Poetry*. This dialogue occurred when Confucius was difficult at State of Wei around 493 BC at his 59.

冉有曰:"夫子为卫君乎?"子贡曰:"诺,吾将问之。"入,曰:"伯夷、叔齐何人也?"曰:"古之贤人也。"曰:"怨乎?"曰:"求仁而得仁,又何怨?"出,曰:"夫子不为也。"(07.15)

【白话译文】

冉有问:"我们的老师赞同卫君的行为吗?"子贡说:"噢,我去问他。"他进入孔子房里,问孔子:"伯夷、叔齐是什么人呀?"孔子说:"他们是古代的贤人。"子贡问:"后来他们对他们的行为遗憾吗?"孔子说:"他们追求仁德,并且得到了仁德。那么,他们遗憾什么?"子贡离开孔子,对冉有说:"我们老师不赞同卫君的行为。"(07.15)

【注释】鲁哀公三年(前492年),孔子60岁,卫灵公卒,其子蒯聩被逐在外,立其孙蒯辄为君,后父子争位,孔子答子贡问。冉有:姓冉名求,字子有。为(音wèi谓):本意是帮助,这里译成"赞成"。卫君:卫出公,姓姬,名蒯(音kuǎi扻)辄(音zhé哲),卫灵公之孙,因其父聩(音kuì愧)杀南子未遂而被逐,被立为君,后父子争位。子贡:姓端木名赐,字子贡。诺:好,缓缓地回答。入:进屋。伯夷、叔齐:北方小国孤竹国君两子,相互推位让国。怨:(因让位而)怨恨。夫子:孔子。

【英译】

Ran You(1) asked, "Does our Master agree with the actions of the Sovereign(2) of the State of Wei?" Zigong(3) said, "Oh! I will ask him." Coming into the Master's room, he asked, "Who were Bo Yi and Shu Qi(4)?" The Master said, "They were ancient sages." Zigong said, "Did they have regrets for their actions?" The Master said, "They pursued superior benevolence and they actually obtained it. Why did they have

【英译注】(1) Ran You: Surname Ran, first name Qiu, style name Ziyou, Confucius's disciple. (2) the Sovereign: Surname Ji, first name Kuaizhe, the grandson of Duke Ling of the State of Wei. His father Kuaikui failed to murder Nanzi, the wife of Duke Ling, and escaped to the State of Jin. After Duke Ling died in 492 BC, he was sent home by the State of Jin for invasion of the State of Wei. The father and son thus fought for the throne. (3) Zigong: Surname Duanmu, first name Ci, style name Zigong, Confucius's disci

regrets?" Zigong left the Master and said to Ran You, "Our master does not agree with the actions of the Sovereign." (07.15)

ple. (4) Boyi and Shuqi: Boyi was the elder son of a monarch of the State of Guzhu in the Shang Dynasty, and Shuqi was his younger brother. Their father appointed Shuqi as his successor. After their father died, Shuqi gave the throne to Boyi, while Boyi respected their father and refused it. They all fled to the State of Zhou.

子在陈曰:"归与!归与!吾党之小子狂简,斐然成章,不知所以裁之。"(05.22)

【白话译文】

孔子在陈国说:"回家吧!回家吧!在我故乡的年轻弟子们志向远大,但行为粗疏,显示出引人注目的文学才干,能够用华丽的词藻创作文章,但他们不知道以什么合适的方式和标准来裁度和解决所遇到的问题。"(05.22)

【注释】陈国被楚国、吴国侵伐,民不聊生。鲁哀公三年(公元前492年),孔子60岁,在陈国,鲁国召冉求(冉有)时,思乡。陈:陈国,都城在今河南淮阳。归:回家。与:吧。党:一党500家,家乡。小子:学子。狂:志向远大。简:行为粗疏。斐(音 fěi 匪):有文采。然:样子。成章:作成文章。斐然成章:文采可观,才干显耀。所以(裁之):用来(裁之)的东西。裁:裁剪、割正、处理。之:问题、事情。不知所以裁之:弟子不知正确处理事情与认识问题的尺度和方法。

【英译】

When the Master was in the State of Chen(1), he said, "Oh, Come home! Oh, Come home! My young disciples in my hometown are ambitious but crude and careless, show outstanding literary talent and the capacity to compose articles with beautiful words, but they do not know the proper

【英译注】(1) the State of Chen: A fief of the Zhou Dynasty. Its capital was Wanqiu, currently at Huaiyang County of Henan Province. Its first sovereign was Wei Man, an offspring of Saintly Emperor Shun, surname Wei. Confucius stayed in it for many years and said this when he was 60 years old in 492 BC.

methods and criteria to judge and solve the problems they meet." (05.22)

在陈绝粮,从者病,莫能兴。子路愠见曰:"君子亦有穷乎?"子曰:"君子固穷,小人穷斯滥矣。"(15.02)

【注释】鲁哀公六年(前489年),孔子63岁离开陈国,经蔡国去楚国见叶公,返回陈国,在陈、蔡边界,楚国下聘礼,孔子应聘。陈、蔡大夫惊恐,派人围攻孔子7天,子贡使楚,得救,至楚。绝:断绝。粮:粮食。从:随从。者:的人。莫:不。兴:站起。子路:姓仲,名由,字子路。愠(音 yùn 运):内心的愤怒、怨恨,尚未表现出来。见:来见。亦:也。穷:穷困潦倒(的时候)。乎:吗。固穷:穷困时,仍保持优秀的道德情操。斯:就。滥:大水溢出,胡作非为。

【白话译文】

孔子在陈国断绝了粮食,他的随从弟子病倒了,站不起来。子路心怀不满来见孔子说:"君子也有穷困潦倒的时候吗?"孔子说:"一名君子在穷困的时候,还能保持他的道德节操,而一个小人在穷困的时候已经胡作非为了。"(15.02)

【英译】

The Master once ran out of food while in the State of Chen(1), and all his disciples were so sick that they were unable to stand. Angry in heart, Zilu went to see the Master, saying, "Does a superior man also encounter a time when he is poverty stricken and down and out?" The Master said, "Even when a superior man is destitute, he will maintain his moral code and integrity, but an inferior man in the same straitened circumstances may commit all kinds of outrages." (15.02)

【英译注】(1) the State of Chen: A state of the Zhou Dynasty. Its capital was Wanqiu, currently at Huaiyang County of Henan Province. Confucius was confined for 7 days because he wanted to accept an appointment from the State of Chu in 489 BC at age of 63. He was rescued by Zigong who came to the State of Chu for help. (2) Zilu: Surname Zhong, first name You, style name Zilu, Confucius's disciple.

楚狂接舆歌而过孔子曰:"凤兮!凤兮!何德之衰?往者不可谏,来者犹可追。已而!已而!今之从政者殆而!"孔子下,欲与之言。趋而辟之,不得与之言。(18.05)

【注释】鲁哀公六年(前489年),孔子63岁,在陈、蔡绝粮7天,到楚国未被重用,闻此言,离开楚国再到卫国。楚狂:楚国狂人。接舆:假名,非姓非名,接近车子的意思。歌:唱歌。过:走过。歌而过孔子:一边唱歌,一边路过孔子。兮:啊、呀。凤兮:凤凰啊。何:怎么。德:德运。衰:衰弱。何德之衰:社会仁德之风为何这么衰落。往:过去。者:的人、的事。谏:纠正。来:未来。追:补救。已:止、息。而:吧。已而:算了吧。从政者:执政者。殆(音dài代):危险。孔子下:孔子下车。与之言:同他谈。趋:快走。而:用以。辟:避开。之:前指孔子,后指接舆。

【白话译文】

楚国的狂人接舆,唱着歌,路过孔夫子的车子说:"凤凰啊!凤凰啊!社会的德风怎么这样衰落?过去的无法挽回了,但是未来的还可以追求。一切都结束了!一切都结束了!今天一个人从事行政管理的官员是多么危险啊!"孔夫子下车,想与他说话。他快走,避开了,所以孔夫子没有机会与他说。(18.05)

【英译】

Jie Yu(1), a madman of the State of Chu singing and passing by Confucius's carriage said, "Oh, Phoenix! Oh, phoenix! How in a decline the virtues of society are! The past cannot be retrieved, but the future can still be pursued. All is over! All is over! Oh, it is dangerous for a man to work as a government official today!" Confucius descended from his carriage and wanted to talk with him, but he walked away quickly and shunned him, so Confucius had no chance to speak with him. (18.05)

【英译注】(1) Jie Yu: He was an assumed name for a hermit of the State of Chu, meaning "a man approaching to a carriage'. Confucius came to the State of Chu and encountered him after he was rescued from starvation in the State of Chen in 489 BC when he was 63.

子曰:“鲁卫之政,兄弟也。”(13.07)

【白话译文】

孔子说:“鲁国和卫国是兄弟之国。”(13.07)

【英译】

The Master said, “The State of Lu and the State of Wei(1) are brother states.” (13.07)

【注释】鲁哀公七年(公元前488年),孔子64岁,在陈、蔡绝粮7天,到楚国未被重用,离开楚国再到卫国,说此言。鲁:鲁国,是周公的封地。卫:卫国,是周公少弟康叔姬封的封地。之:的。政:国事,鲁卫两国衰乱相似。兄弟:像兄弟一样。

【英译注】(1) the State of Wei: Confucius returned to the State of Wei in 488 BC at age of 64 and said this when he was not hired in the State of Chu. Both states had similar state affairs and government administrations.

子曰:“吾自卫反鲁,然后乐正,《雅》《颂》各得其所。”(09.15)

【白话译文】

孔子说:“我从卫国返回鲁国后,开始编修音乐作品,恢复《雅》乐、《颂》乐,使每个篇章分别回到它适当的位置。”(09.15)

【英译】

The Master said, “After I returned(1) to the State of Lu from the State of Wei, I began to compile the works of music in their correct order and restored the *Odes and Epics* and *Hymns* music to their proper positions.” (09.15)

【注释】鲁哀公十一年(公元前484年),孔子68岁,自卫国结束14年周游列国的旅程,回到鲁国。自卫反鲁:鲁哀公十一年冬,孔子68岁,从卫国回鲁国,修《春秋》、删《诗》、正乐。乐正:调整乐曲的篇章。雅、颂:《诗经》所配《雅》乐、《颂》乐。其所:自己的位置。

【英译注】(1) I returned: Confucius returned to the State of Lu, his motherland in the winter of the Year 11 of Duke Ai (484 BC) after 14 years traveling through all states. He then completed the edition of *History of Spring and Autumn*, *Poems and Odes*, the poems and music works, currently named *Book of Poetry*. Two parts of *Poems and Odes* are "Odes and Epics" and "Hymns".

子曰:"从我于陈、蔡者,皆不及门也。"(11.02)

【白话译文】

孔子说:"跟随我到陈国、蔡国受饿的弟子们,今天都没在我的身边。"(11.02)

【注释】鲁哀公十六年(前479年),孔子73岁,病,子贡(端木赐)请见。孔子方负杖逍遥于门,曰:"赐,汝来何其晚也?""昨暮予梦坐奠两柱之闲,予始殷人也。"后七日卒。(《史记》)此言时间不详,是老人盼亲人之言,孔子去世前,随他周游的颜回、子路已过世,子贡曾不在身边。从(音zòng纵):跟随、随从。于:在(到)。陈:陈国。蔡:蔡国。皆:都。及:到。门:受教的场所。不及门:不在身边。

【英译】

The Master said, "All the disciples who followed me to the State of Chen(1) and the State of Cai suffering hunger are not beside me today." (11.02)

【英译注】(1) the State of Chen: A state of the Zhou Dynasty, where Confucius was starved for 7 days in 489 BC at age of 63. The State of Cai was at the south boundary of the State of Chen. These words were spoken when Confucius was ill and longed to see those disciples following him to these states.

十五
Fifteen

生老病死
From Birth to Death

73

生 Birth

子曰:“人之生也直,罔之生也幸而免。”(06.19)

【白话译文】

孔子说:“一个人的生命是建立在正直之上的。如果建立在邪恶之上,这个人只能凭侥幸才能避免灾难。”(06.19)

【英译】

The Master said, “The life of a person is founded on righteousness. If it is founded on iniquity, he can avoid calamities only by luck.”(06.19)

【注释】生:出生时。而:就,便。知:懂得、掌握。之:知识、学问。生而知之:一出生就有知识学问。好(音 hào 号):喜爱。古:古代典籍。敏:勤奋敏捷。求:获得。

子曰:“我非生而知之者,好古,敏以求之者也。”(07.20)

【白话译文】

孔子说:“我不是生下来就有知识的人。我喜爱古代典籍,我是勤奋敏捷、追求掌握知识的人。”(07.20)

【注释】之:的。生:生存。也:句中停顿语气词,引起下文。直:正直。人之生也直:人生靠正直。罔(音 wǎng 往):诬罔不直,欺骗。幸:侥幸。而:才。免:免除、避免(灾祸)。罔之生也幸而免:人生不正直,只能凭侥幸才会避免灾祸。

【英译】

The Master said, "I am not a person born with knowledge. Loving the ancient doctrines, I am the one who masters them and acquires knowledge creatively and industriously." (07.20)

孔子曰:"生而知之者,上也;学而知之者,次也;困而学之,又其次也;困而不学,民斯为下矣。"(16.09)

【注释】生:生来。而:就。知(音 zhī 织):明白,懂得。之:知识、道理。生而知之:不经过学习,就感悟出自然与社会的发展规律或知识。者:的人。上:上等,最好的。学:学习、读书。次:排序上低一等。困:遇到困难。又:再、更。民斯:此民,这种人。为:是。下:下等,最差的。矣:呀、啊。困而不学,民斯为下矣:遇到困难还不学,这种人就太差了。

【白话译文】

孔夫子说:"那些与生俱来就有知识的,是最上等的。那些通过学习获得知识的,是次等的。那些遇到困难而学习掌握知识的,又次一等。那些遇到困难还不学习的,是最下等的了。"(16.09)

【英译】

Confucius said, "Those who are born with knowledge are the highest class of men; those who gain knowledge through study are the next highest; those who master knowledge through encountering difficulties are the next; those who does not learn even when they encounter difficulties are the lowest class of men." (16.09)

74

老 Aging

叶公问孔子于子路，子路不对。子曰：“女奚不曰：其为人也，发愤忘食，乐以忘忧，不知老之将至云尔。”(07.19)

【白话译文】

大臣叶公向子路了解孔子的情况，但是子路没有回答他。孔子说：“你为什么不这么说：他的为人是这样，他如此勤奋，经常忘记吃饭，他如此快乐，经常忘记忧愁的事，但他不知道老年将要来到。如此这般就是了。”(07.19)

【英译】

Senior Official She[(1)] asked Zilu[(2)] about the Master, but Zilu did not answer him. The Master said, "Why didn't you say: his conduct is such that he is so diligent that he often forgets his meals and he is so happy as he often forgets his anxieties, but he is not aware of his old age approaching. And so on and so forth." (07.19)

【注释】鲁哀公六年（公元前489年），孔子63岁离开陈国去楚国，见叶公，子路陪同。叶(shè社)公：楚国大夫，姓沈名诸梁，字子高，封地在叶城(今河南叶县南30里)，叶公是叶地方的县长，楚君称王，那县长便称公。问：了解。于：向。子路：姓仲名由，字子路。对：答。女(音rǔ辱)：汝，你。奚：为何。其：他。愤：愤闷。发愤：因愤激而决心努力。忘：忘记。食：吃饭。乐(音lè勒)：高兴。以：而，就，连词。老：老年。将：快要。至：到来。云：如此。尔：耳，而已。

【英译注】(1) Senior Official She: Surname Shen, first name Zhuliang, senior official of the State of Chu and his fief was given at She City, currently Ye County, Henan Province. (2) Zilu: Surname Zhong, first name You, style name Zilu, Confucius's disciple.

颜渊季路侍，子曰："盍各言尔志？"子路曰："愿车、马、衣、轻裘与朋友共，敝之而无憾。"颜渊曰："愿无伐善，无施劳。"子路曰："愿闻子之志。"子曰："老者安之，朋友信之，少者怀之。"（05.26）

【注释】颜渊：姓颜名回，字子渊。季路：仲由，字子路。侍（音 shì 事）：恭敬站立陪同。盍（音 hé 何）：何不。尔：你的。子路：季路，姓仲名由，字子路。愿：愿意拿出。轻裘：皮袍。与：给与。共：共享。敝：用破。憾：恨。愿：愿意。伐：夸耀。善：（自己的）长处。施：表白。劳：功劳。子：老师，孔子。老：年老。者：……的人。安：安逸、安心，（使老者）安心。之：他、他们。信：（给予）信任。少：年少。怀：（给予）关怀，施之以恩惠。

【白话译文】

颜渊、季路站在孔子旁边服侍他。孔子说："何不各自讲讲你们的理想？"子路说："我愿意拿出车、马、衣服、皮袍，与朋友分享，即使用坏了，也不遗憾。"颜渊说："我的理想是，不吹嘘自己的优点，不表白自己的功劳。"子路问："我们愿听听老师您的理想。"孔子说："我的理想是，让老年人安心舒适，给予朋友信任，给予青少年人关爱和照顾。"（05.26）

【英译】

Yan Yuan(1) and Jilu(2) stood by the Master to attend upon him. The Master said, "Why don't you mention your ambitions respectively?" Zilu(3) said, "I wish to share my carriages, horses, clothes, and leather coats with my friends and I will not regret it even if they might wear them out." Yan Yuan said, "My ambition is that I neither boast of my merits nor display my accomplishments."

【英译注】(1) Yan Yuan: Surname Yan, first name Hui, style name Ziyuan, Confucius's disciple. (2) Jilu: Surname Zhong, first name You, style name Zilu, also called Jilu, Confucius's disciple. (3) Zilu: Jilu.

Zilu asked,"We would like to hear my Master your ambitions." The Master said,"I wish to make the elders safe and comfortable,give trust upon my friends,and offer love and care to the young."(05.26)

子曰:"凤鸟不至,河不出图,吾已矣夫!"(09.09)

【白话译文】

孔子说:"凤凰没有再来了,黄河上没有再出现八卦图了。啊!恐怕我的一生就要结束了!"(09.09)

【英译】

The Master said,"The phoenix does not come again and there are no more trigrams[(1)] emerging from the Yellow River. Oh,I am afraid that my life is to be over!"(09.09)

【注释】凤鸟:神鸟,传说在舜和周文王时出现过。至:来。河:黄河。图:龙马背负的八卦图。已:完了。矣:了。夫:吧。吾已矣夫:我一生(恐怕)完了吧。

【英译注】(1) trigrams:It is said that Chinese trigram figures were drawn on the dragon horse emerging from the Yellow River.

75

病 Disease

伯牛有疾，子问之，自牖执其手，曰："亡之，命矣夫！斯人也而有斯疾也！斯人也而有斯疾也！"（06.10）

【注释】伯牛：姓冉名耕，字伯牛。疾：重病。问：慰问、探视。自：从。牖（音 yǒu 有）：窗户。执：握着。亡：死。之：相当于语气词，不是代词，不是"亡"的宾语。命：天命。矣：了。夫（音 fú 扶）：吧，语气词。亡之，命矣夫：（他）要死了，天命啊。斯：这。而：竟然。疾：疾病。有斯疾：这样的病。

【白话译文】

伯牛生病了，孔子探视他。他从窗户握着他的手说："活不了啦！这是命啊！这样的人，居然有这种病？这样的人，居然有这种病？"（06.10）

【英译】

Boniu(1) was ill, and the Master visited him. Holding his hands through the window, the Master said, "Oh, dying! Oh, this is fate! How could such a person suffer this disease? How could such a person suffer this disease?" (06.10)

【英译注】(1) Boniu: Surname Ran, first name Geng, style name Boniu, Confucius's disciple.

子疾病，子路请祷。子曰："有诸？"子路对曰："有之。《诔》曰：'祷尔于上下神祇。'"

【注释】疾：生重病。病：病重。子路：姓仲，名由，字子路。请：请求。祷（音 dǎo 导）：祈祷。诸：之于的合音，这事。对曰：敬

子曰:“丘之祷久矣。”(07.35)

答。诔(音 lěi 垒):祈祷文,颂扬某某生前德行的文章,与悼念死者的诔不同。尔:你。于:向。神:天神。祇(音 qí 旗):地神。丘:孔子,姓孔名丘,字仲尼。之:的。祷:(如此)祈祷。

【白话译文】

孔子得了重病,子路请求允许他为孔子祈祷。孔子说:“古代有这么做的吗?”子路敬答:“有呀。《诔》说:‘为你向天神、地灵祷告。’”孔子说:“我丘这么祷告已经很长时间了。”(07.35)

【英译】

The Master was critically sick and Zilu(1) requested that he be allowed to pray for the Master. The Master said, “Did people do this in ancient times?” Zilu replied respectfully, “Yes. *The Prayers* says: ‘Pray to the deities of the heavens and earth for you.’” The Master said, “Well, I, Qiu(2), have been thus praying for a long time.” (07.35)

【英译注】(1) Zilu: Surname Zhong, first name You, style name Zilu, Confucius's disciple. (2) Qiu: The first name of Confucius.

曾子有疾,召门弟子曰:“启予足!启予手!《诗》云:‘战战兢兢,如临深渊,如履薄冰。’而今而后,吾知免夫!小子!”(08.03)

【注释】曾子:姓曾名参(音 shēn 申),字子舆,鲁国南武城人。疾:得病。召:召集。门:门下。启:掀开(被子看);《说文》有“启”云“视”。予:我的。启予足:掀开被子看我的脚(身体受之父母,不能毁伤,孝之始)。战战:小心,出自《诗经·小雅·小旻》。兢兢:谨慎。临:临近。履:踩。而:从。而后:以后。免:避免。而今而后,吾知免夫:从今以后,我知晓自己可免了刑戮。小子:弟子(你们要注意啊!)。

【白话译文】

曾子得了重病,召集弟子说:“看看我的脚!看看我的手!《诗经》说:‘心惊胆战啊!就像站在悬崖深潭边缘上,也像步

行在薄薄的冰面上。’从今以后，我知道我可以免于杀戮和刑罚了，弟子们！这一点，你们一定要注意啊。”（08.03）

【英译】

Master Zeng[1] was sick seriously. Calling his disciples together, he said, "See my feet! See my hands! *Poems and Odes*[2] says, 'Do tremble with fear like standing at the edge of an abyss and a sheer precipice, and also like walking on thin ice.' From now on, I recognize that I can be spared from massacre and criminal punishment, my disciples! You must pay attention to this!" (08.03)

【英译注】(1) Master Zeng: Confucius's disciple (505 BC – 436 BC), surname Zeng, first name Shen, style name Ziyu, a person from Nanwucheng City, the State of Lu, current Pingyi County, Shandong Province. (2) *Poems and Odes*: Currently named *Book of Poetry*. These sentences were from *Counselors*, *Fourth Decade of Odes* of this book.

子疾病，子路使门人为臣。病间，曰：“久矣哉，由之行诈也！无臣而为有臣。吾谁欺？欺天乎？且予与其死于臣之手也，无宁死于二三子之手乎？且予纵不得大葬，予死于道路乎？”（09.12）

【白话译文】

孔子病危。子路让孔子的弟子装扮成家臣，设立预备治丧委员会。当孔子的病情好转时，他说：“好久了，由！你在给我

【注释】疾：生病。病：病重。子路：姓仲，名由，字子路。使：让。门人：孔子门弟子。臣：（装扮成）家臣，仅适用于诸侯以上官员，孔子无此资格；由家臣组成预备治丧会，相当于今天的治丧处、治丧委员会，不同之处是治丧如今是在高官去世后，而当时是在王侯去世之前开始工作。病间：病情减轻。久矣：很久了。哉：啊。由：姓仲，名由，字子路。之：的。行：做。诈：做假、骗。无臣：没有家臣，孔子不是大夫，不能有家臣。而：却。为：表现成。谁欺：骗谁。天：苍天。且：况且。予：我。死于：死在。无：不如。宁：宁可。二三子：弟子们。乎：吗。纵：即使。大葬：大夫

弄虚作假啊！我没有资格设立预备治丧委员会，但他们却为此一直冒充家臣。我在欺骗谁呀？我在欺骗天啊！我与其死在所谓的家臣之手，宁可死在我弟子的手中！即使我不能有宏大的葬礼，难道我会死在道路上，没有人照看我的尸首吗？”（09.12）

之葬礼。死于道路乎：死在路边，没人埋吗。

【英译】

The Master was critically ill. Zilu(1) asked the Master's disciples to disguise themselves as retainers and set up a probationary funeral committee(2) for him. When his condition improved, the Master said, "You(3)! For what a long time you have been deceiving me! I am not qualified to have a probationary funeral committee. You have been, however, pretending to be retainers. Whom am I cheating? I am cheating Heaven! I would die rather in the hands of my disciples than in the hands of so-called retainers! Even if I cannot have a grand funeral, shall I truly die on the road without anyone to care for my body?" (09.12)

【英译注】(1) Zilu: Surname Zhong, first name You, style name Zilu, Confucius's disciple. (2) a probationary funeral committee: It was similar to the current funeral committee, but it was set up for a duke before he died. It was composed of home officials (retainers). As Confucius was ranked as a senior official, he was not qualified for such a committee. (3) You: First name of Zilu.

疾，君视之，东首，加朝服，拖绅。（10.19）

【注释】疾：（孔子）重病。君：国君。视：探视。之：孔子。东首：头朝东；古人的卧榻一般设在西边，国君进屋，从东边走到床前，头朝东表示礼貌。加：盖在身上。朝服：上朝礼服。拖：附加，束在身

【白话译文】

孔子病重时,国君探视他。他的头朝东。他的朝服盖在他身上,他的礼带束在身上,垂下来一截。(10.19)

上。绅:束在腰间的大带子。

【英译】

When the Master was seriously ill, the sovereign visited him. He was put with his head oriented to the east(1). His court clothes were covered over him and a ritual belt was tied on him with a part hanging down. (10.19)

【英译注】(1) to the east: Confucius was in bed due to illness and could not sit up. At Confucius's time, the bed was put close to the window in the west room that had a door and windows to the south. The visiting sovereign came from the door. He was moved with his head to the east so that the sovereign first encountered his head other than his feet. This was a courtesy.

76

药 Medicine

康子馈药,拜而受之。曰:"丘未达,不敢尝。"(10.16)

【注释】康子:季康子,姓季孙名肥,谥(音 shì 是)号康,鲁哀公时任正卿。馈:赠送。药:药物。拜:拜谢,拱手礼。而:并且。受:接受。丘:孔子,姓孔名丘,字仲尼。未:不曾,没有。达:了解。尝:试服、试吃,这是当时的礼节。

【白话译文】

康子给孔子赠送药,孔子向他鞠躬,接受了它。他说:"我丘对药性没有完全理解,(当你的面)不敢试服它。"(10.16)

【英译】

Master Kang[1] presented some medicine as a gift and the Master bowed to him and accepted it. He said, "I Qiu[2] do not thoroughly understand the nature of the medicine and do not dare to try it[3] (before you)." (10.16)

【英译注】(1) Master Kang: Surname Ji, first name Fei, posthumous title Kang, the general senior official of the State of Lu. (2) Qiu: First name of Confucius. (3) try it: It was a courtesy for one to try anything editable once it was presented to him.

77

死 Death

曾子有疾,孟敬子问之,曾子言曰:"鸟之将死,其鸣也哀,人之将死,其言也善。君子所贵乎道者三:动容貌,斯远暴慢矣;正颜色,斯近信矣;出辞气,斯远鄙悖矣。笾豆之事,则有司存。"(08.04)

【注释】孟敬子:孟孙捷,鲁国大夫。问之:探视他。之:他。其:它的、他的。哀:悲痛。贵:重视。道:道德。三:三个方面。动:调整、严肃。容貌:表情、神态、仪容;容指内心的活动,貌指外在的举止。斯:这样。远:避免、远离。暴慢:(自己)粗暴、放肆。正:庄重。颜色:脸色、面容。近:接近。信:诚信、信任。斯近信矣:这样,要使自己更加诚信。出:发出。辞:言辞。气:和气。鄙:粗陋。悖(音bèi背):背理、违反。斯远鄙悖矣:要避免粗野和谬误。笾(音biān边):祭祀礼器。豆:盛食物的礼器,像高脚盘,汉代后为豆类作物的总称。则:就。有司:主管官吏。存:负责。则有司存:就由主管部门及具体人负责。

【白话译文】

曾子得了重病,孟敬子探视他。曾子对他说:"鸟将要死的时候,它的鸣叫是悲哀的;人将要死的时候,他说话是和善的。一名君子倡导道德的三个方面:调整他的容貌,表情恰当,避免粗暴放肆;端正自己的神态，表示诚信；说话使用适当的言辞和柔和的声调，远离鄙俗和错误。至于如何摆放祭祀器物的事务，由具体人员负责。”（08.04）

【英译】

Master Zeng[1] was critically ill and Master Meng Jing[2] visited him. Master Zeng talked with him, "As a bird dies, it cries mournfully; as a man dies, he speaks kindly. A superior man advocates three aspects of his moral character: adjust one's appearance to have a proper expression on his face to avoid rudeness and uncivil behavior; correct his manner to show faithfulness; speak properly with a gentle voice, so as to avoid vulgarity and mistakes. As for the matter of sacrifice vessels and other ritual articles, there are specific persons taking care of them." (08.04)

【英译注】(1) Master Zeng: Confucius's disciple (505 BC – 436 BC), surname Zeng, first name Shen, style name Ziyu, a person from Nanwucheng City, the State of Lu, current Pingyi County, Shandong Province. (2) Master Meng Jing: Surname Zhongsun, first name Jie, posthumous name Jing, a senior official of the State of Lu.

颜渊死。子曰：“噫！天丧予！天丧予！”（11.09）

【白话译文】

颜渊去世了。孔子说：“唉！老天爷要了我的命呀！老天爷要了我的命呀！”（11.09）

【注释】颜渊生于鲁昭公二十一年（公元前521年），卒于鲁哀公五年（公元前490年），去世时年仅31岁，孔子悲痛至极。颜渊：姓颜名回，字子渊，鲁国（今山东）人。噫：唉。天：苍天、上天。丧：毁灭。予：我。天丧予：老天爷要了我的命。

【英译】

Yan Yuan[1] died. The Master said: "Alas! Heaven drives me to death! Heaven drives me to death!" (11.09)

【英译注】(1) Yan Yuan: Surname Yan, first name Hui, style name Ziyuan, Confucius's excellent disciple, dead at 31 years old in 490 BC.

季路问事鬼神。子曰:"未能事人,焉能事鬼?"曰:"敢问死?"曰:"未知生,焉知死?"(11.12)

【注释】季路:仲由,子路。问:请教。事:(如何)侍奉。鬼:人死后的灵魂、逝去的祖先。神:神灵,或者天地万物的创造者。焉:怎么。敢:冒昧;以卑触尊。死:死是怎么回事。未:不曾,没有。生:生命之理。

【白话译文】

季路问如何侍奉鬼和神。孔子说:"还不能很好地侍奉人,那么怎么能够侍奉鬼和神?"季路又说:"我可以冒昧请教死是怎么回事吗?"孔子说:"连活着的原理都没有理解,怎么能够理解死的道理?"(11.12)

【英译】

Jilu[1] asked how to serve ghosts and gods. The Master said, "As we cannot serve the living well, how can we be able to serve ghosts and gods?" Jilu said further, "May I dare to ask advice about death?" The Master said, "Even if the principles of life are not understood yet, how can principles of death be understood?" (11.12)

【英译注】(1) Jilu: Zilu, surname Zhong, first name You, style name Zilu, also style name Jilu, Confucius's disciple.

子曰："君子疾没世而名不称焉。"（15.20）

【白话译文】

孔子说："一名君子担心的是，到死，他的所作所为不配君子这个称号。"（15.20）

【英译】

The Master said, "A superior man is worried that all his deeds will not deserve the title of a superior man at his death." (15.20)

【注释】鲁哀公十一年（公元前484年），孔子68岁，周游列国回鲁，担心身后儒道不传，始作《春秋》。疾：担心。没世：死亡之后。而：却，但。名：名字。称：一解"音chēng撑，（被）赞扬、称颂"；二解"音chèn衬，相称、符合"。焉：啊。疾没世而名不称焉：一解"痛恨名声终生还不被人称颂啊（相当于白活了一生）"；二解"痛恨死后名声与生前所作所为不相当啊"。此处取后者。

78

哭 Weep

子于是日哭，则不歌。（07.10）

【白话译文】

孔子哪一天哭泣了，那一天就不唱歌。（07.10）

【注释】于：在。是日：这天。则：就，便。歌：唱歌。

【英译】

The Master did not sing that day when he wept. (07. 10)

颜渊死，子哭之恸。从者曰："子恸矣！"曰："有恸乎！非夫人之为恸而谁为？"(11. 10)

【注释】鲁哀公五年(前 490 年)，孔子 62 岁时，颜渊去世，时年 31 岁，孔子痛哭。子：你。之：的。恸(音 tòng 痛)：极悲哀。矣：了。从者：随从人员。乎：啊。有恸乎：极为悲痛啊。夫(音 fú 扶)：此。夫人之为恸：为此人悲伤。谁为：为谁。非夫人之为恸而谁为：不为这个人哀痛，还为谁哀痛呢。

【白话译文】

颜渊去世了，孔子哭得极为伤心。他的随从弟子说："啊，先生！你太伤心了！"孔子说："我确实太伤心了！如果我不为这样的人伤心，我应为谁伤心呢？"(11. 10)

【英译】

When Yan Yuan died, the Master wept with deep grief. His attendant disciples said, "Oh, Master! Your grief is too much!" The Master said, "My grief is truly too much! If I am not extremely grievous for this man, whom should I be grievous for?" (11. 10)

79

葬 Funeral

颜渊死,颜路请子之车以为之椁。子曰:"才不才,亦各言其子也。鲤也死,有棺而无椁。吾不徒行以为之椁。以吾从大夫之后,不可徒行也。"(11.08)

【白话译文】

颜渊去世了,颜路请求孔子把他的车卖了,为颜渊买一个棺椁。孔子说:"别说有没有木材做棺椁,我们讲一讲我们各自的儿子吧。鲤去世的时候,有棺材但没有棺椁。我不能卖了我的车给颜渊买棺椁而徒步行走。因为我必须跟在卿大夫行列的后边,按照礼仪要求不能徒步行走啊。"(11.08)

【英译】

When Yan Yuan(1) died, Yan Lu(2) asked for the Master to sell his carriage and

【注释】颜渊生于鲁昭公二十一年(公元前521年),31岁去世于鲁哀公十四年(公元前490年),当时孔子62岁在蔡国、陈国。孔鲤于鲁哀公十二年(公元前483年)50岁去世,而当时颜回已去世7年。除非此处孔鲤有棺无椁是孔子在做事先安排,那么人去世7年,再议棺椁之事,有些不可能。

颜渊:姓颜名回,字子渊,31岁去世,其父为其求椁,孔子婉言拒绝。颜路:颜无繇(音yóu邮),字路,颜回的父亲。请:请求(卖掉)。子:孔子。车:车子。以:用来。为:做。之:他(颜渊)的。椁(音guǒ果):套棺,套在棺材外的大棺材。才:才能,通"材"字,也指木材。不才:没才能或没有木料意;此译文取后者,因为椁需要木料,与才能、才干无关。各:各人。言:说,讲。其子:他的儿子。鲤:孔子之子,姓孔名鲤,字伯鱼。也:语气词,表示停顿。而:却,但是。徒行:徒步行走。以为之椁:用来换得他的椁。以:因为。从:跟随。大夫:大夫行列。之后:后面。也:句末语气词。

【英译注】This passage may contain an error for the date of Li's death unless Li's funeral was as-

buy an outer coffin for him. The Master said, "To mention whether wood is available for the outer coffin or not, we first talk about our own sons. When Li(3) died, he had a coffin without an outer coffin. I cannot walk on foot by selling my carriage for Yan Yuan's outer coffin. Because I have to follow behind senior officials, I cannot walk on foot as required by the Rites." (11.08)

sumed here by Confucius. Because Yan Yuan died in 490 BC while Li died in 483 BC, the coffin of Yan Yuan normally could not be discussed after he died 7 years later.

(1) Yan Yuan: Surname Yan, first name Hui, style name Ziyuan, Confucius's excellent disciple, dead at 31 years old in 490 BC when Confucius was at the State of Cai. (2) Yan Lu: Surname Yan, first name Wuyou, style name Lu, Confucius's disciple, the father of Yan Yuan. (3) Li: Son of Confucius, surname Kong, first name Li, style name Boyu, died at 50 in 483 BC when Confucius was 69. Character "Li" here means a carp in Chinese.

颜渊死,门人欲厚葬之。子曰:"不可。"门人厚葬之。子曰:"回也视予犹父也,予不得视犹子也。非我也,夫二三子也。"(11.11)

【白话译文】

颜渊去世了,孔子的弟子想给他举办丰厚的葬礼。孔子说:"不可以这么办。"他的弟子依然给颜渊举办了丰厚的葬礼。孔子说:"回啊!你平时对待我像父亲,但我没有能力对待你像儿子。这违背了我的意愿呀,弟子们。"(11.11)

【注释】颜渊生于鲁昭公二十一年(公元前521年),卒于鲁哀公十四年(公元前490年),去世时年仅31岁,孔子(当时在蔡国)悲痛,但不主张厚葬。门人:孔子弟子。厚葬:隆重地安葬。予:我。犹:如。视予犹父也:待我如父亲。得:情况允许,指能够、可以。视犹子:我对待颜回如父亲对待儿子。非:违背、不符合。非我也:违背我的意愿了。夫:语助词。二三子:弟子们。

【英译】

When Yan Yuan died, the Master's disciples desired to hold an elaborate funeral for him. The Master said, "You may not do that." His disciples, however, held an elaborate funeral for Yan Yuan. The Master said, "Alas, Hui[2]! You ordinarily regarded me like your father, but I cannot be able to treat you like my son. This is against my will, my disciples!" (11.11)

80

丧 Mourn

宰我问:"三年之丧,期已久矣。君子三年不为礼,礼必坏;三年不为乐,乐必崩。旧谷既没,新谷既升,钻燧改火,期可已矣。"

子曰:"食夫稻,衣夫锦,于女安乎?"

曰:"安。"

【白话译文】

宰我向孔子请教:"给父母的守孝期

【注释】宰我:姓宰名予,字子我。丧:服丧。期(音 qī 七):时间。已:太、过分。久:太长。为:实行。必:一定。坏:败坏、破坏。乐(音 yuè 月):乐曲、乐舞。崩:荒废。既:已经。没:完了,吃完。升:上场。燧(音 suì 岁):取火器具、石头。钻燧:钻木取火。改火:四季所用木头不同,每年轮换一遍。马融引用《周书·月令》称春取榆柳、夏季取枣杏(季夏取桑柘)、秋取柞楢、冬取槐檀。期(音 jī 基):一年。可:可以。已:完成。矣:了。

食:吃。夫:这。稻:米,好吃

三年太长了。君子三年不演习礼仪,礼仪就会败坏。三年不演奏礼乐舞蹈,礼乐就会荒废。用一年时间,旧粮食吃完,新粮食存入粮仓。适合钻木取火用的木头,每季节轮换一次,用一年时间这些木头轮换一遍。因此,丧期满一整年就可以了。"

孔子说:"(三年丧期没有过完)你吃香稻,穿锦缎,你心安理得吗?"

宰我说:"(一年丧期结束后)心安理得。"

的。衣:穿。锦:锦缎,好穿的。于:在,对于。女:汝(音 rǔ 辱),你。安:心安。乎:吗。何晏注:宰我言,既期除丧,即食稻衣锦,其心安也。

【英译】

Zai Wo[1] asked the Master's advice, "The mourning period of three years for one's parents is too long. If a superior man does not practise the Rites of Proprieties for three years, the Rites of Proprieties must be undermined. If he does not perform the Ritual Music for three years, the Ritual Music will fall into disuse. In a year's time the old grains will be used up, and new grains will be stored in granaries. Different wood[2] is used in each of the four seasons for making fire by drilling. In one year's time these kinds of wood are shifted for a round. Therefore, one year is sufficient for the mourning period."

The Master said, "Do you feel at ease and justified to eat good rice[3] and wear silk brocade (when the three year mourning period is not over)?"

【英译注】(1) Zai Wo: Surname Zai, first name Yu, style name Ziwo, Confucius's disciple. (2) Wood: One ancient book recorded that willow or elm was used for spring; date, apricot or mulberry for summer; Chinese mulberry for autumn; and ebony for winter. (3) Good rice: Rice was precious food at Confucius's time when millets were commonly cooked for food.

"女安,则为之。夫君子之居丧,食旨不甘,闻乐不乐,居处不安,故不为也。今女安,则为之。"

宰我出。子曰:"予之不仁也。子生三年,然后免于父母之怀。夫三年之丧,天下之通丧也。予也有三年之爱于其父母乎?"(17.21)

【注释】则:就,那么。为:做。之:此,这样。居丧:守丧。旨:甜,美味,好吃的。甘:甜。闻乐(音yuè月)不乐(音lè勒):听音乐不快乐。

出:离开、出去。予:宰我,姓宰名予,字子我。子:小孩。生:出生。免:离开。于:从,对,在。怀:怀抱。免于父母之怀:离开父母的怀抱。通丧:通行的丧礼。予也:宰我、宰予呀。有:存在。三年之爱:三年的爱护或敬爱,与"三年之丧"相当,据说是三年之丧的出处。于:对或来自。乎:吗。

【白话译文】

孔子说:"你心安理得,你就按你的想法做。君子在三年守丧期间,吃美食感觉不到香甜;听音乐感觉不到快乐。平时生活,他都不舒服。这是他为什么不那么做的原因。现在你心安理得,你就做。"

宰我走后,孔子说:"予的说法,不符合仁德的要求啊!孩子出生后三年,才离开父母的怀抱。所谓三年的丧期,是天下人共同遵守的做法。予曾经像其他孩子一样享受过他父母三年怀抱的爱吗?"(17.21)

【英译】

"At ease and justified (after one year mourning period is over)," said Zai Wo.

"If you feel at ease and justified, then do as you wish. In the three years of mourning, a superior man does not enjoy fine food; nor

【英译注】(1) Yu: First name of Zai Wo.

does he take pleasure from listening to music. He does not feel comfortable living in his home. That is why a superior man does not do these things. If you feel at ease and justified now, just do as you wish."

After Zai Wo left, the Master said, "What Yu[1] said does not meet the requirements of superior benevolence! Children do not leave the bosoms of their parents for the first three years of life. The mourning period of three years is a general practice commonly observed by everyone under heaven. Did Yu ever enjoy three years of love in the bosoms of his parents like other children?" (17.21)

子游曰:"丧致乎哀而止。"(19.14)

【注释】子游:姓言,名偃(音yǎn眼),字子游,吴人。丧:丧事。致:极致、竭尽。哀:悲伤。止:停止、止息,不要过分悲伤而自伤、自残等,因为此过激行为违背孝道。

【白话译文】

子游说:"一个人守孝期间,他保持悲痛就可以了。"(19.14)

【英译】

Ziyou[1] said, "It is acceptable that one must grieve throughout the period of mourning." (19.14)

【英译注】(1) Ziyou: Surname Yan, first name Yan, style name Ziyou, from the State of Wu, Confucius's disciple.

曾子曰:"吾闻诸夫子:人未有自致者也,必也亲丧乎!"(19.17)

【注释】诸:之于。夫子:先生,孔子。未有:没有。自:自己。致:极、尽。自致:自致其诚,自动充分发挥感情。必也:(如果)一定有的话。亲:父母,至亲之人。丧:去世(时)。

【白话译文】

曾子说:"我从我的老师那里听到:平时,没有人会自动地充分显露他的全部感情。如果有这种情况,一定是他父母去世的时候!"(19.17)

【英译】

Master Zeng(1) said, "I have heard my Master say, 'Ordinarily, no one can give free rein to his emotions unless it is when his parents pass away!" (19.17)

【英译注】(1) Master Zeng: Confucius's disciple (505 BC – 436 BC), surname Zeng, first name Shen, style name Ziyu, a person from Nanwucheng City, the State of Lu, currently at Pingyi County, Shandong Province.

81

鬼 Ghost

子曰:"非其鬼而祭之,谄也。见义不为,无勇也。"(02.24)

【注释】其:本人的。鬼:一般指逝去的祖先,也泛指应当祭祀的鬼神。而:却。祭:祭祀。之:其鬼。谄(音 chǎn 产):谄媚、阿谀。谄也:这是献媚。义:道义、符合道义的事。为:做。勇:勇气。

【白话译文】

孔子说:"祭祀的鬼神不是他的祖先,

这种祭祀是一种谄媚。在一个人应当正义地挺身而出的事情面前,他袖手旁观,是一种怯懦。”(02.24)

【英译】

The Master said, “It is flattery when a man offers sacrifices to the ghosts(1) that are not his own ancestors. It is cowardice when one stands by with folded arms at affairs that he should righteously and bravely step forward.”(02.24)

【英译注】(1) ghost: A dead man was called a ghost in ancient China. Normally it was specifically referred to one's deceased ancestors.

樊迟问知。子曰:“务民之义,敬鬼神而远之,可谓知矣。”问仁。子曰:“先难而后获,可谓仁矣。”(06.22)

【注释】樊迟:名须,字子迟。知(音 zhì 治):智,智慧。务:致力于(提倡)。民:百姓。之:的。义:道义。务民之义:致力于从事百姓认为符合道义的事。敬:尊敬、恭敬对待。鬼:人死后的灵魂、逝去的祖先。神:神灵,或者天地万物的创造者。而:并且。远:久远,非空间上的远,而是时间上的远,“‘慎终追远’之远,追孝、思孝、思远”[J13]。之:鬼神。远之:久远地追思祖先。先难:困难时自己吃苦在前。后获:得利时自己收获在后。可谓:可以称作。仁:仁德。矣:了。

【白话译文】

樊迟请教什么是智慧。孔子说:“一个人致力于一件事,教育、领导人民有正义之心,以敬重的心情祭祀鬼神,而且深远地缅怀他的祖先,这就可以称作智慧。”他请教什么是仁德。孔子说:“克服困难时,他第一个走在别人前面,在收获果实时,他走在最后一个,这就可以称作仁德。”(06.22)

【英译】

Fan Chi(1) asked advice about wis dom.

【英译注】(1) Fan Chi: Surname Fan, first name Xu, style name

The Master said, "One dedicates oneself to a thing that teaches and leads the people to be righteous, offers sacrifices to the ghosts and gods[(2)] respectfully, and far back reminisces about his ancestors. This can be called wisdom." He asked advice about superior benevolence. The Master said, "One is first before others in overcoming difficulties and he is last after others in getting benefits. This can be called superior benevolence." (06.22)

Zichi, Confucius's disciple. (2) Ghosts and gods: They are one's deceased ancestors. They were placed in the tablets at ancestral temple or sacrificial table at home, very close to the family members.

82

祭 Offer Sacrifices

曾子曰:"慎终追远,民德归厚矣。"(01.09)

【白话译文】

曾子说:"慎重对待父母的葬礼,虔诚地祭祀自己的祖先,这样老百姓的道德风尚就可以变得淳厚了。"(01.09)

【英译】

Master Zeng said, "Carefully undertake a funeral for one's parent, piously offer sacri

【注释】终:(父母)去世。追:追念。远:祖先。归:导向。厚:淳厚。

fices to one's ancestors so that morals of the common people can become pure and excellent." (01.09)

季氏旅于泰山。子谓冉有曰:"女弗能救与?"对曰:"不能。"子曰:"呜呼!曾谓泰山不若林放乎?"(03.06)

【白话译文】

季氏要祭祀泰山。孔子向冉有问:"你不能想办法阻止他做此事吗?"冉有敬答:"不能。"孔子说:"哎呀!难道泰山神在理解礼仪方面竟然还不如林放吗?"(03.06)

【英译】

The Ji Family[(1)] was going to offer sacrifice to Mount Taishan. The Master said to Ran You[(2)], "Cannot you think out a remedy to prevent him from doing it?" He replied respectfully, "No, I cannot." The Master said, "Alas! Is the God of Mount Taishan really no better than Lin Fang[(3)] in understanding the Rites of Proprieties?" (03.06)

【注释】季氏:鲁国正卿季孙氏,季康子,姓季孙,名肥,谥号康,鲁哀公时任正卿,违礼祭祀泰山;冉有为其家臣。旅:祭祀山川,天子之职。于:在、向。泰山:五岳之长,在山东中部,高1545米,受天子或君王封禅祭祀。冉有:姓冉名求,字子有,当时季康子的家臣。女(音 rǔ 辱):汝,你。弗:不。救:挽救、劝阻住、谏止。呜呼:哎呀。曾:难道。谓:说。泰山:泰山神(喻:泰山不会接受不合礼仪的祭祀)。若:如、胜。不若:不胜。林放:鲁国(今山东)人。乎:吗。

【英译注】(1) The Ji Family: Master Ji Kang, the prime minster of the State of Lu. He was not qualified to sacrifice Mount Taishan. (2) Ran You: Surname Ran, first name Qiu, style name Ziyou, the manager of the Ji. (3) Lin Fang: A person from the State of Lu. His life is unknown. It seemed that he understood the Rites that only the Emperor or Duke of a state might sacrifice at Mount Taishan.

子曰："禘，自既灌而往者，吾不欲观之矣。"(03.10)

【白话译文】

孔子说："对于盛大祭祀典礼禘，在第一次向灵魂献酒以后，我不想继续观看下去了。"(03.10)

【英译】

The Master said, "For the grand sacrificial ceremony of *Di*(1), I do not desire to continue watching it after the first drink is presented(2) to the spirits." (03.10)

【注释】禘(音 dì 帝)：极为隆重的祭祖大礼，只有天子能举行。灌：第一次献酒，祭祀中的一个节目，本作"祼"(音 guàn 贯)，用童男童女代表受祭者，让其闻到酒香。而往：以后。观：欣赏。吾不欲观之矣：我不想看它了；鲁国为周公封地，特许此礼，周公去世后，为鲁君沿用，实为越礼。

【英译注】(1) sacrificial ceremony of *Di*: This grand sacrificial ceremony should be presided over by the Emperor. The Emperor King Cheng of the Zhou Dynasty specially permitted the first duke Dan of the State of Lu to do it for his great contributions. The following dukes of the State of Lu in fact were not qualified to do it, but they just followed this custom. (2) ... drink is presented: The spirits of ancestors were played by small boys and girls. The drink was presented to them many times so that they could smell its fragrance.

或问禘之说。子曰："不知也。知其说者之于天下也，其如示诸斯乎！"指其掌。(03.11)

【白话译文】

有人问孔子盛大祭祀禘的制度。孔子说："我不知道。知道它的人，治理国家就像把一个东西展示在手掌里一样容易！"

【注释】或：有人。问：请教。禘(音 dì 帝)：天子祭祖典礼。说(音 shuō)：规定、理论。不知也：我不知道；实际上孔子不便评论，因为此祭祀礼只有天子能举行，鲁国为周公封地，周公去世后，鲁君沿用这一传统，已越礼。其说：这个理论。之于天下：对于(治理)天下。其：大概。如：好像。示：展示，指、置，摆放之意，或同"视"。诸：之(它)于(在)。斯：这里。其

他一面说着,一面指着他的手掌。(03.11)

如示诸斯乎:大概如同把东西展示或放在此处(一样容易)吧。指其掌:(一边说,一边)指着他的手掌。

【英译】

Someone asked the Master advice about the institution of the grand sacrificial ceremony of *Di*[(1)]. The Master said, "I do not know. The one who knows it can administer the country as easily as he displays a thing on his palm!" Saying this, he pointed to his palm. (03.11)

【英译注】(1) sacrificial ceremony of *Di*: It refers to the remarks of the last passage (03.10,82 Offer Sacrifices).

祭如在,祭神如神在。子曰:"吾不与祭,如不祭。"(03.12)

【注释】如:如同。在:(被祭祀者)就在面前。与(音 yù 预):亲自参加。不与祭:不亲自祭,由人代替。如不祭:如同没有祭祀。

【白话译文】

祭祀祖先时,好像祖先就真的在那里。祭祀神时,好像神就真的在那里。孔子说:"如果我不能亲自参加祭祀活动,我不请别人代劳,因为那样如同没有祭祀一样。"(03.12)

【英译】

When sacrifices were offered to one's ancestors, his ancestors seemed to be truly present there. When sacrifices were offered to the gods, the gods seemed to be truly there.

The Master said, "If I cannot offer sacrifices in person, I will not ask someone else to do it on my behalf because it is as if no sacrifice were offered." (03. 12)

乡人傩，朝服而立于阼阶。(10. 14)

【白话译文】

家乡举行傩仪式时，孔子穿着朝服，立在东侧的台阶上观看。(10. 14)

【英译】

When the exorcising ceremony(1) was performed at the Master's hometown, he dressed in his court clothes and stood on the eastern steps(2), watching it. (10. 14)

【注释】乡人：本乡人。傩（音 nuó 挪）：迎神驱鬼的仪式，古今皆有驱逐疫鬼的风俗，有的是在腊月里以舞蹈表演的形式进行驱逐疫鬼的仪式。朝服：（孔子）穿朝服。而：且。立：站。于：在。阼（音 zuò 坐）：大堂前东面的台阶，是主人所立之处，而宾客从西阶上下。阶：台阶。

【英译注】(1) exorcising ceremony: This was a performance to invite the gods and drive away pestilential demons. This ceremony can be seen somewhere in China even today. (2) eastern steps: Hosts stood on the eastern steps while the western steps were for guests.

十六
Sixteen

岁月
Time Forever

83

岁月 Time Forever

子曰:“吾十有五而志于学,三十而立,四十而不惑,五十而知天命,六十而耳顺,七十而从心所欲,不逾矩。”(02.04)

【白话译文】

孔子说:“15 岁,我立志大做学问;30 岁,我可以独立做事;40 岁,我不被误导也不受迷惑;50 岁,我明白了上天的命令;60 岁,我能清晰平静地听得进任何事;70 岁,我做任何想做的事情都不会越礼违反规矩。”(02.04)

【英译】

The Master said,“At fifteen,I was determined to engage in great learning; at thirty,I could do a thing independently; at forty,I was neither deluded nor perplexed; at fifty,I understood the mandate of Heaven; at sixty, I listened to everything soberly and gently; and at seventy,I did whatever I wanted but never transgressed rules and the Rites.”(02.04)

【注释】子:孔子。吾:我。有:又。十有五:15 岁。而:就。志:立志。学:读书学习。三十:30 岁。立:独立处世立身。惑:被外表迷惑,看不到本质。天命:上天的命令,人力不能支配者,个人意志不能改变者。耳顺:心平气和地听进不同意见,无论好坏、无论批评、赞扬等话,都能正确对待,听得进,不刺耳。从:遵从。逾:越过。矩:规矩。七十而从心所欲,不逾矩:70 岁,规矩已经长在心里,任何念头,随心所欲,不会违规;此言勉人志学,善始善终。

子张问："十世可知也？"子曰："殷因于夏礼，所损益，可知也。周因于殷礼，所损益，可知也。其或继周者，虽百世，可知也。"(02.23)

【注释】子张：姓颛（音 zhuān 砖）孙名师，字子张。世：30 年为一世，或指朝代。十世：十世后的礼仪。也：吗，语气词。殷：商朝。因：沿用、继承。于：从。夏：夏朝。礼：礼仪制度。损：减少。益：增加。周：周朝。其或：大概。继：接续。者：……的朝代。

【白话译文】

子张问："今后十个朝代的礼仪能够提前知晓吗？"孔子说："殷朝的礼仪是因为它是继承了夏朝的礼仪，有些减少，有些增加，是可以知晓的。周朝的礼仪是因为它是继承了殷朝的礼仪，有些减少了，有些增加了，是可以知晓的。因此，如果任何朝代可能作为周朝的继承者，它的礼仪是可以提前知晓的，甚至一百个朝代以后也是如此。"(02.23)

【英译】

Zizhang asked, "Can the institutions and protocols be known in advance for ten dynasties?" The Master said, "The institutions and protocols of the Yin Dynasty could be known as they were inherited from the Xia Dynasty with some abrogated and some supplemented. Those of the Zhou Dynasty could be known as they were inherited from the Yin Dynasty with some abrogated and some supplemented. Therefore, if any dynasty may possibly serve as a successor of the Zhou Dy nasty, its institutions and protocols can be known in advance, and even so far as for one hundred dynasties later. ” (02. 23)

子曰:“加我数年,五十以学《易》,可以无大过矣。”(07. 17)

【注释】鲁哀公十一年(公元前 484 年),孔子 68 岁,周游列国后回到鲁国,开始作《春秋》,整理诗书乐礼,喜欢《易》,为之作序、说,书绳被他读断多次(三绝)。加:增加。年:岁。加我数年:(如果)多给我几年时间。五十:在 50 岁时。以:用来。《易》:当时称《易》,后来称《易经》。过:错。矣:了。

【白话译文】

孔子说:“假如能够多给我几年时间,我会用这些时间在 50 岁时钻研《易》,这样就可以让我不会犯大错了。”(07. 17)

【英译】

The Master said, “If I might be given several extra years more, I would have used such years to study *The Changes*(1) at fifty. This might make me free from big errors. ” (07. 17)

【英译注】(1) *The Changes*: Currently called *I Ching*, or *Book of Changes*, the anicient Chinese book of fortune telling and philosophy.

子在川上曰:“逝者如斯夫! 不舍昼夜。”(09. 17)

【注释】川:河。川上:河边。逝:消逝,一去不返。者:的时光。斯:这。夫:啊。逝者如斯夫:消逝的时光,如同这河水一样一去不返啊。舍:止息。昼夜:白天、晚上。不舍昼夜:白天、晚上都不停止。

【白话译文】

孔子站在河岸上说:“啊! 飞逝的时光如同这河水一样一去不返啊,白天和晚上都不停息。”(09. 17)

【英译】

The Master stood at a river bank and said, "Oh, time flies like this water, never returning, unceasing, regardless of day and night!" (09.17)

子曰:"后生可畏。焉知来者之不如今也?四十、五十而无闻焉,斯亦不足畏也已。"(09.23)

【注释】后生:年轻人。畏:值得敬畏。焉:怎么。来者:下一代。今:当今一代。也:呀。四十:40岁。而:还,依然。闻:闻名。无闻:不著名,无仁德功绩。斯:那么。亦:也就。已:了。

【白话译文】

孔子说:"年轻人值得敬畏。怎么知晓后来的人不胜当今的人呢?但是,当他们到40岁、50岁时还没有大成就,他们就没什么可敬畏的了。"(09.23)

【英译】

The Master said, "The young deserve to be held with awe. How can we know that the new generations will not be better than the current generations? But when they reach forty or fifty, and have no great achievements, then they may not be held in awe anymore." (09.23)

孔子曰:"君子有三戒:少之时,血气未定,戒之在色;及其壮也,血气方刚,戒之在斗;及其老也,血气既衰,戒之在得。"(16.07)

【注释】三:三种。戒:戒除。少之时:年轻。定:稳定。色:贪色。其:他的。壮:壮年。方:正在。刚:强壮。斗:好胜逞强。及:到。老:老年。既:已经。衰:衰弱。得:贪得无厌。

【白话译文】

孔夫子说:"一名君子要戒除三件事:年轻时,血气没有完全发育,戒除贪色;壮年时,充满血气,戒除争斗;老年时,血气衰弱,戒除贪得无厌。"(16.07)

【英译】

Confucius said, "A superior man has three abstentions: abstention from lust in his teens when his vigour and vitality are not fully developed; abstention from fight in adulthood when he is full of vigour and vitality; and abstention from avarice in his old age when his vigour and vitality are weak." (16.07)

子曰:"年四十而见恶焉,其终也已。"(17.26)

【注释】年:年龄。四十:40岁。而:还。见:被,被人。恶(音 wù 务):厌恶。焉:啊、呀。年四十而见恶焉:到 40 岁还被人厌恶呀。其:他、他的。终:一辈子;终生。已:止、完。其终也已:他这辈子呀,算完了。

【白话译文】

孔子说:"一个人到了 40 岁时还让人讨厌,他这一辈子就快完了。"(17.26)

【英译】

The Master said, "When a man is detested at the age of forty, his whole life is nearly over." (17. 26)

附录:《论语》篇章在本书的分类表

说明:以第一条“01.01 / 24 学 / 24 Learn”为例,01.01 表示《论语》第一篇“学而第一”的第一章,“24 学”表示此书在第 24 节“24 学”,“24 Learn”为其英译。

Note: Take item one “01.01 / 24 学 / 24 Learn” as an example. “01.01” indicates the first passage of “Book One Xue Er” of *The Analects of Confucius*, and “24 学” and “24 Learn” show the section number and new classification in this book in Chinese and English respectively.

学而第一 Book One Xue Er

01.01 / 24 学 / 24 Learn
01.02 / 17 孝 / 17 Filial Piety
01.03 / 10 仁 / 10 Superior Benevolence
01.04 / 05 人 / 05 Human Being
01.05 / 45 政 / 45 Politics
01.06 / 24 学 / 24 Learn
01.07 / 24 学 / 24 Learn
01.08 / 16 忠 / 16 Loyalty
01.09 / 82 祭 / 82 Offer Sacrifices
01.10 / 23 师 / 23 Teacher
01.11 / 17 孝 / 17 Filial Piety
01.12 / 12 礼 / 12 Rites of Proprieties
01.13 / 05 人 / 05 Human Being
01.14 / 24 学 / 24 Learn

为政第二　Book Two Wei Zheng

八佾第三　Book Three Ba Yi

03.02 / 35 天子 / 35 The Son of Heaven
03.03 / 10 仁 / 10 Superior Benevolence
03.04 / 12 礼 / 12 Rites of Proprieties
03.05 / 37 君 / 37 A Duke
03.06 / 82 祭 / 82 Offer Sacrifices
03.07 / 58 射 / 58 Archery
03.08 / 26 诗 / 26 Poems and Odes
03.09 / 12 礼 / 12 Rites of Proprieties
03.10 / 82 祭 / 82 Offer Sacrifices
03.11 / 82 祭 / 82 Offer Sacrifices
03.12 / 82 祭 / 82 Offer Sacrifices
03.13 / 01 天 / 01 Heaven
03.14 / 12 礼 / 12 Rites of Proprieties
03.15 / 12 礼 / 12 Rites of Proprieties
03.16 / 58 射 / 58 Archery
03.17 / 12 礼 / 12 Rites of Proprieties
03.18 / 38 臣 / 38 An Official
03.19 / 37 君 / 37 A Duke
03.20 / 26 诗 / 26 Poems and Odes
03.21 / 37 君 / 37 A Duke
03.22 / 38 臣 / 38 An Official
03.23 / 15 礼乐 / 15 Ritual Music
03.24 / 01 天 / 01 Heaven
03.25 / 15 礼乐 / 15 Ritual Music
03.26 / 66 气 / 66 Enrage

里仁第四　Book Four Li Ren

04.01 / 53 住 / 53 Residence
04.02 / 10 仁 / 10 Superior Benevolence
04.03 / 10 仁 / 10 Superior Benevolence

公冶长第五　Book Five Gongye Chang

05.06 / 40 仕 / 40 Officialdom

05.07 / 65 笑 / 65 Laugh

05.08 / 10 仁 / 10 Superior Benevolence

05.09 / 24 学 / 24 Learn

05.10 / 67 骂 / 67 Scold

05.11 / 22 志 / 22 Ambition

05.12 / 34 修身 / 34 Moral Cultivation

05.13 / 24 学 / 24 Learn

05.14 / 24 学 / 24 Learn

05.15 / 24 学 / 24 Learn

05.16 / 07 君子 / 07 A Superior Man

05.17 / 38 臣 / 38 An Official

05.18 / 38 臣 / 38 An Official

05.19 / 10 仁 / 10 Superior Benevolence

05.20 / 31 思 / 31 Think

05.21 / 38 臣 / 38 An Official

05.22 / 72 周游 / 72 Interstate Travel

05.23 / 70 高士 / 70 Eminent People

05.24 / 11 义 / 11 Righteousness

05.25 / 70 高士 / 70 Eminent People

05.26 / 74 老 / 74 Aging

05.27 / 47 讼 / 47 A Lawsuit

05.28 / 24 学 / 24 Learn

雍也第六　Book Six Yong Ye

06.01 / 40 仕 / 40 Officialdom

06.02 / 45 政 / 45 Politics

06.03 / 24 学 / 24 Learn

06.04 / 11 义 / 11 Righteousness

06.05 / 11 义 / 11 Righteousness

06.06 / 40 仕 / 40 Officialdom

06.07 / 10 仁 / 10 Superior Benevolence

06.08 / 40 仕 / 40 Officialdom

06.09 / 40 仕 / 40 Officialdom

06.10 / 75 疾 / 75 Disease

06.11 / 20 贤 / 20 Sage

06.12 / 02 道 / 02 The Way of Heaven

06.13 / 06 小人 / 06 An Inferior Man

06.14 / 45 政 / 45 Politics

06.15 / 42 兵 / 42 A Soldier

06.16 / 28 忧 / 28 Anxiety

06.17 / 02 道 / 02 The Way of Heaven

06.18 / 07 君子 / 07 A Superior Man

06.19 / 73 生 / 73 Birth

06.20 / 13 智 / 13 Wisdom

06.21 / 05 人 / 05 Human Being

06.22 / 81 鬼 / 81 Ghost

06.23 / 05 人 / 05 Human Being

06.24 / 02 道 / 02 The Way of Heaven

06.25 / 57 器 / 57 Utensils

06.26 / 10 仁 / 10 Superior Benevolence

06.27 / 07 君子 / 07 A Superior Man

06.28 / 72 周游 / 72 Interstate Travel

06.29 / 03 德 / 03 Morals

06.30 / 10 仁 / 10 Superior Benevolence

述而第七　Book Seven Shu Er

07.01 / 71 孔子 / 71 Confucius

07.02 / 71 孔子 / 71 Confucius

07.03 / 28 忧 / 28 Anxiety

07.04 / 55 起居 / 55 Daily Behaviors
07.05 / 56 梦 / 56 Dream
07.06 / 05 人 / 05 Human Being
07.07 / 23 师 / 23 Teacher
07.08 / 23 师 / 23 Teacher
07.09 / 52 食 / 52 Foods
07.10 / 78 哭 / 78 Weep
07.11 / 42 兵 / 42 A Soldier
07.12 / 49 贫富 / 49 Poverty and Wealth
07.13 / 71 孔子 / 71 Confucius
07.14 / 15 礼乐 / 15 Ritual Music
07.15 / 72 周游 / 72 Interstate Travel
07.16 / 71 孔子 / 71 Confucius
07.17 / 83 岁月 / 83 Time Forever
07.18 / 25 言 / 25 Speech
07.19 / 74 老 / 74 Aging
07.20 / 73 生 / 73 Birth
07.21 / 69 忌 / 69 Taboo
07.22 / 23 师 / 23 Teacher
07.23 / 72 周游 / 72 Interstate Travel
07.24 / 23 师 / 23 Teacher
07.25 / 23 师 / 23 Teacher
07.26 / 22 志 / 22 Ambition
07.27 / 59 钓 / 59 Fishing
07.28 / 71 孔子 / 71 Confucius
07.29 / 21 恕 / 21 Forgiveness
07.30 / 10 仁 / 10 Superior Benevolence
07.31 / 30 过 / 30 Mistake
07.32 / 15 礼乐 / 15 Ritual Music
07.33 / 71 孔子 / 71 Confucius

泰伯第八 Book Eight Tai Bo

子罕第九 Book Nine Zi Han

09.02 / 54 行 / 54 Travel

09.03 / 12 礼 / 12 Rites of Proprieties

09.04 / 69 忌 / 69 Taboo

09.05 / 72 周游 / 72 Interstate Travel

09.06 / 71 孔子 / 71 Confucius

09.07 / 71 孔子 / 71 Confucius

09.08 / 71 孔子 / 71 Confucius

09.09 / 74 老 / 74 Aging

09.10 / 71 孔子 / 71 Confucius

09.11 / 23 师 / 23 Teacher

09.12 / 75 疾 / 75 Disease

09.13 / 44 商 / 44 A Merchant

09.14 / 53 住 / 53 Residence

09.15 / 72 周游 / 72 Interstate Travel

09.16 / 62 酒 / 62 Drink Liquor

09.17 / 83 岁月 / 83 Time Forever

09.18 / 72 周游 / 72 Interstate Travel

09.19 / 34 修身 / 34 Moral Cultivation

09.20 / 25 言 / 25 Speech

09.21 / 24 学 / 24 Learn

09.22 / 41 农 / 41 A Farmer

09.23 / 83 岁月 / 83 Time Forever

09.24 / 25 言 / 25 Speech

09.25 / 16 忠 / 16 Loyalty

09.26 / 22 志 / 22 Ambition

09.27 / 51 衣 / 51 Clothes

09.28 / 04 自然 / 04 The Nature

09.29 / 05 人 / 05 Human Being

09.30 / 13 智 / 13 Wisdom

09.31 / 31 思 / 31 Think

乡党第十　Book Ten Xiang Dang

10.01 / 71 孔子 / 71 Confucius
10.02 / 71 孔子 / 71 Confucius
10.03 / 71 孔子 / 71 Confucius
10.04 / 71 孔子 / 71 Confucius
10.05 / 71 孔子 / 71 Confucius
10.06 / 51 衣 / 51 Clothes
10.07 / 52 食 / 52 Foods
10.08 / 52 食 / 52 Foods
10.09 / 52 食 / 52 Foods
10.10 / 55 起居 / 55 Daily Behaviors
10.11 / 52 食 / 52 Foods
10.12 / 55 起居 / 55 Daily Behaviors
10.13 / 62 酒 / 62 Drink Liquor
10.14 / 82 祭 / 82 Offer Sacrifices
10.15 / 60 友 / 60 Make Friends
10.16 / 76 药 / 76 Medicine
10.17 / 63 火灾 / 63 Fire Disaster
10.18 / 52 食 / 52 Foods
10.19 / 75 疾 / 75 Disease
10.20 / 54 行 / 54 Travel
10.21 / 12 礼 / 12 Rites of Proprieties
10.22 / 11 义 / 11 Righteousness
10.23 / 12 礼 / 12 Rites of Proprieties
10.24 / 55 起居 / 55 Daily Behaviors
10.25 / 71 孔子 / 71 Confucius
10.26 / 54 行 / 54 Travel
10.27 / 04 自然 / 04 The Nature

先进第十一　Book Eleven Xian Jin

11.01 / 12 礼 / 12 Rites of Proprieties
11.02 / 72 周游 / 72 Interstate Travel
11.03 / 24 学 / 24 Learn
11.04 / 25 言 / 25 Speech
11.05 / 17 孝 / 17 Filial Piety
11.06 / 61 嫁 / 61 Marriage
11.07 / 24 学 / 24 Learn
11.08 / 79 葬 / 79 Funeral
11.09 / 77 死 / 77 Death
11.10 / 78 哭 / 78 Weep
11.11 / 79 葬 / 79 Funeral
11.12 / 77 死 / 77 Death
11.13 / 28 忧 / 28 Anxiety
11.14 / 64 翻修 / 64 Reconstruction
11.15 / 24 学 / 24 Learn
11.16 / 24 学 / 24 Learn
11.17 / 48 税 / 48 Taxes
11.18 / 24 学 / 24 Learn
11.19 / 44 商 / 44 A Merchant
11.20 / 19 善 / 19 Goodness
11.21 / 07 君子 / 07 A Superior Man
11.22 / 27 惑 / 27 Perplexity
11.23 / 72 周游 / 72 Interstate Travel
11.24 / 40 仕 / 40 Officialdom
11.25 / 67 骂 / 67 Scold
11.26 / 22 志 / 22 Ambition

颜渊第十二　Book Twelve Yan Yuan

12.01 / 10 仁 / 10 Superior Benevolence

子路第十三　Book Thirteen Zilu

13.06 / 45 政 / 45 Politics
13.07 / 72 周游 / 72 Interstate Travel
13.08 / 53 住 / 53 Residence
13.09 / 09 民 / 09 Common People
13.10 / 72 周游 / 72 Interstate Travel
13.11 / 19 善 / 19 Goodness
13.12 / 36 帝 / 36 Emperor
13.13 / 34 修身 / 34 Moral Cultivation
13.14 / 45 政 / 45 Politics
13.15 / 25 言 / 25 Speech
13.16 / 45 政 / 45 Politics
13.17 / 45 政 / 45 Politics
13.18 / 50 盗 / 50 Robbery
13.19 / 16 忠 / 16 Loyalty
13.20 / 39 士 / 39 A Scholar
13.21 / 05 人 / 05 Human Being
13.22 / 22 志 / 22 Ambition
13.23 / 06 小人 / 06 An Inferior Man
13.24 / 05 人 / 05 Human Being
13.25 / 06 小人 / 06 An Inferior Man
13.26 / 06 小人 / 06 An Inferior Man
13.27 / 10 仁 / 10 Superior Benevolence
13.28 / 39 士 / 39 A Scholar
13.29 / 42 兵 / 42 A Soldier
13.30 / 42 兵 / 42 A Soldier

宪问第十四　Book Fourteen Xian Wen

14.01 / 33 耻 / 33 Shame
14.02 / 10 仁 / 10 Superior Benevolence
14.03 / 39 士 / 39 A Scholar

14.04 / 02 道 / 02 The Way of Heaven

14.05 / 03 德 / 03 Morals

14.06 / 36 帝 / 36 Emperor

14.07 / 10 仁 / 10 Superior Benevolence

14.08 / 16 忠 / 16 Loyalty

14.09 / 38 臣 / 38 An Official

14.10 / 38 臣 / 38 An Official

14.11 / 29 怨 / 29 Complain

14.12 / 38 臣 / 38 An Official

14.13 / 05 人 / 05 Human Being

14.14 / 65 笑 / 65 Laugh

14.15 / 38 臣 / 38 An Official

14.16 / 37 君 / 37 A Duke

14.17 / 38 臣 / 38 An Official

14.18 / 38 臣 / 38 An Official

14.19 / 38 臣 / 38 An Official

14.20 / 37 君 / 37 A Duke

14.21 / 25 言 / 25 Speech

14.22 / 37 君 / 37 A Duke

14.23 / 38 臣 / 38 An Official

14.24 / 06 小人 / 06 An Inferior Man

14.25 / 24 学 / 24 Learn

14.26 / 72 周游 / 72 Interstate Travel

14.27 / 45 政 / 45 Politics

14.28 / 31 思 / 31 Think

14.29 / 33 耻 / 33 Shame

14.30 / 07 君子 / 07 A Superior Man

14.31 / 25 言 / 25 Speech

14.32 / 34 修身 / 34 Moral Cultivation

14.33 / 20 贤 / 20 Sage

14.34 / 25 言 / 25 Speech
14.35 / 03 德 / 03 Morals
14.36 / 03 德 / 03 Morals
14.37 / 01 天 / 01 Heaven
14.38 / 02 道 / 02 The Way of Heaven
14.39 / 20 贤 / 20 Sage
14.40 / 71 孔子 / 71 Confucius
14.41 / 72 周游 / 72 Interstate Travel
14.42 / 36 帝 / 36 Emperor
14.43 / 12 礼 / 12 Rites of Proprieties
14.44 / 34 修身 / 34 Moral Cultivation
14.45 / 67 骂 / 67 Scold
14.46 / 24 学 / 24 Learn

卫灵公第十五　Book Fifteen Wei Ling Gong

15.01 / 72 周游 / 72 Interstate Travel
15.02 / 72 周游 / 72 Interstate Travel
15.03 / 24 学 / 24 Learn
15.04 / 03 德 / 03 Morals
15.05 / 36 帝 / 36 Emperor
15.06 / 16 忠 / 16 Loyalty
15.07 / 70 高士 / 70 Eminent People
15.08 / 25 言 / 25 Speech
15.09 / 10 仁 / 10 Superior Benevolence
15.10 / 43 工 / 43 A Workman
15.11 / 36 帝 / 36 Emperor
15.12 / 05 人 / 05 Human Being
15.13 / 72 周游 / 72 Interstate Travel
15.14 / 70 高士 / 70 Eminent People
15.15 / 29 怨 / 29 Complain

15.16 / 13 智 / 13 Wisdom
15.17 / 28 忧 / 28 Anxiety
15.18 / 07 君子 / 07 A Superior Man
15.19 / 07 君子 / 07 A Superior Man
15.20 / 77 死 / 77 Death
15.21 / 06 小人 / 06 An Inferior Man
15.22 / 07 君子 / 07 A Superior Man
15.23 / 07 君子 / 07 A Superior Man
15.24 / 21 恕 / 21 Forgiveness
15.25 / 25 言 / 25 Speech
15.26 / 14 信 / 14 Faith
15.27 / 05 人 / 05 Human Being
15.28 / 32 察 / 32 Observe
15.29 / 02 道 / 02 The Way of Heaven
15.30 / 30 过 / 30 Mistake
15.31 / 24 学 / 24 Learn
15.32 / 02 道 / 02 The Way of Heaven
15.33 / 36 帝 / 36 Emperor
15.34 / 06 小人 / 06 An Inferior Man
15.35 / 10 仁 / 10 Superior Benevolence
15.36 / 23 师 / 23 Teacher
15.37 / 07 君子 / 07 A Superior Man
15.38 / 38 臣 / 38 An Official
15.39 / 23 师 / 23 Teacher
15.40 / 02 道 / 02 The Way of Heaven
15.41 / 25 言 / 25 Speech
15.42 / 15 礼乐 / 15 Ritual Music

季氏第十六　Book Sixteen Ji Shi

16.01 / 42 兵 / 42 A Soldier

16.02 / 35 天子 / 35 The Son of Heaven

16.03 / 37 君 / 37 A Duke

16.04 / 60 友 / 60 Make Friends

16.05 / 65 笑 / 65 Laugh

16.06 / 25 言 / 25 Speech

16.07 / 83 岁月 / 83 Time Forever

16.08 / 01 天 / 01 Heaven

16.09 / 73 生 / 73 Birth

16.10 / 31 思 / 31 Think

16.11 / 19 善 / 19 Goodness

16.12 / 03 德 / 03 Morals

16.13 / 24 学 / 24 Learn

16.14 / 08 女 / 08 Women

阳货第十七 Book Seventeen Yang Huo

17.01 / 40 仕 / 40 Officialdom

17.02 / 05 人 / 05 Human Being

17.03 / 13 智 / 13 Wisdom

17.04 / 65 笑 / 65 Laugh

17.05 / 71 孔子 / 71 Confucius

17.06 / 10 仁 / 10 Superior Benevolence

17.07 / 72 周游 / 72 Interstate Travel

17.08 / 24 学 / 24 Learn

17.09 / 26 诗 / 26 Poems and Odes

17.10 / 26 诗 / 26 Poems and Odes

17.11 / 02 道 / 02 The Way of Heaven

17.12 / 67 骂 / 67 Scold

17.13 / 03 德 / 03 Morals

17.14 / 03 德 / 03 Morals

17.15 / 67 骂 / 67 Scold

17.16 / 09 民 / 09 Common People
17.17 / 10 仁 / 10 Superior Benevolence
17.18 / 15 礼乐 / 15 Ritual Music
17.19 / 01 天 / 01 Heaven
17.20 / 66 气 / 66 Enrage
17.21 / 80 丧 / 80 Mourn
17.22 / 55 起居 / 55 Daily Behaviors
17.23 / 18 勇 / 18 Courage
17.24 / 07 君子 / 07 A Superior Man
17.25 / 08 女 / 08 Women
17.26 / 83 岁月 / 83 Time Forever

微子第十八　Book Eighteen Wei Zi

18.01 / 10 仁 / 10 Superior Benevolence
18.02 / 70 高士 / 70 Eminent People
18.03 / 72 周游 / 72 Interstate Travel
18.04 / 72 周游 / 72 Interstate Travel
18.05 / 72 周游 / 72 Interstate Travel
18.06 / 66 气 / 66 Enrage
18.07 / 41 农 / 41 A Farmer
18.08 / 70 高士 / 70 Eminent People
18.09 / 15 礼乐 / 15 Ritual Music
18.10 / 36 帝 / 36 Emperor
18.11 / 39 士 / 39 A Scholar

子张第十九　Book Nineteen Zi Zhang

19.01 / 39 士 / 39 A Scholar
19.02 / 03 德 / 03 Morals
19.03 / 60 友 / 60 Make Friends
19.04 / 22 志 / 22 Ambition

19.05 / 24 学 / 24 Learn
19.06 / 10 仁 / 10 Superior Benevolence
19.07 / 43 工 / 43 A Workman
19.08 / 06 小人 / 06 An Inferior Man
19.09 / 07 君子 / 07 A Superior Man
19.10 / 14 信 / 14 Faith
19.11 / 03 德 / 03 Morals
19.12 / 24 学 / 24 Learn
19.13 / 40 仕 / 40 Officialdom
19.14 / 80 丧 / 80 Mourn
19.15 / 10 仁 / 10 Superior Benevolence
19.16 / 10 仁 / 10 Superior Benevolence
19.17 / 80 丧 / 80 Mourn
19.18 / 17 孝 / 17 Filial Piety
19.19 / 46 法 / 46 The Law
19.20 / 36 帝 / 36 Emperor
19.21 / 30 过 / 30 Mistake
19.22 / 71 孔子 / 71 Confucius
19.23 / 71 孔子 / 71 Confucius
19.24 / 71 孔子 / 71 Confucius
19.25 / 71 孔子 / 71 Confucius

尧曰第二十　Book Twenty Yao Yue

20.01 / 36 帝 / 36 Emperor
20.02 / 45 政 / 45 Politics
20.03 / 05 人 / 05 Human Being

参 考 书 目

1. 儒家经典编委会. 儒家经典:论语[M]. 北京:团结出版社,1997.

2. 杨伯峻. 论语译注:第3版[M]. 北京:中华书局,2010.

3. 张以文. 四书全译:论语[M]. 长沙:湖南大学出版社,1989.

4. 朱熹. 论语集注[M]. 济南:齐鲁出版社,1992.

5. 薛贻康,等. 中国智慧精典:论语[M]. 济南:山东大学出版社,1993.

6. 理雅各. THE FOUR BOOK · 四书:第2版[M]. 杨伯峻,今译,刘重德,罗志野,英文校注. 长沙:湖南出版社,1996.

7. 王力,等. 古汉语常用字字典:第4版[M]. 蒋绍愚,等增订. 北京:商务印书馆,2005.

8. 于丹. 于丹《论语》心得[M]. 北京:中华书局,2006.

9. 于丹. 于丹《论语》感悟[M]. 北京:中华书局,2008.

10. 老铁. 中国帝王辞典[M]. 济南:明天出版社,1989.

11. 何晏. 论语注疏[M]. 邢昺,疏. 北京:中国致公出版社,2016.

12. 司马迁. 史记:孔子世家[M]. 长沙:岳麓书社,1988.

13. 左丘明. 左传:汉英对照和文白对照[M]. 胡志挥,英译,陈克炯,今译. 长沙:湖南人民出版社, 1996.

14. 何新. 孔子年谱[M]. 北京:时事出版社,2007.

15. 赵阳. 回归孔子—论语细译[M]. 郑州:河南人民出版社,2010.

16. 中国社会科学院语言研究所. 新华字典[M]. 北京:商务印书馆,2004.

17. 北京外国语学院英语系《汉英词典》编写组. 汉英词典[M]. 北京:商务印书馆,1980.

18. 吴光华. 汉英大辞典[M]. 上海:上海交通大学出版社,1993.

19. STEIN J. The random house dictionary[M]. New York:Random House, Inc. ,1980.

20. 中国社会科学院语言研究所词典编辑室. 现代汉语词典[M]. 北京:商务印书馆, 1983.

21. 辞海编辑委员会. 辞海:历史分册:中国古代史[M]. 上海:上海辞书出版社,1981.

22. 辞海编辑委员会. 辞海[M]. 1979 年版. 上海:上海辞书出版社,1987.

23.《新英汉词典》编写组. 新英汉词典[M]. 上海:上海译文出版社,1981.

24. 郑易里,等. 英华大辞典[M]. 北京:时代出版社出版,1965.

25. 王健. 儒学三百题[M]. 上海:上海古籍出版社,2001.

26. COVEY S R. The 7 habits of highly effective people[M]. 1st ed . New York:Fireside Press, 1990.

27. 辜鸿铭. 辜鸿铭讲《论语》[M]. 天津:天津社会科学院出版社,2014.

28. 辜鸿铭. 辜鸿铭讲《论语》[M]. 英文版. 天津:天津社会科学院出版社,2014.

29. 孔子. 论语[M]. 韦利,英译. 北京:外语教学与研究出版社,1998.

30. WEBSTER N. Webster's new universal unabridged dictionary [M]. New York:Dorset & Baber,1996.

31. 赵佶. 宋徽宗道德真经解义[M]. 万曼璐,点校. 上海:华东师范大学出版社,2017.

32. 潘麟.《大学》广义[M]. 上海:复旦大学出版社,2015.

杂志文献目录

[J01]吴肖惠,吴菊芳,吴成达.《论语·里仁》篇“富与贵,是人之所欲也”章浅释[J].哈尔滨学院学报.2010,31(10):95—97.

[J02]林源.“岁寒,然后知松柏之后凋也”正诂[J].广州广播电视大学学报.2008,10(6):74—76.

[J03]盛义.中国古代婚龄考释[J].西南民族学院学报(哲学社会科学版).1990(3):73—79

[J04]张晓英,吴敏.论“知之为知之,不知为不知”的人生智慧[J].阿坝师范高等专科学校学报.2014,31(1):64-67.

[J05]朱康有.“学固”的君子形象[J].月读.2018(2).

[J06]曹文心.《论语·侍坐》章注释质疑[J].淮北师范大学学报(哲学社会科学版).1992(3):87—91.

[J07]杨欢.“鼓瑟希”“异乎三子者之撰正误[J].绵阳师范学院学报.1996(2):6—6.

[J08]邱衍云.“萧墙”辨[J].教师教育论坛.1995(5):7—8.

[J09]罗唯嘉.谁家的萧墙——读《论语》“季氏将伐颛臾”章小札[J].文史知识.2019(9):96—102.

[J10]廖名春.《论语》“听讼”章与《大学》篇的误读[J].社会科学战线.2014(6):18—24.

[J11]毕宝魁.《论语·公冶长篇》“无所取材”本义考论[J].沈阳师范大学学报(社会科学版).2009,33(3):67—69.

[J12]徐前师.《论语》“夫子矢之”之“矢”及相关问题[J].孔子研究.2007(5).

[J13]何凡.敬鬼神而远之刍议[J].学术月刊.1987(6):78—81.

[J14]尹赋."君子无所争"再解——兼论儒家"尊让"问题[J].社会科学研究.2019(6):119—125.

[J115]吴进生,吴红红.孔子生卒年月日新考[J].贵州文史丛刊.1997(4):50—50.